Tales from the Sausage Factory

Tales from the Sausage Factory

Making Laws in New York State

Daniel L. Feldman
and
Gerald Benjamin

excelsior editions

An imprint of State University of New York Press
www.sunypress.edu

Published by State University of New York Press, Albany

For information, contact State University of New York Press, Albany, NY
www.sunypress.edu

Production by Kelli LeRoux
Marketing by Anne M. Valentine

Library of Congress Cataloging-in-Publication Data
Feldman, Daniel L.
  Tales from the sausage factory : making laws in New York State /
Daniel L. Feldman and Gerald Benjamin.
      p.   cm.
  "Excelsior editions"
  Includes bibliographical references and index.
  ISBN 978-1-4384-3401-8 (hardcover : alk. paper) 1. Feldman, Daniel L.
2. Legislation—New York (State) 3. Legislators—New York
(State)—Biography. 4. New York (State). Legislature.
Assembly—Biography. 5. New York (State)—Politics and government—
1951- I. Benjamin, Gerald. II. Title.
  F128.3.F45A3 2010
  328.73'092—dc22
  [B]   2010015999

10 9 8 7 6 5 4 3 2 1

Dedications

To Asher Benjamin Feldman and Leah Madeleine Gardner Feldman,
who may someday wish to know what so preoccupied their father.
—Dan Feldman

To Andrew Anthony Reder and Samantha Sophia Reder, who will no
doubt read this as soon as they can . . . right after they learn to read.
—Gerald Benjamin

To achieving representative government, as conceived in the
constitutional ideals of the United States.
—DF and GB

Contents

Acknowledgments

I owe this book to my political career. I owe my political career to my love for my country. Had it not welcomed my ancestors in the late nineteenth century, their descendents would likely have been murdered in Europe.

My political career has ended. My gratitude to the United States is eternal.

I also remain deeply grateful to a much smaller, but still quite large, political construct: the people of the 45th Assembly District in Brooklyn, who chose me to represent them between 1981 and 1998. My wife Cecilia thinks it is somewhat indicative that in my unmarried days I ignored years of entreaties from girlfriends to do something about the large chips off my two front teeth, but made an appointment with the dentist immediately upon entering my neighborhood Assembly District office after encountering an elderly gentleman voter on my way in, who said—in one breath—"Feldman. You're doing a good job. Why don't you get your teeth fixed?"

In recent months, my thoughts have turned to a great man I met 44 years ago, Dr. Mphiwa Mbatha, who taught an anthropology course sponsored by the National Science Foundation in the summer of 1965 to a select group of high school students. In some ways, this book reflects the participant-observer notions Dr. Mbatha inspired.

I have more recent debts as well. There could be no better co-author than Jerry Benjamin. I've had other co-authors, so I have a basis for comparison. I may have been a participant observer, but I was also enough of a politician to have too much ego for me ever to have been selfless enough to do what he did here—to invest enormous talents and efforts into the telling of someone else's stories. He knew what to cut out, what to redesign, and especially what to add. When what we needed to add was buried somewhere in the crevices of my memory, he knew what to ask me for. Without him, neither you nor I could proceed with confidence in the belief that we are embarking on a journey into more than a self-serving, historically unreliable memoir of a former small-time politician. Perhaps the foremost scholar of New York State government, he has also had enough "participant-observer" experience himself as an elected official to understand and communicate the nuances of political life, and the drama.

Before Jerry joined in this effort, Enid Stubin, professor of English at Kingsboro Community College in Brooklyn and "Our Spy in New York" for *The Reader*, a British literary magazine, edited an earlier version of this manuscript. The present version, although substantially different, continues to benefit greatly from her close and fine line-by-line review. Professor Jeffrey Stonecash, Maxwell Professor of Political Science at Syracuse University, and two anonymous reviewers for SUNY Press made extremely helpful comments, and our book benefited from changes we made in response. We thank the League of Women Voters of the City of New York for permission to use the map on page 16. Jerry and I are very grateful, as well, to the staff of SUNY Press not only for choosing to publish our book, but for many very worthwhile suggestions during the publication process. We also owe a special thank you to Bradford Scobie and Amane Kaneko, the wonderfully talented artists who gave us the perfect graphics for our cover. I don't think I'd mind at all if people judge *this* book by its cover. I am obligated to add that the opinions expressed herein are those of the authors, and in no way purport to represent those of the Office of the New York State Comptroller or any other institution.

Finally, although Cecilia has often commented on my consistent choices of, in her words, "unremunerative and incredibly time-consuming" leisure activities, with this book first and foremost among them, she continues to put up with them and with me generally—and be assured she has many other valid complaints.

A very large thank you to all the above.

Daniel L. Feldman
Port Washington, New York

I met Dan Feldman one evening about three years ago at the New York City Bar Association. I was on a panel that he chaired. I can't remember the subject; maybe it was reapportionment. If not, it no doubt had something to do with legislative reform.

At the close of the session Dan asked me if I would "take a look" at a book manuscript he had written based upon his experiences as a member of the New York State Assembly. I admired his reputation as a smart, thoughtful, tenacious, policy-oriented legislator; one of the "good guys." So I agreed.

The offer to coauthor came after I first gave Dan a memo on how I thought his already very good draft might be strengthened. I demurred at first. Most of the work was already done. A great strength of the draft, I thought, was that it was written in the first person. But it was a fine project; one that held the potential if published to enrich scholars', practitioners', and citizens' understanding of the New York legislature and state legislatures generally. I have devoted myself to the subject of New York government over decades, and thought I might add some value. And during my years in academic administration I had not done a scholarly project of this scope. It was time.

Dan rejected the idea of a book by Feldman *with* Benjamin. He agreed to leave the book in his voice (which we have done, except for the Preface, the Prologue, and the final chapter). The rest, as they say, is history.

Of all that has thus far come out of this project, or may result from it, I value most that it has brought me the friendship of Dan Feldman.

Even a casual observer of its performance, or more accurately non-performance, for much of the time during the 21st century's first decade will understand why the New York State legislature is hard to love. Nonetheless, I am a lover of representative democracy, and therefore of legislatures. This affection extends especially to New York's legislature, its often infuriating, profoundly disturbing behavior notwithstanding. One easy explanation is that there is no accounting for the vagaries of the human heart. Another is that we tend to value most what we know best, warts and all.

But there is also the mind to consider. The workings of our state legislature both require and elude our understanding. Our legislative institution is at once opaque and transparent, the province now and through history of both scoundrels and statesmen. To walk through the halls of the capital and talk with the people who work there is to experience the talent, energy, and diversity of New York. It is a place where together we more-or-less publicly address our great challenges, have our occasional successes, and are diminished by our frailties.

Its disabilities notwithstanding, our legislature is routinely caricatured, and therefore misrepresented, in its operations and performance. I for one have spent far more time debunking our legislature, and pressing for reforms to its practices and processes, than I have praising it. The second thing I value about having worked with Dan on this book, therefore, is that it has helped me, I think, to come to a more nuanced, balanced understanding of our New York legislature, and given me the chance to offer that understanding for the consideration of others.

I am grateful for the support of the staff of the Office of the Dean, College of Liberal Arts and Sciences, and the Center for Research, Regional Education and Outreach (CRREO) at SUNY New Paltz for helping create the time and intellectual space for me to work on this project. The value of the Sojourner Truth Library at New Paltz and all who work there in helping me to find what I need as I research and write, always great for past projects, has not been diminished by the onset of the internet era. Three anonymous readers provided valued guidance in improving this work. The extraordinarily skilled surgical intervention of Dr. Bertrand Guillonneau at the Sloan Kettering Memorial Hospital assured that I could be sitting here, writing this, and looking forward to other projects.

Conversations with Liz Benjamin make me smarter every day about politics and government in Albany. Claudie Benjamin understands what drive me as a professional, but also makes sure that there is balance and joy in my life beyond work (not to mention travel!). And all in the family regularly provide that joy in great measure.

Thank you.

Gerald Benjamin
New Paltz, New York

Preface

"Laws are like sausages. It's better not to see them being made," Otto von Bismarck is said to have remarked. Though perhaps apocryphal, this famous quote is likely accurate in capturing the German Chancellor's sentiment that detailed knowledge of process diminished the human appetite, whether for sausages or for representative democracy. We disagree. Sausages may be one thing. But Bismarck's warning notwithstanding, we have devoted careers to penetrating the fog and mist, with the conviction that there is positive good for our politics and governance in revealing how laws are actually made.

Those outside the Legislature imagine a black or white legislative world; entirely corrupt, or entirely virtuous. Both are wrong. Lawmakers fight intense and dramatic battles. Victory and defeat; anger, frustration, and satisfaction; friendship and betrayal—all the elements of human drama infuse the legislative process. In fact the legislator's is a gray-shaded world, with ambition, constituent service, interest group needs and demands, deeply-held social and constitutional values, ignorance, fear, symbolism, loyalty, pettiness all playing important roles.

The problem of seeing clearly is a powerful clue. It arises, in part, because the manipulation of perceptions is at the core of politics, intentionally causing outsiders to see the legislative world through fog and mist.

The New York State Legislature has been widely and roundly condemned in recent years as non-democratic in the election of its members and its internal procedures, dominated by a few powerful leaders and, in general, non-responsive to the economic and social needs of the state's people. Defenders have responded that critics simply do not understand the intricate workings of the legislative institution, the time and effort required to produce the compromises necessary in the governance of a highly diverse complex polity.

We offer neither a knee jerk condemnation of the Legislature, nor an uncritical panegyric. Rather we seek here to present a nuanced and textured presentation of the flaws and virtues of the New York State Legislature, along with the human relationships and emotions that make it a place of flesh and blood and drama. This is a book that deeply values the legislative experience, and embraces the potential of deliberative democracy, but also understands that we have miles to go before fully realizing that potential.

Neither legal treatises nor legislative process manuals are notable for holding reader attention. The "war stories" centered on New York State politics and policy making in this book are gripping, and frequently involve leaders still in office. But because of our combination of practical experience and scholarly background, we think that we have been able in this book also to convey insight into principles, techniques, and broader lessons applicable to any legislative battle.

Our approach is to dramatize those dimensions of key political/legal controversies, in courts or in legislatures, which reflect a clash of legitimate values. Equality against liberty, liberty against security, equality against property, liberty against efficiency—Americans cherish each value enough so that the inevitable sacrifice of one to another entails pain and upset. Sometimes these case studies we offer enter upon the terrain of litigation: there, as in legislative battle, the underlying value conflict exposes the true legal conflict.

"Tales from the Sausage Factory" is not the conventional third person account of state government and politics. Though purposefully written in the first person, Feldman's voice, this book is a fully collaborative product throughout, one that seeks to integrate decades of experience and scholarship. The idea is to allow the reader to vicariously experience legislative life—placing himself or herself not only in the shoes but inside the head of the Assembly member. We think that the rich detail of this text provides both students and interested citizens access to the contemporary-law making process, and the interactive political and policy considerations that inform and drive lawmakers, in a way that will both interest and inform them.

Though memoirs of legislative leaders are not uncommon, this sort of intense collaboration—between a scholarly practitioner and a scholar with some practical political experience—is rare in the study of New York politics, or legislatures more generally. One author is a Democrat; the other is Republican. One author fought those battles as a member of the New York State Legislature. The other has achieved prominence as a widely-published leading academic expert on New York State government. But also the legislator has written several books on law and government, and the professor has served as an elected member of his county legislature for twelve years, two of them as the county's chief elected official.

Though heavily reliant on stories drawn from Dan Feldman's experience, this book is not a memoir. One important and self-conscious reason for our collaborative authorship was to help avoid the pitfalls of "memoirism," the tendency of old politicians to ramble on with tales colored to make themselves look good, at the expense of historical accuracy and intellectual rigor.

Reflecting our desire for focus and rigor, this book is not loosely structured. Each of the first nine chapters concerns itself with one or more key questions of how politics works in New York State, how the Legislature operates, and how major public policy questions are decided in the Legislature and through the courts. All of this is presented within a consistent general framework—the clash of values, the legislator as a utilitarian, the interplay between politics inside the Legislature with politics in the broader society.

Our first two chapters clarify the elements of legislation: legal principles, values, the internal politics of legislative life, and the politics of external pressures that bear on legislators from constituents, lobbyists, and the press. The next two chapters set forth the "rules of the game": the laws, politics, customs and traditions that govern the legislative process in Albany, illustrated with actual incidents that bring the rules to life. To illuminate by comparison, they also take brief glances at the national legislature in Washington, D.C. and occasionally at state legislatures around the country.

Four major public safety battles form the core of the book, enriched with material drawn from hundreds of other legislative controversies (in the course of which the state legislator/author won enactment of over 140 laws). It took six years of struggle in the New York State Legislature to overcome criminal defense lawyers' opposition to a powerful new legal tool against organized crime, the enterprise corruption statute. A decade later, the Speaker's opposition had to be overcome to establish New York State's Megan's Law. In 1987, the author began the drive to repeal the State's harsh drug laws. And the early 1990s saw the first efforts to make gun manufacturers financially accountable for injuries to victims of gun violence, only to be crushed by the NRA.

These stories reflect a somewhat unusual perspective, in that many who identified themselves as liberal opposed the first two efforts, while those who tend to identify as conservative opposed the extensive efforts to reform the Rockefeller drug laws and to make gun manufacturers subject to tort liability.

All four elements—law, values, inside politics, outside politics—play a role in each story. Each of the five core chapters, though, offers its own unique slant. Changes in outside politics played an especially noticeable role in putting the Organized Crime Control Act on the table, while its ultimate fate depended on the success of highly delicate negotiations across that table. The drugs and prison story shows the powerful consequence of the interaction between the inside politics of the Legislature and the broader movement to reform the Rockefeller drug laws. Outside politics would enable a lone legislator to overcome the opposition of the Speaker both to Megan's Law and to its sponsor; careful attention to legal principles in its drafting and in its presentation in floor debate enabled it to survive a serious post-enactment constitutional challenge in court. The legislative failure to impose financial accountability for gun violence illustrated the power of small but well-organized groups to defeat larger but less intense constituencies; the transfer of the effort to the judicial arena helped show where the lines between courtrooms and Legislatures are properly drawn, and where they are not.

Throughout, *Tales from the Sausage Factory* persistently addresses the kinds of questions that long have been front and center for students of the New York State Legislature and legislatures generally, for example:

1. How are legislators recruited? What motivates people to seek elective office?
2. How do legislators get elected? How do they act in their districts to build support once elected?
3. How do legislators "take ownership" of issues? How do they advance them?
4. How do legislators interact with each other?
5. How do legislators interact with staff?
6. How do personal relationships across houses and party lines help make things work?
7. What is the nature of the mutually dependent/adversarial interaction between legislators and the media?
8. Are members who are in non-contested districts dominated by one party still accountable to those who elect them?

9. How do interest groups affect legislators' behavior? What does each expect of the other?
10. How are legislative leaders elected? What are the stakes for members in the selection process?
11. How powerful really are legislative leaders in New York?
12. May those leaders be resisted with success?
13. How do legislators seek to advance their careers?
14. Where do policy ideas come from?
15. Why do some ideas take off, and other languish?
16. How are bills really negotiated?
17. How do legislative rules work, and how might they be changed?
18. How do policy goals and politics within and outside the Legislature interact with personal ambition in its every-day workings?
19. How does the prospect of court challenges affect lawmaking?
20. What strategies do lawyers use to challenge legislation? To defend legislation? To make policy in courts?

Our penultimate chapter, still from Feldman's perspective, seeks to draw overall lessons from the first nine. The final chapter, written by Benjamin, though hardly an apology for the institution, suggests that evidence presented in this book provides the basis for a less condemnatory reconsideration of the record of the modern legislature in New York.

Prologue—The Senate Scandal of 2009

The book you just picked up took us many years to write. As we worked, the reputation of the New York State Legislature declined. A 2004 study of the respected Brennan Center for Justice made "dysfunctional" the most common description of it used in public discourse. The Legislature's public reputation could get no worse, it seemed. Then in June 2009, as we put the final touches on our manuscript in response to readers' comments, the State Senate became deadlocked for more than a month in an ugly, despairing dispute over its control. To borrow the sports vernacular, the Senate "ratcheted it up a notch," achieving a whole new level of disrepute (even disgust) for itself, and thus for the State Legislature a whole.

So we were putting a new set of final touches on the book some months into 2010 when Governor David Paterson announced that he would not run for a full term later that year. He was caught up in three investigations, one a domestic violence dispute involving one of his closest aides in which he may have acted inappropriately to discourage the victim from pursuing legal recourse, the second a question of possible perjury concerning expensive baseball tickets for which he may or may not have intended to pay, and the third looking into whether political considerations influenced his choice of a contractor for video gambling machines at Aqueduct racetrack. There was therefore considerable pressure for the governor to resign even before completing his own term. Thus, as of 2011, New York will have had at least three and possibly four governors within five years, while the previous three governors served for a total of 32 years.

Paterson's troubles, in the midst of agonizing budget woes, capped an amazing series of embarrassments brought on New York by officials of its state government. These seemed to signal such a breakdown in that government that by March 2010, one State Senator darkly joked that he longed for the days of "dysfunction"—at least it "has function in its title."

Problems with governors have by no means been confined to New York in recent years: see, e.g., Rod Blagojevich of Illinois, Mark Sanford of North Carolina, James McGreevey of New Jersey, and John Rowland of Connecticut. These generally pass with the tenure of the governor in question. Legislatures are forever.

It is hard to imagine, but about forty years earlier the New York Legislature, operating under rules, if anything, granting even more central control to leadership than at present, was considered a model of institutional professionalism. In a 1971 report, it was one of four that received the highest ranking available from the Citizens Conference on State Legislatures. (The others were California, Illinois and Florida.)

In immediately following years, the Legislature in New York was regarded as notable not only for its functioning, but for its leadership. Though they were often at odds, former Governor Mario Cuomo in 1997 noted a "consensus" that the Assembly's Speaker between 1979 and 1986, Stanley Fink, "was one of the best Speakers this century." Warren Anderson, the Republican Senate Majority Leader longest serving in modern history (1973–1988), is remembered as a giant, notable for example for suspending partisanship to assure the fiscal rescue of New York City in 1975.

This book tells stories that took place in and around the New York State Legislature during the last thirty years. In an apparent paradox, this was a time of reassertion of power by the legislative institution, led by Fink in the Assembly and Anderson in the Senate, while also a time of steady decline in the Legislature's reputation, and performance. There were a number of reasons for this. One was a change in the political recruitment process. Aspirants for legislative service were no longer screened by strong county party leaders capable of assessing individuals' readiness for elective office or advancement. They now succeeded in a more atomized, less mediated candidate- and money-centered politics in which individual wealth and interest group resources counted for much more than in the past.

Perhaps ironically in light of events since control came fully into Democratic party hands in 2008, the decline in legislative performance and reputation was also attributed to bi-partisan gerrymandering. This practice both arose from and resulted in institutionalized long-term divided partisan control, and contributed to a very high member reelection rate, entrenched incumbency and—it was argued—insulation from the public will.

The professional resources provided the Legislature that led to praise in 1971 were controlled by the leaders of the partisan majorities in each house, reinforcing their hold on power. Staff and public money—member items doled out from the "pork barrel"—were consistently used to reinforce the majorities in each house. Beginning in the 1970's, the rise of leader-dominated Campaign Committees in each chamber devoted to political resource gathering and used to assure majority continuity reinforced the Senate and Assembly as centers of reelection politics.

All these developments lead to increased independence from executive leadership, making reaching decisions in tough times and on tough issues harder. But most important, they raised the stakes of having and holding the legislative majorities in each house.

The bizarre events of 2009, apparently the results of a "perfect storm" of unlikely coincidences, may be seen as the result of pent-up forces in the State Senate that had been gathering for decades. As of 2007, all statewide elected offices in New York were in Democratic hands. A large Democratic majority in the Assembly was entrenched. Only the State Senate remained Republican. Notwithstanding their control of the year 2000–census–based reapportionment, as described in this book, the Republican Senate majority had been shrinking steadily as the decade advanced. Key factors were an aging membership, a declining "farm team" in parts of the state, Governor Eliot Spitzer's aggressive partisanship in support of the Democratic Senate minority, and—most of all—continued demographic change.

Democrats who left New York City to move into the old Republican suburban strongholds downstate, on Long Island and in Westchester County, stopped changing their party registrations as the political machines weakened: as fewer and fewer suburbanites needed patronage favors, the incentives to register Republican disappeared. The upstate rural population, reliably Republican, shrank both absolutely and proportionally, as manufacturing that sustained the state's smaller population centers left and the economic environment for farming became more challenging. Upstate, too, Republicans grew increasingly disillusioned with the failure of their party to revive the economies of their region during a twelve-year period when a Republican governor, George Pataki, enjoyed control of the Senate by his co-partisans.

What Happened in the New York State Senate in 2009

Finally, in 2008, with Barack Obama leading the ticket with more than 62% of the vote, New York's voters elected 32 Democrats and 30 Republicans to the State Senate. But the new Democratic majority in the Senate did not find it easy to organize the body in order to govern. Politics in New York had long been an avenue for the succession to status and power for leaders of ethnic, racial and religious minorities, and for the realization of personal ambition. It also has been an arena for ethnic conflict: the new Senate Democratic conference was far more diverse than the Republican one it displaced. David Paterson, an African-American, had served as Senate Minority Leader before becoming Lieutenant Governor, and then succeeding to the Governorship. His successor as Minority Leader and the principle aspirant for the Majority Leadership, Malcolm Smith, was also African American. Meanwhile, Hispanic-American legislators' ambitions for top leadership posts were unrealized.

Early on, a "Gang of Four" Democratic members—Carl Kruger from Brooklyn, Hiram Monserrate from Queens, and Pedro Espada and Ruben Diaz Sr., both from the Bronx—delayed the organization of the Senate by refusing to caucus with the Democrats or commit to supporting Malcolm Smith for Majority Leader.

Kruger, first elected in a special election in 1994, had already established a record of party disloyalty: he was the only Democrat in recent memory to chair a committee under Senate Republican leadership.

Espada, elected to the Senate in 2008 after two previous periods of service, had narrowly escaped indictment some years earlier when other members of a Bronx health-care non-profit, which had paid him over $400,000 in annual salary through 2007, and to which he funneled state taxpayer dollars, were indicted and convicted for improper use of such funds. The State Attorney General continued to investigate whether Espada had used employees of the group in his election campaign; other investigators questioned his compliance with election law residence and campaign contribution filing requirements.

Diaz, an ordained evangelical minister, former member of the City Council and member of the Senate since 2002, was an avowed opponent of gay rights in all its public policy manifestations, and especially gay marriage.

Monserrate, a former police officer and New York City Council member, achieved some recognition for his advocacy for illegal aliens. He ran a close primary race for a Senate nomination in 2006 against John Sabini, a four-year incumbent. When Sabini stood down to take the chairmanship of the State Racing and Wagering Board in 2008, Monserrate was unopposed for the Democratic nomination. He achieved notoriety shortly before assuming his new position with his arrest for allegedly cutting his girlfriend's face with a broken glass, an action for which he was convicted ten months later, in October 2009, only of a related misdemeanor, but on the basis of which he was expelled from the State Senate in February 2010 by a vote of 53 to 8.

Because Republicans added a seat in their reapportionment for the 2002 election to bolster their majority, the Senate had an even number of members. With the Democratic margin only two votes, any one of these four could therefore produce a leadership deadlock. Monserrate, the least senior of the group, which came to be called "the Amigos," came over relatively quickly, his reward the chair of the Consumer Protection Committee. But the other three held out for bigger stakes. January came with the remaining three holdouts more or less explicitly threatening to elect a Republican Senate leader, the general election outcome notwithstanding.

Democrats last won the New York State Senate majority during the 1964 Lyndon Johnson landslide victory over Barry Goldwater (and before that in 1938). In 1965 it took the intervention of a Republican Governor, Nelson Rockefeller, to facilitate their organizing both the Senate and Assembly. After a complex fight over reapportionment, the Democrats lost control of both houses after a single year. Now, after forty years in the wilderness, same as the biblical Hebrews, the Senate Democrats were doing it again—or not doing it—much to the disgust of commentators across the state.

Malcolm Smith, thirsting mightily for that majority leadership, with a daunting fiscal crisis looming and to end an impasse that was bringing into question Senate Democrats' capacity to govern even before they began, decided to pay the necessary price. Kruger, who had chaired the Social Services Committee under the Republicans, now got the ultimate plum committee assignment, chairmanship of Finance. Diaz got a pledge of some sort that the Senate would at least "slow-track" the gay marriage bill, notwithstanding promises made by the Senate Democrats to the gay community during the election that this measure would quickly be brought to a vote. (When the Senate finally brought the bill to a vote in December 2009, gay activists were surprised and deeply disappointed by its 38 to 24 defeat.) Espada would be Vice President of the Senate for Urban Policy—a newly invented job—and chair of the Housing, Construction and Community Development Committee. These decisions clearly left a residuum of unhappiness about Smith with a number of the loyal members in the Democratic majority, exacerbating his later problems.

Meanwhile Republican Senator Dean Skelos of Nassau County on Long Island looked on in frustration. After 26 years in the Senate, Skelos finally got to serve as Majority Leader when Joseph Bruno, the long-time Republican holder of that post, resigned just after the 2008 session adjourned. Then the prize was snatched from him by the results of that year's election. (Bruno had been under investigation at the time. More than a year later, in December 2009, he was convicted on two federal felony counts of depriving his constituents of the "honest services" he owed them by secretly accepting several hundred thousand dollars from a client with an interest in matters under consideration by the Legislature. The United States Supreme Court at the time was planning to consider whether the "honest services" statute was unconstitutionally vague.)

Skelos and his Republican colleagues also had a longer term problem. With the loss of their majority for the first time in over forty years, with a number of the older, now powerless remaining GOP incumbents tempted by retirement, and with the demographic cards stacked against them, they faced an uphill climb to return to power in 2010. And if they remained in the minority in that year, the future was very bleak indeed. A persuasive study published in 2009 predicted that six more Senate seats would go Democratic at the 2012 post-reapportionment election if the Democrats got to draw the district lines after the results were in from the 2010 census. Only if the Republicans could reestablish control of the Senate in 2010, and therefore control the reapportionment, might they hold on. This was a slim chance, but the GOP's only chance, to retain a political bastion in New York over the longer term.

Sensing that Espada and Monserrate were not happy with the outcome of their deals with Smith as the session progressed, Skelos very quietly courted them. In developing these relationships, Skelos and his colleagues were assisted by upstate billionaire and former gubernatorial aspirant Tom Golisano and his political advisor, Steve Pigeon. Golisano had given $5 million to Democratic legislative campaigns in 2008, only to be deeply disappointed at his lack of influence with the new leadership, and what in his view was continued-tax-and spend budgeting.

On June 8, 2009, in a surprise legislative maneuver, Tom Libous, Republican of Binghamton, offered a resolution in the Senate that at first seemed innocuous. As the clerk completed reading the title, however, it became clear that it allowed for the vote on a new Senate leadership. Before the result of this vote was recognized by the Senator then presiding, Democrat Neil Breslin of Albany, Democrat Jeffrey Klein of the Bronx and Westchester moved for adjournment. Breslin then adjourned the house, but without a vote. He and 27 other Democrats walked out. The 30 Republicans remained, along with Espada, Monserrate, Diaz, and Kruger. With the votes of Espada, Monserrate, and all thirty Republicans (but not Kruger and Diaz, who abstained) a resolution passed electing Espada as temporary president and Skelos as majority leader of the Senate, separating jobs that were formerly joined. Though great tumult ensued, it was clear that Smith and his Democrats had lost operating control of the body.

Democrats sought to use their remaining physical control of the Senate chamber to block the conduct of business. Monserrate again proved a weak link for the "coalition": at first he refused to participate in substantive votes until, he said, more Democrats could be attracted to their ranks. Working Families party and Democratic party activists pressured him fiercely. When on June 15, 2009 the Democrats voted for an alternative to Smith as leader in their conference, John Sampson of Brooklyn, Monserrate returned to their ranks. This left the Senate divided evenly: 31 members in each camp.

Ordinarily, the Lieutenant Governor would have been able to cast a procedural vote to end such an impasse. But when Eliot Spitzer resigned as Governor in 2008, his Lieutenant Governor, David Paterson, automatically became Governor, leaving the Lieutenant Governor position vacant. No provision in the state constitution existed specifically to cover this circumstance. Since the requirement was passed in 1953 that the governor and lieutenant governor be elected at the same time, on the same ballot, vacancies that had previously arisen were left unfilled until the next gubernatorial election. Changes to the constitution concerning this requirement were considered but not adopted. Calls for a constitutional amendment to remedy this problem began to be heard. The need for a provision concerning filling a vacancy that might arise in the lieutenant governorship was even used to further justify emerging arguments for the need for a constitutional convention.

Meanwhile, however, the Democrats and the Republican-dominated coalition each claimed control of the Senate, but neither could conduct any business. When Governor Paterson ordered the Senate into special session every day, including weekends, starting on June 21, Espada and Smith each tried to preside, each with his own gavel. Simultaneous "sessions" proceeded, with each side trying to out shout the other. Capturing the level of public disgust, on June 24, 2009 the New York *Post* published a front-page picture of seven senators sitting in the Chamber with clown faces superimposed over their own, under the caption "State Senate holds emergency meeting."

Traditionally, both houses, the Assembly and the Senate, pass most of the year's legislation, and virtually all the controversial bills, in late June. The Senate deadlock meant that important revenue-sharing grants could not go to local governments; the City of Yonkers came within days of bankruptcy as a result. New York City and upstate counties lost tens of millions of dollars as the Senate could not pass required reauthorizations of existing sales taxes and a promised quarter percent increase authorization for the City's sales tax. Legislation empowering New York City Mayor Bloomberg to control the City's school system through his appointee, Joel Klein, expired, forcing school governance there to revert to the old, failed, Board of Education. The editorial pages excoriated the entire Senate, noting that even those members who usually merited some measure of respect would not abandon the stop-at-nothing efforts to seize power.

Governor Paterson directed Comptroller Tom DiNapoli to withhold expense checks and paychecks from the Senators. After a few days, DiNapoli complied, while also noting that he asked the courts to rule on whether such an action was legal. On July 8, Paterson claimed the legal authority to appoint a lieutenant governor, against the advice of Attorney General Andrew Cuomo that such a move was unconstitutional. Paterson appointed Richard Ravitch, a 76-year old former chair of the Metropolitan Transportation Authority and successful businessman.

This move might have restored the Democratic majority to power without Espada. However, even when the State's high court, the Court of Appeals, found Ravitch to be legitimately in office in a narrow 4–3 decision, he, as Lieutenant Governor, could vote only on procedural questions. Thus, had the controversy persisted, a 31–31 deadlock still would have been left in place even with a Democrat "leading" the body.

Though constitutionally questionable, the appointment of Ravitch was good politics. It seemed to break a psychological roadblock, and start things moving. Also, rumors emerged that other blocks of legislators were threatening to switch sides: whether such moves would have helped the Democrats or the Republicans, they could have rendered Espada irrelevant. Then, on July 9, Espada returned to the Democratic fold—as majority leader. Smith remained as temporary president, but apparently temporary was the operative word, since Monserrate's return had been conditioned on Smith's replacement by John Sampson. Sampson emerged as "caucus leader," presumably preparatory to his eventual ascension to temporary Senate president.

What the Senate Scandal Meant—Two Almost Opposite Interpretations

A legislative leader faces extraordinary challenges. That leader must discern the will of the majority on matters large and small, and even more, the compromises that the majority will accept. To do so, the leader must also know what each individual that comprises the majority wants and needs, for the State, for his or her district, for himself or herself, and even for his or her family and friends. Over time, the skilled leader comes to an intimate knowledge of the members, their strengths and weaknesses, and to the range of action they will permit. And while doing all this, the leader must take a statewide perspective, and also be mindful of guarding the institutional interests of the Legislature.

Let us return to Warren Anderson and Stanley Fink.

Warren Anderson once told one of us:

If the Conference really feels strongly about something, I could not or would not go around them. But I have gotten to know when I could just go ahead. . . . You have to develop the confidence of the members that you're leading in the right direction. They may not all immediately see it or they may see it and not want to vote for it, but if they have the confidence that you're not going to do something stupid, they'll support you.

Similarly, Fink remarked to one of us:

Leadership is a two way street. I think a leader in the Legislature these days in New York would be foolish to underestimate the collective power of the individual members, to ignore their concerns, their intellect, their preferred solutions to problems. People want to have an opportunity to be heard and take part in the process. . . . I used to hold Democratic Conferences where all members were given an opportunity to be heard and no one was cut off . . . After spending a great deal of time in the Conference room and having the patience for them to hear me and me to hear them . . . I was generally very aware of the parameters of what I could or could not negotiate on behalf of this group of men and women.

To do the leader's job in the way Anderson and Fink did it requires tolerance of colleagues with vastly different backgrounds and values. (Fink, in particular, gloried in the diversity of his Conference.) But it also required a willingness to stand firm for the whole group, and mobilize it on behalf of a collective purpose.

Malcolm Smith had never led a majority; Dean Skelos had barely done so. Smith faced the task of leading a group largely comprised of members that had long served in the minority, people who perhaps had become comfortable with having the perquisites and status of office without the responsibility of governing, people who had never really faced the need of foregoing individual goals in favor of collective purposes. Skelos had experience being in the majority, but acted out of the desperation of having lost personal power on the cusp of grasping it, and with his colleagues, facing its permanent loss.

Both gave too much to a few opportunistic individuals—some of them likely corrupt—and by doing so each proved himself unworthy of achieving the balance required of first-rate legislative leaders. Smith did not insist on the collective purpose in meeting unreasonable individual demands; in doing so he undid his majority and plunged New York into further difficulty at a time of great crisis. Skelos sacrificed the integrity of his Conference to the single priority of restoring a temporary Republican power base and, he hoped, creating a path to future power for himself and his party at virtually any cost.

Both authors learned through legislative service at the state and local level to admire the good qualities of legislators whose bad qualities, in another life, might have turned us utterly against them. Both know that in legislative life, the perfect is the enemy of the good. Both also know, however, of the need to stand up for fundamental democratic values in order to defend the Legislature's reputation and, in doing so, its policy-making purpose. Arguably, acceding to political extortion does not even pass the test of good practical politics: as with blackmail, the victim never finishes paying the price. In seeking both personal and institutional power, both Smith and Skelos showed they never knew or had forgotten that a leader who fails to take a stand in favor of institutional integrity is, in the end, destructive of the democratic purpose of legislatures.

Maybe ethics, ultimately, is good politics, after all. We don't share the notion of ethics as clearly denoting good and bad. Principles must indeed be compromised, to a point—but no further. Whatever sound bites the legislative leader may feed the public, he or she must bear in mind the greater complexities of governing through the institutions we have so arduously created, and must nurture, to serve us.

However, one may take a dramatically different view of the Senate proceedings of June/July 2009, drawing conclusions that may be quite different but equally valid, and even—perhaps—heartening. The 2008 election truly shook the status quo. Lobbyists and government insiders who benefited from that status quo—the winners when public authorities remained patronage troughs for political favorites and the State maintained high incarceration rates of low-level drug offenders—were shaken when power in the State Senate shifted. Among the powerful tabloid voices decrying the Senate scandal, with the stately *New York Times* largely in chorus, a lone critical reporter, Tom Robbins of the *Village Voice*, was barely noticed suggesting that the din about the "petty internal dispute" in the Senate drew public attention away from much, much larger issues: that the new Democratic majority threatened long-entrenched power centers.

While the Democrats had not distinguished themselves in their short period of dominance prior to the June coup—enacting a deeply-flawed budget with the traditional three-men-in-a-room secrecy, delaying and jeopardizing the passage of numerous other important pieces of legislation—they had included in that budget the first increase in the basic welfare grant in eighteen years, and they had enacted the Rockefeller drug law reforms, stalled for decades previous by the Republicans. On tap, although not assured of enactment, was legislation protecting some New York City tenants against rent increases, assuring minimally decent working conditions for domestic workers and temporary farm workers, and imposing some more reasonable limits on campaign contributions.

In fact, in December 2009, the Governor signed into law another measure long stifled by the former Republican majority, submitting public authorities' contracts to the State Comptroller for approval or rejection, making it harder for them to burden the State with more debt, and forcing them to reveal their relationships with lobbyists—a significant victory in the effort to control abuse by this too-secretive "phantom government."

The actual process of restoring control to the Democrats, ugly though it was, included important Senate rules reform. Pedro Espada, the new Senate Majority Leader, taking credit for insisting on rules reform as a condition of his return to the Democratic fold, said "it was never about power, but empowerment of 62 members [of the Senate] . . . and through them, all of the people of the State of New York." In fact, with their return to the majority problematic, one default Republican goal for the month-long coalition "insurrection" might have been redistribution of institutional power and resources to individual Senators in anticipation of their permanent minority status.

However implausible Espada's claimed priority may have been, the Senate Majority Leader, whoever it may be in the future, will find it hard to reverse some of these reforms: one rule change takes some control of committee staff away from central leadership and gives it to committee chairs and (minority party) ranking members. Another takes some control over the bill calendar away from the Majority Leader by assuring a bill supported by a majority of Senators the right to a floor vote. Other reforms may be somewhat easier to overturn: providing a greater share of the body's resources to each individual senator; eight-year term limits on Senate leadership posts; committee composition proportional to the overall proportions of Democrats and Republicans in the Senate. Still, revolutions are built on rising expectations, so these real steps forward mean something.

Governor Paterson described the competition between the Democrats and the Republicans for the support of Espada and Monserrate as "so blatantly quid pro quo that it borders on the boundaries of illegality," in other words, sale to the highest bidder—a process that brought Espada, a junior senator with notorious ethical problems to a title, if not a position, historically held by the actual leader of the State Senate, and placed him in line for the governorship. The party caucuses found themselves competing for the support of legislators that a spokesperson for Malcolm Smith had earlier called—when they sided with the Republicans—"a thief and a thug."

Thus actual enactment of some needed reform legislation, real hope for the future of further reform, and some rules changes with the potential of great significance, resulted from a truly nauseating process. Whether Otto von Bismarck really did first utter the phrase we borrowed for the title of our book, or whether as current scholarship now suggests, a nineteenth century lawyer and poet should get the credit, whoever said it was not joking: there are times, at least, when legislation you like will emerge from a process the sight of which would make you sick.

Nonetheless, we reject the advice to avoid looking closely at how it is made. We assume, if you have read this far, you do too.

After all, we have the memory of Warren Anderson and Stanley Fink, two great legislative leaders, able—when times and circumstance required—to transcend partisanship in the interests of New York State.

Might what once was, be again?

CHAPTER I

Getting the Job and Starting It: Politics, Ethics, Values

For 18 years, between 1981 and 1998, I was New York State Assembly Member Dan Feldman. I represented District 45 (of the state's 150) in the southern part of the borough of Brooklyn, in the City of New York. If one superimposed a clock face on Brooklyn, my district would be the slice between 5:30 and 6:30, including parts or all of the neighborhoods of Sheepshead Bay, Manhattan Beach, Brighton Beach, Gerritsen Beach, Plumb Beach, Marine Park, Ocean Parkway, Kings Highway, and Midwood. (See map on page 16).

Brooklyn is legendary. My piece of Brooklyn was and is best understood not for any building, or event, or sports team, but as the home of 118,000 down-to-earth, hard-working people—a big part of the heart, soul, and backbone of middle-class New York.

As I write, I think: "One paragraph and I have already—if not entirely intentionally—told you something very important about the way legislators see the world." It was always, to me, *my* district. I took ownership when I won my first election. I kept ownership by dint of close attention and hard work for all the years I served. Other Assembly members deferred to me on matters where (just) my district was concerned, as I did to them for theirs.

Winning in My *District*

My first campaign for my Assembly seat in 1980 was decided in a Democratic primary. Inter-party politics barely counted. (Later, when I got to Albany, I learned that inter-party competition pervaded all, and

Brooklyn STATE ASSEMBLY DISTRICTS

■■■■■■■■■■■■■■■■■■■■■■■■■■■■■■■■■■■■

38 Frederick D. Schmidt (D-R-C-RTL)
    (Also in Queens)
39 Stanley Fink (D-L)
40 Edward Griffith (D-L)
41 Helene E. Weinstein (D)
42 Harry Smoler (D)
43 Rhoda S. Jacobs (D-L)
44 Melvin Miller (D-L)
45 Daniel Feldman (D)
46 Howard L. Lasher (D-L)
47 Frank J. Barbaro (D-L)
48 Samuel Hirsch (D)

49 Dominick L. DiCarlo (R-C-RTL)
50 Florence M. Sullivan (R-C-RTL)
51 Joseph Ferris (D-L)
52 Eileen C. Dugan (D-L)
53 Woodrow Lewis (D-L)
54 Thomas S. Boyland (D-L)
55 Thomas R. Fortune (D-R-L)
56 Albert Vann (D-L)
57 Roger L. Green (D-L)
58 Joseph R. Lentol (D)
59 Victor L. Robles (D-L)

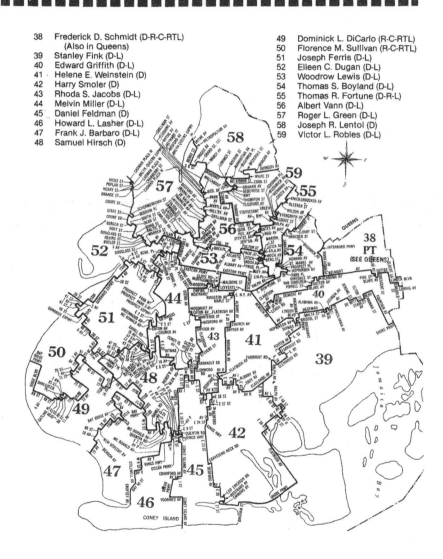

was defining of everyday legislative life.) My Republican opponent in the general election that followed was Barry Kaufman, a very pleasant and articulate man roughly my own age. He knew the district's proclivities. When he campaigned alongside me, Kaufman told the voters that he was the Republican candidate and I was their next Assembly Member. He was right. Like most local Democratic candidates in the area before me and since, I won the general election with 80 percent of the vote.

In the primary, however, I had had serious competition. New York State's political party structure is county-based. (Brooklyn, a borough for city purposes, is the County of Kings for state purposes.) Each party in each county has a county committee. Within New York City, assembly district boundaries are used to define the sub units of the county party, from which county committee members are chosen. Each Assembly district contains a "regular" party club, and many also are the homes of "reform" clubs organized at some time in history around a candidate, issue or issues, in opposition to the regulars within the party. One or the other or both may send elected members to the county committee.

Although my candidacy had the support of the district's reform Democratic club as well as the main body of the regular Democratic organization, a significant disgruntled faction of the regular organization supported my principal opponent, Ruben Margules. Margules, an Orthodox Jew, was a wealthy landlord, a graduate of the Harvard Business School, and a very aggressive campaigner. He also had the support of the Midwood Development Corporation, then a powerful community organization in the district, created to maintain neighborhood housing quality and street safety. Although my primary opponent campaigned as one who understood tenant problems and was sympathetic to their needs, a legitimate computer printout of the violations in the buildings he owned—including rats, cockroaches, falling ceilings—ultimately emerged, and essentially destroyed his candidacy. I won with about 10,000 votes; he had about 5000, and Bill Rothman, a third candidate with little organized support, garnered about 2500.

I never again faced a serious political threat to my Assembly seat. Perhaps my legislative record protected me. It ultimately included the enactment of the more than 140 laws I wrote, many resulting in quality-of-life improvements for my constituents. More likely, it was my district office, personally helping thousands of constituents get their lost Social Security checks, their garbage picked up more regularly, a crossing guard at their children's school, or any of a plenitude of other services. Or it was my personal leadership of a series of battles like picketing the opening of a new X-rated movie theatre on a busy shopping street down the block from St. Edmund's School and the Ocean Avenue Synagogue, till it closed for good; or collecting ten thousand petition signatures against the dumping of toxic dredging material in the ocean less than a mile from the shore of my district, and delivering them to the Governor, who then persuaded the Port Authority to back off; or arranging for the 8000 members of a beach club in my district to get about $100 each in refunds from a tax illegally collected from them. Or it may have been my attendance at literally thousands of community meetings, weekday evenings and Sunday mornings, of the East 14th Street Block Association, the Brighton Neighborhood Association, the Ocean Avenue Synagogue Men's Club, the Atlantic Towers Tenant Association, the Resurrection Parish Home School Association, the P.S. 254 Parent-Teachers Association, the 61st Police Precinct Council, Community Board 14, School Board 21, etcetera, ad infinitum. Or perhaps I can attribute it to meeting and greeting voters on their way to work between 6:30 a.m. and 8:30 a.m. three times a year at each of the eleven subway stop entrances in my district. And then there were the two dozen or so presentations of Dan Feldman's John F. Kennedy Memorial Citizenship Award at June graduation ceremonies each year, $25 or $50 bonds supplied by neighborhood banks, each given to a student selected by one of the elementary, junior high, and high schools in my district.

Here's the point. Critics have said that the overwhelming majorities run up by incumbent legislators seeking reelection in New York are a sign of failed democracy. And they are surely right in saying that we should not design legislative districts to discourage competition, assure the perpetuation of particular people in office, or cement partisan majorities in place in the Assembly or Senate. But the geographic concentration of voters' partisan preferences militates against real competition between major parties in most of Brooklyn, and across much of New York State. Also, critics tend to overlook the prospect of intra-party competition that helps keep incumbents alert and accountable. And some of an incumbent's advantage, a lot of it, arises from doing exactly what he or she is supposed to do—working hard, in and for the district.

When I came to office in 1981, my constituents were overwhelmingly second-, third-, and fourth-generation Americans of Jewish, Italian, Irish, and German ancestry. My district also included a small but interesting pocket of upper middle-class African Americans, whose ancestors had come up from the South a century earlier to work at what was then the Sheepshead Bay Racetrack. There were also remnants of what had been, prior to the ascension of Astoria, Queens, the largest Greek-American community in New York City, and a few old-stock Americans of British descent, whose ancestors here dated back to the Colonial period.

At least half of my constituents were tenants, mostly in multiple dwelling apartment houses, but some in smaller two- and three-family structures. The rest owned private homes. My immediate predecessors in the Assembly were Charles Schumer and Stephen Solarz, who were both considered liberal at the time and had gone on to the U.S. Congress. Schumer's popular predecessor in Congress was another liberal, Elizabeth Holtzman.

Many of these characteristics changed over the eighteen years I served. Orthodox Jews began to replace many of the more assimilated Reform and Conservative Jews; Russian immigrants in large numbers replaced the older residents of Brighton Beach and, to a lesser extent, Sheepshead Bay; Chinese immigrants replaced Italians and Jews both as residents and shopkeepers on Avenue U.

Many of the apartment buildings converted to cooperatives, so many tenants transformed themselves into owners of their own apartments.

The district's political coloration became far more conservative. While residents had occasionally voted for Republicans at the top of the ticket even early in my tenure, at least most had voted Democratic for Bill Clinton over the first George Bush and Bob Dole, for Mario Cuomo over all his opponents, and of course for Ed Koch. But as time went on, voting Republican become more of a habit, with the district giving majorities to Rudy Giuliani over David Dinkins in 1989 and 1993, George Pataki over Carl McCall in 2002, and the second George Bush over Al Gore in 2000 and over John Kerry in 2004. In 1993, to my intense annoyance, the leaders of the Democratic party organization in my Assembly District endorsed Rudy Giuliani for election as Mayor.

I never consciously altered my position on an issue to suit my constituents. It may be that I adjusted my beliefs to theirs without conscious awareness, but I doubt it. While the views of my constituents were generally more conservative than my own, and became increasingly so over the years, for the most part they allowed me the leeway to act as my conscience dictated. Rent control was the only issue that would have endangered my seat, had I disagreed with my constituents on it. A City Council Member, Leon Katz, who represented much of the same area, actually lost his seat on that basis. Even when conversion of rental units to cooperatives reduced the tenant percentage in my district, the vehemence and intensity of support for rent control might have sufficed to assure the defeat of a politician who opposed it.

While particular groups of constituents vehemently objected to my support of gay rights, my efforts to ease the Rockefeller drug laws, or any number of other liberal stances I took, the same constituents generally approved of my support for the death penalty, mild and nuanced though it was, my support for other changes in the law to strengthen police and prosecutors, and certainly my consumer protection and environmental protection efforts. And all of them loved my fight to curb the parking ticket excesses of the New York City Parking Violations Bureau.

A First Crusade to Change the Law: The Battle of the Parking Violations Bureau

When I was a college senior in 1970, a fellowship from the Alfred P. Sloan Foundation allowed me to work at a fairly high level of New York City government in the Lindsay Administration. I helped design the Parking Violations Bureau. Our goal was to get parking tickets out of the criminal courts, where they clogged a process that needed more time for more serious problems, and into an administrative agency, where they would presumably be handled more quickly and efficiently.

Eleven years later, as a first-term legislator, I encountered some unintended consequences of my labors. When I tried to register a new car, the New York State Department of Motor Vehicles, based on a computer message it received from the City Parking Violations Bureau, insisted that I owed $200 in unpaid tickets. Since I rarely got parking tickets, and this was a lot of money for me, I remembered these several tickets (for one late registration sticker) and I also remembered that I had paid them by check. I found the cancelled check, but I had to spend another day straightening out the problem before I could return to the DMV to register my car, a very annoying experience.

As it turned out, the PVB had a computer with a record of my payment. It had a second computer, however, that *only* had the record of what I owed, and that forwarded that information to the DMV. The second computer did not have the information in the first computer and the two computers were altogether incompatible.

After I told my story to the press, over a hundred furious citizens told their stories to me. Realizing that the PVB must be doing this sort of thing a lot, I brought suit to force it to mend its ways. The judge offered a lesson in government. He told me in these exact words, "You're a leg-islator—change the law!"

So in 1982 I began a crusade to give the PVB a financial incentive to be more careful. That is, I wrote, introduced, and pressed for enactment of a bill to make the PVB pay the motorist—beyond reimbursement for paying the ticket—on proof by cancelled checks, copies of filed stolen motor vehicle forms, or the like, that the PVB continued its harassment beyond reason after receiving proof that the motorist had already paid the ticket or shouldn't have gotten it in the first place. Note that I was trying to change a practice in New York City by altering New York state law. The Home Rule provision of the state constitution notwith-standing, one of the worst kept secrets of New York government is that this is not only possible, but a regular practice. That's why the city maintains a substantial lobbying office in Albany. The lobbyists for the mayor of New York City quietly but effectively fought my efforts.

I figured the City opposed the bill so tenaciously because it needed the $20 million a year it was collecting at the time from people who did not owe the money but who found it less onerous to pay than to jump through the hoops the City set up for anyone who challenged a ticket. The City lobbyists argued that penalizing government for its errors, even these extraordinarily egregious ones, would set a dangerous precedent that would hamstring efforts to govern. Little did I know that powerful political leaders in New York were profiting personally—and illegally—from the magnitude of New York City's parking fine collections. (This became important to my later battle to win enactment of New York's Or-ganized Crime Control Act, as explained in Chapter Five.)

I won the PVB battle. The press loved the bill, so I was able to embar-rass the Koch administration regularly with newspaper accounts of the PVB's egregious behavior and the City's stubborn resistance to reform. In 1987 the City gave up, and the bill became law. Years later, when I ran for Congress, Ed Koch endorsed me and graciously added, based in part on the PVB battle, that we had had "big fights" over legislation, but I had been right.

Changing the World by Changing the Law—Values: Origins and Perspectives

My fellow citizens chose me to be one of the lucky people who got to change the laws to make the world more like what we thought it should be. My colleagues in legislatures and I picked the ideas we liked, or dreamed them up ourselves, and made them into legislation. We persuaded our fellow-legislators to vote for our bills, and governors or presidents to sign them. Often, we didn't succeed, but when we did, we felt very good about it. Something real in the world had changed because we were there, and acting to make change happen. Often these were small things. But sometimes they altered the daily lives of literally millions of people.

After I left the Legislature, six years as New York State Assistant Deputy Attorney General gave me the opportunity to continue to help shape policy in a different way. Drawing upon our experience as the people's lawyers in New York State, we in the Attorney General's office proposed changes in the law, and sought to define or alter law through litigation.

The roles overlapped. As a legislator, I sometimes needed to use the courtroom to defend one of my public safety statutes, and I almost always needed to be aware of the courtroom implications of my legislative initiatives as I advanced them. As an assistant to the Attorney General, from time to time my public safety suggestions were reflected in the Attorney General's legislative program and others of the Office's responses to public safety controversies.

The public safety battles recounted in this volume spanned both roles. It took until 1986 to enact the Organized Crime Control Act, six years after I was first elected. It only took me about three years to get Megan's Law enacted in 1995. My crusade against the Rockefeller drug laws, which I began in 1987, only achieved dramatic success in 2009 under the leadership of others, eleven years after I left the Legislature and four years after the end of my service for the Attorney General. I began my effort to impose negligence liability on handgun manufacturers in the early 1990s and continued it in the Office of the Attorney General in the first few years of the twenty-first century; success remains beyond our grasp.

LIBERALS AND CONSERVATIVES: VALUES IN BALANCE

At first blush, my role in those stories may seem puzzling. The first two would generally be regarded as conservative initiatives, while the second two would conventionally be labeled liberal. My strong efforts on behalf of both "liberal" and "conservative" changes in policy occasionally puzzled my fellow legislators. But as I worked in the field of criminal justice I felt no inconsistency, because here it was most evident that the ferocious policy conflicts between "liberals" and "conservatives" in the United States arise from common values.

Let me draw upon my own personal history to illustrate this point. I was a small child during the McCarthy era of the early 1950's, but I remember my parents' strong civil libertarian views on criminal justice. They were sharply aware of the potential for oppression of the innocent by government prosecutors. No spy had been executed in peacetime in the United States, and no woman had been executed by the federal government since the Civil War, when Ethel and Julius Rosenberg went to the electric chair in 1953 after their conviction for spying for the Soviet Union. At the time, it was by no means clear that they were guilty. Serious doubts remain to this day about Ethel's guilt. Prosecutorial and judicial misconduct deprived the Rosenbergs of a fair trial. Irving Kaufman, the trial judge, engaged in improper *ex parte* communications with Irving Saypol, one of the prosecutors (such communications, excluding counsel for the defendant, violate the procedural laws). He had even more egregiously improper off-the-record conversations with Justice Department officials during the course of the trial. Given doubts at the time that the Rosenbergs were guilty at all, this provided a particularly clear example of how the constitutionally guaranteed rights of defendants on trial work to safeguard against abuse by government, and therefore to assure fairness

Later, during my own formative years in the 1960's and my early adult years in the 1970's, crime in New York City reached pandemic proportions. Well-publicized stories of vicious attacks on innocent citizens by criminals appeared almost daily. It became very clear to me that the criminal, at least at the moment of the crime, had more power than the victim. This experience made me relatively more sensitive to the predations of criminals, and the consequent need for increases in prosecutorial and police power necessary to curb criminal behavior. Inevitably, I came to put a high value on protecting citizens against attacks by criminals, even if it required some increase in the power of government.

So because of one fundamental value—a desire to resist oppression of the less powerful by the more powerful, whatever its source—I was sensitive to the possibility of abuse of power by government, and retained a distrust of government power, while also recognizing the need for strong, effective government to assure public safety. The ferocious clashes between liberals and conservatives about criminal justice policy in the states and nation would certainly be mediated more effectively if the two sides acknowledged their shared dislike of oppression, which surely constitutes more than a minor point of agreement.

The balance we all must strike, more or less self-consciously, between security against criminals on the one hand, and security against government abuse on the other, constitutes just one small part of a larger value system. Relatively few people in the United States, academic studies show, act in accord with internally consistent value systems structured to reflect a particular ideology. Most Americans, and like them, most legislators, come to decisions with sets of values that arise from their backgrounds and life experiences. There are, of course, some broad commonalities. For example, people generally tend to dislike pain and tend to like happiness and security, the latter in both its senses of freedom from want and freedom from attack. Because of deeply rooted historical and cultural experience, most United States citizens tend to place particular value on individualism and personal autonomy. This contrasts, say, with the balance in societies like China and Japan, where—though things are changing—the group traditionally is given greater weight than the individual, and there is consequently far less stress on personal political autonomy.

What Motivates Legislators?

Drawing upon economic theory, "utility maximizers" among political scientists argue that almost all legislative behavior can be explained by members' self-interest. In fact, it is fair to say that this is the predominant view among contemporary scholars of legislative behavior. It certainly finds resonance in New York in the media, and among reform critics of state government. There are still many scholarly voices, however, that insist that legislators are motivated to a substantial degree by a strong commitment to public service, and to the public interest—as each of them understands it.

The critics have it right. Legislators certainly include self-interest, whether political, financial, or in some other form, among the values upon which they act. In New York, as in many other states, most legislators are what political scientists categorize as "professionals." They work at the job full-time; often they aspire to advancement in public life. The kind of work I described for constituents was not only good representation; it built my job security. People whom I helped were grateful and supportive; they were also less likely to oppose me for reelection if they came to disagree with me on one or another policy matter.

The Legislature was organized along party lines. Meeting expectations for party loyalty on most matters was necessary for achieving stature and leadership in the Assembly majority conference, and therefore within the body. It also built a chance for advancement in and outside the Legislature in state government, or to higher office.

But the critics have it wrong, too: legislators not only act in accord with values other than self-interest, but may sometimes even knowingly act against their own self-interest when they prize other values more highly. To cite just one of many possible examples, George Michaels, a Democrat from Auburn, a small city in the Finger Lakes region of New York, served in the New York State Assembly starting in 1961. In 1970, he felt that his conscience required him to cast the deciding vote in favor of legalizing abortion, although he believed that it would end his political career. It did.

Finding Balance Among Values:
Liberty, Equality, Property, Security, and Efficiency

On most issues, most of the time, legislators make policy decisions on the basis of some kind of utilitarian calculation, otherwise characterized as cost-benefit analysis. That is, legislators weigh the costs and benefits of competing options to determine which option, on balance, produces the outcome that is "best" for most people (with their own personal or political interests, of course, figuring into the mix). Needless to say, there are exceptions. On a few issues—those that touch more directly on emotional or religious commitments, like the death penalty and abortion, for example—some legislators abandon utilitarian calculations in favor of "intuitionism"—the uncalculated adherence to what they regard as overriding ethical concerns.

Apart from personal and political considerations, when a typical American legislator does approach an issue as a utilitarian, he or she more or less consciously seeks to balance five fundamental values: liberty, equality, property, security, and efficiency, each value weighed against the others. Though Americans have in the past given less weight to security and efficiency than to liberty, equality and property, there are signs that political and economic events since the turn of the 21st century are causing this to change.

Efficiency in this context is tricky. It means the use of resources most productive of desirable values, including the legislator's less fundamental ones. Thus the formula really encompasses more than five values. An unusual example might help. The anthropologist Ruth Benedict in 1959 described the potlatch ceremony during which Kwakiutl Indians of what is now the northwest United States consumed and destroyed huge quantities of their own property. If the Kwakiutl find ego reinforcement a scarce and important commodity as compared with property, and if the ritual of the potlatch produces more ego reinforcement than any other marginal use of property, the ritual generates efficiency, in the Kwakiutl context. In the United States, we can generally understand "efficiency" in the ordinary sense of getting the most out of available resources. But one American may define "getting the most" very differently from another.

American prosperity has tended to reduce concerns about efficiency. Throughout much of our history, the United States has enjoyed extraordinary prosperity. The structure of our government of "checks and balances" purposely allows inefficiency as a bulwark against tyranny. There are innumerable examples of the ability of one part of government to prevent action intended by another part. One that received great publicity just as this chapter was being drafted was the federal judiciary's action in March 2005 to thwart the intent of an emergency weekend session of Congress that Terry Schiavo's feeding tube be reinserted. A lesser known but far more expensive example: legal requirements imposed to prevent government agencies from riding roughshod over interest groups caused the Food and Drug Administration to spend almost a decade and to produce a transcript of over seven thousand pages of testimony in the effort to determine what percentage of peanuts a producer must maintain in a foodstuff in order to be permitted to designate it as "peanut butter."

Security means the human tendency to preserve a people's society as they know it. It also means freedom from physical attack or illegal deprivation of property, whether perpetrated by a foreign enemy or a domestic criminal.

Until recently, and especially until 9/11, our relative geographical isolation in the United States tended to reduce concerns about security, at least on the international level. We Americans thought that with oceans separating us from Europe and Asia, and with no threats to our national security on our northern or southern borders, we need concern ourselves relatively little with the possibility of attack. While we did worry about nuclear war with the Soviet Union from the 1950s through the 1970s, we had not experienced a foreign enemy on the mainland since the British troops burned Washington in 1814.

Anyone who has seen heavily armed National Guard units patrolling Wall Street or Pennsylvania Station in recent years can appreciate the difference the attack on the World Trade Center of September 11, 2001 has made in the willingness of the American public to accept what looks like a police state, at least on the surface and at least compared to the past, in return for the illusion of security. Given my own values, I believe and hope that Americans still, nevertheless, value Benjamin Franklin's advice that those who would sacrifice essential liberty for temporary security will end up with neither.

Liberty, equality and property are intertwined, core constitutional values in the United States. History unique to our national experience leads us to give heavier weight to these values. In the first modern nation to win its independence through revolution, the importance of the legitimacy of dissent (liberty) can scarcely be overlooked, notwithstanding whatever embarrassing episodes may stain our nation's history in this regard. That each individual holds a part of the power of government, and that no one may deprive another of life, liberty, or property other than by due process of law, were the lessons built upon the concept of equality. Due process of law also, of course, is the essence of fairness, which includes the right to be heard (liberty). From the twentieth-century point of view, the original U.S. Constitution incorporated hideous elements of inequality, at least with respect to slavery and limited suffrage. But those elements were, as Frederick Douglass said of slavery, "only as scaffolding to the magnificent structure, to be removed as soon as the building was completed."

Finally, a people inspired to revolution in substantial part under the slogan "no taxation without representation" clearly had embraced the right to property as a basic value; the revolutionary generation, and later Americans, closely linked liberty and equality to the protection of individual property rights.

Representativeness, Fairness, Dissent . . . and Finding Balance Among Values

Most Americans, and their legislators, regard these three values— liberty, equality, and property—as basic. To understand the difficulty in reconciling them with the more universal values of security and efficiency, we might examine very briefly how liberty, equality, and property are bound up with one another in three key aspects of our underlying expectations of government: representativeness, fairness, and the right to dissent.

Representativeness. If liberty entails self-government, and each individual equally asserts part of the power of government but can do so practically only through representativeness, then liberty and equality translate in this context into representativeness.

Fairness. If equality requires each person to be subject to the rule of law, and the law must operate with respect to the liberty and property of persons only within certain standard formal rules of procedure, then the three values in this context translate into fairness.

Right to dissent. If representativeness is to be meaningful, individuals must have access to information relevant to policy issues, and government's ability to suppress dissent must be very limited. Liberty limits government's power to suppress expression, and equality limits government's power to suppress expression for reasons of bias against particular content. In this context, liberty and equality translate into the right to dissent, in which we must include the right of access to information relevant to public-policy issues.

Representativeness and fairness can conflict with efficiency. Dissent can conflict with security. Legislators must find some reasonable balance among them. While, as noted above, legislators do not devise, much less follow, strict mathematical formulae balancing these values, virtually all American legislators have in their minds some sense that they should attempt some such balance. Differences among legislators can be explained by the different choices they make in how they weight each value. But by "plugging in" some constants to weight the variables of liberty, equality, property, security, and efficiency, each provides his or her own usable, fairly consistent utilitarian theory, a value matrix on which to base policy decisions.

All this may seem far too abstract and theoretical, reconstructed retrospectively with the benefit of analytic distance from the hurly-burly of daily events and pressures. But I am quite certain that it correctly describes my considerations as I did my job as a New York State Assemblyman, and fairly confident as well that it captures something like the calculus used by a majority of my legislative colleagues over the years. For greater clarity, some illustrative examples are provided in the next chapter.

CHAPTER II

What Counts When Legislators Decide

Each legislator brings to the job a unique combination of values. These are rarely systematized; they are an unexamined and (often) inconsistent hodgepodge. Is it most important to achieve greater equality? Or increase overall economic well-being? Or advance personal liberty? Or promote safety? Indeed, legislators may make unconscious adjustments to their values as they try through successive approximation to reach necessary compromises with erstwhile opponents.

But in addition to values, legislators almost always take a number of personal, political, and other considerations into account in decision making.

Outside Politics, Inside Politics, and the Law

Even the least sophisticated citizens assume that politics affects the lawmaking process. For a clearer picture of the process, though, it helps to separate "inside" and "outside" politics.

Commonly, discussion of the role of politics in public policy controversies really addresses "outside politics." The public generally understands the roles of interest groups such as the Christian Right, the American Association of Retired Persons, trial lawyers, the American Medical Association, unions, big business, big campaign contributors; and they understand the role of the press. These are the outside forces that apply pressure to legislators.

They generally don't understand how outside politics is separated from, but intertwined with, inside politics; and they really do not understand inside politics. Friendship among legislators is at the core of inside politics. Considerations of the legislative power structure, and how to advance oneself within it, provides the other important component.

Outside politics. First is the outside politics, the impact of potential actions the legislator may take in the world beyond the Legislature. Most particularly, "How will it play in my district?" is a question of overriding concern, for legislators legitimately pay attention to the wishes of the people they represent. Though the idea of representation is not a simple one, certainly any definition must include taking into serious account the interests of those represented, if not their wishes. But as earlier noted, most matters on which I had to vote drew little attention from the people in my district, giving me great leeway for action.

Organized groups may be powerful in shaping the opinions of citizens in a legislator's district. They are also an important source of campaign funds. In some districts, the views of the teachers' union may be influential; in others, religious leaders, the American Association of Retired Persons, the Farm Bureau, or General Electric. In most districts, various interest groups play important roles. Legislators must keep them all in mind.

The power of the media should not be overlooked. The daily and weekly press, radio, and especially television are not only major—and credible—channels through which voters may be reached, but important sources of influence over the behavior of many. A legislator may want to please the editorial pages of local newspapers or of *The New York Times*, either because those editorial pages influence his or her current constituents, or because they influence a wider constituency that may be important to the legislator's political ambitions for the future.

Loyalty to the political party may dictate a particular policy position. The strength of that loyalty varies. With respect to the political party organization back in the home district, it depends on how much the party helped elect the legislator, and how much support the legislator thinks he or she will need from the party in the future.

Inside politics. Then comes the inside politics. The party is not only present in the district, but has a structure within the Legislature. It may be important to please the Speaker, the Majority Leader, the Minority Leader, or even important committee chairs or other legislative leaders, not only to enhance a legislator's chances of getting elected or appointed to higher office, but also to improve the legislator's life within the Legislature. Only with the support of those leaders will a legislator get better committee assignments, appointment to a committee chairmanship or a better committee chairmanship, a bigger staff budget, or even just bills passed.

Friendships count, too. The Legislature is small community; members get to know each other quickly and well. In considering which position to take on a matter of public policy, legislators will be influenced by the views of other members, and may vote "yes" or "no" on a particular matter simply to avoid disappointing their friends.

Legislative friendships differ in some measure from ordinary friendships among non-politicians. Tom Wolfe, in his book *Bonfire of the Vanities*, used the image of the "favor bank" to explain the way a participant in the New York City legal system—a defense attorney, say, or a prosecutor—will call upon another—a police officer, or a clerk—for help in the expectation that the doer of the favor will later call upon the beneficiary of the favor for one in return. A participant who too often announces inability to make favor "deposits" when called upon, will find the bank closed for favor "withdrawals." Legislators make these kinds of withdrawals and deposits with each other constantly.

Because each of them does it, every legislator knows that his or her colleagues must weigh the values in a particular decision for him- or herself, and that the resulting judgment, or even just political self-interest, is likely to trump political debts. More than once I've had a colleague who was trying to call in a favor say to me, "But if I were in your shoes I might not give this vote. If you can't, I will understand." Legislators, after all, are all politicians. Since politicians have friendships with many politicians, their political judgments, interests, and ambitions are very likely eventually to clash. This makes the requirements of friendship complicated, though it still counts heavily.

The law. Then, finally, there is law. The separation of the "values" element from the "law" element requires a complicated explanation. Clearly, legal principles and law derive from values. The Framers protected their prized values of liberty, equality, and property by incorporating them, to the extent they could, into our most basic law, the Constitution's provisions for the structure of government and the Bill of Rights.

As illustrated earlier, the core legal principle of free expression, enshrined in the First Amendment, may conflict with provision by government of physical security for its citizens, a fundamental expectationin an ordered society. So there is free expression, and yet newspapers cannot legally report the deployment plans for American troops in wartime. We *could* describe the conflict as between the values of liberty and equality on the one hand, and security on the other. But Americans are so accustomed to translating liberty and equality into representative democracy, and regarding free expression as an essential device to make representative democracy effective, that describing the conflict as between the "law" of free press on the one hand and the "value" of security on the other best avoids confusion.

When values have evolved into complex legal principles—and policymakers feel sufficiently attached to those principles to adhere to them in the face of conflicting values or despite contrary political pressures—it makes more sense to talk about "law," rather than attempting to break it back down into values. So we discuss such "law" as the non-delegation doctrine, which holds that legislatures, the people's own representative branch of government, should not abdicate power unduly to bureaucrats who are not elected; or the Second Amendment, which certainly says something about the right to bear arms, however controversial its meaning; and due process, that guarantees citizens a degree of fairness when facing government action against them.

One can easily criticize this distinction as arbitrary and overlapping. Similarly, the lines between values, inside politics, and outside politics may seem narrow and faint at best. Ambition, for example, could be included in the list of values. Or it might manifest itself as "inside politics"—as in a politician's desire to advance within the legislative structure. Or it could be seen in "outside politics"—the desire for reelection or advancement to higher office. We do think, however, that these distinctions are useful for separating, and thus understanding, the various simultaneous developments in the progress of a controversy over public policy in the lawmaking arena.

Clash of Values: Abortion and the Death Penalty

In considering most issues, legislators, like the citizens they represent, approach decision-making with an unexamined, perhaps incoherent, set of ethical attitudes. There are some social issues, however, where this is not the case. Historically, divorce law was one such issue. More recently it has been abortion and the death penalty. It is when these sorts of issues are involved that legislators are most likely to identify and act upon the fundamental principles that motivate them. That is why—from an inside politics perspective—party discipline, so defining of life in the New York Legislature, is most challenged when these hot-button social issues are being decided.

Since they were very likely elected by constituencies with whom they generally share values, legislators' political considerations on these kinds of issues, from an outside politics perspective, most often comfortably coexist with ethical imperatives. Where the two conflict, career considerations may outweigh their ethical instincts. But not always, as illustrated by the story we earlier told about Assembly Member Michaels's 1970 abortion vote.

The ferocity and violence that sometimes characterizes debate over abortion and the death penalty stems from the fact that strongly held values underlie opposing points of view. Those values are not always made explicit, so neither party to the debate is necessarily aware, or willing to concede, that the other is operating out of fundamental ethical principles that are worthy of respect, although their principles differ. Moreover, the worst misunderstandings probably arise out of debate in which one party takes a conventional utilitarian (cost-benefit) approach, while the other approaches the issue as involving overriding and narrower ethical concerns (that is, takes an intuitionist position).

Although the intuitionist/utilitarian conflict creates misunderstandings if the two sides do not understand each other's premises, when those premises are presented clearly, that match-up can produce the most elegant of the various confrontational patterns that arise in the Legislature. The "intuitionist" legislator, much influenced by Western religious traditions, whose argument is informed by a commitment to the absolute sacredness of human life, will, in this particular formulation, oppose both abortion and the death penalty. This is the position, for example, that the New York State Catholic Conference, the lobbying arm of the Catholic bishops of the State of New York, consistently put forward in the 1980s.

The symmetrically opposite position is that of the utilitarian who believes that the costs of abortion and the death penalty, in terms of pain, injustice, and damage to society's respect for life, are more than outweighed by the benefits in terms of those elements. But the intuitionist will not be persuaded by the utilitarian's argument based on the benefits, even if (as is rarely the case) the intuitionist concedes that all the claimed benefits would accrue. To the intuitionist, nothing, no matter how valuable in its own terms, can justify violating the prohibition against the taking of innocent life, whether it be the life of the fetus or the life of the statistically inevitable innocent victim of capital punishment. Even the deterrence argument for the death penalty, were it accepted as valid, would not suffice for many intuitionists who could not accept their own participation in the taking of life through acquiescence in the State's policy.

The religious arguments against the legalization of abortion and against the death penalty that are most difficult to answer depend, in their purest form, on the premise that the sanctity of life is infinite and may not be weighed against other values. For example, the Talmud, second only to the Bible as a foundational document in the Jewish tradition, states that one who saves a single human life is to be regarded as though he had saved a universe. No arguments about deterrence or justice can very well persuade someone who must equate executing a human being—any human being—with destroying a universe.

A fortiori, for one to whom a fetus is a human being, no argument about a woman's right to control her own body or any other argument, indeed, can support a decision to declare, as a matter of State policy, that abortion is legal. In fact, one who single-mindedly applied the Talmudic principle would have grave doubts about legalizing abortion even if he or she were not necessarily convinced that a fetus is a human being, since another Talmudic principle speaks of "making a fence around the Law," meaning that one should not even come close to violating a biblical commandment, and surely a fetus is no more than nine months away from being a human being.

In today's world, where science and technology have allowed us to sustain life in babies with congenital defects so severe that they would have had no chance in previous eras, this argument takes on greater salience. Some observers have worried that our society more readily accepts the withholding of life support from infants with serious birth defects because of a decrease in respect for the sanctity of human life as acceptance of abortion has grown.

This absolutist "pro-life" position is relatively easy to lampoon: do we ban the automobile because of highway accidents that take lives? Do we outlaw electricity because from a statistical point of view, inevitably some children will stick their fingers into sockets with fatal results? And indeed, the very Talmudic tradition from which the foregoing principles were extracted is much less absolute, hardly mentioning and restricting but not barring abortion, and restricting but not barring use of the death penalty (branding as "destructive," for example, any court that condemns to death one man in seven years, or according to other commentators, seventy years).

The orthodox Roman Catholic position includes an absolute ban on abortion. Twentieth-century papal pronouncements, as well as older ones, preclude abortion even when necessary to save the life of the mother. Of course, thoughtful Roman Catholics hold other points of view. Mario Cuomo, who was the governor of New York from 1983 to 1994, considered himself an observant Catholic, conversant with Catholic theology. He argued in a well-publicized address at Notre Dame University that although he personally rejected abortion as an ethical alternative, Roman Catholic ethics did not require him to impose this belief on others. Some Roman Catholic legislators also took this position. But to the more orthodox Roman Catholic legislators, and citizens, a fetus is a human being, and therefore abortion is murder. No argument based on suffering or difficulties exacerbated by making abortion illegal could persuade one who holds that view to accept legalization of this "taking of innocent life."

Those who find such moral absolutism anathema might consider that rational arguments can usually be found for most points of view and can be used to attack the intuitionist position on any given issue. Robert Caro, in *The Power Broker*, memorably reported the 1912 New York State Assembly debate on a bill requiring one day off a week for women and children. The legislators who "pleaded for the canneries" argued that those employees especially needed the money that they might be able to earn only with a seventh day of work. Further, if the canneries were forced to lose their services for that one day, their tight margins of profit might force them to close, throwing out of work altogether and into the direst of poverty the very people the legislation was designed to help. Sometimes only moral absolutism, as then Assembly Member and later Governor Al Smith exhibited that year, can supply an appropriate response to the hubris of intellect. "I have read carefully the commandment 'Remember the Sabbath Day to keep it holy,'" he said. "I am unable to find any language in it that says, 'except in the canneries.'" Who is to say that the future may not show the Catholic Conference to have been the true moral progressives in the Assembly debates over abortion in the 1970s and 1980s, as Smith—it is clear to us now—was in 1912?

But the utilitarian perspective appears to offer the more responsible position to most legislators. Legislators who regard their responsibility as the effort to maximize human happiness and minimize human misery appear to premise their policy choices on utilitarian cost-benefit analysis, which is not compatible with intuitionist moral absolutism, even one as life-affirming as that which makes paramount the sanctity of human life itself. Of course, many utilitarian cost-benefit analysts could argue persuasively that their philosophies also make paramount the sanctity of human life, but they express their commitment to that value a different way: not by prohibiting the abortion of a fetus or the execution of a person convicted of murder, but by attempting to assure the highest quality of life for the general population. As noted in the opening chapter, this requires an assessment of a wide range of factors, and therefore precludes the possibility of decisions made on the basis of a single variable, such as "does the policy involve State complicity in the taking of any innocent life?" It would also bar decisions made on the basis of an arbitrarily selected small number of variables. Single-variable or small-number-of-arbitrarily-selected-variable assessments characterize intuitionist approaches, at least at their fundamental level, although basic intuitionist premises sometimes lead, not arbitrarily, to highly complex, multivariate decision-making matrices.

Several other confrontational patterns in the death penalty debate pit various kinds of utilitarians against each other, but when they differ, at least they can find some common ground and trace their disagreements to factual disputes. Does the death penalty kill more innocents wrongly accused than it saves innocents by deterring potential murderers from killing them? Does legalized abortion encourage more than enough abortions to make up for the mothers killed in furtive self-abortion attempts or "back-street" jobs? Or if the death count is the same, or unknowable, or slightly higher, do the qualities of justice and respect for the individual benefit enough from one policy choice or the other to balance the scales? For the sanctity-of-life intuitionist, nothing can balance the loss of human life in which the intuitionist, indirectly through a vote on State policy, has implicated himself or herself, not even the saving of another human life. For the State to take or condone the taking of a human life, to this kind of intuitionist, is unacceptable notwithstanding any other factor. For cost-benefit utilitarians, some things *might* "balance the scales," though they may differ over whether the benefits of death penalty statutes and legalized abortion *actually* do so. Indeed, many liberals take the position that abortion does and the death penalty does not. That is precisely why we've presented this argument in this way, to highlight the inconsistent positions held by some, and encourage others to identify the common themes that may underlie the positions they have taken, but that they may never have previously considered deeply.

Finally, there may be intuitionist positions in support of the death penalty and legalized abortion. The argument that the death penalty does not work and may be counterproductive, even were compelling evidence to be adduced in support, would fail to convince someone who believed as a matter of unshakable faith in justice as the highest goal, and that justice demands the possibility of the ultimate retribution. Similarly, the argument that legalized abortion results in a general lowering of society's commitment to human life, even were compelling evidence to be adduced in support, would fail to convince someone who believes that personal liberty is a transcendent value, and that therefore everything going on inside a woman's body must remain under her control in order to avoid infringing on her rights as an individual.

An explicit understanding of the ethical premises underlying one's own and one's opponents' policies on matters of conscience (indeed, we would argue, on all matters) makes discussion and debate more productive, and also makes for greater consistency in one's own point of view. A legislator, for example, may consciously decide that the sanctity of human life is not to be weighed against other social or economic values. Further, whether or not a fetus is a human being, that legislator may believe that it is at least close enough so that to legalize abortion would intolerably damage our society's adherence to that principle. If so, that legislator would have a great deal of intellectual work to do before convincing himself or herself to vote with his or her pro-death-penalty or pro-war constituency.

Alternatively, and this is but one of innumerable alternatives, a legislator may choose to accept the cessation of brain activity as a definition of the termination of one's status as a human being. This legislator may well find it difficult to define as a human being a fetus of fewer than twenty weeks, which is prior to the onset of brain activity, and therefore may not be able to justify legal opposition to abortions performed before that stage of pregnancy.

Hot-button social issues arise relatively infrequently. Most other issues with which legislators must deal do not provoke a compelling values-based analysis. Moreover, legislators who feel they must apply ethical standards to a special subset of issues may not think to apply them (or choose to apply them) to other issues they address.

Indeed, few legislators impose on themselves an absolute requirement of consistency. Wayne Morse, four-term United States Senator from Oregon through 1968, was known as "the conscience of the Senate" for his courage and integrity. It is said that on one occasion when he guest-lectured at Columbia Law School, a student asked him why, since year after year he strongly advocated free international trade, he also invariably voted in favor of the tariff on wheat. "Son," the story has him reply, "it's true I like free trade. But I also like being Senator from Oregon."

Few familiar with Wayne Morse's history would wish he had done otherwise. Indeed, a perfectly legitimate utilitarian calculus can easily justify Morse's exceptional protectionist vote on the basis of all the other things it enabled him to accomplish. Other legislators may justify similar assessments, assuming a utilitarian stance. (Of course, this can be a slippery slope, given the natural propensity to rationalize what is in one's own interest.)

While legislators may not adhere to any particular set of consistent utilitarian principles, at least utilitarianism can take into account the wide variety of values that their constituents—and presumably they themselves—would like to pursue as objects of their policy efforts. The formula of life, liberty, and the pursuit of happiness includes a great many values, and Americans tend to want all of them. Normal policy-making in the United States involves efforts to have as much of prosperity, liberty, equality and security as possible, with fewest possible sacrifices. That effort uses a process called "cost-benefit analysis," readily translated into utilitarianism.

Law and the Clash of Values

Arguments on "law" as well as on "values" frequently appear on both sides of a legislative issue. When principles of law collide in a courtroom, a judge must decide which prevails. When principles of law collide in a legislature, the legislature decides. A principle of law, in that context, is not a rule of law that must be obeyed, nor does a principle of law necessarily prevail if it opposes only a "value," or a political need. Legislators may honor values that courts may not regard as binding. Consider two examples.

No Smoking Rules. In the early 1980s, the New York State Legislature on several occasions, for several years running, considered and rejected legislation restricting the smoking of cigarettes in restaurants and other public places. (The Legislature eventually, years later, approved the bill.) Although the legislation regularly went down to defeat, I was among those who voted for it, reflecting a simple preference, in that context, for the value of a reduction in human suffering in terms of improved health and reduced death and disease, over the value of liberty and autonomy for those who choose to smoke.

In the mid-1980s, however, the New York Public Health Council, a State agency, promulgated regulations essentially incorporating the thrust of the legislation. That is, the Council attempted to do administratively what the Legislature had refused to do legislatively. Since agencies are "agents" of the Legislature, empowered by the Legislature to act within the boundaries of powers delegated by the Legislature in law, it seemed to some—me included—that the Public Health Council's actions constituted a usurpation of legislative authority.

The principle barring such *ultra vires* actions, actions outside an agency's legitimate scope of authority, is known as the "non-delegation doctrine." It reflects deep-seated ideas about who might legitimately do what to limit liberty in a democratic society. In this case the legislature's deliberate refusal on several occasions to pass a law encompassing a value or combinations of values (as earlier explained), came into clear conflict with the straightforward value of reducing human suffering that an executive branch agency had adopted in regulation.

A lawsuit ensued. The New York Court of Appeals decision on the matter, *Boreali v. Axelrod*, 71 N.Y. 2d 1 (1987), invalidating the Public Health Council's regulations as *ultra vires*, or beyond the scope of its powers, more or less tracked the present author's *amicus curiae* ("friend-of-the-court") brief arguing on behalf of the Legislature.

Free Speech in Shopping Malls. During the first half of the twentieth century, virtually anyone without big money to buy advertising and with no special skills in manipulating the media, could print up a few thousand flyers on a mimeograph machine for very little money, stand on a busy street corner, and reach most of the local population to express a point of view or collect petition signatures for a cause, whether mainstream, minority, or bizarre. But in the 1970s and 1980s, the decline of the traditional small town village square or even big-city Main Streets as busy shopping locations and their replacement by large, privately-owned shopping malls, created a real-life decrease in the degree to which average people could effectively exercise their First Amendment rights in a political context. People have to drive to these malls, and once they get into the parking lot, they are on private property, where mall owners can decide whether or not to permit political activity, depending on whether they like the point of view in question or not.

In the early 1980s, Long Island environmentalists petitioning against the Shoreham nuclear power plant sought to reach significant numbers of their neighbors by protesting at the Smith Haven Mall, a large shopping center in Suffolk County. The owners of the mall expelled them. In 1985, New York's highest court, the Court of Appeals, held that the protesters had no constitutional right to the exercise of their expressive rights at this privately owned mall. This ended the first round in New York of the "free speech in shopping malls" debate, a classic conflict between two great American principles of law: freedom of speech versus property rights.

In the course of its opinion, however, the Court of Appeals did advise the State Legislature that it could enact a law permitting petitioning and other similar political activity at malls, if it chose to do so, without violating constitutional private property rights.

Indeed, in 1946, the United States Supreme Court had gone further. The religious group known as "Jehovah's Witnesses" includes door-to-door proselytizing in their practices, and through their courageous efforts have "pushed the envelope" of religious freedom through numerous courtroom challenges. *Marsh v. Alabama*, 326 U.S. 501, was a case involving the exercise of expressive rights by a Jehovah's Witness in a "company town," where the whole town was owned by a private company. There, the Court explained that private property rights consisted of a variety of powers, not all of which were necessarily absolute. A person has close to absolute property rights as to his shirt. He or she has fewer absolute rights as to his car, which he cannot drive without insurance and adherence to certain performance standards assured by inspection. And that person has still fewer rights to his house, on which he or she must pay taxes, in which he or she usually cannot manufacture explosives or store huge piles of stinky garbage, and which he or she must surrender to the State should it be condemned in an eminent domain proceeding.

The point is that as private property takes on more characteristics of public space, the owner may be obliged to take on some of the responsibilities of public ownership. The U.S. Supreme Court asked, What if all private property in the United States were to come under the control of private companies? Would those companies then be permitted to abrogate First Amendment rights entirely? The Court ruled that while the town remained private property, the company must accommodate the exercise of First Amendment rights in the equivalent of what ordinarily would be public space.

In that pre-World Wide Web era, it seemed to some that New York State should not permit socioeconomic forces to effectively eliminate an important component of traditional political rights, and that the political health of our society required maintenance of the free and robust exchange of political viewpoints. That principle outweighed the relatively minor incursion on private property rights necessary to provide a reasonable accommodation, under reasonable time, place, and manner restrictions, for petitioners in privately owned shopping malls. So I introduced legislation to that effect and fought for it from 1986 until 1998, my final year in office.

At least one eloquent advocate on the other side of the issue, James Quaremba, then president of New York's Retail Council, perceived increasing state incursions on private property rights as more serious than the threat to expressive rights, and stood up to me in lengthy and highly substantive debate in a private setting. The Assembly passed the bill four or five times. Senator John Marchi, a Republican from Staten Island who retired in 2006 after over 50 years service and was one of the most respected members of the State Senate, introduced it there. However, the Senate leadership never brought it to the floor. Marchi's position differed from that of most of his Senate majority colleagues on this issue, whose value systems placed far more weight on the rights of property owners than did the members of the Assembly majority.

The battle for "free speech in shopping malls" exemplified the clash of legitimate legal principles, almost without reference to simpler values or to "inside" politics. (One exception: when I first introduced the bill, in 1986, then-Speaker Stanley Fink independently introduced virtually the same bill. As Speaker, he rarely introduced legislation. Until he retired at the end of 1986, he, not I, was the lead sponsor of the bill.)

"Outside" Politics

Lobbying against the free-speech-in-shopping-malls bill by business interests did play a role, but oddly: reliable surveys showed that shopping malls tended to do more business where state law or mall policy protected expressive rights. The business interests apparently were not protecting their "business interests," but rather their power, or their ideological commitment to the legal principles in question. "Outside" politics also provided support for the bill in the form of petitioning at shopping malls by "good government" groups like Common Cause, League of Women Voters, and anti-abortion *and* pro-choice groups, but they did not seem much to influence its fate in the Legislature. So the battle stood as a remarkably pure clash of legal principles, and it served to heighten awareness and increase sensitivity to the importance of both sides of the debate.

Most people think they understand how "outside" politics affects the legislative process, and they are usually right. When an issue heats up, coverage hits the front page and the nightly television news. The editorial and op-ed writers step in. Constituents start to call, or ask questions at meetings in the district. Lobbyists step up their visits. As the activity (and noise) mounts, so does pressure on legislators to "do something."

Sometimes, however, the press gets excited about an issue, but the public refuses to share its excitement. In the mid-1980s, for example, then-Governor Cuomo tried to lead a crusade against alleged legislative corruption, seeking creation of an ethics commission. My response, suggesting that the investigative commission Cuomo was proposing should also be empowered to investigate executive branch ethics, prompted a tirade by Cuomo in his one-and-only telephone call to me ever. Both response and tirade garnered news coverage, but citizen concern stayed minimal. Of the roughly three thousand constituents I greeted at subway-stop entrances every morning the next week, two hundred or so commented on one matter or another. Of those, only four mentioned the ethics issue at all, and those four all commended me for standing up to the Governor.

The Legislature eventually did establish an ethics commission, headed by the well-respected and eminently reasonable John Feerick, at that time Dean of Fordham Law School, instead of Cuomo's choice, Joe Califano, then at Columbia University and formerly President Lyndon Johnson's Secretary of Health, Education, and Welfare. Califano would have been expected to "hit" the Legislature. The Feerick Commission unearthed some major problems with local government in the state but launched no major assaults on the Legislature. Cuomo did not get what he wanted because his effort—ferociously supported by the press—did not resonate with the public, and therefore resulted in no pressure on the Legislature.

Continuing concerns about corruption and ethical lapses in the state legislature, driven by a number of very high profile cases discussed elsewhere in this volume, made mechanisms for oversight of legislators' behavior a persistent reform issue. Two decades after Mario Cuomo's effort came an astonishingly scandal-ridden period in New York State government. For several years, reaching a peak in 2009, the non-stop drumbeat of news stories reporting the criminal convictions of numerous members of the Legislature, including the Senate Majority Leader, strongly suggested that the Legislature lacked the will to monitor its members' behavior effectively.

One of the changes effected by the Public Employee Ethics Reform Act of 2007 was the replacement of the Legislative Ethics Committee, comprised only of Assembly members and Senators, with a Legislative Ethics Commission that included five non-members with the four legislator members. Each of the four legislative leaders appointed one colleague and one non-member, with the fifth non-member jointly appointed by the Assembly Speaker and the Senate Majority Leader. Of course this meant that the legislative leaders still completely controlled appointments to the Commission ostensibly responsible for overseeing them.

With the public at long last awakened to the problem, in the spring of 2009 Governor David Paterson proposed farther reaching ethic reforms in a bill that, among other provisions, placed oversight of the legislature in an agency responsible for maintaining ethical standards across all of state government. The members of this commission were not controlled by appointees of the leaders. The Legislature, perhaps predictably, refused to enact Paterson's bill. Early in 2010, with near unanimity in each house, it passed a different reform package, one that did not relinquish leadership control of appointees. This bill was vetoed by the governor. The veto was overridden in the Assembly. However, it was sustained in the Senate, where many Republicans who had supported the legislation—now in the minority—did not vote to override.

In February and March 2010, Paterson's own ethics became the focus of several serious investigations, leading him to abandon his bid for election to a full term and causing others to call for his immediate resignation. These events demolished any remaining credibility or influence he might have exercised in support of reform.

In every one of the public safety policy case studies offered later in this book, when "outside" politics plays a major role the press is an important part of the action, and sometimes the most important part. Yet the Legislature feels the pressure of "outside" politics far more from organized groups of citizens—interest groups—than from the press. This is because the primary currency of politics is votes, and legislators perceive the Catholic Conference, Agudath Israel, the AFL-CIO, the teachers' union, the Farm Bureau, the National Rifle Association, the Business Council, and numerous other groups as influencing large numbers of voters. Many of these organizations, of course, are also significant sources of campaign contributions and other forms of political support that may be used to reach voters.

The political influence of interest groups can be measured as a function of intensity as well as numbers. Thirty rabid volunteers can outdo three hundred voters who care mildly about an issue, because the thirty can persuade more than three hundred to vote for a candidate, while the three hundred may not even cast their vote for a candidate based on that particular issue.

Well-timed interventions by interest groups can increase the likelihood that legislation to change policy will succeed. New York State, not parents, pays the bus fare of handicapped elementary children to non-public schools. The federal and state Constitutions neither prohibit nor require this. The Legislature enacted a law to do it, but the law included a one-year "sunset" provision. That is, if the Legislature didn't reenact it each year, it would expire.

Each year, New York State United Teachers, the public school teachers' union, in its discussions with legislative leadership in both Houses, would agree not to oppose the extension in return for some legislative item of its own. Wanting to keep the issue as a bargaining chip, the teachers' union insisted on the annual sunset provision.

Because this was a small and technical issue, it didn't generate much public attention until the parents of the children somehow found out that the process created a danger. If the Legislature failed to reenact the law they would be hit with the heavy burden of paying for this extremely expensive transportation themselves. Each year, the parents became more and more nervous in the late spring, as the negotiations seemed to leave the cost of transportation for the following school year hanging in the balance.

By the late 1980s, some of the parents seemed to be suffering annual anxiety attacks. As a representative of many such parents, I introduced a permanent version of the law and gave the issue enough publicity to make it uncomfortable for the teachers' union to oppose it too vigorously, because the more vigorously it opposed the bill, the more public attention the effort would generate. So both Houses passed the bill and sent it to the Governor.

Under the state constitution the Governor has ten days (Sundays not included) after he or she actually receives a bill either to sign or veto it if the Legislature is in session, and 30 days if it has adjourned. (The modern legislature has taken to recessing rather than adjourning, which shortens the bill signing period, but bills are sent to the governor in stages, not all at once, to spread out the time available for their review by him or her.) Late in the bill-signing period my office got a courtesy call from the Governor's Counsel's office notifying us that Governor Cuomo would be vetoing the bill. Shortly thereafter, we called New York State Catholic Conference and Agudath Israel, the two principal lobbying organizations representing the religious Catholics and Jews in

New York who tend to send their children to religious schools, informing them that the Governor intended to perpetuate the annual fear suffered by some of the most vulnerable of their parents, those already dealing with the challenges of caring for handicapped children. These organizations influence hundreds of thousands of voters.

When the representatives of the State Catholic Conference and Agudath Israel called the Governor's office to express their extreme concerns that the Governor might possibly veto the bill, no explicit threat had to be made. Had they only found out about the bill after a veto, the Governor could have claimed that he had been unaware of their concerns. But their timely intervention gave Cuomo no "wiggle room." If he vetoed the bill now, he would, at the very least, have to mollify the groups with some subsequent favor, perhaps one even more costly than signing this bill. Otherwise, he might eventually face their wrath at the polls. Some days later, in mid-summer 1992, the Governor signed the bill.

"Inside" Politics versus "Outside" Politics: DC #37 and the Speaker.

As a newly elected Assemblyman in 1981 I quickly learned that inside legislative politics, lesser known to most citizens, can and does sometimes prevail over outside politics, even when a very powerful interest group is involved. District Council 37 (DC #37), the New York City local of the American Federation of State, County and Municipal Employees (AFSCME), represents a wide range of civil service jobholders, from clerks, non-teacher school aides, and cafeteria workers, to engineers, pharmacists, and architects. DC #37 provided campaign worker volunteers and an endorsement mailing in my successful campaign for the office in 1980. It was the only major union to help me. Its political director, Norman Adler, who had lined up the union's support for me, had been a political science teacher of mine in college and was still a good friend.

Because of his extraordinary intelligence and skill, Adler's influence extended well beyond that of his own union, to the other powerful public employee unions in New York. Teachers, police, firefighters, and sanitation workers, through their unions, looked to him for guidance and leadership. In addition, he provided often crucial campaign support to many legislators, and so was owed a degree of loyalty by an unusually large group of Democrats in the Assembly. (At that time he had just begun to provide support to some carefully selected Republican legislators in the Senate, as well).

1981 was also the year that the statewide contract provisions for government employees in a category known as "Tier III," also including New York City civil servants, came up for renewal. Adler led the coalition of government employee unions seeking wage increases for Tier III workers.

In 1975, after many years of unsound fiscal practices by New York City's government, banks lost confidence in the City's ability to repay its debts, and refused to allow it any further short-term borrowing. Left to its own devices, the City would have gone bankrupt. It was saved by a financial plan to which contributions in the hundreds of millions of dollars were made by New York State, major financial institutions, and the municipal unions.

The unions also voluntarily sacrificed workers' pay increases for several years after the fiscal crisis to help New York City recover. Most important for this story, they agreed that new union members hired after 1976 (designated as Tier III employees in the pension system) would have to accept less generous contracts than their predecessors, with larger chunks taken out of their salaries to pay for smaller pension benefits. Five years later, the City was doing better and the civil service unions felt that the State now owed their Tier III employee members some recompense for the way they felt they had been unfairly treated.

Given his perception of the financial needs of the State, then-Governor Hugh Carey said that he would sign an extension of the contract but would veto any new contract that included changes costing the State more money. Norman Adler believed that Carey was bluffing. The governor too owed political debts to the municipal unions; Adler insisted that rather than face their wrath, he would ultimately sign a better contract.

Adler pressed those many legislators he had helped over the years to reject the governor's plan for a simple extender of the existing contract. The matter dragged on until the end of the legislative session, when the old contract was due to expire. Since the contract included the workers' insurance benefits, any day without a contract exposed workers to financial calamity should they or a dependent fall ill or otherwise incur a loss during a time in which their insurance was lapsed.

At the deadline, Assembly Speaker Stanley Fink called an Assembly Democratic Conference to discuss the matter. Fink, even smarter and more eloquent than Adler, believed that Carey was not bluffing, and would in fact veto an enriched contract. Since Carey had earned a reputation for willingness to do outrageous things (dyeing his hair orange, offering to drink a glass of the toxic chemical PCBs, marrying a flamboyant society lady who turned out to have been divorced four times previously) Fink's assessment was plausible.

In a private discussion, I said to Fink, "Stanley, I really owe Norman." Fink said to me, "Fine. When you need money for staff, ask Norman." As discussed below, in 1981 and now, the Speaker of the Assembly held roughly the position in that institution that Joe Cannon held as Speaker of the House of Representatives in 1910: absolute control. Money for staff, or the authority to let a bill come to the floor, or your committee assignments, or someday your committee chairmanship could come only from the Speaker.

Senior members of the conference, such as Frank Barbaro, chair of the Labor Committee, and Jose Serrano, later to become chair of the Education Committee and subsequently a Member of Congress, with well-established pro-labor records over many years, stood up in conference to explain why they had agreed to vote for the simple extender of the existing contract, essentially repeating Fink's position. I faced a more difficult dilemma. This was my first tough vote on a matter crucial to labor. Labor had supported me, and this would signal whether or not I paid my debts. On the merits, of course, it was impossible to tell who was right, Fink or Adler. So I got on the list to speak, preparing to explain the difficult position of a new member and asking for guidance.

Just as I was called on, Fink asked if I would "suffer an interruption." He said he was sure I would find it worthwhile. I waited as he left the room for a few minutes. Much later I found out where he had gone and what he had done. He laced into Adler, with whom he had been—and later remained—closely allied, asking Norman if he thought that he was running the Democratic majority in the Assembly.

As much power as Adler had, Fink obviously had more. When Fink returned to the room, he announced, "Adler says it's okay to vote for the bill." The collective sigh of relief was audible.

The story has a coda. A handful of Assembly Democrats grandstanded by voting against the extender, knowing that it would now pass anyway. One union local apparently had not gotten the marching orders. A few months later, when I was back home in my district office recovering from session, I was deeply annoyed to see in the local's latest newsletter high praise for those whose "no" vote reflected nothing more than a gesture designed to elicit such praise from the gullible. My name, in contrast, appeared on a long list of those who had voted for the simple extender, headed something like "Traitors."

I saw that Barbaro, Serrano, and some of the other senior members, who had also voted for the bill, were not on that list, and so I got much angrier. Knowing that its members knew and trusted Barbaro, Serrano, *et alia*, I reasoned that perhaps the local had refrained from attacking them so as not to complicate the message to their members to be angry with people like me. But when I turned the page, I felt much better. There, on a much shorter list, were the Barbaro, Serrano group. That list was headlined "Lickspittles."

Notwithstanding the disgruntled local union newsletter, "inside" politics triumphed over "outside" politics on this occasion. Despite all the power of the municipal unions behind him, in a direct confrontation with the Speaker of the Assembly, Adler was forced to remove the pressure he had been applying to legislators indebted to him, even at the possible cost of losing credibility with his own union members and the other unions who had trusted him to lead the fight for them. He understood that life is long and he would need the Speaker too many times in the future to risk his relationship with him over one issue.

"Inside" Politics

Legislators and Staff: Dramatic confrontations like the one in the Tier III story rest on the kinds of friendships and relationships that build most inside politics over the course of years. Immediately prior to my service in elective office, I worked for my predecessor in the New York State Assembly, the current U.S. Senator Charles Schumer. In the late 1970s I had drafted a bill for him to reform one aspect of New York's local finance law that I thought had contributed to New York City's 1975 fiscal crisis, a provision that permitted the City to repay over decades money it had borrowed to buy items that were only used or useful for short periods of time. Since the law allowed this abuse of the "periods of probable usefulness" rule, the City had regularly given in to the temptation to mortgage its future to meet current expenses.

Schumer was perhaps too preoccupied with other matters at the time for him to push this one hard, so when I took office I introduced it as part of my own legislative agenda. As a finance bill, it was referred to the Assembly Ways and Means Committee, where it would either die or be reported out favorably. A few months into my first session, noticing that the bill had not been reported out, I asked Jerry Kremer, then chair of Ways and Means, what was happening to my bill. He asked, "What bill?" I told him, and he said he'd check.

With the hundreds or even thousands of bills considered by a powerful committee like Ways and Means, which must pass on any legislation with fiscal impact, neither the committee chair nor the other members can possibly operate intelligently without staff support. To provide such support, experienced staff analysts review each bill in detail and report back to the chair the staff's expert judgment about whether the bill will accomplish the sponsor's goals, whether the sponsor's goals make sense, and what unintended consequences the bill might trigger were it to become law. Such staff members also draft bills on complex issues for the Speaker and committee chairs, sometimes in conjunction with drafting specialists on the Legislative Bill Drafting Commission.

The next week Kremer came back to me with a report. "I don't know exactly how to say this," he said, "but the staff says it's a pretty technical bill and not really the sort of thing a Member of the Assembly should get too involved with." What he meant was that "nuts and bolts" legislation dealing with complex issues that matter, but not the sort of bills that get public attention, was considered by staff members to be *their* domain. The implication was that legislators, who were after all the elected officials for whom the staff worked, would only cause problems by interfering in matters they did not understand.

I said, "Jerry, do me a favor—let me meet with the staff guy." A few days later, the staff analyst, Alan Billingsley, whom I later got to know as one of the best and most technically proficient budget experts on the Assembly staff, came to my office to discuss the bill. I said, "Let me explain something. I wasn't always a moron: I used to be a staffer." Shortly thereafter, the bill was reported out of committee. That was my first successful use of "inside" politics, the politics of legislators' relationships with other influential players within the system, be they other elected officials or staff.

Friendship. I had come to the Legislature having been raised in what was called the "reform" wing of the Democratic party, with the notion that political corruption associated with "the organization" was even worse than Republicans. When I first ran for office, unsuccessfully, for New York City Council in the early 1970s, the reformers backed me against the "regular" Democratic clubs. In my successful run for the Assembly, my first backers were the reformers. Then the regulars came

g me as the lesser of two evils: they feared that the seat
in a primary to someone allied with a rebellious faction of
ization.

came to office seriously skeptical about the regular party ma-
n New York City, and with an active distrust of political organ-
izat.   in areas of the City where their corruption had come under fire.
One such area was East Harlem. The Assembly member representing that
district, Angelo del Toro, had done nothing to dispel the persistent rumors
about the nature of the Democratic organization under his control.

To my great surprise, after a few years serving with him, I discovered that del Toro was a person of considerable intelligence, charm,
generosity, and humor. A man of strikingly unattractive physical appearance, with a huge nose, bad complexion, and sparse but greasy
black hair, Angelo sometimes commented on the unfairness of the
strong tendency of both the public and the press to attribute better character and more intelligence to better-looking politicians.

During particularly boring budget sessions, the chess players in the
Assembly would retire to the Members' Lounge for a game or two.
There were only three relatively serious players—Del Toro, Richard
Brodsky, and me—and half a dozen others who would play an occasional game. Chess players do not ordinarily heckle each other. It is still
more uncommon for a bilingual chess player to needle his opponent in a
language the opponent does not speak. Del Toro would heckle me hilar-
iously in Spanish across the chessboard. I came to like him very much.
While I still believed that he used his political organization in inappropriate ways to provide personal enrichment for himself and his inner
circle, I thought I was able to compartmentalize and appreciate his other
good qualities. Perhaps I overcompensated for my partial disapproval
by accepting what seemed to be the strong arguments he made on a
matter of public concern.

Over the chessboard, Del Toro explained to me the plight of the proprietary schools. These business schools, he noted, had a wonderful
record of training hitherto unskilled, usually minority-group students
and placing them as secretaries, computer operators, and technicians of
various kinds into good jobs where they could prosper. The schools also
benefited from government reimbursement on behalf of these students,
the overwhelmingly number of whom were poverty-stricken. But they
had gotten a bad name, Del Toro said, because of a few "rotten apples"
that shortchanged their students on educational quality while enriching
themselves with government reimbursement. Also, he insisted, they

were the victims of slander by jealous accredited institutions of high learning that could not match their job placement record but were influential with *New York Times* editorial writers, and were unduly harshly treated by the New York State Education Department (SED) bureau which funded its monitoring activities with the fines it imposed on the very schools it was monitoring.

One particular group of schools, according to Del Toro, headed by a talented Iraqi immigrant, Michael Alharmoosh, did an especially good job, but was hounded mercilessly by the State Education Department (SED). I was primed to be skeptical of the SED, because in 1975 and 1976 my investigation of the federal Summer Food Service Program for Children on behalf of then-Member of Congress Elizabeth Holtzman uncovered its remarkably inept administration of the New York version of the program. At Del Toro's urging, I was treated to a number of visits to Alharmoosh's schools, where he and his associates set up persuasive demonstrations of their fine record of achievement. Over the next year or two, with Del Toro's constant support, Alharmoosh and his chief associates became very friendly with me, contributed hundreds of dollars to my campaign fund, and armed me with arguments against the constant complaints that the SED made about their operation.

Matters came to a head when the SED bureau's legislative mandate for monitoring the proprietary schools came up for renewal. With del Toro and Tony Genovesi—a colleague from Brooklyn and a close friend of the Speaker (and Fink's successor as the Assembly Member from Brooklyn's Canarsie neighborhood) who had been won over to our point of view—I met with the SED representatives and the chair of the Assembly's Higher Education Committee, Ed Sullivan, a supporter of the SED's viewpoint. Del Toro, Genovesi, and I insisted on a mitigating condition to any extension of SED's power to levy fines on the proprietary schools for technical violations. Consideration had to be given, we said, to the success of these schools in providing training to those who had not previously held jobs that resulted in their remaining employed for respectable periods of time.

Del Toro died in office in 1994, after struggling bravely and without complaint for many years with kidney failure and then dialysis. Genovesi died in an automobile accident in 1998. But Alharmoosh and his top associates fled the country shortly before the SED closed down all their schools, giving considerable credence to the suggestion that perhaps the SED had been right all along. I miss Del Toro and Genovesi, who had many fine and impressive qualities. I still think we fought for

legislative change. But to the extent that my efforts
to protect Alharmoosh from the SED for a while, I
d, and the "inside" politics of the Legislature was to
onal friendship aspect of "inside" politics broadened
g of human nature in a way that matured me, but also
elping people I should not have helped.

Balancing Law, Values, Inside Politics and Outside Politics— Non-Action on "Baby" AIDs

Unhappy though I am to shine the spotlight twice on my one truly cowardly moment as a legislator, it is worth anticipating the story of my non-vote on the "baby AIDS" bill described in Chapter Four. There the story illustrates the use of the procedural rules for political advantage. But the story also provides an unusually clear example of the dilemma a legislator may encounter when faced with a particular convergence of the four elements of the legislative process treated in this chapter: considerations of law; counterbalanced considerations of values; inside politics; counterbalanced outside politics. For me under these cross-pressures the best option available seemed to be to avoid voting at all. That is what I did.

As a strong advocate of information privacy, I had originated laws protecting consumers' rights to withhold their Social Security numbers from merchants in credit card transactions and laws prohibiting carbon copies of credit card slips which could otherwise be filched by the unscrupulous to acquire personal identifying information about the customer; and I had fought for the extension of the Fair Credit Reporting Act and other privacy protections for consumers. Although it is common to think of privacy as a value, from a legal point of view it is not only a complicated set of values, it is also a somewhat mysterious derivative of laws and values. Justice William O. Douglas famously (or infamously, for those who did not like the decision) decided that a right to privacy could be found in the "penumbras" around certain provisions of the Fourth Amendment to the Constitution in *Griswold v. Connecticut*, 381 U.S. 479 (1965), the birth control decision that provided the main foundation for *Roe v. Wade*, 410 U.S. 113 (1973), the decision invalidating most laws against abortion. So in the classification system we have been applying, the privacy concerns that prompted opposition to Assembly Member Nettie Mayersohn's bill to require AIDS tests of newborns in public hospitals, really constitute legal principle, which here we categorize as "law."

The simple and powerful value of saving lives provided support for Mayersohn's bill. Factual disputes clouded both sides of this debate. Opponents questioned whether the bill would truly save lives; advocates questioned whether the bill would truly invade legitimate privacy concerns. I could not, at the time, decide whether the legal principle or the value carried more weight.

My campaign for Congress was then under way. The congressional district included my Brooklyn Assembly district and other parts of Brooklyn; it also included part of Assembly Member Mayersohn's Queens district; and one of my opponents was another Assembly Member from Queens, with whom Mayersohn had a rocky relationship. Mayersohn made her "baby AIDS" bill the crusade of her career, and she made it very plain that opposition to or support for that bill would be the litmus test she would apply in determining her political endorsements. At first glance one might consider my interest in Mayersohn's endorsement an aspect of outside politics, but our long and multifaceted collegial relationship made it unmistakably a "family" matter: this was "inside" politics.

On the other hand, my relationship with gay and civil liberties groups was also delicate. I had always been a leading advocate for gay rights and civil liberties. When gay rights had no vocal support and loud and strenuous opposition in my district, I had strongly and publicly supported gay rights legislation. Regarding civil liberties, I was one of a handful of New York legislators to vote against a resolution calling for an amendment to the Constitution allowing the imposition of criminal penalties for flag-burning. The true test of our commitment to freedom, I believed then as I do now, is our toleration of the most offensive forms of dissent.

However, in 1989, when I ran unsuccessfully for District Attorney in Brooklyn, someone in my campaign, without my authorization or knowledge, had issued a flyer implying that a gay Democratic club's support for my chief opponent, Charles ("Joe") Hynes, was a reason to vote against Hynes. This had soured my relationships with gay rights groups and civil liberties groups for some time. Although by now those relationships had been restored for the most part, I remained particularly sensitive to any issue that might hurt them again. Whatever might have been going on in my own psychology, an observer would have concluded that my concerns about those relationships fell into the category of "outside politics."

Mayersohn might never forgive me if I voted against her bill; the gay and civil liberties groups might never forgive me if I voted for it. While Mayersohn might be annoyed that I failed to support the bill, at least on that basis she could not accuse me of opposing it. While the gay and civil rights groups might be annoyed that I failed to oppose the bill, at least on that basis they could not accuse me of supporting it. So I neither opposed it nor supported it. I didn't vote. I ducked.

All the elements—values, law, inside politics, and outside politics— produced this legislative behavior. Not my proudest hour.

CHAPTER III

How Things Work

At 2 P.M. on the second Monday in January 1981, I entered the Assembly Chamber for my first official session as a Member. I knew that no one could take my new job away from me any time in the next two years (unless I was convicted of a felony, and I also knew I was not going to commit one). One of those 150 big leather Assembly chairs was mine, in that huge Moorish-Gothic room with its fifty-six-foot-high ceiling, hailed by the leading American architect Henry Van Brunt when it was dedicated in 1879 as "the most monumental interior in the country."

Initiation

The Speaker presided from a raised podium at the front of the members' desks arrayed in a two-thirds circle. Well, as it turned out, not exactly. Usually, he designated a temporary Speaker to preside, while he sat in his own special office, behind a closed door on the members' left front, working the telephone and simultaneously listening to the Assembly proceedings and debates, emerging to take the podium away from the Speaker *pro tempore* only in the rare situation that called for a personal display of authority.

The Majority Leader sat four rows from the front on the right aisle seat facing the podium, with a telephone on his desk connected to the Speaker's, the only such telephone in the room. Democrats generally sat to the right and Republicans to the left, except for a special section on the far left needed by the extra Democrats, since we—who had captured control of the Assembly in 1974—had 86 members to the Republican's 64.

About an hour before the session started I had joined the other Assembly Democrats in the Speaker's Conference room, a more normal room, albeit one with nice wood paneling and rugs and a conference table big enough for about thirty comfortable upholstered chairs, in which the more senior members sat. The rest of us sat in folding chairs at the two long sides of the room. Assembly Members William Passanante and Arthur Eve shared the honors of presiding and nominating Stanley Fink for re-election as Speaker. Passanante, an Italian-American from Greenwich Village in New York City, had served since 1955. In 1956, championing the cause of mothers and their babies in strollers, he was one of the first politicians to back down Robert Moses when the famed "master builder" tried to widen a road through Washington Square Park. Instead, Passanante, Jane Jacobs, and other community leaders got the park closed to traffic entirely. Eve, an African-American Assembly Member from Buffalo since 1967, was most famous for attempting to negotiate on behalf of the inmates after they seized control of Attica prison in September, 1971. He was unsuccessful; forty-three hostages and inmates died when, acting on Governor Rockefeller's orders, state troopers retook the facility by force. Stanley Fink, who represented a district near mine in Brooklyn, entered the Assembly in 1968. He became the Speaker in 1979, after a brief two-year stint as Majority Leader. Unopposed, he was re-elected by our unanimous vote.

The Democratic Conference. Over the next eighteen years I spent hundreds of hours in that conference room. Under Fink and his successor Mel Miller, the Democratic members of the Assembly would regularly announce "conference" breaks from legislative session, during which most of the Democrats would repair to the Speaker's Conference Room. Meanwhile, most of the Republicans would convene in their quarters for their respective strategy sessions. These huddles were a much longer version than the football game variety.

During these conferences, usually chaired by a senior Member not considered competent enough to chair a substantive committee, the Speaker would outline his plan to bring some significant legislation to the floor that day, or in the near future. Members would often question the substantive merits of the legislation, or its politics, or the wisdom of the particular legislative tactics intended.

Democrats from Manhattan's Upper West Side tend to hold political views to the left of most other people in the United States, while parts of Queens remain Archie Bunker territory. Democrats representing black and Latino areas in Brooklyn and the Bronx often hold dramatically different positions from the Democrats representing ultraconservative German- and Polish-American neighborhoods in Lackawanna, near Buffalo, in western New York, or the farmers living near Amsterdam, in New York's Mohawk Valley. For that matter, Democrats representing black and Latino ghettos in Brooklyn and the Bronx often hold dramatically different positions from those Democrats representing middle-class black and Latino voters in Queens or Rochester. Uniting such a group behind almost any particular policy presents a challenge to any Speaker.

Reporting emphasizing that New York is governed by "three men in a room"—the Governor, the Speaker, and the Senate Majority Leader—gives little credence to leaders' claims that they are far less autonomous actors than representatives of the collective will of the majority party conference. Actually, the record is mixed, with the importance of the conference at any particular time a function of the expectations and assertiveness of members and the style and responsiveness of particular leaders.

At their best, as they were under Stanley Fink, the majority conference discussions were uninhibited, free-wheeling, honest and ferocious exercises in intellectual combat, resulting in policy decisions that had survived that form of trial by fire. Certainly they were, then, truly deliberative.

Fink dominated the conference by force of his intellect and personality, but on the rare occasions that he failed to persuade the conference, he followed the will of the majority. Miller succeeded as often as Fink, probably because he tended to judge accurately the mood of the Conference, and did not try as frequently to bend it to his will. During my time in the Assembly, Saul Weprin and Shelly Silver were far less responsive to the will of the Conference and predisposed to making decisions on their own. More recently, perhaps in response to the attempted coup by then Majority Leader Mike Bragman in 2000, Silver has been reported to be more willing to allow the Conference to guide his decisions. One good example in 2005 was his push to include civil rape cases in the legislation disallowing the use of the statute of limitations by many defendants, a matter on which Silver took the Conference's direction though his personal views diverged from those of the majority.

Because they are (actually or potentially) key venues for policy-making, some of those in favor of more open government have argued that the majority and minority conferences in the New York State Legislature should not be closed to the press and public. There is a degree of inconsistency, they argue, in the Legislature requiring more openness in decision making in state agencies and local government in New York than they are willing to embrace for themselves. If these meetings were not closed, however, elected legislators could not have expressed themselves as honestly. Indeed, if they were public the locus of real decision-making would no doubt have moved to a different, non-public venue—like telephone conversations among three or four people, rather than debates involving eighty or ninety people. In fact, that's more or less what happened anyway after Weprin and then Silver became speaker.

By analogy, the same degree of confidentiality should be available to legislative caucuses at the local level. Different standards for openness for legislatures than for executive agencies, however, are justifiable: the legislative policymaking process benefits from uninhibited exchanges among its participants, and—at least in theory—if the public does not like the results, it can fire the legislators. There is less argument for the benefits of uninhibited exchanges among those who are supposed to be carrying out policy, and with the protections given in law it is much harder to fire them.

Liberals *could* outvote conservatives in the Democratic Conference, but everyone in the Conference understood that the Democrats would lose their majority altogether if they alienated the voters enough so that the conservative neighborhoods of the State elected only Republicans. That is, if too many conservative and moderate Democrats lost their seats to more conservative Republicans because voters got sick of "ultraliberal" Democratic policies, the next Speaker of the Assembly would be a Republican. So liberals refrained from pressing their advantage. That's how the Conference operated: not just voting policies up or down but hashing out what seemed best for the people of the State of New York and for the future of the Democratic Party in the Legislature.

Of course, members of the Democratic Conference usually thought that what worked best for the latter also worked best for the former. From time to time, however, the more liberal members would object to the cautious approach in the following terms: What is the point of maintaining our Democratic majority if not to address the serious social ills of our time?

The Life. Constituents most often interact with their Assembly member in the district. Others—lobbyists, legislative staffers, state agency officials—are likely to see him or her in the capitol. Few share the legislator's experience of constant movement, weekly and sometimes more frequent travel back and forth between the district and Albany.

Some attribute the apparent loss of moral compass by legislators and other elected officials in part to the somewhat strange and disconnected life they lead in Albany. Elected officials walk the halls as princes of the domain, away from their families, attended by non-unionized employees who serve entirely at their pleasure and by interns one step still lower on the hierarchical ladder, and constantly beseeched by lobbyists.

When I first came to the Legislature there was talk of the "Bear Mountain Compact," the hypothetical agreement that shenanigans in Albany, generally assumed to be sexual, were not talked about south of Bear Mountain (about two-thirds of the way down the New York State Thruway from Albany to New York City). This was the legislative version of "what happens in Vegas, stays in Vegas." Of course, it ceased to be true long ago, as recent scandals demonstrate.

Some elected officials in New York do indeed lose moral compass. Most, I think, don't. Moreover, as news accounts make abundantly clear, unethical and illegal behavior is hardly unique to Albany. It bedevils government at all levels and in all branches. Mark Twain commented, famously, "The only native American criminal class is the Congress."

But Albany has in recent years supplied an impressive list of elected officials who have been convicted of crimes or otherwise had their moral standards publicly called into question: former Assembly members Gloria Davis, Roger Green, Brian McLaughlin, Clarence Norman, Diane Gordon, Anthony Seminario, Sam Hoyt, Ryan Karben; State Senators Efrain Gonzalez, Hiram Monserrate, Guy Velella, and Majority Leader Joseph Bruno; State Comptroller Alan Hevesi, and Governors Eliot Spitzer and David Paterson. The length of this list has caused more than one observer to comment that incumbents in state elected office are more commonly removed by indictment and conviction than by failure of reelection.

If that list in fact reflects ethical standards inferior to those of professions whose practitioners experience less scrutiny, most likely Lord Acton's maxim that power corrupts has some relevance. In his benchmark work on political culture, political scientist Daniel Elazar included "private regarding" New York as among those states in which self-interest is accepted as a legitimate motivator for seeking public office. Especially in New York and states like it in that respect, one attracted to politics by the opportunity to repair the world may underestimate the role that sheer access to upward economic mobility may play in bringing others into the public arena. To the extent that the latter is a driving force, strict adherence to ethical standards may of course be less correlative. Clearly, however, judging from the personal circumstances of some of those on our list, that latter motive insufficiently explains at least some of the lapses we have seen, and has no relevance whatsoever to others.

The relationship between political office and morality may have deeper and more complex dimensions. Even at the highest and more admired levels, effective governing does not necessarily allow practitioners to do what is immediately ethical. Lincoln's refusal to free the slaves, except—from the point of view of contemporaries—gradually and slowly, often elicited the wrath of Frederick Douglass. FDR's paltry assistance to Jews targeted by Hitler was just one of many possible examples of his refusal to take ethical positions demanded by Eleanor. Lyndon Johnson for years stymied the efforts of paragons of the civil rights movement like Paul Douglas and Hubert Humphrey. But Frederick Douglass eventually acknowledged that Lincoln had been right, and himself wrong, for otherwise Lincoln could not have brought the country along with him. The great achievements of FDR and LBJ likely had parallel roots. In contrast, President Jimmy Carter, arguably, tried to impose the "right" policies, but generally was unsuccessful.

I found my colleagues in the Legislature to be largely representative of the public in terms of adherence to ethical standards as in many other ways, though—as political life requires—a good deal more gregarious. But perhaps the disposition toward utilitarianism in political life does generate a certain relativism, a disposition too toward independence from usual moral standards. If so, such independence does not usually operate to produce the accomplishments of a Lincoln, an FDR, or an LBJ. More often, it likely produces the escapades of a McLaughlin or a Seminario.

Like many of my colleagues, my travel to Albany during my first nine sessions was by car up the Thruway. I often picked up colleagues along the way, who occasionally spelled me at the wheel. During my last nine years in office I turned to traveling by train, most often catching the 7:15 from Penn Station each Monday morning (it stopped leaving from Grand Central shortly after I became a regular on it) as did others heading to Albany for the session. The train's ultimate destination was Montreal. On the first leg to Albany, it was a place to talk business with staff, other members or lobbyists. Quite often, I would read the *Times*, fall asleep, and wake up just as we pulled into Albany. One morning I felt a hand pulling my shoulder and heard a voice saying urgently, "Monsieur, monsieur, c'est Montreal!!" Of course it was my good friend, then-State Senator Donald Halperin. Don was one of the funniest people I knew, and an all-round great guy.

Only the members of the Legislature (except those representing Albany or districts in commuting distance from the capitol) and a few others experience the displacement of having to live in two places for much of the year. In the old days, when sessions were shorter and legislative service more an avocation than a profession, Republicans, when in the capitol, lived in the Ten Eyck Hotel (the current location of the Crowne Plaza), while Democrats took over the DeWitt Clinton Hotel, for decades now, sadly, an abandoned hulk. Informal interaction in a generally shared accommodation did a good deal to help build friendships and reinforce party cohesion.

By the time I reached the Assembly many members were working full-time as legislators. With sessions longer, they were far less inclined to hotel living, and were making housing arrangements all over town. This, of course, cut down considerably on members' interaction with each other after work. For my first six two-year sessions I rented a small bedroom in an apartment on Peyster Street in Albany's Pine Hills section from a friend-of-a-friend. I also briefly owned this house, but sold it in 1992 and rented rooms in town for my remaining three sessions. This was truly just a place to sleep. I ordinarily got to work in the capitol at 8:30 and often did not return until 10 or 11 at night.

Committees. The day after we selected the Speaker, a Tuesday, I attended my first committee meetings. Partially in response to the preference list I had sent to the Speaker and partially in response to needs as he saw them, I had been assigned to five committees: Cities; Judiciary (dealing with judicial matters and questions of evidence, but also with a variety of substantive areas of the law, including landlord-tenant relations, trusts and estates, and marital property); Corporations, Public Authorities, and Utilities; Education; and Real Property Taxation. This number of assignments was typical.

The number of committees in each house of the New York State Legislature reflects the range of business before the state, but also a desire by leadership to have sufficient committee chairmanships with which to recognize and reward majority party members. Not insignificantly, chairmanships carried with them added compensation. The size of the Senate majority compared to that of the Assembly assured that almost every Republican Senator could be given a chairmanship (or other position that carried with it a "lulu," payment in lieu of expenses), while Democrats in the Assembly had to wait their turn. When asked about this, Stanley Fink remarked that the relative scarcity of leadership posts in the Assembly as compared to the Senate actually gave him a subtle advantage as leader in his House because his members knew that "when your turn comes you want it to be there for you."

Though the larger Assembly might have gotten by with fewer assignments per member, the leadership wanted the same ratio of Democrats to Republicans on each committee as on the floor. That way, marginal Democratic members would enjoy the benefit of not having to vote for bills harmful to them in their districts while the Democratic majority still retained enough votes to report the bills that the leadership, or the chair, wanted to reach a vote. Most members participated only nominally in some of their committees and some—like Dov Hikind—assiduously avoided any committee responsibilities.

A few weeks after the session began, at the suggestion of Kenneth L. Shapiro, the Speaker's Counsel, I left the Cities Committee, which focused mostly on the needs of jurisdictions outside New York City, for an assignment to Codes, which dealt mostly with criminal law—and which the Speaker himself had chaired earlier in his legislative career.

My First Bill. At the Judiciary Committee meeting, the committee clerk called up one of the bills I had "pre-filed," or written and introduced a few weeks in advance of the new year, as all legislators are permitted to do prior to the beginning of a new two-year session. My predecessor in the Assembly, Charles Schumer, had introduced a similar bill; I was familiar with the problem it addressed and therefore comfortable with the subject. I explained that the bill would prevent a landlord from evicting a tenant for nonpayment if the tenant alleged that he or she had paid in cash and could prove, presumably through testimony by other tenants, that the landlord customarily refused to provide receipts for rent paid in cash. The committee chair, a small, unassuming, kindly, middle-aged member from Queens, Saul Weprin, a Democrat (as were all the Assembly committee chairs—Democrats that is, not necessarily small, kindly or middle aged), quickly said "Motion to report. All in favor?" Many hands went up. "Any opposed?" I do not remember if any of the seven or eight Republicans out of the Committee's twenty-five or so members raised their hands. Certainly none of the Democrats voted against. The Committee reported my bill and about a dozen other bills to the floor in similar manner. So somehow I was off to a fast start.

I later learned why. The leadership had to call up *some* bills early in the session; pro-tenant bills were easy for the Democratic leadership in the Assembly. The Senate usually killed these, but I lucked out. The Senate actually passed this bill, thanks to the support of the aforementioned Donald Halperin, a Democratic Senator uniquely popular on both sides of the aisle.

The following Monday the Assembly held its first "working" session of the year. As the Members filed in, the Assembly Clerk recorded their presence. The presence of a bare majority of the House, 76 members, satisfied the quorum requirement, and the clerk called the House to order.

The majority leader was Daniel Walsh, from the town of Franklinville in western New York's Cattaraugus County. In New York State, the Majority Leader is appointed by the Speaker. Speaker Fink, who (as noted) was from New York City as were most Assembly Democrats, established the modern practice of choosing Democratic Assembly Majority Leaders from upstate.

Walsh called the "consent calendar," uncontroversial bills extending existing funding for government programs, providing technical assistance for local governments, designating state birds or flowers, and the like. As Walsh called each bill number in turn, any Member could yell "lay aside," which would postpone consideration of such a bill for the "debate calendar." Otherwise, the clerk would ask for negative votes on the bill. The Member who introduced the bill would be far happier with a negative vote by some other Member who had some reason to dislike it than with a "lay aside," because negative votes on consent calendar bills were never very numerous, but once a bill came up for debate—if indeed it was not postponed to some other date, because other controversial bills took up the day's debating time—its fate would be somewhat less certain.

My bill got laid aside, by Dominick DiCarlo. With the exception of Stanley Fink, DiCarlo, a conservative Republican Assembly Member from Bay Ridge, Brooklyn, was possessed of the sharpest mind and debating skills in the House. I knew enough to be frightened of DiCarlo; I didn't know that custom suggested that new Members be treated gently, particularly with respect to their first bill on the floor.

There were few enough bills on the debate calendar that early in the session so that mine was not put over to another session, but was in fact called up for debate that very afternoon. After Walsh asked the clerk to put the bill up for debate, DiCarlo stood, the Speaker *pro temp* recognized him, and DiCarlo asked me if I would yield for a question. I said I would. He asked me if I had seen any instances of the kind of problem my bill addressed. Indeed I had, back in my district, and I said so. "No further questions," said DiCarlo. The bill passed overwhelmingly, and all my colleagues, Democrats and Republicans, gave me the traditional round of applause accorded a new Member upon passage of the Member's first bill.

New York Geography And Political Demographics

New York City is not New York State. (Most of the outside world does not know this . . . or seems not to.) The City of Albany, not New York City, is the state's capital. Most city residents know this; but many figure that, somehow, a mistake has been made.

By the census of 2000, the one on which the last legislative reapportionment was based, New York City had 8,008,300 of New York State's almost 18,976,500 people. The city's population was extraordinarily diverse. Only 35% of its residents—2,801, 267 of them, to be exact—were white, while 2,160,554 were Hispanic (separately counted, but not a race), 1,962,154 African American, and 780,229 Asian. And, of course, there was enormous variety within these categories, as New York has been renewed in recent years by a wave of immigration from around the globe unparalleled since the early part of the twentieth century.

In contrast, though all counties reported some residents who were not white, and there were important concentrations of minority group members in a number of other cities, towns, and villages throughout the rest of New York, whites constituted 85% of New York's population outside New York City.

Its numbers in the 2000 census entitled New York City to 65 of the 150 members of the Assembly and 26 of 62 state Senators. These numbers were not dramatically different in 1981, so this was a key point for a new Assembly Member from Brooklyn to learn: a majority of representatives in both houses are not from New York City. In fact, it turned out that some legislators from far western New York State represent fans who could more easily drive to Cleveland or even Pittsburgh to see a major league ball game than to the Bronx or Queens.

There were 3,103,947 enrolled Democrats in New York City in 2008. The city's 533,761 enrolled Republicans were outnumbered even by the 730,395 voters who chose to have no party affiliation at all. In contrast, Democratic (2,727,498) and Republican (2,520,759) enrollments in the rest of the state were more evenly balanced, reflecting a great shift over earlier years when Republicans outside New York City enjoyed a heavy majority. Even two years earlier, non-New York City Republicans outnumbered non–New York City Democrats by a small margin.

The idea of an "upstate/downstate split" defines the old way of looking at New York politics, with Democrats, overwhelmingly dominant in New York City, battling Republicans, overwhelmingly dominant in the rest for the state, for control of state government. These days 41 percent of Assembly Democrats are from the suburbs of New York City, the Hudson Valley, the state's other major cities, and even some very rural areas; there would be no Democratic majority in that House without at least some out-of-city seats. The Senate would have had a Democratic majority even earlier if the Republicans lost their New York City members. In my time, the Democrats in the Assembly needed upstate Democrats, and the Republicans in the Senate needed New York City Republicans, to keep their respective majorities, and to get things done.

The 2008 elections enabled the Democrats to command a majority in the New York State Senate in 2009 for the first time since their single year of control in 1965—only the second time since the Great Depression era. This Democratic victory ended the longest period of continuous divided party control of a state legislature in the United States. As of 2009, all but one of New York City's 65 Assembly members and all but three of its 26 state senators were Democrats. Outside New York City there were 45 Democratic and 40 Republican members of the Assembly, and 9 Democratic and 27 Republican Senators.

As was the case in 1965, the new Senate Democratic majority in 2008, so long out of power, had some initial difficulty organizing itself. For reasons of ideology, ethnic politics, and personal advantage, not necessarily in that order, four members—Ruben Diaz, Sr. and Pedro Espada of the Bronx, Hiram Monserrate of Queens, and Carl Kruger of Brooklyn—resisted endorsing the sitting Minority Leader, Malcolm Smith, for Majority Leader. At least one member of this "gang of four"—Carl Kruger, who was the only Democrat in modern history to be awarded a committee chairmanship in the Republican Senate—threatened to enter into a coalition with the Republicans to organize the body. The Democrats ran the Senate when it convened in January, 2009.

This historic change, giving one party control of the Assembly, the Senate, and the governorship in New York for the first time since 1974, held out the prospect that New York might be entering into in era of "responsible party government" favored by some political scientists. That is, with one party in control, there would be less buck-passing. The electorate could now hold the Democrats accountable for the performance of state government. Others bemoaned the loss of the additional "checks and balances" that divided control had provided.

Certainly with the Democratic victory in 2008, the demographic character of the Senate majority changed dramatically, and its geographic and ideological center shifted. The Republican majority before 2008 had no African-American members and included persons of Hispanic descent only briefly (as a result of party changes by sitting members, later defeated in primaries). Fourteen Democratic members, more than forty percent of the Democratic majority in 2009, were African American or Hispanic. The Republican majority in 2008 included three women; the Senate Democratic conference in 2009 had six. The Republican majority was suburban- and rural-based. The Democratic majority in the Senate was even more urban-centered than the long-term Democratic majority in the Assembly.

As a result of these differences, policy priorities of the Senate shifted. But inter-institutional differences between the Senate and Assembly remained, and negotiations remained necessary. Moreover, neither the internal dynamic of the Assembly nor its leadership changed in 2008. In sum, the essential nature of the legislative process persisted.

The historic shift of the State Senate to Democratic control was the culmination of a long-term trend. Partisan political change in New York State in recent decades has followed population movement north and east from New York City and outward from other major cities. The rural area north and west of Albany—the true Republican heartland of New York State—elected the bulk of the Senate Republican majority. It was extraordinary, therefore, when Democrat Darrell Aubertine, a dairy farmer, beat his assembly colleague Will Barclay for a North Country senate seat in a special election in 2008 and held on in the general election that year. This was a clear case of redistricting for partisan advantage by Assembly Democrats in rural areas providing the basis for a later successful move to erode the Republican Senate majority.

The major northern and western cities—Rochester, Syracuse, Schenectady, Utica, Niagara Falls, Troy, and Binghamton—usually elect Democratic Assembly members, but are swallowed up into Republican state senate districts. However, Democrat David Valesky broke through against Nancy Larraine Hoffman, who had earlier switched from Democrat to Republican, in a three-way race in 2004, retained his seat against a spirited challenge in 2006, and was a comfortable victor in 2008.

All of Long Island's nine state senators were Republican in 2006, while 10 of its 21 Assembly members were Democratic. (See the "Drawing the Lines" subsection of this chapter, below, for a discussion of how this startling result was achieved, again and again.) The Republican monopoly in the Island's Senate delegation was cracked in 2007 when Craig Johnson won a special election to fill a vacancy created after a longtime Republican Senator, Michael Balboni, resigned to become the new Democratic Spitzer administration's homeland security Czar. Johnson was re-elected in 2008. Also in that year, the 82-year-old 36-year incumbent Caesar Trunzo, lost to Brian Foley. Trunzo had beaten Foley's father in 1984, when Trunzo had only been in the Senate for ten years.

Westchester County, not so long ago a Republican bastion, has gradually become so Democratic that a remaining Republican Senator from the district encompassing a large part of it, Nicholas Spano, was re-elected in 2004 in such a close race that it took three months to determine the outcome. Spano lost his seat in 2006 in a second race against Andrea Stewart-Cousins.

Also in the first decade of the new century, Republicans lost seats within New York City. These were initially gained by exploiting a (diminishing) Republican base in some neighborhoods. They were retained by a combination of artful district design and relentless use of majority status and incumbent advantage in resource allocation and fundraising to preempt and discourage opposition. Roy M. Goodman relinquished the East Side Manhattan seat long held by Republicans to Democrat Liz Krueger in 2002. In May of 2004, Guy Velella left his Bronx/Westchester Senate seat as part of a plea bargain in a corruption trial, and was later replaced by a Democrat. Also in 2004, Olga Mendez of the Bronx, like Nancy Larraine Hoffman first elected as a Democrat but induced to change parties and join the Republican majority, lost her reelection bid. And in 2008, Republican Serphin Maltese relinquished his Queens district to City Councilman Joseph P. Addabbo Jr.

The Mid-Hudson Valley, formerly all GOP, is now a partisan battleground. Albany itself not only elects Democrats to the Assembly, its suburbs in recent years have become Democratic enough so that Albany's one senator is also a Democrat. Buffalo, which declined in population from more than half a million in 1950 to under 292,648 in 2000, remained solidly Democratic, with an African-American Democratic State Senator representing most of the city, and only Democrats representing it in the Assembly.

Of course, the electorate can depart strikingly from its usual partisan preferences, especially for highly visible jobs. Republican George Pataki finished twelve years as governor of Democratic New York State at the end of 2006. In overwhelmingly Democratic New York City, the mayoralty had been won for two consecutive terms each—the legal limit—by celebrated Republicans, Rudolph Guiliani and Michael Bloomberg. (In 2007, well after his reelection, Bloomberg changed his registration so that he belonged to no political party. After a tough battle, in October 2008 he got the New York City Council to suspend the two-term limit that had been imposed by a public referendum after Ed Koch's mayoralty, and in 2009 won re-election to a third term.) Nonetheless, both the state's U.S. Senators were Democrats, and New York emerged from the 2006 elections with all its statewide elected officials members of a single party (the Democratic party) for the first time since before World War II.

New York Republicans have traditionally been more moderate or liberal than the national Republican party, going back at least to Tom Dewey's years as governor, from 1943–1954, and those of Nelson Rockefeller, 1959–1973. Other prominent liberal or moderate Republicans elected statewide in New York in the latter half of the twentieth century included U.S. Senators Jacob Javits, Kenneth Keating, and Irving Ives; Attorney General Louis Lefkowitz; and, arguably, Governor Pataki. Only U.S. Senator James Buckley provided a relatively recent example of a notably conservative statewide elected official in New York, and he won in 1970 on the Conservative Party line with less than a majority of the vote in a three way race with Democrat Richard Ottinger and Republican Charles Goodell.

The State Senate was the one consistent bulwark of power for New York Republicans over the decades. Though the Senate majority generally approached issues from a more conservative set of premises, like successful GOP statewide candidates its members were drawn to the center by the imperatives of state politics in New York. Staying in power to advance a conservative agenda in some areas of policy required taking more liberal stands on others. Thus while New York Republicans may have been adherents of "trickle-down" economics, curbing government spending on such programs as welfare and Medicaid, and supporting tax cuts and the death penalty, they often supported environmental causes and civil liberties. The New York State Senate Republican leadership fought to increase state spending above the levels proposed in Governor Pataki's executive budgets in every year of his governorship, and continued on this line in Democratic Governor Eliot Spitzer's year. The Senate has passed increases in minimum wage legislation, gay rights legislation, and significant protective legislation for the environment.

If New York State Republicans were more liberal than national Republicans, New York State Democrats are, for the most part, more liberal than national Democrats. Although the New York State Senate enacted some liberal legislation, it usually was in the role of blocking or delaying progressive initiatives by the State Assembly. Thus the Republican-led Senate consistently resisted consumer protection efforts opposed by banking and insurance interests. It enacted bills like the aforementioned gay rights, environmental, and minimum wage legislation years, even decades, after the Assembly brought them forward. And it made New York one of the last states to reduce harsh criminal penalties for nonviolent drug offenses. On the other hand, the Senate majority enthusiastically advanced initiatives for tax cuts, regulatory relief for business, school choice and economic development subsidies.

No legislation may be enacted unless it is passed by both Houses. New York does eventually enact a budget each year, and other laws. So the chambers must and do reach agreement fairly often. Nonetheless, the Democratic Assembly and the Republican Senate clashed in fierce conflict virtually without end. Battling was the norm in a Legislature in which partisan control had been continuously divided for a third of a century. And therein lies a tale.

Legislative Districts, New York Politics, And Party Control

New York has about 19 million people. Under the Supreme Court's one-person one-vote rulings in *Baker v. Carr*, 369 U.S. 186 (1962) and *Reynolds v. Sims*, 377 U.S. 633 (1964) its Assembly members must represent approximately equal populations. Thus each Assembly district has to include about 126,000 people (this is somewhat larger than the number I originally used because of population growth in New York). For the same reason, each of the 62 members of the State Senate represents about 300,000 people. However, Supreme Court decisions allow state legislative districts a larger percentage of population variation than they allow to congressional districts. As a result, when the Senate leadership succeeded politically in making seven of its districts in Queens represent over 2,200,000 people, and seven upstate districts represent under 2,044,000 people (based on the census of 2000), it faced no legal problem in doing so. A smaller number of upstaters, presumably more Republican, received as much representation as a larger number of New York City residents, presumably more Democratic.

Democrats controlled the New York State Senate for only 14 years between 1900 and 2007, only one of these—1965—since the end of World War II. The Assembly was in Democratic hands for only three years in the 20th century prior to the U.S. Supreme Court's reapportionment decisions. Since that time they have been in the Assembly majority for all but six years (1969–1974).

Partisan control of the New York State Legislature was closely contested in the post-Civil war period. Then in 1894, seizing the opportunity, a GOP-controlled state constitutional convention acted to assure that the Legislature thereafter would be—as the great Democratic Governor Alfred E. Smith later described it—"constitutionally Republican." They wrote into the constitution that each county except Hamilton in the Adirondacks would have at least one of the 150 Assembly members (increased from 128), with those having more than 1½ but less than 2 "population ratios" getting another before the remainder of the seats were distributed according to population. For the Senate they provided for a minimum of 50 members, with no county allowed more than one-third the membership and no two counties "adjoining or separated only by public waters" (Manhattan and Kings, or Brooklyn) more than half. Moreover, counties with four or more Senators could add a seat only when they achieved an additional "complete ratio," and then seats were added, not redistributed, as was and is the case for the Assembly. Finally, and to the great disadvantage of New York City, according to the 1894 constitutional provision, apportionment of both the Senate and Assembly was to be on the basis of citizenship, not population. (Then as now the City had a large proportion of immigrants who were not yet citizens.)

One of the most prominent Republican delegates to the 1894 Constitutional Convention, Elihu Root, later Secretary of State under presidents William McKinley and Theodore Roosevelt, defended this arrangement at the Convention on the grounds that "the more sparsely populated portions of the state have diverse interests and, therefore, should have relatively more legislators to represent those varied interests. Although a great city may have more inhabitants, it has a unified interest and, consequently, requires fewer legislators to represent that interest in Albany."

The 1894 constitutional provisions resulted at first in a Legislature apportioned roughly in accord with population. But after the creation of metropolitan New York City in 1898, and as time passed and the City population grew, rural areas became more and more over-represented. By 1963, just before implementation of the one-person one-vote rulings, ". . . a majority of New York's senators represent[ed] only thirty-eight per cent of New York's citizen population . . . while a majority of New York's assemblymen c[a]me from districts where only 36.5 per cent of New York's citizen inhabitants live[d]."

Beginning in 1930 the state constitution required that the Legislature be reapportioned every ten years on the basis of the decennial federal census. (Previously a separate state census was used, because citizenship, not population, was prescribed as the base for apportionment under New York's constitution.) Partisan differences, however, resulted in this requirement not always being honored. After the U.S Supreme Court established the one-person-one-vote standard in the mid-1960's, state legislatures could no longer allow "cow districts" to outvote "people districts." So now for elections in years ending in "2" (1982, 1992, 2002, 2012) Assembly and Senate districts must be adjusted to assure that they are "substantially equal in population" and, as a result, most legislators find themselves running in districts with altered boundary lines.

In 1970, just a few years after the U.S. Supreme Court's landmark reapportionment decisions, amendments adopted by Congress to the Federal Voting Rights Act (VRA) introduced additional criteria that were to shape redistricting in New York. These amendments provided that the U.S. Department of Justice or a Federal Court could review electoral practices in any state or locality in which less than half the voting-age population had registered or voted in 1968. Manhattan, Brooklyn and the Bronx in New York City were all covered jurisdictions under this act.

Republicans, who controlled both houses of the Legislature in 1971, sought—while acting within the constraints of one-person-one vote—to carve out districts that would assure their dominance for the next decade. In this they had help from certain Democratic Assembly members: those with strong support from regular party organizations in New York City sought to protect themselves at the expense of reformers. The resultant redistricting worked for the GOP in the Senate but not for the Assembly, where Republican plans were overwhelmed by a combination of rapid demographic change and adverse public reaction in 1974 to the Watergate scandal. Notwithstanding litigation brought by the NAACP Legal Defense Fund under the VRA that forced the mid-decade redrawing of lines within Manhattan and Brooklyn for both the Senate and Assembly, the number of minority group legislators increased only incrementally over the balance of the decade.

Democrats controlled the Assembly in 1981. This gave the party a key role in reapportionment of the Legislature for the first time since the adoption of the 1894 state constitution. The result was the establishment of New York's infamous bi-partisan gerrymander, with the Republican Senators designing the districts for their house and the Democratic Assembly members for theirs—and the governor going along. The "non-retrogression rule," established by the Supreme Court in *Beer v. United States,* 425 U.S. 130 (1976), assured that reapportionment would not diminish minority representation in jurisdictions covered by the Voting Rights Act. But one-person-one-vote and the VRA notwithstanding, the Senate Republicans entrenched a 34 or 35 seat majority (of 61) that they were able to protect for the entire decade. As for the Assembly, before the 1981 reapportionment there were 81 Democrats in the body; after there were 96, and in no time during the decade did the number fall below 92.

Reapportionment is done by law, and thus subject to gubernatorial veto—and, therefore, influence. Like his co-partisan Hugh Carey before him, however, Democratic Governor Mario Cuomo was not willing to enter into this thicket. The Assembly majority did not want the governor in their intimate family business. Taking on the Republican Senate would put major gubernatorial agenda items at risk. The reapportionment following the 1990 census gave the Assembly Democrats 101 seats in 1992, a so-called "veto proof" majority. The number of Democrats in that body fell back to 94 after the next election, but rose again by increments to 99 at the end of the decade. Republicans in the Senate were able to keep their numbers between 35 and 36 for the entire decade.

The reapportionment for the 2002 election produced 103 Democratic seats in the Assembly and—partially as a result of Democratic defections—a 36–26 Republican majority in the Senate (again the Republicans sought added advantage by creating an additional seat in their house). The next year the Assembly Democrats' number went up by one more to 104, while the Senate Republicans fell back to 35.

Unlike his Democratic predecessors, Eliot Spitzer made electing a State Senate controlled by his party an explicit electoral goal; this was, in fact, a major source of the tension between him and the Republican

Senate majority. As a result, far fewer incumbent Senators got a "free ride"—were unopposed—in 2006 than in earlier years. After Spitzer's big win that year, there were 108 Democrats serving in the Assembly and 34 Republicans in the Senate. Special elections in 2007 and 2008, for which Spitzer raised funds and provided key operatives, reduced the Republican Senate majority to 32. After a honeymoon period with the Republican Senate Majority, Spitzer's successor David Paterson, himself a former Senate Minority Leader, decided to persist in placing gubernatorial muscle behind the effort to produce a Democratic Senate Majority. This, and the great national Democratic tide in the 2008 election, carried the day. Just 30 Republican Senators were left standing.

A District's Disappearance. I was first elected in 1980, was a much more senior member in 1990, and therefore served through two redistricting cycles. Neither changed my district more than peripherally. But I was witness to the high stakes nature of the game, and the sometimes draconian effects of the process on others.

Shortly after I was elected in 1980, my predecessor, Chuck Schumer, jokingly explained to me that the responsibilities of the Assembly Member from the 45th district included chauffeuring the Assembly Member from the 42nd district to session in Albany each week. Harry Smoler, then 69 years old, a real-estate broker and insurance agent, represented the 42nd District in the Assembly.

David Greenberg, a "hero cop," served one term in that seat, in 1977 and 1978, before rumors began circulating that he had legal problems of his own (he was convicted of conspiracy and fraud charges in 1990). When it became clear that Greenberg would not be able to run for re-election in 1978, Liz Holtzman called me to suggest that I consider running for the seat. Having just lost two City Council races in Queens in 1973 and 1974, I was not ready to run again, and had no special connection to the 42nd anyway. (I had actually moved into the 45th Assembly district in 1977, into the third-floor apartment of my aunt's house, after my father sold our own family house in Queens.) No strong candidate emerged in the 42nd.

Harry Smoler was one of the great "captains" in the regular Democratic club of the 42nd; he had hundreds of friends in the enormous middle-income housing cooperative in which he lived. He relied on them, year in and year out, for their signatures for the club's nominating petitions, and to turn out their votes for the club's candidates. Harry decided that he himself should be elected, and ran three unsuccessful campaigns for office before winning the Assembly seat in 1978.

Although Harry had already served a term, he quickly began to seek guidance from me on numerous aspects of legislative life—such as how to introduce a bill.

When the Democratic members of the Assembly held our conference to discuss the reapportionment process, Speaker Fink explained that each member would confer privately with Fink to review the member's political needs, as he or she saw them, and Fink would do the best he could to accommodate those needs. Eddie Sullivan (not the famed TV personality of the 1950s and 1960s, but the extremely liberal, voluble, and good-hearted Assembly Member from the Columbia University area on the Upper West Side) worried about the growing black population in his district. He feared competition in a primary from a potential black opponent, either from outside the Legislature or from within, if his district had to be merged with that of an incumbent. Although usually intelligent, Eddie could on occasion become simple-minded. He said, "Stanley, instead of us coming us to see you individually, wouldn't it be a good idea for us to come in groups [by geographical area], so we could have the benefit of each other's information?" (Obviously, he was interested in learning details of his neighbors' districts to try to negotiate the strongest possible new district for himself.) Stanley replied, "Eddie, that's a very good idea. When you come in to talk with me about your district, you can bring in anyone you want to listen."

Oliver Koppell, the highly intelligent, extremely ethical, and eloquent but sometimes preachy voice of reform, said, "Citizens Union, the League of Women Voters, and the New York Public Interest Research Group [various good-government civic organizations] have pointed out that the public would benefit greatly from a reapportionment process that was independent of political considerations. We should establish an objective process . . ." Oliver went on at considerable length along these lines. Stanley listened impassively. When Oliver finally concluded, Stanley said "No." He then called on the next speaker.

Because of population shifts, Brooklyn needed to lose two Assembly districts. The district in the Bay Ridge area, the only one in the borough then represented by a Republican, Florence Sullivan, was the most obvious target for the Democratic leadership. Florence gracefully ended her elective career by running as the Republican party's sacrificial lamb against U.S. Senator Daniel Patrick Moynihan.

The other district targeted was Harry Smoler's. It was divided among mine, the Speaker's, and Helene Weinstein's, the latter originally based in East Flatbush. Helene got the biggest piece. When Harry looked at the new map, he continued to inquire, with honest curiosity, "But where is my district?" After he figured it out, he ran in a primary against Helene that year and two years hence, and against me in 1988. He did not do well in any of those efforts.

Drawing the Lines. The 1981 reapportionment was the first for which the Joint Legislative Task Force on Demographic Research and Reapportionment (LATFOR) drew the lines. The Task Force formally consists of six members—two each (one a legislator and one a non-legislator) appointed by the Temporary President of the Senate and Speaker of the Assembly and one each appointed by the Minority Leaders of the Assembly and the Senate. In fact, however, it is responsive to the needs of the majorities of each house. Through the sophisticated use of both demographic and election outcomes data LATFOR seeks for each house to maximize the strength of the majority parties and assure incumbent reelection while also meeting federal and state constitutional requirements. Opposition party voting strength was concentrated (packed) or dispersed (cracked) to maximize the majority party's seat totals. Permissive judicial interpretation of the New York State Constitutional requirement for compactness and contiguity in legislative districting has resulted in the acceptance and implementation of districts quite bizarre in shape and appearance. Because there are so many more Democrats than Republicans in New York State, the task of producing comfortable majorities without wasting supportive votes was particularly challenging for the Senate. In fact in 2004 there were nine Senate districts won by Republicans in which enrolled Democrats outnumbered enrolled Republicans, sometimes by very wide margins.

It is the rare New York governor who serves for fewer than two terms. The governorship was open in 2006, and reformers realized that the person elected was therefore very likely to be in office when the next redistricting of the state Legislature occurred. As the 2006 gubernatorial election approached, they therefore sought and obtained pledges from all the major candidates that they would block another bipartisan gerrymander of the Legislature if they were in still office in 2011. Though Governor Paterson, as candidate for Lieutenant Governor, made no such pledge, he did, as Minority Leader, involve his conference in 2002 in litigation seeking to overturn the Senate's redistricting plan.

Reapportionment by independent commission, the practice in twelve states and advocated by Oliver Koppell in the Democratic conference a quarter of a century earlier, remained a reform objective. The establishment of a five member bipartisan redistricting commission, with one member appointed by the Court of Appeals, was included in the state constitution offered to the voters at the polls in 1967, but it failed when the entire document failed of adoption. In 2006, good government groups got behind a bill introduced by Michael Gianaris in the Assembly and Nick Spano in the Senate, both majority party members, that would create an independent districting commission for the state modeled on that in use in Iowa. Though this proposal received some criticism because it achieved change by statute—not constitutional amendment, which would have made it harder for the Legislature to later alter—and left the final say on districting with the Legislature, it is clear that the establishment of such a commission would go a long way toward reducing public cynicism about politics and politicians in Albany.

CHAPTER IV

Playing by the Rules, and Changing Them

The New York State Assembly and Senate passed and sent to the Governor for his signature (or veto) on July 19, 1990, a bill concerning "the siting of solid waste management-resource recovery facilities within agricultural districts." A day after the transmission of this bill to the executive, the Assembly (with Senate agreement) passed a resolution to recall it from the governor's desk. This was in accord with an internal Assembly parliamentary rule that allows a member who introduces a bill to "move," or officially ask, the body for a vote to recall the bill from the governor "for correction." Presumably, some participant in the legislative process had learned late in the day that either a signature or a veto would cause political embarrassment to the Governor, the Legislature, or both.

The Governor returned the bill to one of the houses. But a prospective beneficiary of the legislation sued. In *King v. Cuomo*, 81 N.Y. 2d 247 (1993), the New York Court of Appeals, the high court in the State's judicial system, decided to invalidate the Assembly's rule as unconstitutional, although it did so prospectively, allowing its use for this one last time. The court found that although the Legislature itself acts as the ultimate arbiter in deciding whether it has operated in accordance with its own rules of procedure, and courts cannot overrule such legislative determinations, legislative rules cannot contradict constitutionally mandated processes. The constitutional provisions requiring presentment of bills after passage by the Legislature, the state high court found, do not include an authorization to the governor to return bills to the Legislature without signing them.

New York's constitution, like the federal constitution and those of all the states, sets forth familiar, fundamental procedures for law making.

At the most basic level, to become law a bill must be passed by both houses and presented to the executive (president or governor) for approval. (One state, Nebraska, has only one house, and so provides an exception to this rule.) Also, each house needs a majority of its membership—a quorum—to do business. The constitutions allow for vetoes by the executive, and for overrides by specified majorities of each house.

Unlike the national constitution, state constitutions have frequently been revised, amended, or wholly replaced, often in response to legislative abuse or excess. As a result, contemporary state constitutions are substantially more defining of legislative procedure than is the U.S. constitution. Like the constitutions of many states, the New York constitution requires that a bill's title states the subject matter of the bill; that bills, other than budget bills, address only a single subject; and that bills further some public purpose. These requirements have given rise to numerous controversies. The New York state constitution also directs that a bill must be on members' desks in final form for three days before it comes to a vote, except if the governor issues a "message of necessity" to allow earlier action. The routine, non-emergency use of this gubernatorial power has also been controversial in recent years. (More on this below.)

In addition to these constitutional requirements, each house of every legislature—whether the U.S. Congress, the state legislature, a county legislature, a city council or a town board—adopts its own rules of order, or parliamentary rules. As we have seen, it is not unknown for these to conflict with the state constitution. But so long as they don't violate constitutional requirements, legislative bodies set their own rules, and legislators must follow them.

Legislative leaders often cause rules to be adopted that consolidate, enhance, and protect their power. Legislators can and do also use the formal constitutional and parliamentary rules to their advantage.

Finally, there are the informal norms of behavior that operate in each legislative house, the "political" rules. As we shall see, these are as important, sometimes more important than the formal rules, as legislators seek to win passage of their bills.

House Rules, Formal and Informal—Knowing Them and Using Them

Early in my legislative career, a strange thing happened on the Assembly floor. At the beginning of one session, Bobby D'Andrea, a somewhat eccentric Republican from Saratoga, who in later years I found to be a pleasant person, "laid aside" every single bill on the consent calendar. Notwithstanding absolute dominance by the majority parties, in those days the leadership of the respective Houses commonly allowed those in the minority—Republicans in the Assembly and Democrats in the Senate—to introduce bills in their own names, as lead sponsors, on "local" matters, that is matters affecting only their own districts. Such bills might allow a county to impose a sales tax, or permit a town to build on some parkland in exchange for setting aside an equivalent area for park use. Apparently, not only had the Democratic leadership of the Assembly found fault with a local bill of D'Andrea's, but his own Republican minority leadership wasn't happy enough with it to intervene with the Democratic leadership on his behalf. This barrage of lay-asides was D'Andrea's way of protesting this treatment.

The debate calendar that day included another local bill of D'Andrea's. No one debated it, but a Member stood and asked for a "slow roll call." At least fourteen other members stood to signal their support for the request. When fifteen members ask for a slow roll call, their demand prevails. At that time, the Assembly clerk tallied the votes manually. It was not until much later that the Assembly installed and actually used an electronic voting system, with buttons to push. (An electronic voting system was installed in the Assembly in 1968, but the machines were removed in 1971. As of 2005, the Senate still used the manual system.) Under the manual system in use in 1981, for a fast roll call, the clerk would call out "Emery, Walsh, Abramson, Zimmer": these were the Republican minority leader, James Emery, the Majority Leader, Dan Walsh, the first name on the alphabetical list of Assembly members, Eddie Abramson, and the last name, Mel Zimmer. Any member wishing to vote "no" would raise his or her hand, and be recorded in the negative. If a Member was checked in, but out of the Chamber—in the Members' Lounge, the telephone room, or back in his or her office in the Legislative Office Building listening to the debate on the "squawk box" while doing other work—he or she would be recorded as a "yes."

This rule worked to the advantage of the leadership. Since the legislative leadership, as we shall see, has tremendous power in keeping bills off the floor, bills that did get to the floor were virtually always intended for passage. Since legislators could be recorded in the affirmative while doing other work on the telephone, or even back in their offices, many could be counted on to absent themselves from the floor, both increasing the number of guaranteed "yes" votes and decreasing the number of legislators who might find something objectionable about a bill, were they actually there to follow the debate.

For a slow roll call, the clerk would actually call each of the 150 members' names, and each would have to respond "Aye" or "Nay." A member not present in the room would be marked "absent." The clerk got up to D'Andrea's own name. Not one member, Democrat or Republican, had voted in favor. D'Andrea said "star the bill." By having the clerk place a "star" on his own bill, a Member could withdraw the bill from consideration until and unless he or she removed the star. D'Andrea had gotten the message. He instructed the clerk to remove each and every one of his "lay asides." His local bill, the one that was blocked, did not pass, but he opened up the hope that, someday, a bill that he sponsored would successfully run the gauntlet.

Baby AIDs: An aspect of my involvement with the baby AIDs issue (discussed in Chapter II) does not describe my finest hour, but does show how the rules may be used to escape a political dilemma. Too many mothers, either through ignorance or fear, bypassed voluntary HIV testing in New York. Infants died, when their lives could have been saved by timely treatment. In 1996, Nettie Mayersohn, an Assembly colleague from Queens, fought a well-publicized battle to change the law to *require* HIV testing of newborn infants, with the mother informed of the results, rather than leaving the program voluntary.

At the time, however, AIDS victims had to deal not only with their illness but also with harassment and prejudice. Gay rights organizations and their political allies (including the Civil Liberties Union), reacting to concerns about possible breaches of confidentiality, therefore vehemently opposed the legislation. They also feared that legislators might take further steps, driven by unjustified public fear of AIDS, to infringe on the privacy and/or freedoms of AIDS sufferers and gays.

As previously noted, my own political interests at the time, as I was planning a race for Congress, appeared to require me to avoid antagonizing either the sponsor of the legislation or the gay organizations. Also, at the time I could not tell who was right. This was not a really good excuse, because by its nature, legislative duty requires decisions to be made on less than complete information. However, under the circumstances I was willing to use a tactic frequently employed by other legislators, but which I had generally found distasteful: I sought to avoid voting on the bill at all.

At the time, and until 2005, the rules of both the New York State Assembly and Senate permitted Members to be recorded as voting in the affirmative once they checked in for the day's session. Starting in the early 1990s, Assembly Members checked in by sliding their legislative identity cards through a machine designed for that purpose. Members have such machines for their own use on their desks in the chambers. Similar machines for general use are placed at the entrances to the bar of the House. Once checked in, the Member did not need to remain in the legislative chamber but could continue to be recorded in the affirmative on votes. The Speaker of the Assembly often cautioned members to remain within "the bar of the House," meaning within the suite of rooms including the legislative chamber and the adjacent rooms: the telephone room, where members can make calls to constituents, lobbyists, journalists, or anyone else; the Members' Lounge, where members can confer with each other, eat a snack, or just relax; the Speaker's Chambers Office; the bathroom; and a few other offices.

However, members often retired to their personal offices in the Legislative Office Building across the street from the Capitol, where they could listen to the debate on the "squawk box," or intercom speaker, and run back in to vote on a "slow roll call" or on a bill that they preferred to vote against. If they didn't mind the risk, they could retire to a restaurant in the Albany area, or even back home to their districts: once the day's session ended, members were automatically checked out of session. Members did not have to put their cards back through the machines to register their departure unless they wished to have their departure registered, for some reason, prior to the end of the day's session. Since members prefer that opponents not be able to attack them on the basis of their attendance record, or record of missed votes, they did not customarily register their early departure.

Most state legislatures do not operate this way. Only about a fifth use fast roll calls at all. In a report issued in 2004, the Brennan Center for Justice at New York University Law School noted that of the nine state legislatures that political scientists have determined to be "professional," like New York's, the only others that use fast roll calls were New Jersey and Pennsylvania. New Jersey rarely did so and Pennsylvania never did for significant bills. In contrast, New York used it for most bills, significant or not.

The machines on each Member's desk also include "yes," "no," and "abstain" buttons. Members are not permitted to abstain unless they can show an actual ethical conflict of interest on a vote. To vote in the negative a Member had to be in the room to push the "no" button. The "yes" button, in contrast, lit automatically when a vote was called once the

Member had checked in. Were the Speaker to call a "slow roll call," however, members would not be recorded affirmatively or negatively unless they indicated their choice in person, in the Chamber.

On a high-profile, highly controversial bill like the "baby AIDS" bill, the Speaker ordinarily called a slow roll call, to make sure that members did not inadvertently find themselves recorded in the affirmative when they needed, for political reasons, to be recorded in the negative, or to "duck" by not voting. I made sure, therefore, to absent myself from the Chamber, in order to avoid pressure from either side to vote one way or another, and in order to "duck" the vote with the least possible embarrassment.

To my surprise, the Speaker let the bill go on a fast roll call. Apparently, too many members had the same idea I did. Most of the Republicans had supported the bill from the beginning. Democrats responding to gay and civil liberties groups had been reluctant. Indeed, the Speaker himself had long opposed the bill and only recently reversed his position. Democratic speakers do not enjoy passing legislation on the basis of a majority of Republican votes, because it makes them look weak. With a fast roll call, any Democrat not alert or spry enough to notice would find himself or herself voted in the affirmative. Both alert and spry, I ran over to the machine at the back entrance to the bar of the House, slid my card through, and checked out for the day. I was recorded as "absent" for that vote.

Use of House Rules by "Leadership"

Toward the end of my tenure in the Assembly, in the late 1990's, I used to explain to new colleagues that the committee system existed to kill their bills. While I was exaggerating a little for the purpose of shock treatment, my comment contained an element of truth.

A legislator's life encompasses many distractions. Something—a constituent's complaint, a newspaper article, a stray thought—prompts a legislator to introduce a bill. It gets referred to a committee and stays there. Maybe the legislator will remember to ask committee staff about the bill; the staff may mention some problem with it. The bill never emerges. In fact, the member may have little interest in it moving through the process. Introducing a bill is easy, and in New York there is no limit on the number a member may enter. If the bill was introduced in response to some request or organized pressure, he or she may regard the mere act of introducing it as a sufficient response, at least initially.

The key point is that the legislative process is fundamentally conservative. Producing change through it is far harder than protecting the status quo. But if interest groups, editorial boards, energetic and effective sponsors, some combination of these, or even, occasionally, the logic of the situation (*mirabile dictu*) exercise enough force to move a bill out of committee, inertia now operates to keep the bill moving. Like other objects governed by Newton's Second Law of Dynamics, a bill in motion tends to remain in motion, unless it encounters an obstacle that stops it.

Most often that obstacle is the Speaker and his staff. The Speaker of the Assembly, like the Majority Leader of the Senate, has his own vision of the direction he wants the House to take. Events and political necessity may require concessions, but ordinarily the Speaker has no interest in moving bills dreamed up by someone else, that might create unanticipated problems. Committee chairs can be counted on by the Speaker or the Majority Leader to stop most bills, especially Republican bills in the Assembly and (until 2009) Democratic bills in the Senate. Staff members understand that their jobs, from time to time, require them to come up with some kind of substantive arguments to justify holding bills.

If a bill with fiscal implications escapes its committee of initial reference, it must then go to the Ways and Means Committee in the Assembly, or the Finance Committee in the Senate, where the State's financial difficulties can almost always be counted on to kill it. Bills emerging from committees of initial reference or from the fiscal committees after March 31—and very few bills emerge before then—must go to the Rules Committee. Until 2005, the Assembly Rules Committee met almost always inside the skull of the Speaker.

Only Leaders Change the Rules. When I was head of the Criminal Justice Committee of the National Conference of State Legislatures, I learned that in 1985 Tennessee had adopted the practice of measuring the cost of proposed increases in prison sentences. Any bill passed there that increased sentences had to include an appropriation to pay for the increase in prison costs. Informed in this way, Tennessee reduced sentences for low-level drug sales while increasing them for violent sex offenses. Impressed, I tried to do the same thing in New York.

My goal was to give visibility to the costs of the boom in prison construction in New York, driven in turn by what I regarded as wrongheaded mandatory sentencing of non-violent drug offenders to state prison after their second felony offenses under the Rockefeller Drug

Laws. (See Chapter VI.) It was already the case under Rule III that to submit a bill in the Assembly, the sponsor had to provide "fiscal impact" information, but there was an exception for bills imposing or changing criminal penalties. When New York spent too little on prisons to affect the State budget in a major way, this exception meant little. But when State spending on Corrections began to cut deeply into our ability to make other spending choices, I argued that we could no longer justify this "ostrich" approach, and drafted a resolution to adopt a rules change.

Resolutions are one-House actions usually used to commemorate things like the Smiths' Fiftieth Wedding Anniversary or to commend the Bensonhurst Kiwanis Club on its fine contribution to the community. These fly through to unanimous passage on the Assembly floor. Because all legislative bodies control their own rules, however, rule changes in the Assembly were a one-house matter, also submitted by resolution. Saul Weprin was the Speaker; I had not supported him for the post. I recruited Shelly Silver, whom he had appointed as chair of Ways and Means, and Joe Lentol, whom he had appointed as chair of Codes, to join with me in a resolution to amend Rule III so as to require financial impact information for bills that changed criminal penalties.

Rule change proposals that are actually adopted invariably come from the Speaker. These also fly through, unless the Republican minority chooses to debate them, in which case they are adopted by majority vote after debate. Rule changes submitted by a mere individual member follow a more difficult route—in fact, a hopeless one. I had neglected to notice this political reality.

Weprin referred the matter to Silver's Ways and Means Committee. Although Silver co-sponsored the resolution, I accepted his explanation that since it was new and introduced late in the session, his Committee hadn't had time to consider it adequately. This became less believable the following year, when Silver became Speaker (I did not support him, either) and refused to add his name when I reintroduced the resolution to amend Rule III. He referred the matter to Codes.

When committees report bills—or resolutions—late in the session, the Rules Committee gets them before they go to the Assembly floor for a vote. As Chair of Codes, Lentol reported the resolution to Ways and Means, now chaired by Herman "Denny" Farrell. This occurred in June, late in the session, so although Farrell's committee promptly approved it as well, the resolution went to Rules . . . and stayed there.

In the 1990s, the Speaker not only chaired the Rules Committee, he *was* the Rules Committee. That is, the committee very rarely met, but nonetheless selected bills and resolutions to go to the floor. My resolution amending Rule III never made it to the floor that year, or any year thereafter. Sometimes in the Legislature, indeed a lot of the time, it is who you backed that counts, not what you are backing.

How Leaders Use the Rules to Get What They Want. "Leadership"— the Speaker and the Senate Majority Leader—not only use the rules to kill legislation they don't like; they use them to effectuate legislation they do like. As earlier noted, the New York State Constitution requires that bills must sit on the desks of Assembly members and state senators in final form for at least three days before they may be voted on, in order to give legislators sufficient time for review. However, the Constitution allows for an exception if the governor issues a "message of necessity," presumably because some pressing circumstance requires immediate enactment to avoid calamity. The Governor and the legislative leaders have often used this constitutional rule to short-circuit the possibility that legislators, the press, and the public might raise an uproar and apply political pressure when a deal they reached was particularly "stinky."

For example, in late November 2001, a year before his reelection, Governor Pataki felt that he needed a quick infusion of cash into the State treasury as well as the support of Dennis Rivera, the powerful leader of Local 1199, the hospital workers' union in New York. Assembly Speaker Sheldon Silver was accustomed to receiving campaign contributions and endorsements for his Democratic Assembly Campaign Committee from Local 1199; Senate Majority Leader Joe Bruno was anxious to become more accustomed to such largesse.

Rivera and Pataki worked out a deal whereby Empire Blue Cross-Blue Shield, until then a state-subsidized and partially state-controlled health insurer, would be "privatized"—bought out by private owners, reducing the State's control but giving New York a "one-shot" infusion of cash for the sale. Without a solid basis for doing so, they also counted on a major increase in federal Medicaid assistance to the states for part of the costs they incurred by agreeing to a large pay increase for Rivera's hospital workers. When Congress ultimately failed to provide that increase, county governments in New York were left with large budget shortfalls.

Less than two months after Pataki and Rivera began discussing the $1.8 billion deal, they were joined by Silver and Bruno in announcing it. James McKinley, covering the story for *The New York Times*, wrote,

No public hearings were held on the bill . . . The details changed day to day. The Insurance and Health Committees in each house never saw the bill or voted on it.

Rank-and-file lawmakers learned of developments only through private meetings with the leaders or by talking to lobbyists.

On January 15 . . . Mr. Rivera, the governor and the two legislative leaders stood on the Capitol steps and said the bill would pass that day, even though it had yet to be printed, much less introduced, and few lawmakers had read it. The governor had provided "a message of necessity" to skirt the constitutional requirement that bills sit at least three days in each house before a vote. The bill passed at 12:30 the next morning.

McKinley further reported that Silver and Bruno "say that secrecy and a quick vote are necessary on important bills. Otherwise, they argue, the advocates for special interests, like unions or particular industries, will pick a bill apart before it goes to a vote." Of course, members of the Legislature, the press, and the public might also pick the bill apart. The core idea of a well functioning legislative process in a democracy is to allow interested parties to have the opportunity to examine and criticize legislative proposals. It's called deliberation.

Sadly, in the case of *Maybee v. New York* decided in 2005 (4 N.Y. 3d 415 (2005) the state's highest court, the Court of Appeals, upheld the routine use of the message of necessity power to expedite passage of a law banning internet cigarette sales. Plaintiffs argued that the governor issued such a message in this case without offering any reason why the immediate passage of the legislation was needed. The Court of Appeals held that even though the facts stated were no more than the content of the bill—that is, that there were no facts at all related to the timing—the message of necessity power was still appropriately used. In her concurrence, then Chief Judge Judith Kaye said that even though she believed that the state constitution meant for such messages to be used only in exceptional circumstances, they had become the "practice of government" and "to put in doubt legislation enacted on such messages would lead to great unsettlement." But she would have restricted such abuses as to all future legislation.

The Speaker Makes a Difference — But the System Is the System

"Reform" is a natural issue for members of any legislative minority, Democrats or Republicans. When in the minority in the Assembly, frustrated Democrats cried out for reform, and the outspoken reformers among the Democrats, the Democratic Study Group, constituted a substantial bloc within the minority. Stephen Solarz, who served as a minority Democrat in the Republican Assembly between 1968 and 1974 (when he entered Congress) described his service as being in "the American political equivalent of the Gulag Archipelago." When the tables were turned, and Republicans became the Assembly minority, they became voices for reform. John Sheffer, a thoughtful GOP member from western New York who later served in the Senate, personally paid in 1985 for publication of the Republican Study Group's *Project 1990: The Challenge of Effective Legislative Management in the State of New York* to detail an Assembly reform agenda.

Steingut. In New York State "reform" necessarily meant reducing the powers of the Speaker. When Democrats took majority control in New York, as in many state legislatures in the national wave of revulsion after the Republican Watergate scandal in 1974, the Democratic Study Group finally had an avenue through which to achieve their long-suppressed goals. Members pressed Stanley Steingut, newly elevated from minority leader to Speaker, to implement the reforms they had advocated. Steingut acceded to a few of their requests. He reduced his own power by abandoning the right of the speaker to unilaterally "star" bills already on the Calendar, thus preventing the House from considering or passing them. He guaranteed each Assembly member, majority and minority alike, a minimum budget (about $7,500 at that time) with which to staff both a home district office, if the Member had one, and the Albany office.

Steingut's accession occurred when electoral power was shifting away from county and local political party organizations and toward individual candidates for and holders of elective office. So the new Speaker also agreed that he would abandon the tradition of using Democratic county leaders, including at the time Meade Esposito of Brooklyn, Matthew Troy of Queens, and Pat Cunningham of the Bronx, to line up Assembly members in support of legislation, but would deal directly with the Members for their votes.

The Democrats could hardly refuse to elevate Steingut, their leader in the minority, when they became the majority party. Steingut, however, was a fairly typical, "finger to the wind" cautious politician, noted for horribly mixed metaphors like "This session has been hit by an avalanche of creeping paralysis" or "the ship of state has gone off track." When Steingut lost his own re-nomination primary in 1978 to Murray Weinstein, the Democrats chose Stanley Fink to succeed him as speaker. There is some evidence, in fact, that the primary challenge to Steingut was not unrelated to the desire to elevate Fink to the speakership.

Fink. Stanley Fink, although a party regular, shared the Study Group's frustration with the conservative policies the Republicans had imposed when they controlled the Assembly. He brought energy and enthusiasm to the Democrats' battles for the environment, the poor, education, civil liberties, and racial justice. He urged each Assembly member to contribute his or her own creativity and ideas to the policymaking process. But as he sought to cement his majority and assure its future dominance in the Assembly he did not countenance any additional significant changes in the Assembly rules to decentralize power away from himself as Speaker. Under Fink and his successor, Mel Miller, the issue of excessive power in the leadership was defused by the manner in which that leadership was used.

Fink's quick wit and perfect timing added much to his powers, whether within Democratic party conference or presiding over Assembly sessions. When Assembly member Jerry Nadler, in closed party caucus, once inadvertently referred to a disloyal Democrat as a "fink," he halted in a rare and sudden silence which spread over the rest of the room, until Stanley remarked, "Oh, that's perfectly all right. When I don't like someone, I call them a 'Nadler.'" Toward the end of one very lengthy Assembly session, Assembly Member Ed Sullivan, an amateur rhymer ("poet" is too strong) and often quite long-winded in debate, recited to the Chamber his fairly lengthy verse recounting the year's frustrations with a recurring refrain, a line to the effect of, "So why are we still here?" Stanley, from the podium, in his classic Canarsie-Brooklyn inflection and without losing a beat, said "Eddie, I got a poem for you too. 'Roses are red, violets are blue, the reason we're here so long is YOU!'"

Democratic party conferences frequently became loud and angry as Assembly members argued about bringing controversial bills to the floor, but as noted earlier, on the rare occasions that Fink's view did not prevail, the Democratic leadership of the Assembly—Fink—followed the will of the conference. Policy differences did not necessarily remain within the conference, either. Roger Robach, chair of the Commerce and Industry Committee under Fink, and one of the speaker's close confidants, regularly sponsored legislation and took public positions reflecting Roger's conservative business orientation. None of this hurt his relationship with Fink, or resulted in any reductions in his power. Frank Barbaro, chair of the Labor Committee and the Assembly member furthest to the left—far to the left of Fink—regularly sponsored legislation and took public positions reflecting his own views. Barbaro remained chair of the Labor Committee throughout Fink's tenure as Speaker, and throughout Mel Miller's tenure as well. Saul Weprin took away Barbaro's chairmanship.

Warren Anderson, the Senate Majority Leader at the time, followed a similar route. His Republican committee chairs ranged from liberal Roy Goodman of Manhattan to conservative upstaters like Dale Volker, and they, too, publicly expressed a fairly wide variety of views.

Miller. When Fink decided that it was time to leave public life, Mel Miller succeeded him as Speaker in 1987 and followed in his footsteps to the best of his ability. I had had a very public policy dispute with Miller in 1984. This did not stop him from making me one of his very first committee chair appointments. Nor did he protest when I, or others, continued to give public expression to policy views different from his own. Shortly after assuming my Correction Committee chairmanship, I expressed my public opposition to the lengthy sentences imposed by the Rockefeller drug laws on low-level non-violent addict/sellers years in advance of the emergence of the Assembly majority's support for that view. Speaker Miller and most of my Democratic colleagues could not afford to advance such a position at that time, even if they agreed with it (and many did not). But the chairmanship was my pulpit to use as I saw fit.

There were many other examples. Mel Miller certainly did not fund my initiatives for specially-staffed supportive prison units for the mentally ill at the level I wanted (and to this day such services are woefully inadequate) but he did fund them, so a few were established. Miller never tried to impede my investigations of prison staffing levels, even though they put more pressure on him to increase funding. My medical parole bill became law shortly after Miller's departure. And Miller left entirely to me the three-way negotiations with the Governor's criminal justice coordinator and the Senate's Crime and Correction Committee chair that resulted in the "earned eligibility" program for early parole, the "boot camp" program for young offenders, and other initiatives.

Although the rules of the Assembly did not permit the actual process of amending bills to take place during committee meetings, I would sometimes submit amendments to my bills to the Legislature's Bill Drafting Commission that reflected criticisms I heard during the committee meetings I chaired, and would recommend to members of my committee that they do the same. While I would rarely report Republican-sponsored bills out of my committee, I did do so occasionally, and I would often allow Republican Assembly members to co-sponsor bills of mine.

Miller was forced to leave the Assembly in 1991 after conviction for a felony in connection with his private legal representation of a client. The conviction was later reversed on appeal, but such a reversal could not restore Miller's former status. Saul Weprin became Speaker.

Weprin. Perhaps out of insecurity, Weprin attempted to enforce a new policy couched in a phrase popular among political professionals at the time: Democratic members were expected to "stay on message." So, for example, if the Assembly pollsters found a negative voter reaction to Rockefeller drug laws reform, and the Speaker chose not to spend political credits on that issue, Assembly Democrats were expected to offer public support, and not diverge from this line.

Whether on his own initiative, or more likely at the urging of Sheldon Silver and Michael Bragman, who had united behind Weprin's candidacy for Speaker, Weprin expanded the power of his central staff at the expense of individual Assembly committee chairs. This played out in practical terms. As a fairly senior Member, in addition to my personal staff of five or so serving constituent needs in Brooklyn and three working on legislative issues in Albany, as well as a number of interns, I had two full-time professional staff for the Corrections Committee. Speaker Miller had kept all committee staff on his central payroll, but in practice they answered primarily to the committee chair, unless the committee was chaired by a nitwit incapable of providing meaningful direction.

Weprin, perhaps masking an illness already under way, often seemed to want to hide from the members. Many strongly suspected that Bragman and Silver were pulling the strings from behind the curtain. The Speaker also delegated far more power to his chief counsel, Ben Chevat, than Fink or Miller had delegated to Chevat's far more experienced predecessors. Committee staff took orders from "team leaders," who took orders from Weprin's chief staffer. Chevat attempted to compensate for his lack of sophistication by imposing a dictatorship. He told the team leaders that they answered to him, not to the committee chairs.

On one occasion early in the Weprin regime, my committee staff reported that their team leader, Carol Gerstl, had informed them that they reported to her, not to me, and indeed that my instructions on a particular piece of legislation had been countermanded. In addition to the team for my Committee (Corrections), Gerstl headed those for Judiciary, under Oliver Koppell (the earlier mentioned independent-minded reformer from the Bronx and later briefly, Attorney General of New York State); Codes under Joe Lentol; and Government Employees, under Eric Vitaliano, then the bright young chair of the Government Employees Committee, and now a federal judge.

The four of us all bitterly resented the interference of the team leader "responsible" for our committees and demanded a meeting with the Speaker. Though Ben Chevat sought to take the meeting with us, we insisted on meeting with Weprin, and informed him that he would have four major committee chair resignations unless we regained control of our staff. Weprin overruled Chevat and Gerstl backed off.

Silver. We won the battle. But later we lost the war. Weprin died in 1994, and was succeeded by Sheldon Silver. Silver completed the job that Weprin started. After George Pataki became governor in 1995, the Democrat-led Assembly faced Republican control of two of the three key policy making institutions, the governorship and the State Senate. This offered Silver further justification for expanding his power. It was, he said, a necessary defense against Republican efforts to divide and conquer.

Central staff, under Silver, assumed full control over committee staff. Committee chairs got a clear message that the expression of public disagreement with Silver would not co-exist with their continued exercise of power. The Democratic party conference became an opportunity for Silver to announce what the Assembly would be doing, instead of an opportunity to decide what the Assembly would be doing. Creative dissent became a thing of the past. An internal memo to staff by Silver's chief counsel Fred Jacobs warned the rest of the Speaker's staff not to share information even with other Assembly leaders such as Ways and Means Committee chair Denny Farrell or Majority Leader Mike Bragman.

I continued to go my own way, pressing for New York's Megan's law, voting against the Speaker's deal with the Governor to fund more prison expansion (a significant protest from the chair of the relevant committee), proposing rule changes to require fiscal impact statements for criminal justice bills, and doing my own investigations into prison abuses. Occasionally, staffers would tell me to withdraw a bill, or retreat from a policy position, because staff analysis had "determined" that my approach would not work. But by then I had worked hard at Correction for six or seven years, learned much from Correction Commissioner Tom Coughlin and many others, and had acquired the knowledge and self-confidence to overrule the staff, because I really did know better. Although my independence clearly displeased Silver, stripping me of my chairmanship would only have made me more outspoken and contrary. But against the Speaker, I could only occasionally win; and few if any other committee chairs or members continued to flout the Speaker's wishes. When I left the Assembly to run for Congress in 1998, I had no support from the Speaker.

In 2000, Mike Bragman attempted to overthrow Silver in a coup. Queens Democratic County Leader Tom Manton publicly supported Bragman's bid, and with him so did most of the Queens delegation to the Assembly. Bronx Democratic County Leader Roberto Ramirez and much of his delegation also appeared to be in support, along with many of Bragman's fellow upstaters and a variety of members, like Brooklyn's Jim Brennan, who were disturbed by Silver's use of the Speaker's power to move the Assembly majority away from internal democracy.

While Brennan and other reformers stayed put, Manton and his followers switched sides to Silver four days later, and apparently the Bronx leadership did as well. Observers variously attributed the switches to Hillary Clinton's need for Democratic party stability during her Senate race that year, Silver's switch of his support for the 2002 Democratic primary for Governor (then down the road) from Andrew Cuomo to Carl McCall, or New York City power brokers' fear of leaving the "ruling triumvirate" of Speaker, Majority Leader, and Governor without a downstate participant.

After the failed coup, Silver removed Bragman as Majority Leader and Brennan as chair of the Mental Health Committee. Other supporters of the coup were punished in less public ways. Any effort to reform the Assembly seemed dead in the water, although Silver promised to be more open and available to individual Assembly members. But lobbyists Patricia Lynch and Brian Meara, whose wealthy clients could be counted on to continue supporting Silver's control of the Democratic Assembly Campaign Committee, continued to enjoy vastly greater entrée to Silver's decision-making process and to Silver than rank-and-file members or even committee chairs.

Change the Leader, or Change the Rules?

One rationale often given for strong legislative leadership in an economically complex and socially diverse state like New York is that it is necessary to produce results. But New York had strong leadership with few results. By the mid-1990s, editorials and academics were criticizing the lawmaking process in New York's capital, and with increasing frequency and ferocity after the turn of the century complained of legislative inaction, gridlock, unresponsiveness, and autocracy. In fact, the New York State Legislature did indeed become increasingly dysfunctional between 1981 and 2009, the period in which this book's stories took place. An editorial in *Newsday* in 2002 noted,

Legislative committees, where lawmakers should make their mark developing big ideas, have become as irrelevant as individual members. In a body renowned as recently as 25 years ago for spirited and, yes, suspenseful policy debate, most lawmakers—especially in the Assembly—know little about what they're asked to vote on.

The context was therefore right for the aforementioned report of New York University Law School's Brennan Center for Justice, issued in late July 2004, to strike a nerve. It led with a remark made in 1918 by Republican State Senator George F. Thompson from Middleport in Niagara County: "Six years of experience have taught me that in every case the reason for the failure of good legislation in the public interest and the passage of ineffective and abortive legislation can be traced directly to the rules." The Center called the New York Legislature the most dysfunctional in the nation and urged changes in its operating rules as the remedy.

Given that the Legislature operated effectively, even impressively, with virtually the same rules under the leadership of Fink and Anderson, this approach might be open to question. Maybe the answer was to change the leaders, not the rules. Not so, for three reasons.

First, there's the principle: the proper operation of a legislature should be hardwired into the system. It should not depend upon the good will or particular style of one or another individual leader.

Second, it is very rare for legislative bodies to promote leaders with Stanley Fink's extraordinary personal strengths.

Third, there's the practical point. Changing sitting leaders is too hard, and may in the end have little effect on day-to-day realities of legislative life.

The leadership revolt that put Joseph Bruno into the Majority Leadership the Senate—successful because it was supported by the newly elected governor George Pataki—was a truly rare event. Moreover, following experience showed little real improvement in legislative performance, nor did internal democracy in that body result. The abortive revolt against Speaker Silver showed the great risks and likely futility of seeking leadership change without the help of a governor angry at the incumbent and willing to pull furiously on strings behind the scenes.

Silver, now the second-longest serving Speaker in Assembly history, and Bruno, until his resignation in 2008 one of the longest-serving Senate Majority Leaders ever, were deeply entrenched. From 1975 until 2009, when the Democrats took the majority in the Senate, a Democratic majority ruled the Assembly while a Republican majority had ruled the Senate continuously since 1966. That arrangement had a number of implications.

Richard Perez-Pena, a very capable reporter for the *New York Times*, researched and analyzed the roots of New York's notorious problems of legislative gridlock in 2002. The issues that year included: a halt in New York's toxic waste clean-up program for lack of refunding; the loss of federal highway aid for failure to enact a decrease in the legally permitted blood-alcohol level; and the tardiest state budget in the nation by far, which not only imposed operating uncertainty and interest costs for local school districts across the State but called into question the fundamental competence of state government.

Perez-Pena noted that in no other state had the legislature remained split between the parties, with comfortable majorities on each side and without change, for so long. (After his article, of course, that record was extended by six years.) Across the United States throughout that period of time legislative re-election rates hovered around 92 percent. In New York they "hovered" above 98 percent until the 2004 elections, when three Republicans among the 62 incumbent members of the State Senate were replaced by Democrats.

The Albany stories in this book took place starting in 1981, only seven years after the beginning of that arrangement, before the system grew barnacles. The ferocious criticisms leveled against the New York State Legislature in more recent years reflected the increasing sclerosis, to switch metaphors, which came with the aging of the arrangement. The problem persisted though both Democratic and Republican governorships, even through Eliot Spitzer's initial session as chief executive in 2007, notwithstanding the new governor's electoral mandate and campaign commitment that "On Day One, Everything Changes." The stories in the book themselves reflect changes over time, with individual members seeking meaningful progress against forces of inertia—and centralized leadership power—that grew stronger as the years went on.

Although the Democratic leader of the Assembly and the Republican leader of the State Senate often hurled vicious verbal attacks at each other, they managed to reach agreement quickly and apparently easily when the political advantages of doing so favored both sides. The rest of the time, observers noted, they each provided the other a handy excuse for the State's failure make progress on legislation.

Even the resurrection of Fink and the restoration of Anderson would not alone have returned the Legislature to the glory days of the late 1970s and early 1980s, because the political culture took its toll on the membership. Most of them accommodated: life is easier when the leadership makes the decisions and takes the heat. Moreover, reports of current conditions in Albany discouraged the candidacies of many with the energy and independence to strive to change the world for the better.

However, public criticism and the discussion of rule change and reform has given encouragement to such candidates. On the run-up to the 2004 legislative elections, Tom Suozzi, the Nassau County executive, embarked on a "Change Albany" campaign. Charles Lavine, one of his designated candidates, defeated a six-term incumbent Democrat, David Sidikman. (Interestingly, after just over two years in office Lavine was showing sure signs of being socialized into the Albany system. "Reform, he said to an interviewer, is "much like pornography and beauty: it's in the eye of the beholder.")

Others also ran, and won, on a "fix Albany" platform. In the Assembly Robert Reilly, an Albany Democrat, unseated a five-term Republican and made noises like he was going to give Silver some trouble. In 2006, in a letter to the Speaker and his Assembly colleagues later made public, Assemblyman Mark Schroeder called for a change in the speakership, or at least an open discussion of the need for such a change.

Rule-Change Proposals and Rule Changes

Broad editorial support for the Brennan Report and widespread criticism of the legislative leadership apparently reached some level of critical mass. Bruno, the only legislative leader in the United States with the power to unilaterally prevent bills from reaching the floor by placing a "star" on the bill's entry on the Legislative calendar, in November 2004 said he would give up that power, a mere thirty years after Stanley Steingut relinquished the same power in the Assembly (although to be fair he had not actually exercised it for some years). In any event Bruno surely remained aware that the Assembly Speaker still unilaterally prevents bills from reaching the floor by "holding" them in the Rules Committee, and that he could do the same.

In early January 2005 the Assembly announced that its Rules Committee meetings would be public, with members not only in attendance but with recorded votes. With this new practice, it became somewhat harder for the Speaker to keep bills bottled up in Rules until after the end of the legislative session. Now, the Speaker must rely more on his influence with committee chairs to hold bills there, preventing them from getting as far as the Rules Committee in the first place. By making the Speaker even slightly more dependent on the good will of the committee chairs, this rule effects at least some decentralization of power.

The Assembly adopted a version of the Brennan Center recommendation to make it easier for the minority to make floor motions to discharge committees from their responsibility to consider a bill—that is, floor motions to get a bill out of committee and onto the floor, despite the committee's decision not to report the bill. Such motions will continue to fail; they rarely if ever succeed in Washington and never succeed in Albany. In this respect Albany follows the legislative mainstream, and with fairly good reason. Motions to discharge attack the legitimacy of the committee system itself, as well as the power of the leadership. The mere ability to make the motion, however, probably does more good than harm by increasing the minority's ability to bring public attention to its dissatisfaction. But legislative reform efforts should improve the committee system, not undermine it.

Motions to amend bills already on the floor, like motions to discharge, never pass in Albany. But even in Washington, a floor amendment, newly offered to a bill that had already been approved by the subcommittee and committee with jurisdiction, starts out with two strikes against it. One cannot do better to illustrate the problem than quote the typical speech Eric Redman, in his 1973 classic, *The Dance of Legislation*, imagined might have been offered against such an amendment:

Mr. President, the amendment in question may have much to recommend it . . . I do not say it is a bad amendment; I merely say that it is impossible for me to know much about it, one way or the other, without hearing from the Committee on Labor and Public Welfare first. I would say to the distinguished Senator from Washington, my able colleague, that if I were not forced to choose today, if I could first see some hearings or a report from the Committee, I might very well wish to associate myself with this program he proposes, as I have on so many occasions in the past.

But Mr. President, why must the Senate rush to create this program without having a chance to learn more about it? If it is a worthwhile program, as well it may be, then the Committee will certainly act upon it, and in the process the Senator's bill will undoubtedly benefit from the wisdom of the Committee and from the testimony of expert witnesses . . . but if we must decide now, on the basis of a mere amendment we have hardly seen, then—and I say this with all respect for my friend, the distinguished Senator—I am afraid I must oppose it.

Or, if the amendment's sponsor failed to provide a confident and convincing response to virtually any question raised about the measure, "Since a number of uncertainties seem to surround this proposal, perhaps it would be wise for us to send it to the Committee on Labor and Public Welfare for study instead of trying to make a final judgment here this afternoon."

But unlike the realities in Albany, in Washington, at least in Redman's era, support from the Committee chair and other members of the Committee, and mastery of the subject matter sufficient to satisfy any technical questioning or criticisms put to him on the floor, could have enabled the sponsor to withstand that kind of attack.

The Assembly also moved in the direction of ending its abuse of "messages of necessity" as in the Empire Blue Cross–Blue Shield deal of early January 2002, described above. This abuse allowed the Speaker, Majority Leader, and Governor agree to send bills reflecting their own political deals immediately upon drafting to the floors of each house for votes, without meeting the constitutional mandate otherwise required for three days of consideration first. The Assembly's new rule as of January 2005 requires an on-the-record vote by the Assembly to accept any message of necessity. Of course, the Speaker retains sufficient influence to make it likely that he will still be able to persuade his Democratic majority to approve the message. Such a message from Governor Spitzer facilitated timely adoption of the 2007–2008 budget even though its contents were a mystery to most members. Nevertheless, at least a few independent-minded members will now have the opportunity to cause a considerable uproar, should new abuses justify it.

The Senate also instituted significant rule changes in January 2005, a few weeks after the Assembly. Like the Assembly, the Senate ended the practice of "voting" in the affirmative members who had checked in for the day but were not actually present in the Senate Chamber at the time of a fast roll-call vote, although the Senate retained a loophole by allowing Majority Leader Bruno to personally authorize a Senator to be "voted" in absentia.

The Brennan Center urged that each committee chair be empowered to hire his or her own committee staff, so that staff members would not be dependent on the Speaker or the Majority Leader to sign their paychecks. Unlike Silver in the Assembly, Bruno in the Senate adopted this proposal formally. To the extent that he actually allowed Senate committee chairs to hire and fire their own personnel, the Senate decentralized power more meaningfully than the Assembly. Finally, the new Senate requirement of committee reports on bills held some promise for progress to a higher level of openness and transparency.

But most of the Brennan Center rule change proposals were not adopted. For example, the Center proposed rules that would provide for the markup of bills in committee, in public session. This change would radically alter the workings of the Legislature, again decentralizing power away from the Assembly Speaker and Senate Majority Leader, but also focusing press and public attention on the push and pull of political forces and policy arguments openly jousting to shape legislation. Members of the House and Senate in Washington amend bills in open, public committee meetings, in mark-up sessions.

The public and the press may attend committee meetings in Albany, but much less happens. When a bill in Albany is amended "in committee," staff members write the amendments while the committee is in the process of "considering" the bill—but considering it mentally, one is to presume, not publicly, during the actual committee meeting. Only two other states, Delaware and Idaho, do not allow the amendment process to take place in the context of open, public debate in committee.

Amendments to bills may be instigated by members of the New York State Legislature, but generally those amendments are written by the central staff of the Assembly or Senate, who report respectively to the Speaker or Majority Leader, not by the elected representative or even by staff responsible to the legislator; and they are usually written behind closed doors, out of the presence even of the legislators who introduced the bills, much less other legislators or the public. And the amendments may well be instigated by the staffs of the Speaker or Majority Leader, with the implicit or explicit message that the bill will not be reported out by the committee without such amendment.

The proposed Brennan changes would end the power of committee chairs, often exercised at the leader's behest, to schedule votes on bills they don't support in late June or July on one huge end-of-session "kill" agenda, the one time when committee members are truly too busy to listen to debate with staff on each of the 200 bills, say, on that agenda. It's not as if committee chairs don't have enough power to control their committees' output without scheduling bills for the kill calendar. Committee clerks or chairs call bills up, with brief explanations by the chair or by staff counsel, followed by up or down votes by the committee members, almost without exception as the chair wishes.

Sometimes committee members may discuss or argue about the bills. Having attended between one thousand and two thousand committee meetings, I can remember only one occasion when the members of a committee flatly rejected a chair's request. It was the Education Committee headed by Leonard Stavisky. Stavisky was very smart, but commanded neither strong backing from the speaker nor personal loyalty from his peers. He was one of relatively few members in the history of the Legislature to voluntarily move from membership in the majority in one house (the Assembly) to the minority in the other (the Senate). That committee also had an unusually eloquent and brilliant ranking minority member, the late Jack Flanagan of Suffolk County (the father of current State Senator John Flanagan).

On perhaps one hundred occasions, a chair would postpone consideration of a bill if he or she needed more time to persuade majority members or to get enough majority members in attendance. At the next meeting, the bill would be approved. When I was a committee chair, I too would occasionally postpone consideration of bills of mine in response to criticism by members of my committee, redraft them, and then get my members to approve the redraft at a subsequent meeting. Sometimes I would just postpone consideration of a bill in order to round up enough supportive Democratic votes to approve the motion to report.

Another rules change proposed by the Brennan Center would require conference committees to iron out technical differences between bills addressing the same subject passed by both houses, when the bills' respective sponsors so desire. In Washington, when the House of Representatives and the Senate pass different versions of legislation on the same subject, the rules of each House allow the selection of representatives for a "conference committee," which the Houses empower to negotiate a compromise. Although the creation of the conference committee is not inevitable, as the procedural rules provide opportunities to object and prevent conferencing, the conference committee plays a prominent and frequent role in the federal legislative process. The Houses then vote again to accept or reject the compromise legislation. Should both Houses approve, the bill goes to the president for signing or veto. Many state legislatures have similar procedures, designed to produce compromise bills for submission to their respective governors.

If the sponsors of bills in the New York State Legislature could require the convening of conference committees, they would end the leadership's ability to subsume negotiations on any bills into their overall negotiations on everything—a power that was at least partly responsible for twenty straight years of late budgets coming out of Albany, but that solidifies the leadership's control over the policy initiatives of individual members. Edward Schneier and former Assembly Member John Brian Murtaugh, in their *New York Politics* (2001), described this problem vividly:

. . . [P]olicies keep bumping into each other. Party leaders link policies together, not because they have any tangible relationship to each other, but to secure bargaining points. Thus, in recent years, budgets have been held up long after the major actors have agreed in principle on the major money issues. These budget agreements have, in effect, been held political hostage to such seemingly unrelated issues as workmen's compensation reform (in 1996) and the extension of New York City's rent control laws (in 1997).

In Albany, until 1995 no such thing as a conference committee existed, unless negotiations between the Assembly Speaker and the Senate Majority Leader counted as such. In response to editorial pressure that continued to grow as a reaction to the lengthening history of frustration with Albany's processes, the leadership agreed in 1995 to institute conference committees. However, these conference committees come into existence only at the pleasure of the House leaders. The 2002 session, for example, saw no conference committees, and most sessions after 1995 saw them operate only rarely and with respect to relatively unimportant legislation, like a change in the blood alcohol level necessary to trigger conviction on a "driving while intoxicated" charge.

Although in December 2004 Senator Michael Nozzolio credited the criminal justice conference committee of the two Houses, on which he served, for the mild step in the direction of Rockefeller drug law reform then enacted into law, other close observers believed that this conference committee, like others, danced on the end of strings pulled by Silver and Bruno.

In comments he made a few days before the 2008 election that elevated his Democratic caucus to the majority and thus himself to the Majority Leader position, Malcolm Smith pledged that under his regime conference committees would have more authority in negotiating bills, among other reforms including empowerment of standing committees, allowing more discharge motions, and narrowing the wide disparity of resources and authority between minority party and majority party senators.

In the Assembly, one of the few legislators still willing to take on the leadership is Assembly Member Sandra Galef, who was first elected in 1992. She introduced legislation to require conference committees whenever bills addressing the same substantive issue are passed by both Houses. Ninety of 150 Assembly members co-sponsored the bill with her. On the strength of this co-sponsorship they can all tell their constituents they favor reform of the institution. But since the bill's original introduction in 1999, it has never gotten to the floor for a vote. Clearly, the members have not signaled the Speaker that the price of his opposition will be a different candidate for Speaker.

Commenting on this and other disappointments, a 2002 editorial in *Newsday* referred to above explained that many legislators have come to accept their "humiliating" impotence as an acceptable price for political security, "perks," and "pork":

Frequently, members are informed of leaders' decisions a few hours before a vote and don't get actual bills to read until minutes before, leaving no time for reading, much less analysis. There is no process, as in Congress and most other states, for "marking up" bills in public to work out erroneous or confusing passages.

In the end, most vote the way their leaders tell them. They hardly raise their voices if a bill they are pushing gets buried in the rules committees, which are controlled by the leaders.

Some of these criticisms have antecedents in history. Consider the sentiment about the British Parliament William S. Gilbert wrote into the lyrics of his First Lord of the Admiralty's song in *H.M.S. Pinafore*, the nineteenth-century operetta he created with Sir Arthur Sullivan:

I grew so rich that I was sent
By a pocket borough into Parliament
I always voted at my Party's call
And I never thought of thinking for myself at all
I thought so little, they rewarded me
By making me the Ruler of the Queen's Navy.

The longevity of this kind of criticism of legislative behavior may suggest a degree of skepticism about the likelihood of effective reform. Perhaps the glory days of Fink and Anderson were no more than a strange aberration. But the world has seen effective reform in other times and places. No power structure lasts forever. Thomas Jefferson said, "the tree of liberty must be refreshed from time to time with the blood of patriots," and Mao called for "continuing revolution." Legislative reform is not as exciting as revolution. Certainly it is not as risky. But reform, like revolution, most often tends to emerge out of rising expectations.

The key is staying power. George Washington Plunkitt, the Tammany Hall politician, famously remarked at the turn of the century that reformers were "mornin' glories—looked lovely in the mornin' and withered up in a short time, while the regular machines went on flourishin' forever, like fine old oaks. . . ." But we are in an era in which political organizations are far weaker than in Plunkitt's day, and some people who make careers in politics are committed to reform over the long term. Under these conditions, the modest reforms of January 2005 (and those of July 2009, described in the Prologue), may well start a positive cycle, encouraging legislators, or aspiring legislators, to press for more reform. And eventually, if they persist, more substantial reform.

CHAPTER V

The Organized Crime Control Act

There were 1,812 murders and 3,711 forcible rapes in the New York region in 1980, the year I was first elected to the Assembly. The FBI crime index for New York State and City had been rising rapidly since the mid-1960s, and its level far exceeded that for the rest of the country. Although most of the increases in murder and other violent crime in Brooklyn were in African American and Latino neighborhoods, and did not directly affect my mostly white, middle-class district, there were also 100,478 car thefts and 210,703 burglaries in the region in 1980. Many of my constituents had experienced these directly; all felt the impact in their rising insurance rates.

The Context: The Death Penalty Debate

Certainly the dramatic television news coverage of violent crime, almost nightly gave New Yorkers in the City and throughout the State the feeling that they were personally threatened. Emotions ran very high. Fear transmuted into hatred of criminals. The effort to reinstate the death penalty, which along with the death penalties of other states had been overturned as unconstitutional as a result of the Supreme Court's 1972 decision in *Furman v. Georgia*, became the touchstone issue for large numbers of outraged citizens. They besieged the Legislature to re-enact the statute in a form that would meet constitutional requirements.

In the late 1970's, increasingly large and angry crowds came to Albany to protest Governor Carey's vetoes of death penalty legislation and the Assembly's failure to override them. Police and prosecutors added their voices, letters, resolutions, and influence, as did editorial writers for the New York *Post* and *Daily News*. Although reasonable people disagreed on this issue, and some highly cultivated, educated, and intelligent people defend the death penalty, many legislators could not help but notice some of the more bloodthirsty, vicious, and irrational among its supporters.

Conservative Democrats and Republicans, known as the "law and order crowd," allied themselves with police and prosecutors not only in support of the death penalty, but also in support of conservative challengers who threatened to defeat at the polls the shrinking band of liberals serving in the Legislature. While most emotion and attention centered on the death penalty, other legislative goals sought by police and prosecutors, such as longer sentences and reductions in the procedural protections of the rights of criminal defendants, also received almost automatic editorial support from conservative editorial pages and columnists. Legislators, mostly Republicans, who supported such legislation, also won plaudits and political support.

While the Republican-dominated State Senate passed much of the legislation that the "law and order" coalition sought, under the leadership of Speaker Stanley Fink the Assembly for the most part refused to accede to majority opinion. Fink's leadership resonates through the stories in this book. The public knows and will always remember the names of two George Bushes, Ronald Reagan, and Bill Clinton. Many will also remember the state's chief executives, Nelson Rockefeller, Hugh Carey, Mario Cuomo, and George Pataki. But few knew and fewer will remember Stanley Fink, Speaker of the Assembly in New York State from 1978 through 1986. Most of those who served under his leadership in the Legislature, however, consider him much superior, as a leader, to those better-known politicians—yes, even including Bill Clinton—and regret that he never became governor, where his extraordinary capacities might have served the state in an even larger role.

POLITICS IS NOT A MERIT SYSTEM.

Fink sounded like a "dese, dems, and dose" guy from Canarsie, Brooklyn, and in many respects, he was. A lawyer and former Army captain in the Judge Advocate General corps, he no doubt shone among the other denizens of the Thomas Jefferson Regular Democratic Club in Canarsie, but certainly he was one of them. The legendary Brooklyn Democratic political boss, Meade Esposito, who was also the local Democratic leader in Canarsie, selected Fink in 1968 as the Club's candidate for Assembly, thus assuring his election, when the former Assembly Member from Canarsie, Leonard Yoswein, realized the ambition of many lawyers who enter upon legislative service and became a judge.

In an era when moderately liberal Jewish and Italian American communities like Canarsie radically shifted rightward, with overtones of racism sometimes emerging loudly as major themes, Fink remained an unreconstructed liberal. Liberals, at least as the term was commonly understood in the last quarter of the twentieth century, remain sympathetic to the struggles of minorities, support government assistance to the poor, value government efforts to mitigate what they see as the excesses of the free market, and oppose government efforts to regulate private sexual behavior.

Reformers are often but not always liberals, objecting to political organizations that extract jobs and favors from government for their loyal supporters, and thereby sustain themselves in power. Fink was a liberal but emphatically not a reformer. Under his leadership, the Jefferson Club's officers used all the traditional patronage and community service tools of the political machine to remain in power despite their ideological position well to the left of the community they represented.

The Democratic Conference elevated Stanley Fink from chair of the Assembly Codes Committee (the committee that handles changes in the criminal law), first to Majority Leader in 1977 and then to succeed Stanley Steingut as Speaker in 1979. Once the Republicans lost the majority, they tried to win political points by painting the Democrats as "soft on crime." As chair of the Codes Committee, Stanley Fink had spoken eloquently and effectively for the Democrats on issues of crime and criminal justice. The Republicans' verbal assaults on the floor of the Assembly usually backfired disastrously when he was in the Chamber.

When Fink became speaker, a majority of Democrats in the Assembly opposed the death penalty. However, enough supported it so that— when added to the Republican minority—the death penalty won a majority of votes. Often, Assembly Speakers and Senate Majority Leaders refused to bring a bill to the floor if it did not command a majority of the votes of the majority party's own members. However, on an "issue of conscience" like the death penalty, as Fink called it, the Speaker would have been subject to great criticism had he followed that course. So the Assembly, as well as the Senate, regularly passed death penalty bills under Fink's leadership, as well as under the leadership of his successors. Governor Hugh Carey and then Governor Mario Cuomo, however, regularly vetoed these bills over the twenty year period from 1975 to 1994. Having let it come to a vote, and having lost on the floor, Stanley Fink nevertheless continued to oppose the death penalty energetically, and carried with him enough fellow Democrats to defeat all efforts to override the vetoes.

So noticeable were the more strident supporters of the death penalty that by the time Fink became Speaker in 1979, he and the fellow liberals who formed most of his leadership team had begun to see themselves as the defenders of civilization against the barbarian mob. Although the Democrats now had a majority in the Assembly, pro-death penalty Democrats and Republicans together still constituted a majority. Thus, only Fink and his small band of liberals, enough to prevent a two-thirds majority of the 150 Assembly Members from overriding the Governor's veto (it was sometimes unclear, if push came to shove, whether the Senate would have enough votes to override), stood between New York State and the death penalty.

Based upon these experiences, Fink and his allies grew to distrust the "law and order" crowd with increasing intensity. With each new attack by the pro-death penalty alliance, they became increasingly committed to preventing the abuse of power by government through its police and prosecutors. This was the context for my efforts as a newly elected liberal Democratic Assembly member from Brooklyn, the Speaker's home borough, to put new powers into the hands of prosecutors in New York.

Use Immunity: Losing the First Round, and Learning

I knew about rising crime rates and the fear of crime. After I was nominated (with election assured) my first order of business was to try to do something that would really make New Yorkers safer. But what?

To get some ideas, I surveyed my prosecutor friends in District Attorney and United States Attorney offices, asking them to identify the legislative changes in the criminal law that would provide the most practical and useful assistance in combating crime. They had no major legislative answers to ordinary street crime, but they recommended two changes to strengthen prosecutors in their efforts against more sophisticated criminals, including organized crime: changing New York's grand jury immunity standard from "transactional" to "use" immunity, and adopting a New York version of the federal RICO (Racketeer Influenced and Corrupt Organizations) Act.

Now I knew what I wanted to do. But by the time I arrived in Albany with the intention of pressing for such prosecutor-supported changes in the law, Speaker Fink and his successor as Codes Committee chair, Mel Miller, yet another Brooklynite, were not likely to receive them with enthusiasm.

I had not asked for assignment to the Assembly Codes Committee. As a supporter of the death penalty, albeit a quiet one with some reservations, I did not want to start my career by highlighting the conflict between my position and that of the Assembly leadership on that issue. Since Codes is the committee of origin for death penalty bills, as well as for other criminal justice legislation, I was afraid that my assignment there might focus a spotlight on that conflict.

However, as earlier noted, six weeks after I took office Fink's chief counsel, Kenny Shapiro, asked me to consider assignment to Codes. To this day, I do not know whether Fink and Shapiro assumed that because I had worked for two liberal Brooklyn politicians, the former U.S. Representative Elizabeth Holtzman and the former occupant of my Assembly seat, Charles Schumer, I would also vote as a liberal on criminal justice issues. They did know that Mel Miller had endorsed me in my hard-fought primary battle for the Democratic nomination for the Assembly seat. Perhaps, as Shapiro said, they simply thought a Harvard-trained lawyer would add useful intellectual firepower to the Committee's deliberations. Miller, I suspect, came to regret the decision to add me to the Committee when he saw the kind of bills I was introducing.

Use or Transactional Immunity. Under federal law and the law of most states, witnesses subpoenaed and forced to give testimony to grand juries get a guarantee that their testimony will not be used against them. This process honors their Fifth Amendment right against self-incrimination. The prosecutor must not cite their statements as evidence to be used against them in criminal trials, and must not initiate an investigation to find evidence against the witness to support whatever the prosecutor already knows based on the witness's testimony. If Witness X said, "I sold drugs on East 137th Street at 2 P.M. on January 5," the prosecutor cannot send investigators up to East 137th Street to ask locals whether they saw Witness X selling drugs there on January 5. The results of such an investigation would be considered "fruit of the poisoned tree," and thus inadmissible as evidence. The court would probably also sanction or at least scold the prosecutor for the attempt.

New York law, however, goes further. In our State no prosecutor may indict a witness on the basis of any transaction about which the witness has given coerced testimony to a grand jury. Thus, if Witness X testified that he sold drugs on East 137th Street at 2 P.M. on January 2, and a year later some other witness independently approached a different prosecutor with eyewitness testimony or other evidence that Witness X sold drugs on East 137th Street at 2 P.M. on January 2, Witness X would be immune from prosecution for that transaction. This is called transactional immunity.

Defenders of New York's law note that the foregoing scenario might well be proffered by a prosecutor when the reality was less innocent: how likely was such an "independent" appearance of a new witness? More likely, argued the skeptics, the initial prosecutor covertly used knowledge of the testimony to look for, or have some other prosecutor look for, other witnesses to Witness X's transaction. Thus, defenders argued that in the absence of transactional immunity, prosecutors would cheat on use immunity and probably not get caught, sabotaging the Fifth Amendment privilege.

However, little evidence supported the skeptics' view. Judges in "use immunity" jurisdictions looked hard at prosecutions where they suspected "fruit of the poisoned tree." Indeed, federal prosecutors have had to defend themselves to federal judges against unfounded suspicions by defense attorneys that they had used immunized testimony to shape an investigation.

Transactional immunity, on the other hand, imposed real and heavy costs on the system. One case considered especially egregious was that of Delissa Carter, who in 1981 testified to a Queens grand jury that her husband had murdered her stepmother. Completely independent and conclusive evidence subsequently emerged that she herself had committed the murder. But because she had testified about the "transaction," even though she had testified falsely, under New York law she could not be—*could never be*—prosecuted for it.

Although the Carter case was far from unique (similar results were reported in *People v. Williams*, 56 N.Y. 2d 916 (1982), affirming 81 A.D.2d 418 (1981), and in *People v. Bazemore*, Kings County Indictment 3805/76), it is still relatively rare that cases come up when the witness, hitherto thought completely innocent, turns out to be the chief culprit. More often, prosecutors hesitate to call witnesses who might become suspects—if not for the main crime in question, then for other serious crimes. Particularly with respect to well-lawyered white-collar criminals or organized-crime participants, prosecutors fear an immunity "bath": the prosecutor will ask the wrong question, in response to which the witness will admit to behavior for which he could thenceforth never be prosecuted. A prosecutor could ask, "What were you doing on the night of October 23, 2005?" to which the witness under a grant of immunity could answer, "I was in the process of murdering John Jones."

Perhaps prosecutors should be smart enough not to expose themselves to such risk. But the New York law in this regard may require too much, placing even the capable and careful prosecutor at a disadvantage. In response to this problem, in 1981 I introduced my first version of legislation to change New York's law to use immunity. The issue did not come to a head, however, until 1984.

Death by Committee. Assembly committee procedures and the volume of business account for why it took so long. (For a detailed discussion of Assembly procedure, see Chapter IV) First, the Codes Committee is very busy. About 7,000 Assembly bills are introduced in the first year of the two-year session in Albany, and about 3,000 more in the second year. (The Senate, with fewer members, introduces fewer bills.) The Speaker and his staff refer about 1,000 of these to Codes– those that change the existing criminal law or that establish criminal penalties for the violation of a new law.

Second, available time for consideration of proposed legislation in committee is limited. The legislative session begins in January and ends in July, or earlier. Committees meet only on Tuesdays and some Wednesday mornings for the first few months of the year, and sometimes more often as the session approaches its closing, usually in late June or early July.

Third, and most fatally, there's the Rules Committee process. Committee chairs—who decide which bills to put on committee agendas and when—most often advance uncontroversial bills during the first few months when bills "reported out" (those that get a favorable vote from a majority of the committee's members) go directly to the floor of the Assembly. After April 1 bills must go first to the Rules Committee and do not get to the floor at all unless approved by Rules.

I was a member of the Rules Committee during my final few years as a legislator. It never met. In reality, it was the Speaker and his staff who decided which bills "got approved by the Rules Committee" for floor consideration.

99'ing a Bill. Under a "reform" procedural rule adopted by the Assembly when the Democrats first took the majority after 1974 elections, every Member has the right to have a bill he or she introduced formally considered by the substantive committee to which it was referenced (not Rules) at least once in the two-year session. To exercise that right, the Member must submit to the chair of the committee a request for such consideration on Assembly Form 99. Otherwise, the chair may presume that the Member has waived the right to demand a committee vote on the bill. This process resulted in the creation of a new verb, as in "Have you 99'd the bill?"

Even if a Member 99's a bill, the committee chair picks the particular meeting of the committee at which the bill will be considered. The Codes chair usually puts only twenty bills or so on each agenda for the first few months. As a result, Codes's agendas at the end of the session frequently include over a hundred bills. By this time, the Committee members rarely have the patience or the time to do more than vote on the chair's motion to "hold" or "report" a bill.

Formally, the first is a motion to "hold [the bill] for [further] consideration," but in practice it consigns the bill to oblivion. While the Republican minority may vote against the chair's motion, by definition the minority loses—unless it can bring along some Democratic votes. The Republicans in the Assembly try to embarrass Democrats into coming along by persuading the press that the Democrats are stifling a good bill or promoting a horrible one. In the Senate, where the Republicans had the majority, these roles were reversed.

These minority efforts rarely succeed, and their failure creates a self-reinforcing cycle. The chair's power over the fate of bills in committee makes committee members reluctant to antagonize the chair. Voting with the minority substantially decreases the likelihood that a majority member will get his or her own bills reported out.

Playing the Outside Game. The chair may not feel completely free to delay scheduling a high-profile bill that the press has decided to cover, because delaying tactics might themselves become the focus of bad press. Committee chairs do not enjoy headlines like "Assembly Member Jones Buries Crime-Fighting Bill Needed by Police." But it was not until 1984, my fourth year in the Assembly, that I was able to generate enough press coverage to force the issue in some way.

Of course, my time had been occupied with other matters as well. Despite the Assembly leadership's skepticism, it allowed the law enforcement community a few gains each year. My Oral Search Warrant Law, allowing police to get a search warrant based on a tape-recorded telephone presentation to a judge, had already been credited with enabling the police to crack a big drug-dealing operation where delay in getting the warrant would have meant having key evidence flushed down the toilet or otherwise destroyed soon after the police got the "tip." And I had been busy with matters unrelated to criminal law, helping to enact laws protecting tenants and homeowners which, as "bread and butter" legislation, held even more practical importance to my constituents.

Despite our difference in perspective, and possibly because of our underlying personal and political relationship of ten years standing, I had been able to develop a fairly good working relationship with Mel Miller in committee. (I admired Fink, but had fewer opportunities to get to know him.) Nevertheless, though normally quite ebullient even under fire, Miller resented the pressure on him to change New York's immunity laws. He did not buy my arguments. He had heard from defense attorneys that unscrupulous prosecutors did indeed cheat by using "fruit of the poisoned tree," and he thought this happened frequently enough to justify the New York law. He knew that my many prosecutor friends had persuaded me that they were right. He reverted to his usual good humor long enough to make the friendly suggestion that I acquire "more defense attorney friends."

The *New York Post* began to run editorials supporting my bill, orchestrated no doubt by the District Attorneys Association or by individual district attorneys. The prosecutors assured me that their principals— district attorneys throughout New York run in county-wide partisan elections—could turn up the political pressure locally on Assembly Codes Committee members from their parts of the State. In a virtually unprecedented effort, Manhattan's long-serving District Attorney Robert Morgenthau, the dean of the state's D.A.s and former U.S. Attorney for the Southern District of New York, the most prestigious U.S. Attorney's office in the nation, personally led a delegation of his colleagues from around the State to the halls of the Legislative Office Building to lobby for my bill. By this time, I had also enlisted a strong Republican to sponsor a version of the bill in the Senate, where its passage was a foregone conclusion.

In response to the mounting pressure, Miller had his very shrewd Committee Counsel, Jim Yates, persuade me to cosponsor his "version" of my bill—with some "technical amendments." If the Committee reported a bill by its Chair purporting to cover the same territory as a mere Member's bill, the Member's bill, barring a miracle, would never see the light of day. Signing on to Miller's bill meant giving up the viability of my own bill. However, Miller would confer on me the customary reward, very mild honor though it was, second lead sponsorship of his bill.

Although in years to come I would take advantage of Yates's astute analysis and creativity, after this experience I also learned to take his advice with a grain or two of salt. I should have consulted my friends in the District Attorneys Association first. As soon as they saw the Miller bill, the District Attorneys' offices quickly disabused me of any notion that it constituted anything but an evisceration of the bill I had introduced.

Learning to Count. Embarrassed and chagrined, I told my colleague, committee chair, and campaign supporter Miller, that when he brought it up for a committee vote I would have to vote against his bill. As much as I liked Miller, I believed that his bill would subvert the public interest, and I owed a greater loyalty to the public. Corny as that sounds, those were the thoughts that went through my mind as I made my decision.

I cornered each of the twenty-two members of the Codes Committee, fourteen Democrats and eight Republicans. Not all the Republicans were willing to support use immunity. One or two shared the Civil Liberties Union position, essentially the arguments set forth earlier against the bill, in addition to the argument that even transactional immunity constitutes a subversion of the Fifth Amendment, so use immunity would constitute an utterly outrageous subversion. A few more Republicans had their own hopes of getting an occasional minor bill reported out of Codes, so they, like the Democrats, were anxious not to rile the Chair.

There were, on the other hand, a number of conservative Democrats who had had their own battles with Miller and Fink. They were sympathetic to the law-and-order coalition to begin with, and represented constituencies that may have been particularly attuned to that point of view. Also, they had less to lose in bucking Chairman Miller; they'd done it before and were paying the price anyway. My passionate support of the bill may have swayed one or two to encourage me. By the time I finished lobbying my colleagues, I counted eighteen out of twenty-two votes against the Miller bill.

When the chair called the meeting to order that Tuesday morning, February 22, 1984, I was disappointed to see that four of the members who had committed to vote against Miller's bill had not shown up. Still, I had a margin of votes to spare. The chair called on the Committee Counsel to explain why the chair would be recommending a vote to report. I then explained my opposition to the bill.

Since committees of the Legislature, like the Legislature as a whole, are subject to New York's Open Meetings Law, any member of the public, of course including lobbyists, may attend a committee meeting. Most of the time, only a handful of spectators attend. This morning, though, representatives of the District Attorneys Association on one side of the issue, the Civil Liberties Union and criminal defense lawyers on the other side, and newspaper reporters on every side or no side, jammed the room. They were attracted not only by the subject matter, but also by the prospect of a fight within the Democratic majority. The twenty-two committee members minus the four absentees sat at the long committee table as always—but this time the seats were filled at the far end of the room opposite the chair and his staff, and visitors had to squeeze chairs into the narrow space between the committee members and the side walls.

Most of the time, after the counsel describes the bill, even if some members argue its merits, the chair says "motion to hold," or "motion to report," and any members who wish to vote against the motion raise their hands. The clerk tabulates the vote, and the clerk or the chair announces, "bill is reported," or "bill is held."

Controversial measures, particularly when the press attends, get roll-call votes. Four Republicans and two Democrats voted with me against Miller's bill. Two Republicans and twelve Democrats voted with Miller, for his bill. So much for my eighteen-to-four victory.

Three days later, on February 25, the New York *Post* editorial page, which commanded attention among voters in those days, ran an extraordinary item, almost the length of the page, two columns, headlined "To reform the courts, let's forget Millertime." In the early 1980s, heavy advertising for Miller beer made much use of the term "Millertime," but the *Post* was talking about a different Miller, and not in a nice way. After a lengthy attack on Miller's "so-called compromise bill that would return the criminal justice system to a condition of confusion, frustration and doubt," under the subheads "STACKED DECK" and "CRIME HOLIDAY" and an introductory suggestion that readers "note well these names for the coming election" later in the year, came a listing under the subhead "THE GOOD GUYS." Leading the list of "the seven stalwarts who voted AGAINST Miller's meaningless gimmickry" was my name as "the forthright sponsor of the far more reasonable D.A.s' bill." Under the next subhead, "THE MILLER GANG," the *Post* listed "those who danced to Millertime and voted FOR his so-called compromise," led, of course, by Mel Miller himself.

The newspapers covered the District Attorneys' continued fierce attacks against Miller's bill for the next few months. In May, Miller himself prevented his own bill from coming to a vote on the floor, saying, "if those who want change reject compromise, there is no reason for me to move a bill." Actually, the newspapers reported such strong opposition by law enforcement that passage of Miller's bill would have cost even more politically than the mere failure to enact my bill. But Miller would not even consider bringing my bill to the floor.

Miller called me into his office to complain, not about my opposition to his bill, but about my backing off on my initial support for it. He did not berate me but wondered aloud whether he had done the right thing in supporting me for election. I told him that I valued his friendship but that my own reading of the public interest required me to oppose his bill when I realized that it did not solve the problem I was trying to address. But I also told him that I would send a letter to the *Post* defending his integrity.

Fred Dicker, the very aggressive, acerbic journalist who headed the *Post*'s Albany bureau, called me before I sent the letter to ask me about use immunity, he said. Dicker had not attended the committee meeting regarding the matter that now allegedly interested him. In fact, this was the first time I had heard from Dicker, although I had been passing legislation for four years.

I told Dicker that I was very pleased to discuss the legal issues involved. No, he said, he wanted to hear about the fight between Mel Miller and me. As soon as I said there was no fight, just a substantive difference on the issues, he got off the phone. I don't think he ever called me again.

On March 6, the *Post* published my letter, which seemed to restore Miller's cheerful demeanor toward me.

At the end of every legislative session during which he chaired the Codes Committee, usually in very late June or early July, Miller gave a party for all the committee members. Although we just stood around the committee room and ate cold cuts, we always had fun reminiscing about the year's events. This year, as we left, he gave each of us a parting gift, with a big grin: a framed copy of the *Post* editorial.

The Final Nail. This did not end the war, of course. The District Attorneys and I continued to generate news articles and editorial support. But someone on the other side—I still suspect Miller and Yates—outstrategized us.

The New York City Police Benevolent Association did not ordinarily align itself with the New York Civil Liberties Union in the 1980s, when Ed Koch was mayor, nor did other police unions in New York State. Imagine our surprise, then, when no more than a year later various statewide police organizations, in which the NYPBA was influential, issued a memorandum in opposition to use immunity virtually tracking the memo that the NYCLU had put out in more-or-less the same terms the year earlier. With the police off the reservation, even the Senate, the body that ordinarily responded with alacrity to "law-and-order" legislation, refused to pass the bill. And if the Senate refused, there was hardly any point in expending effort to get it through the Assembly, the body more resistant to such legislation.

How did this happen? Had the police suddenly become staunch civil libertarians?

It seems that from time to time, defendants suffered injuries on their way from arrest to the lock-up. When questioned about such injuries before grand juries, arresting officers sometimes received grants of immunity, after which they explained how the defendants had stumbled and fallen, thereby injuring themselves. Should subsequent evidence emerge suggesting that in fact the injuries had arisen in some other manner, those officers had no need to fear prosecution. Since they had testified about the transaction in question under New York's version of a grant of immunity, they could not be prosecuted for anything having to do with that transaction. Police unions understood the benefits of this situation for their members, and that a use immunity law might make things considerably less comfortable. They might well prefer to set forth some other argument—*any* other argument—as the public rationale for their stance, even if it meant an apparent adoption of the Civil Liberties Union argument.

In any case, the police union memoranda effectively drove the final nails into the coffin of the use immunity bill. I continued to introduce use immunity legislation until 1998, my final year in office, hoping for a miracle. But transactional immunity remains the law in New York.

Organized Crime and the Federal Anti-Racketeering Statute

Organized crime persists, and some think it always will. Today, however, La Cosa Nostra ("LCN"), the traditional Italian-American Mafia, does not dominate as it once did. Though LCN is not fully displaced, Russian, Asian, and Latin-American organized crime groups are offering challenges. It takes time, even generations, to build and cultivate the relationships with business, labor, and government that the Mafia commanded in its heyday. Embellished but widely believed was the story of the new New York City mayor, who, when asked who his new police commissioner would be, responded, "They haven't told me yet." The "they," most likely political bosses, were instead widely believed to be Mafia chieftains.

While the power of LCN was already in decline by 1986, it remained a much more formidable force than it is today. Thus, to understand the significance of the story of the New York Organized Crime Control Act, imagine a time when the Gambino Mafia family still controlled trucking in a still-busy garment district in New York City, when the Provenzano Mafia family indisputably ruled a Teamsters Local in New Jersey, and when Paul Costellano, the head of one Mafia family, was just about to be shot dead at Sparks' Steak House in Manhattan on the orders of John Gotti, a better-known Mafia leader.

My own experience included an encounter with the old-time mob. While investigating bid-rigging in the asphalt industry as Counsel for Chuck Schumer's Assembly Subcommittee on City Management, I received an awkward death threat by telephone from John Cody, then president of Teamsters Local 282, whose members worked in the Queens asphalt plants that dominated the industry in New York. Jack Newfield, the famed reporter who worked until his untimely death in 2004, later found out that Cody also had ownership interests in the plants, a highly unusual role for a man purporting to represent his union's employees. Even more remarkable, one prominent guest at Cody's daughter's wedding was Carlo Gambino himself; Cody's bodyguard, Aaron Kay, indicted for murder, was himself found, in several pieces, in the trunk of someone's car. The union's business agent, Harry Gross, was a relic of an even older—though not, per capita, less murderous—organization called Murder Incorporated, whose members had grown up in the early 1900s on the streets of then-Jewish Brownsville in Brooklyn.

So I knew personally that the Mafia lived, thrived, and continued to steal money from the taxpayers of New York in many ways, including through political connections. Although my work then cost them a few million dollars in lowered asphalt prices, I had no doubt that LCN could easily afford what must have been for them a very minor loss.

The McClellan hearings of the late 1950s exposed to a shocked nation the frightening extent of Mafia control over organized labor. But by the time of J. Edgar Hoover's death in 1972, the FBI had not seriously fought organized crime in decades. One reason was U.S. Senator McClellan's discovery, with the help of a brilliant and creative staff counsel named Robert Blakey, that law enforcement, even when it tried to prosecute the mob, faced a serious legal problem in court.

To avoid prejudicing a jury against an innocent defendant, or a less guilty one, conspiracy law forbade prosecutors from joining together as co-defendants individuals who had not worked with each other to plan or carry out particular crimes. For example, the loan shark's secretary who typed up his records could not, without more, be tried as his codefendant.

This provision in law safeguarded defendants against potential unfairness in trials that presented minor lawbreakers as partners with serious criminals. However, it also enabled organized crime leaders to set up a structure that would prevent prosecutors from ever presenting to juries the full range of crimes for which they truly bore responsibility. That is, the "godfather" would organize the crime family into units—say, illegal drugs, murder, and prostitution—while keeping each unit insulated from the others, and also insulating the godfather himself from the details of the crimes to be committed. Particularly important crimes might elicit the godfather's advice or guidance, but only through intermediaries loyal enough to serve long sentences rather than testify. A top Mafia leader might therefore occasionally be convicted of fraud based on a wiretap, or tax evasion, but he would rarely be caught personally for a more serious crime.

Thus, the Mafia evolved beyond the ability of law enforcement to impose effective sanctions. Blakey devised a comparably evolutionary plan to put law enforcement a step ahead of crime. Rather than require prosecutors to show that defendants had planned or committed crimes together before putting them on trial together, Blakey's approach allowed prosecutors to join for trial a defendant "A" who had committed a crime with "B," together with a different defendant "C" who had committed a different crime with "B," and so forth. Even the godfather might be joined on the basis of some minor crime, like tax evasion or wire fraud, so long as any of the others were involved as well. All of these defendants could be convicted of racketeering and given penalties much heavier than those available for most of the underlying crimes.

Blakey came up with a solution to a second problem as well. When Mafiosi went to prison, their incarceration rarely had much effect on the organization they had served. A former underling would simply move up a notch. So long as the organization retained its financial power, it could hire a replacement, and, indeed, provide for the mobster's family while he served time, usually giving him a nice party and a promotion when he came out.

But if law enforcement could seize the instrumentalities and profits, the tools and the payoffs, the "use and fruits" of crime, they could impoverish the organization and thus truly cripple it. On these two concepts—permissive joinder and criminal forfeiture—Blakey built RICO.

The McClellan hearings, actually conducted by a subcommittee of the Senate Labor Committee, had focused on the corruption of labor unions by the Mafia. The real-life Mafia connections of Teamsters Union President Jimmy Hoffa, and the cinematic portrayal of longshoremen's union corruption by the Mafia in the movie adaptation of Budd Schulberg's novel *On the Waterfront,* helped bring this aspect of organized crime most sharply into the public consciousness. In an era when private-sector labor unions enrolled many more Americans than they do now, and America's obsessive fear of illegal drugs had not yet taken hold, people cared more about the corruption of unions than they did about gangsters merely killing other gangsters, or supplying prostitution or gambling opportunities to those who wanted them.

Even though it took until 1970 for Congress to enact the McClellan-Blakey legislation, labor racketeering still remained foremost among Mafia activities in the minds of Congress and the American public, and that perception was largely accurate. The statute was called the "Racketeer-Influenced and Corrupt Organizations" Act, or "RICO." The acronym was supposedly selected in tribute to a mob character played by Edward G. Robinson in the movie *Little Caesar* ("Mother of Mercy, is this the end of Rico?"). RICO allowed prosecutors to place on trial all those participating in various crimes linked by a pattern of racketeering, even if the various defendants did not actually all conspire together. It also allowed prosecutors to take the racketeers' assets, tools, and gains in forfeiture proceedings without some of the traditional limits on such proceedings. It seemed at the time that the Act directed prosecutorial attention to the efforts of criminals to take control of legitimate organizations, like unions, and not necessarily to criminals' operation of their own organizations. The Act also included provisions enabling victims—private citizens—to sue criminals for triple the economic damages caused by their behavior.

It took about six years for federal prosecutors to begin using RICO. Some of the delay could be attributed to inertia; more, most likely, simply to the learning curve. Shortly after federal prosecutors did begin to use it, however, judges and legal scholars began to question the statute's scope. They reasoned that though the crimes "D" committed with "C" might be minor, if "C" committed crimes with "B" and "B" with "A," "D," a very minor lawbreaker, could be tried together as a co-defendant with "A," a monster of crime. Not only could this inure to D's disadvantage at trial, it would also subject D to the very heavy penalties available under a RICO conviction for racketeering.

Further, although prosecutors might pull their punches in light of potential consequences to their reputations and careers, private litigants, particularly when they see themselves as victims of economic crimes, have fewer compunctions about designating their tormentors as "racketeers," although those tormentors may actually be anti-abortion protesters or white-collar criminals. So criticism of federal RICO mounted.

Meanwhile, state prosecutors sorely felt the lack of RICO-style powers. While federal prosecutors undertook the best-publicized organized crime cases, state and local prosecutors in New York, for example, outnumbered federal prosecutors at least six or seven to one. The main burden of workaday criminal justice fell to local district attorneys, and they needed to prosecute mobsters too. In light of the contrast made apparent to them by the advent of RICO, district attorneys realized that they were attempting to do the job with inadequate tools. Some states had enacted "little RICOs," shortly after Congress acted at the federal level. By 1981, when I first took office, New York had not.

In sum, New York prosecutors were clamoring for a "little RICO" of their own at the same time that federal RICO itself was coming under increasing fire. And I was trying to help the D.A.s in the Assembly, where the leadership generally showed more sympathy toward the critics of RICO.

"Fairness vs. Safety" Or "Fairness and Safety"

In 1983 State Attorney General Robert Abrams, as part of his legislative program, urged introduction of an "Organized Crime Control Act (OCCA)," a "little RICO" for New York. It was easy for me simply to introduce the bill he proposed, even though staff of the New York State Organized Crime Task Force, headed by a joint appointee of Abrams and Governor Mario M. Cuomo, warned me that the Assembly leadership strongly opposed the legislation. Moreover, judges and legal experts continued to level serious criticisms at federal RICO in court decisions and scholarly and popular journals. Clearly, I could expect a long, uphill battle.

They teach you in legislative drafting courses in law school that you should try to imagine every circumstance in which the law you write will be applied . . . and also that this is impossible. Understanding this, legislators and their aides who write criminal law must try to limit both the extent to which criminals escape deserved punishment and the potential for prosecutorial abuse under a law's provisions. If drafters have done their job well, and after the resultant draft legislation is tested by an effective deliberative process, undesirable unanticipated consequences will occur no more than two or three percent of the time at either end of the spectrum.

It is a sobering reality that we have sometimes produced law that falls far short of this standard in New York State. Our rent stabilization laws are a good example. These seek to limit landlords' ability to impose rent increases and provide certain other protections for tenants in many privately-owned apartment buildings in New York City and a few other localities. It is conventional wisdom that these laws operate unfairly to tenants 30 percent of the time and to landlords 30 percent of the time. If this is so, that means the law actually operates fairly only 40 percent of the time.

The press reported the negotiations over OCCA, essentially between the prosecutors and the Assembly leadership, as a conflict between those who wanted a "tough" bill and those who preferred a "weak" bill. While their perceptions reflected an element of truth, the reality was more complicated. The prosecutors wanted the powerful tool available to federal prosecutors, and to prosecutors in some other states, in order to protect New Yorkers most effectively against the harm inflicted by criminals. The Assembly leadership, whatever other motivations it may have had, also wanted to limit the potential for prosecutorial abuse inherent in RICO.

But, less obviously to those involved, the two sides shared each other's values. Most Americans strongly support fairness, particularly in the trial context. Sociological studies show that government professionals prize fairness even more strongly, and prosecutors, as well as legislators, are government professionals. Obviously, government professionals, including legislators, also share an interest in protecting citizens against crime as efficiently as possible, "efficiently" in this context meaning by the most productive use of resources to produce the optimal set of desired values. This, of course, does not mean that all involved in policy making give the same weight or ranking to the values engaged in a particular decision. If I was to produce a result, I thought, I had to help all engaged in the debate to realize their shared values, and find a way to effect them while giving fair consideration to the concern of the others.

The prosecutors did not at first recognize that the early versions of OCCA really did raise "fair trial" problems. Since the prosecutors who actually negotiated the bill never imagined that they themselves would abuse their power, they felt that narrowing the powers to be enjoyed under OCCA unnecessarily sacrificed an important measure of prosecutorial efficiency. The Assembly leadership did not at first recognize that the prosecutors' most important goals were not actually inconsistent with fair trial principles. The prosecutors doubted the Assembly's commitment to fighting crime, and the Assembly leadership doubted the prosecutors' commitment to fairness. Over time, during the very long process of negotiation, the two sides did gradually come to accept that their primary goals were compatible, and did come to understand they really did share values. When this occurred, agreement based on those shared values was possible.

Of course, recognition of political realities provided both sides an incentive to seek common ground. Although the Assembly leadership succeeded in persuading the prosecutors that fair-trial values were still jeopardized in early drafts of the bill, those persuasive efforts were bolstered by their clear message that the prosecutors would get nothing if they failed to compromise. At the same time, the prosecutors were not prepared to settle too cheaply. Morgenthau had garnered considerable attention and support in the media by attacking the Assembly leadership for balking at this legislation, and he would probably have continued to do so, with some relish, had the negotiations failed. For its own part, the Assembly leadership—with its consistent opposition to the death penalty—had some interest in answering the longstanding charge that it had little or no concern for the needs of law enforcement, so it had its own incentive to reach agreement.

The "Law 'n' Order" Crowd, the Civil Liberties Union, Giuliani, and the Press

Before we could get Stanley Fink and Mel Miller to consider the possibility that they shared some values with the proponents of the Organized Crime Control Act, we had to get their attention.

The "outside politics," for the first three years I carried the bill – 1983 through 1985—was that of the warm-up round, my losing battle for use immunity. The law enforcement community, led by the District Attorneys, worked in alliance with the law-and-order Republican leadership of the State Senate. The Civil Liberties Union and criminal defense attorneys gave strong support to the liberal Democratic leadership of the State Assembly, who returned the favor. In the downstate media, there was loud—sometimes outrageous bordering on irresponsible—support for the law enforcement side from the New York *Post*. *The New York Times* generally supported the civil liberties side, but not as consistently and certainly not as vociferously as the *Post* supported the right wing. The *Daily News* tended to line up with the *Post*, but less outrageously; *New York Newsday* (long gone these many years, leaving the original Long Island edition alone to carry the banner), generally supported the civil liberties side.

In 1983 I co-chaired two days of hearings on the legislation with then-Attorney General Robert Abrams, drawing testimony from prominent prosecutors, and attempting to make the case that the forfeiture provisions of the bill would provide crucial help in dealing with a burgeoning illegal drug epidemic. Special Narcotics Prosecutor (later federal judge) Sterling Johnson responded enthusiastically to my line of questioning about the possibility of prosecutors using the kind of legislation we were advancing to seize a building well-known as a locus for illegal drug transactions from an organized crime gang.

The press covered the hearings attentively. Editorial pages, even in the two more liberal of the four major dailies, the *Times* and *Newsday*, supported the bill. But Miller remained adamantly opposed to it, and after my experience with use immunity, I knew that I had no hope of beating him in a committee vote.

While I was pushing my legislation, U.S. Attorney Rudolph Giuliani was investigating kickbacks paid to politicians in return for their help in arranging for a company to win the City contract to collect unpaid—or supposedly unpaid—parking fines. The more fines they collected, the more the collectors got paid, and presumably the bigger the kickbacks the politicians got. As earlier related, simultaneous with these events I was involved in a long battle to try to curb the excesses of New York City's Parking Violations Bureau. At that time, the Bureau was collecting about $20 million a year in parking fines for tickets that had already been paid or should not have been issued in the first place—and the Bureau "knew" this, though the information was tucked into an inaccessible corner of its computer system. Little did I know that powerful political leaders in New York were profiting personally—and illegally—from the magnitude of those parking fine collections.

In 1985, two important allies of then-Mayor Ed Koch, Queens Borough President Donald Manes and Bronx Democratic County Leader

Stanley Friedman, became targets of Giuliani's investigation. In March 1986, Manes stabbed himself to death with a kitchen knife. Friedman later went to prison. With regard to the OCCA stalemate, Guiliani's investigation single-handedly altered the equation.

Early in 1986, a *Post* reporter whom I liked, Deborah Orin, saw me on the train ride up to Albany and asked if I thought I might get OCCA passed that year. I had no reason to think that OCCA would do better than it had in any of the three previous years. She understood the politics of the situation better than I. Something had indeed happened to make 1986 different. Giuliani was in the process of using the Federal RICO statute in the PVB case, arguing that the politicians who had corrupted the PVB had turned it into a racketeering enterprise so that they could get kickbacks.

In other cases Giuliani had also arranged for stockbrokers, even those who would ultimately be acquitted, to be led out of their Wall Street offices in handcuffs. He was a Republican appointee and yet had sent a Republican state senator, Joe Pisani, to prison for what ultimately proved a minor offense. Most of the charges against Pisani were reversed on appeal.

Giuliani Scared the Assembly Leadership. Whatever problems the Assembly leadership had with State prosecutors, they knew that these prosecutors needed to come to both the Assembly and Senate for major parts of their budget. While this did not stop Robert Morgenthau from investigating Fred Ohrenstein, the minority leader of the Senate, for illegally using state employees on his Senate minority payroll for campaign work (Ohrenstein was cleared) or later Guy Velella, a powerful Republican senator, for illegally selling his political influence with state agencies to private clients (Velella was convicted), at least state prosecutors had some reason to talk with legislative leaders, and those leaders had at least some level of comfort in talking with them. This was not so for Giuliani, a federal prosecutor.

If federal prosecutors had RICO, and state prosecutors had nothing comparable, state prosecutors would have no plausible argument to tackle complex corruption cases before federal prosecutors had a chance to jump in. With a state law, political targets at least might have a more accessible state prosecutor to talk with.

The Assembly leadership almost certainly did not consciously fear personal prosecution by Giuliani. (Ironically, years later U.S. Attorney Andrew Maloney of the Eastern District did prosecute Mel Miller after he became Speaker. A conviction based on a real estate transaction cost Miller his Assembly seat and thus his speakership; as previously noted, it was reversed on appeal.) Still, in the context of the general distrust of prosecutors, Giuliani's apparently unprincipled ambition and ruthlessness likely prompted them to reconsider the merits of empowering state prosecutors, if only to level a playing field that otherwise favored Guiliani and other federal prosecutors over state prosecutors.

Drafting a Principled Compromise

None of this meant that the prosecutors and the Assembly leadership were ready to trust each other. And if they failed to bridge the distance between the kind of bill the prosecutors wanted and the kind of bill the Assembly leadership was reluctantly willing to accept, they would not get any law passed at all.

Based on input from the American Bar Association, the 1983 version of OCCA had edged away from RICO in a number of important ways:

- RICO permitted private civil racketeering suits for treble damages. In response to the criticism that private plaintiffs tended to level devastating accusations of racketeering somewhat carelessly, we had no such provision.
- RICO allowed the two predicate crimes to have taken place over a ten-year period; we required three such crimes within five years.
- RICO allowed one incident to give rise to the crimes; we required separate incidents.
- RICO required only two misdemeanors to show that a defendant had engaged in a "pattern of racketeering activity"; even the 1983 bill raised the requirement to at least two misdemeanors and a felony.

Codes Committee Counsel Jim Yates dismissed that aspect of the draft bill as "two misdemeanors, a felony, and a coat of paint."

Clearly, we had knotty issues to resolve. Yates wanted the prosecutors to have to show a substantial connection between the prospective defendant and the criminal enterprise in order to get an indictment under the Act. The prosecutors wanted merely to have to show a common scheme or plan encompassing the defendant's three predicate crimes, particularly in the context of the corruption of a legitimate enterprise.

Yates wanted non-defendants to be protected against dissolution of businesses they owned with defendants. The prosecutors had less concern about non-defendant business partners of defendants. Yates wanted a criminal conviction as prerequisite to any proceeding to take a defendant's property. The prosecutors thought a civil burden of proof standard might suffice—preponderance of the evidence, instead of the criminal conviction standard of proof—beyond a reasonable doubt.

The most important issue, and the one that merited that closest attention during the negotiations, concerned the kind of relationships among the defendants and the criminal enterprise that the prosecutor had to demonstrate in order to indict under OCCA. The constitutional right to due process of law requires that guilt be established on an individual, personal basis. The law supports a right not to be placed on trial, as part of a group, for a variety of crimes mostly committed by others. Rules governing what is called "joinder" prevent prosecutors from casually indicting people as codefendants when they did not necessarily commit crimes together. These rules are intended to prevent inappropriate guilt by association. Of course, if defendants had in fact committed crimes together, they could be prosecuted together. Even if they had not actually committed crimes together but had conspired together in one particular agreement to do so, they could be tried together for conspiracy.

Organized crime adopted a corporate structure in part to take advantage of these rules. Without any explicit conspiracy agreement, subgroups or cells may be kept separate from one another but commit crimes that help the overall organization. A gambling operation and a drug-selling operation, for example, could each provide emergency cash reserves for the other through a higher-up without a representative of one organization ever encountering the representative of the other. Higher-level operatives and street-level criminals might never meet.

Given the traditional rules, prosecutors were often unable to present the impressive panorama of a criminal organization's activity at one trial, in front of one jury. As a result, juries could not see the total impact of certain criminal organizations. This may have guaranteed fairness to some minor defendants. In truth, however, minor criminals who actually committed crimes with more serious criminals probably suffered some guilt-by-association prejudice anyway, so these rules protected fairness for them only to a limited degree, while the costs were considerable. Holding several trials instead of one is expensive. More significantly, juries could not see the true extent and nature of the harm these criminals imposed, preventing effective prosecution of organized crime and diminishing the protection of citizens against dangerous criminals.

RICO allowed a joint trial based on the common involvement of the defendants in "enterprise corruption" through "a pattern of racketeering activity" in which A had committed a crime with B, B with C, C with D, and so forth. The pattern must lead to the corruption of an enterprise by running it or participating in it, by acquiring or maintaining an investment in it, or by investing the proceeds of the pattern of crime in the enterprise.

Since RICO was enacted in 1970 initially to combat the infiltration of legitimate business by organized crime, it seemed that the defendants must have joined to take over whichever legitimate business they were in the process of corrupting. By 1978, however, the courts had often permitted a broader interpretation of RICO, reading the "enterprise" element to include those whose "patterns of racketeering activity" were simply their own methods of doing criminal business on behalf of their own criminal enterprise, that is, their mob family. Thus, a prosecutor could indict for RICO on the basis of the commission of two crimes (from a fairly inclusive list of possible types of crimes) constituting participation in the affairs of a group of individuals associated with each other.

Once criminals infiltrate a legitimate business, that business actually provides some assurance of a continuous criminal scheme. But outside the traditional model of organized crime, criminal gangs often operate in a much looser, sloppier style, with individuals getting involved in one crime and disappearing, the gang itself dissolving for a while and then perhaps cranking up again with only some of the same people. Therefore, RICO as it came to be applied by the courts worked well in terms of efficiency of prosecution. Large groups of criminals could be prosecuted at once, with the full scope of their criminal activity illuminated for a single jury. Some defendants could be convinced to testify against their former colleagues in return for being dropped from the case, while defendants to whom they were the only link could still be forced to stand trial.

In terms of fairness, RICO applied in this manner left something to be desired. A minor criminal, tried on his own, would likely get convicted on only a minor charge. The same minor criminal, branded a racketeer and linked by a RICO indictment to serious bad guys, would likely be seen by a jury in a more ominous light and receive harsher punishment accordingly. Under RICO at that time, defendants did not need to know their co-defendants, need not have worked toward a common specific criminal purpose with them, and for the most part need not have known of or benefited from common participation in an overall organization. Thus RICO violated the tradition of fairness that required a defendant to suffer from his associations with others *only* if he did something criminal with those others in the expectation of gain.

Later, the federal courts would impose on RICO some of the restrictions that we adopted explicitly in the drafting of OCCA. Indeed, some courts had begun to do so even before the enactment of OCCA. But the subsequent judicial history of RICO justified to a considerable extent our commitment to make OCCA the model statute, one that would retain the evolutionary advances that prosecutors needed to attack the modern criminal organization but that would also respect the long-established fair-trial principles that should govern American jurisprudence.

The Assembly leadership came to the OCCA negotiations still reacting to the criticism of RICO and taking some pride in New York's relatively strict pre-RICO joinder rules as a bulwark of fair-trial values. Finding a compromise that enhanced prosecutorial efficiency without jeopardizing those values was like charting a course between Scylla and Charybdis.

In January 1985, well before the Assembly leadership had signaled any real willingness to negotiate, the prosecutors and I agreed to amend the draft I had introduced to exclude the possibility that individuals would be charged jointly if they were related to each other only because they belonged to the same legitimate business or association. Instead, they would have to be associated in an enterprise whose purpose included criminal activity. Jim Yates still objected that "Tinkertoy" connections would still suffice for joint prosecutions: A's crime with B, B's crime with C, and C's crime with D could link them all together.

Serious negotiations in 1986 began with our response to this objection. We changed the definition of criminal enterprise to "a group or association of persons engaged in criminal activity and having a continuity of existence, structure, and criminal purpose beyond the scope of individual criminal incidents." This would exclude the loose, sloppy connection, then allowed by RICO, of an ever-changing "organization" tautologically defined only by the crimes its participants happened to commit with each other. Later, we also required that the defendant must have "knowledge of the existence of a criminal enterprise and the nature of its activities, and be[] employed by or associated with such enterprise." Since RICO did not require even the existence of a criminal enterprise, this constituted a significant limitation.

Yates thought the link between the crimes and the criminal enterprise still needed strengthening. At this point the draft required that the three predicate crimes be performed "with intent to further the common scheme or plan or with knowledge of the criminal enterprise." "Knowledge" was a weak and vague standard. The deal-breaker for the Assembly, without which it could not go forward, became this: the three crimes had to be performed "with intent to participate in or advance the affairs of the criminal enterprise." Without sign-off from the prosecutors, I agreed to amend the bill to include this language.

This refined the law to where it ought to be. Organized crime had profited from joinder principles by use of the cell structure, allowing criminals who really did benefit from their position of cooperation with other criminals to avoid being tried with those other criminals by purposely maintaining artificial separations, by never dealing directly with their counterparts. Federal RICO knocked down the joinder wall too far: minor figures who really did not know of or intend to advance the affairs of the criminal enterprise could also be tried together with more vicious defendants. Now we struck the right balance: if a defendant knowingly benefited from participation in a structured criminal operation, even if he didn't know his co-defendants or commit the same particular crimes with them, that defendant had joined himself in fact in the operation, and no proper legal principle should bar his joinder in law.

But there were to be no exceptions: for a prosecutor to charge defendants with enterprise corruption, he or she had to prove the separate criminal-enterprise connections among the defendants whether they had conducted a criminal enterprise or infiltrated or controlled a legitimate one.

This was the hardest pill for the prosecutors to swallow. They had hoped to replicate the federal model for prosecutions, so that when criminals infiltrated a legitimate enterprise, that enterprise would provide the necessary linkages without the need to establish independently the links between the criminal and the criminal enterprise. The two sides left the negotiations without agreement on this issue, knowing that if the prosecutors continued to refuse to accept the Assembly position, all our efforts would have been in vain.

Before we left, though, we split the difference on another point. Yates wanted each defendant to be chargeable under existing New York joinder rules; the prosecutors wanted no such requirement. We agreed that each defendant would have to have been joinable with at least one other defendant under the old rules, so that each pairing would have to have committed particular crimes together or conspired to do so.

Part of the problem was perception. Yates claimed that the bill already made it clear enough that our draft allowed for prosecution of those in a criminal enterprise who attempted to corrupt a legitimate organization. The political attacks on the Assembly from the Republicans, however, had challenged this point. To make it easier for the prosecutors to endorse the bill, then, the Assembly leadership changed some language to make it clearer. (A subsequent court decision actually did rely on the omission of the old language that required the criminal enterprise to be distinct from the legitimate one.) On that basis, on June 26, 1986, the Law Enforcement Council, reflecting the unanimous decision of the District Attorneys, the Attorney General, major police organizations, the sheriffs, and other law enforcement groups, released a letter endorsing the Assembly draft.

The End Game

Given my very public fight with Miller over use immunity, some might have expected me to be punished—as I surely would have been in later years, under other speakers. Moreover, Fink and Miller's attempt to reach some compromise on OCCA was clearly one of the highlights of the year's legislative session. They could have found a way to take the bill from me so that some more compliant colleague might take credit. But such a move would never have occurred to them.

Customarily, only professional legislative staff participated in negotiations of a highly complex and technical bill like OCCA. At one point, *after* many difficult issues had already been resolved, I counted 31 technical controversies between the Assembly leadership staff delegation, led by Jim Yates, and the Senate/prosecutor coalition, led by Marty Marcus of the New York State Attorney General's Organized Crime Task Force. (Although Ron Goldstock was chief of the Task Force, Marcus had a better grasp of the details.) But after my experience with Yates, I wanted to assure myself that this negotiation would produce a result to my liking. Also, since I truly shared values held by both sides, I thought I could help bring them to a reconciliation. So I dealt myself in.

When I told Yates to include me in the negotiation, he delicately suggested that legislators themselves did not participate "at that level." I said that *this* legislator would, or I would "star" the bill. As previously noted, under the Assembly rules, the prime sponsor of legislation has the right to prevent a vote on that bill by instructing the clerk to place an asterisk, or "star," next to the bill's number listed on the calendar of bills to be voted or debated. Until and unless the Member instructs the clerk to remove the star, the bill simply stays on the calendar, motionless.

In three months, I spent easily over one hundred hours in negotiations on OCCA, playing the role I had anticipated. About twenty of us sat around the table: Yates, three or four of his assistants, Marcus and Goldstock, representatives of the District Attorneys Association, and staff negotiators representing the Republican Senate leadership and even the Assembly Republican minority leadership. Yates was considerably outnumbered but had no trouble holding his own. Governor Cuomo's representative in the negotiations had shown no interest in any substantive issue, making it clear that all he wanted was some bill—any bill—called the Organized Crime Control Act for the Governor to sign.

Once the Law Enforcement Council endorsed the bill on June 26, the outcome was settled. With additional changes for three typographical errors (we were to find more in later years and would correct them with technical amendments), the Assembly renumbered and reprinted the bill on July 1. On July 2, exhausted after weeks of effort, we were at the final day of regular session. (We would come back in December for a special session to deal with mass transit funding and a few other matters, but on the following January 1, Fink would no longer be Speaker. Early in the spring, he had announced that he would not seek reelection.)

The bill was sped through an "off the floor" meeting of the Codes Committee in the Speaker's Conference Room, while the full Assembly proceedings continued in the Assembly Chamber down the hall. The Rules Committee (in political reality, the Speaker) reported the bill out moments after it received the bill from Codes. A "message of necessity" from the Governor waived the otherwise requisite waiting period of three days for a bill to sit on Members' Chambers desks before being presented for a vote. (While in general I object to the collusive abuse of such "messages of necessity" by governors and legislative leaders, I raised no objection in this particular instance.)

Note how sharply this process contrasted with the treatment of my earlier described use immunity bill, the one that the Assembly leadership had decided to kill. There, my bill had been shunted aside completely. Miller took his lumps in the press for his Committee's very public action of reporting out his ineffective version of use immunity instead. But by retaining lead sponsorship of that bill, he controlled it. As the second name on the bill, I had no power whatsoever—to amend it, to restore its integrity, or to stop its progress (although, as it happened, Miller himself chose not to push the bill).

With OCCA the real negotiations took place behind closed doors—not in a public mark-up session, such as Congress uses—but I was allowed to retain control of the bill. Of course, the Assembly would *pass* the bill only if and when Yates, the Assembly's chief negotiator, was satisfied.

Around midnight, before the clerk called OCCA up for consideration, Fink called me over. "Don't talk more than a minute," he said. "I got the Republicans [the minority in the Assembly] to shut up. I want the chapter, and the Senate has the bill up too." If the Assembly passed the bill first, the author of record would be me and by extension, the Democratic Assembly. I don't think that anyone but Fink still cared about this practice; politics had degenerated to credit-grabbing almost without rules. In years to come, three or four different Republican state senators, none of whom had drafted any of it, would claim to have been "the author" of OCCA. Fink, honorable but competitive to the end, still wanted the Assembly "to have the chapter" the right way.

I explained the bill in under a minute. No one debated it. The Assembly beat the Senate to the chapter by three hours.

Three weeks later, Governor Cuomo conducted the signing ceremony, to which he invited, as was customary for such a major bill, the legislative leaders, the D.A.s, the bill's sponsors, the Attorney General, various other law enforcement officials, and Tom Reppetto. Repetto, a former police captain in Chicago, was now the head of New York's Citizens Crime Commission, a private organization that organizes breakfasts and luncheons featuring prominent criminal justice professionals as speakers. Reppetto brought a big baseball bat to symbolize this "weapon" against crime, to the creation of which he had contributed nothing. Naturally, most of the print coverage went to Cuomo; the photo editors, however, found room for Tom Reppetto with his bat.

Losing and Winning in Lawmaking

Lawmaking is a skill. A legislator learns from mistakes, and gets better at legislating with experience. There is a system that must be mastered. The relationships among people, interests and events outside the Legislature with those within it, and their subtle orchestration, are crucial.

Luck, or serendipity, plays a role. Winning a seat in the Assembly provides the opportunity, but not the certainty, of importantly altering life in New York. Above all, a member must want to make policy in order to actually have a hand in doing so.

Without my own close association with the District Attorneys Association and the Law Enforcement Council, the OCCA legislation would not have been enacted. Our experience helped us avoid some of the pitfalls of the use immunity battle. After my earlier experience, Jim Yates was not going to be able to persuade me to cosponsor some ineffective version of the Organized Crime Control Act. After their earlier experience, the prosecutors were willing to engage in serious negotiations instead of merely bludgeoning the Assembly leadership in the press (although they continued a milder degree of bludgeoning simultaneously with the negotiations).

Through all the hotly advanced differences, I persisted in believing that shared commitment to the legal principle of due process as fairness on each side of the negotiations made agreement possible, however remote the prospect seemed at times. Meanwhile, outside politics provided some incentives for agreement, not the least of which was the serendipitous timing of federal prosecutor Rudy Giuliani's indictment of a number of city and state politicians.

During the end game, I got into the room because I read the inside politics right. Notwithstanding Fink's and Miller's well-honed distrust of prosecutors, and despite the initial reluctance of Miller's counsel Jim Yates, I guessed correctly that I could successfully insist on participating personally in the negotiations. Once inside I was able to examine each side closely enough to gauge fairly accurately their respective "bottom lines," and pull them across the table till they met (figuratively speaking). The bill signing ceremony taught me that I had (inadvertently) given away a good deal on the outside—perhaps too much—while gaining my success on the inside. Another learning point . . . but in the end a trade worth making.

CHAPTER VI

Getting into the Prisons and Drugs Business

The 1986 session of the Legislature ended shortly after passage of the Organized Crime Control Act. From that moment in the early morning hours of July 3 there was one big thing on every Democrat's mind: leadership change. It was that change that put me into the prisons and drugs business.

Backing the Winner for Speaker and Getting a Committee

Stanley Fink's announced retirement presented me with my first experience with a contest for selection of a new speaker. I knew that there was both danger and opportunity in the moment. Careers would accelerate for members who backed the winner: committee chairmanships, judicial nominations, and other perks were at stake. In contrast, those who backed a loser would be sidetracked or, I later learned, might be so marginalized that their careers would end.

Fink was backing Mel Miller, upon whom he could count to continue in the direction he had charted. The three of us rode back to the City together right after the close of the session on the state plane. (Fink and Miller somehow got the governor to make it available, and I hitched a ride to make a meeting in Brooklyn the next morning—my one-and-only state plane ride in my eighteen years in office.) In between his jokes and astonishingly precise mimicry of some of the State Senate's most susceptible (Democratic!) members, the outgoing speaker talked to me about my possible role in the next Assembly administration. Fink thought I might be the next Codes Committee chair.

I didn't believe it could happen. I had only six years of service, far less seniority than many of my colleagues. Fink argued that he himself had become Codes chair after his sixth year, in 1975, when the Democrats took the majority and Stanley Steingut went from Minority Leader to Speaker. But I knew that Fink had been the Ranking Minority Member on the Codes Committee, and so had ascended to that chairmanship almost automatically. Also, as noted, Fink had remarkable—perhaps unique—leadership qualities. And he had become Codes Committee chair at a time of an even greater (and in New York, far rarer) change than resulted from turnover in the speaker's job—a shift in the partisan majority in the Assembly itself.

That Stanley Fink was even willing to speculate in this way profoundly flattered me. He did so partly, I'm sure, because I had come out in support of Mel Miller immediately upon his announcement for speaker. In fact, I had done so even before Miller sought my endorsement.

I had a number of reasons. Mel Miller had behaved very graciously toward me in the OCCA saga. At the end, and despite his scathing comments about the bill in earlier years, he became second lead sponsor after me. He had obviously not let our earlier ferocious battle over use immunity mar our relationship, even after I had agreed to support his bill and then changed my mind and opposed it.

Moreover, Miller supported my initial candidacy for the Assembly in 1980. Our cordial relationship dated even further back, to ten years earlier, when I helped Elizabeth Holtzman run for district leader in 1970 (two years before her election to Congress) in the same district and on the same Democratic primary slate on which Miller had first won election to the Assembly. Although Miller and Holtzman quickly became estranged, I stayed friends with both, although I always remained closer with Holtzman.

Also, geography counts. Legislators from the same county tend to stick together. Joint efforts for Brooklyn schools, hospitals, and parks benefited our respective constituencies and brought all of us from the borough closer together. And whatever our policy differences might be, all of us could certainly see the value in retaining the speakership for Brooklyn.

Handsome in a raffish way, brassy, Mel Miller strongly resembled an East Coast version of Drew Pearson's fictional Swinging Sid Stapp, the Hollywood-type Senator from California, in his 1960s novels *The Senator* and *The President*. Although Miller probably had two or three inches over the five-foot, nine-inch Fink, without Fink's tendency toward chubbiness, Fink had a charismatic dimension that Miller could not match. Even Miller's Brooklyn accent sounded watered-down next to Fink's. Prodigiously witty, lethally ironic, and yet somehow lovable, Fink scared—and impressed—everyone. Still, Miller had a kind of "show biz" charm of his own.

Because we had the Assembly majority, the Democrats' nomination for speaker was, in reality, the election. Whoever won in our conference would get unanimous Democratic support on the floor. The math was easy. There were 95 votes; half-plus-one was 48. Brooklyn's nineteen Democrats therefore constituted 40 percent of a majority of the majority.

Though he had Brooklyn's all-Democratic Assembly delegation sewed up, Miller was no shoo-in. Queens had a candidate, Alan Hevesi. That county also had the next largest Democratic delegation, with sixteen. Hevesi, a college professor and later New York City Comptroller for eight years and then New York State Comptroller for four years (until he resigned in the face of indictment for personal use of state employees in the 2006 "chauffeurgate" scandal), eloquently opposed the death penalty and supported abortion rights in Assembly floor debates. By this time the most effective debater in the House after Fink, he often led the dominant liberal wing of the Democratic majority in floor fights against the Republicans. On a personal note, Alan had been helpful to me on several occasions, as a senior colleague to a junior colleague.

Manhattan's twelve votes were up for grabs. A tall man, with the clean-cut image of the college basketball star he had been, Hevesi's style had certain appeal to the Manhattan reform Democrats. But Alan never claimed to be a reformer; he never denied his fealty to the old-fashioned Queens Democratic machine. In fact, Hevesi offered an emotional eulogy for Parking Violations Bureau-scandal-tarred Queens Borough President Donald Manes after Manes's suicide, and was one of the very few Assembly Democrats to oppose my legislation to reform that Bureau. So although I liked and respected Hevesi, he would not get my vote, nor was he likely to be successful with other reformers.

The third aspirant to the speakership was Jerry Kremer of suburban Nassau County, chair of the Assembly Ways and Means Committee. Kramer exercised more power than Miller—if influence over budget allocations means more power than influence over criminal justice legislation, and most people think it does. There were eleven Assembly members from Kremer's home county. But only three were Democrats, and the county's Republicans would (of course) have no say in selection of the speaker. However, Kremer found support from the Bronx

Democratic organization, able to deliver nine of the borough's eleven Democrats (not including two reformers). Many thought too that Jerry might also pick up support from scattered members who owed him budget allocation favors.

As summer turned into fall, Miller retained the edge. Then, somehow, Saul Weprin, another Queens Democrat (perhaps influenced by Miller partisans), decided to enter the race. As obvious as it was that he had no chance, Weprin's decision doomed Hevesi's candidacy. Longstanding stresses within the Queens delegation could be papered over so long as Queens had only one candidate, but with two, feuds began to break out into the open again, cracking Alan's base.

Hevesi saw the writing on the wall and withdrew his candidacy. Nassau is right next door to Queens. Kremer, apparently thinking he could pick up Queens votes, held out until shortly before a unanimous decision by the Assembly Democrats to nominate Miller was finally recorded. And, as noted, with 95 Democrats out of 150 members, the nomination quickly turned into election.

Miller selected Sheldon Silver, not me, as Codes chair (a choice that set Silver on the path that ultimately led to the speakership). Silver was an Orthodox Jew from the Lower East Side of Manhattan and a graduate of Yeshiva University. He kept mostly to himself; few if any members knew him well. However, his competent work on relatively low-profile issues had given him credibility, and he had not seriously offended anyone. Everyone Miller asked, including me, advised the speaker-elect to choose Silver over Mark Alan Siegel, another Manhattanite, this time from the Upper East Side. Siegel, although bright and articulate, was astonishingly abrasive. Though seniority is not an absolute rule for committee leadership selection in the New York State Assembly, each of the alternatives had several years' seniority over me. Had Miller selected me, my relative lack of seniority would have annoyed them and unsettled many other members.

But Miller did not forget me. He created a new committee, Corrections. Jurisdiction over prisons had previously belonged to Codes. The New York prison population had increased from 12,500 in 1972 to 40,000 in 1987. Miller noted that he had been too overburdened as committee chairman with traditional Codes work—judging the merits of bills like use immunity and OCCA—to give the attention he would have liked to the budgetary and oversight responsibilities he thought the prison expansion now warranted. Also, it goes without saying—and it went without saying at the time—he wanted to reward me for early and loyal support. Miller's aide, a young woman friendly to me, brought me the news in these terms: "Congratulations. You have 40,000 new constituents, and none of them votes."

After the battle was over, Miller was magnanimous to Alan Hevesi, who had withdrawn in a timely fashion after his candidacy failed. Hevesi, formerly deputy majority leader, was downgraded to assistant majority leader. In this way the new speaker was able to show that it was dangerous to oppose him but that he was big enough to transcend vindictiveness. Alan stayed in the Assembly until his election as New York City Comptroller in 1993, a post he held until becoming State Comptroller in 2002.

The story with Kremer was different, even though Miller and Kremer had been fairly close. Miller looked so pale and ghastly in the hours before he axed Kremer that I thought he would have a heart attack. But to reward his supporters and energize them into high productivity, he needed to be able to promote them. By removing Kremer, second in the hierarchy only to the Speaker, he could now move everyone else up a notch. And a signal was sent about the consequences of opposing him beyond reasonable limits. Weprin, whose candidacy had doomed Hevesi, replaced Kremer as chair of Ways and Means. Kremer, who had hung on even after the handwriting was on the wall, came away with a meaningless title. He was re-elected in 1988, but resigned shortly before his new term began.

Demand and Supply: Upstate Prisons, Downstate Drug Addicts

It simply does not naturally occur to a New York City legislator, or to one from the nearby downstate suburbs, that some legislators want prisons in their districts. Certainly, it never occurred to me. No downstate communities want prisons. A legislator who promised to bring one to his or her district would be thrown out of office at the next election, if he or she lived that long.

Downstate districts are densely settled. A prison in your district would therefore necessarily put inmates near your home and your children's school. Your constituents want jobs, even correction officer jobs, but they don't want them that much.

Upstaters lived in a different universe. Three months into my chairmanship in 1987 I was already deluged with letters, telegrams and resolutions—seemingly from every town and village north and west of Albany—urging me to give them a prison.

This phenomenon, it turned out, had many sources. In the 1970s and 1980s factory jobs moved away from upstate New York to lower-wage regions of the country and then to lower-wage regions of the world. Thousands of good-paying United Auto Workers Union jobs throughout upstate New York disappeared. General Electric, a huge employer upstate, let ninety percent of its workforce go. The Beech-Nut chewing gum factory closed its doors.

At the same time, agribusiness, the large, capital-intensive, heavily automated farming corporations, began to push out small family farms. Again, jobs were lost. Farmland disappeared, either as a result of development or through abandonment as small farms became unprofitable.

Then the final blow: as the Cold War receded and neared its end in the late 1980s, defense plants closed. These, too, had been major employers in upstate New York.

Throughout northern and western New York, rural communities hungered desperately for jobs. And from the 1970s through the 1990s, New York State built them prisons. According to one study, two thirds of the jobs created in upstate New York between 1990 and 2006 were in the public sector, many of these in state prisons. At the beginning of 2007, five state prisons were located in rural Franklin County; the ratio of residents to prisoners there was 10 to 1. This development was not unique to rural New York. In the United States as a whole over two hundred new prisons were built in rural areas during the same period.

In the late 1950s and through the 1960s, Governor Nelson Rockefeller strung a necklace of State University campuses across the state, offering opportunity and hope. But whether New York and the nation acted out of fear of crime, or simply failed in imagination or in spirit, in the 1980s and 1990s, it seems, the best we could come up with was prisons.

Prior to my experience as Corrections chair, I would never have described the prison-building splurge in such terms. Indeed, as counsel to Assemblyman Charles Schumer's subcommittee, I had written a set of recommendations for reform of the State's criminal justice system that mostly called for more resources. I campaigned in favor of the prison construction bond issue on the 1981 statewide ballot, at one point debating Mel Miller on the subject at a community college campus in my Assembly district in Brooklyn. The bond issue failed by a narrow margin.

Like most New Yorkers, I wanted the State to lock up more criminals, thinking that would make us safer. And, indeed, since downstaters wanted more criminals locked up but didn't want them locked up downstate, and upstaters wanted prisons for the jobs they brought, it worked out fine. Felons arrested and convicted got "sent up the river," and New York built prisons upstate to accommodate them. It just had not occurred to me how intensely and in how many places upstaters wanted prisons built.

This revelation did not, in itself, make me into an opponent of prison construction. It merely planted a seed of doubt in my mind based on the idea that we might be building prisons for reasons other than to make New Yorkers safer.

Locking Up the Little Guys

By 1987 I had frequently fielded constituent complaints about a street corner on Avenue K just outside my district, a minor market for the illegal drug trade by citywide standards, but a big annoyance to my constituents. I would alert the local police captain and the police would respond with a "sweep" of the neighborhood, but a day or sometimes hours after the police made their arrests, the drug traffic would return to normal. I quickly found out, because my constituents would call to say, "They let the dealers out again."

For all I knew, my constituents were right. That is, I used to think, as they did, that the courts were letting the street dealers off the hook. Sometimes they were. Much of the time, however, something else was going on.

These dealers sold crack. The shrewder heroin dealers of the previous era attended carefully to the drug weight they carried to be sure it stayed below the felony level. Judges might keep awarding probation or a short stay at Riker's Island, the New York City jail, for the resultant misdemeanors. But these new addled crack dealers did not pay attention; virtually all of them carried felony weight. And ever since enactment of one part of the Rockefeller drug laws in 1973, a second felony conviction required serious upstate prison time.

For their first felony arrest, these dealers would generally plead guilty, receive a sentence of the time they had already spent in jail awaiting trial, and walk out on probation. With New York City's enormous probation caseloads, supervision was virtually impossible. Thus, according to statistics made available in that era to the late thencommissioner of the New York State Department of Corrections, Tom Coughlin, they would be arrested nine days later (the average) for their second felony. In the late 1980s, the courts had no discretion with respect to such dealers; they were sent upstate. The result was enormous growth in the New York's prison population, and demand for prison construction. As Stanley Fink asked more than once, "If the judges were letting out all the criminals, how did we manage to have 40,000 people in prison?"

But when the police arrested and locked away street-level dealers, others came forward to take their place. There seemed to be an infinite supply of street-level drug dealers, mostly addicts who got guarantees of enough drugs for themselves from the mid-level dealers who recruited them. Mandatory sentencing of second felony offenders meant that second offense street dealers got prison terms of at least two years. Not infrequently, drug dealers drew lengthier sentences than rapists or murderers. We spent millions catching and imprisoning people who were primarily addicts, and then millions more building new prisons. By 1993 we had not 40,000 but over 60,000 inmates in our state prisons, maintained at a cost to New York's hard-pressed taxpayers of over a billion dollars a year. The number of inmates in state prisons peaked at 71,000 in 1999. In 2009 the number was about 60,000.

New York State's rate of incarceration was among the highest in the nation. But the rest of the nation could tell similar stories. Although the United States was locking up unprecedented numbers of addicts for dealing on the street, the overall drug trade continued virtually unabated. Our increased reliance on prisons utterly failed to stem the increase in drug abuse. By 1992 I had become chair of the Criminal Justice Committee of the National Conference of State Legislatures. In that capacity I found that states had generally quadrupled their prison populations since 1970 but still had on average eighteen times as many addicts as inmates. Florida had 46,000 inmates but 500,000 addicts, Nevada had 5,800 inmates and 120,000 addicts. Only two states had addict populations as *small* as 2.9 times their prison populations.

Also, by 1993 I had spent a fair amount of time in New York State prisons as part of my oversight responsibilities as Corrections chair. (Not as an inmate. Remember my agreement with myself on my first day in the Capitol.) There I saw that while the overwhelming majority of the inmates had substance abuse problems, including the muggers, car thieves, and murderers, a substantial percentage had *only* substance abuse problems. That is, but for the sale and use of illegal drugs, they did not otherwise fit any traditional criminal profile. A 1991 study by New York's Office of Court Administration supported my observations: 34 percent of New York's prison population had not been arrested for any crimes other than sale and possession of drugs. In 1990, criminals convicted only of sale and possession of drugs accounted for nearly half the state's new inmates, according to Commissioner Coughlin.

Again, this fit the national pattern. Most states continued to incarcerate many of their inmates for drug offenses alone. On average, of the 28 states that supplied this information in 1992, roughly 20 percent of inmates were incarcerated for drug offenses alone.

A handful of the sale-and-possession group fit the drug dealer stereotype: gold chains, expensive private attorneys, flashy cars. But the vast majority did not. Rather, those incarcerated were mostly addicts recruited to sell drugs in return for guarantees that their own addiction needs would be met—what former Bronx District Attorney and judge Burton Roberts once called the "torn-shoe-and-hole-in-the-pants brigade."

Advocates of mandatory sentencing and more prison construction argued that were it not for all this incarceration, the drug trade would have been larger still. However, the illegal drug business needed only a finite number of low-level street dealers. Imprisoning batches of them simply enabled new addicts to fill their jobs. Obviously New York was not willing or able to incarcerate more than a fraction of our half a million drug addicts. Police officers told me that it could take drug lords anywhere from one to six months to replace a mid-level drug entrepreneur, but two minutes for a mid-level entrepreneur to recruit a new addict-seller.

Thus, if the increased incarceration served only to lock up street-level addicts, with no apparent effect on overall drug traffic, why did the strategy remain so popular?

Clearly, the outpouring of requests for prisons that came to my desk translated into significant political support in other quarters.

The Outside Politics of Prison Construction

As the Speaker's aide had reminded me when I got my new chairmanship, my upstate "constituents" could not vote. All inmates in State prison were convicted of felonies, and felons in New York lose the right to vote. (Voting rights for convicted felons has since become a national issue.) In fact, if I were so inclined, I could ignore the actual upstate voters who sought more prisons. They could not vote for me or against me, and few of them could threaten the tenure of my Democratic colleagues. Remember, heavily Democratic New York City provided the center of political gravity in the Assembly. While the larger urban centers upstate—Buffalo, Syracuse, Rochester, Albany—elected Democratic Assembly members, at that time almost all rural areas—the ones clamoring for prisons—still returned Republicans.

The Senate was a different political reality. The Republican majority of that house—about 35 of the 61 members then—drew its strength from the northern and western rural heartland of the State. Even when Ralph Marino of Long Island's mostly suburban Nassau County served as Senate Majority Leader from 1989 to 1994, he relied on and had to cater to the needs of his northern and western rural colleagues. For them, prisons offered constituents jobs within commuting distance. Thirty miles may be traversed in rural areas in forty minutes or so, but the distance puts a prison at a safe-feeling remove from families, neighborhoods, and schools.

Eight urban and mostly Democratic counties accounted for slightly more than half the State's population: New York (Manhattan), Kings (Brooklyn), Bronx, Queens, Richmond (Staten Island), Erie (Buffalo), Albany, and Monroe (Rochester). My survey in the early 1990s showed that those eight counties held only 9 percent of the State's inmates.

The two large counties that make up suburban Long Island, Nassau and Suffolk, housed about 15 percent of the State's population, and no State inmates.

The remaining one-third of the State's population lived in 52 mostly rural, low-density, Republican counties; those housed 91 percent of the State's prison inmates.

The Republican members then comprised 57 percent of the State Senate, but their districts housed 89 percent of the State's inmates, employed 89 percent of the State's Corrections staff, and absorbed 89 percent of the State Correction dollars.

Assembly district analysis showed an even sharper contrast. Republican members comprised only 36 percent of the Assembly, but their districts housed 83 percent of the inmates, employed 81 percent of the staff, and absorbed 81 percent of the dollars.

None of this has changed much since then. By 2000, the percentage of inmates in Republican Senate districts actually increased slightly, to 93 percent.

This pattern defies the logic of rehabilitation. Sound penology suggests that prisons be built in or near inmates' home communities, to increase access to family, neighbors, and potential employers. At about the same time I published my research on where in New York inmates went, a former inmate with a Ph.D., Edward Ellis, published his study of where they had come from. Not surprisingly, it turned out that about 90 percent were from fourteen urban, high-density, mostly Democratic Assembly districts . . . far from most state prisons.

Hispanics and blacks made up about 80 percent of New York's prison population, as they do today. Housing this population in areas of the State with overwhelmingly white rural populations added racial and ethnic dimensions to the already difficult dynamic between inmates and correction officers.

Unintended Consequences: Drug Laws and Violent Crime. Of course, the parochial economic interests that drove the prison construction boom would not have prevailed without public acceptance of the "lock'em up" school of thought. For a long time, it seemed to people that incarcerating those who engaged in criminal behavior, including the sale of illegal drugs, would make things better, isolating those who were caught and deterring others. But the scale of the addiction problem, with ten times as many addicts as we could conceivably incarcerate, proved an insurmountable obstacle to this strategy.

Again, this phenomenon was by no means confined to New York. In the State of Washington, the respected bar association of King County reported that "drug use generally declined *before* the toughening of criminal sanctions in the 1980s and has since risen *after* the increase in those penalties."

It was true in the 1980's and 1990's, and is still true today, that a large portion of violent crime victims—in most years, well more than half—are attacked not by strangers but by someone they know. Domestic violence takes a huge toll: murders by spouses and unmarried partners in some years outnumbered murders by strangers. But Americans could not easily project their hostilities onto people they knew well, while they could muster real enthusiasm for locking up strangers, particularly those of a different color than themselves. Moreover, with the dramatic weakening of communism throughout the 1980s, culminating in the breakup of the Soviet Union, Americans had no serious external enemy upon whom to focus their hostilities. This would change, of course, on September 11, 2001. But in the 1980s and 1990s the image of the sociopathic minority-group drug dealer who would stab or shoot you generated fierce support for increased mandatory sentences for drug dealers.

The illegal drug trade did indeed generate violent crime, although not the way the public imagined. Starting in 1973 with New York's

Rockefeller drug laws, states imposed harsh and lengthy sentences for selling illegal drugs. Many adult drug dealers, dealing mostly in heroin at that time, became uncomfortable at the prospect and removed themselves from the scene. Instead, middle managers in the illegal drug trade began to hire teenagers, who would not be subject to the heavy penalties imposed on adults.

Drug-dealing involves possession of valuable goods and/or cash. Although many adult dealers carried handguns, adults by nature are more risk-averse than youngsters and used these weapons relatively infrequently. As Alfred Blumstein, one of the nation's leading analysts of crime statistics pointed out, as the average age of the street-level dealers decreased, the proclivity toward gun violence increased. In later years, urban ghetto teenagers told us in public hearings that handgun possession had reached such proportions that the unarmed teenagers in those neighborhoods considered themselves to be at risk. Some teenagers who found out how to acquire these weapons then became points of "infection" themselves, supplying massive quantities to other local teenagers. Between 1986 and 1993, gun-related homicide among urban ghetto teenagers quadrupled compared to rates in the previous decade.

Middle-class Americans saw only the crime wave, not the reasons for its development. In response, they called for ever-increasing sentences for drug-dealing, and legislators obliged.

Satisfying these emotional demands did not come free or cheap. In effect, classrooms were being traded for cell blocks. In an important study for the Rand Institute, Peter Greenwood found that by 1994 the state of California—where the prison population grew to be even larger than New York's—had systematically reduced support for its State University while it was expanding its prison system, until it was spending more on prisons than on colleges.

The same was true in New York, which in fact decreased real-dollar support for higher education substantially between 1988 and 1998, while it expanded its prison system. The state spent twice as much to operate its higher education system than its prison system in 1988. After the prison expansion of the following ten years, it spent $300 million less on higher education than on prisons.

Race and Drug Enforcement. It was inescapable, too, that white people went to jail far less for drug related offenses than African Americans. The Sentencing Project in Washington, D.C. reported in 2000 that one out of three black American men between the ages of 20 and 29 was serving time in prison, on parole, or on probation, with one out of nine aged 20 to 34 in prison or jail. This was in part a consequence of the enforcement of the drug laws in minority neighborhoods. No statistics suggested higher use of illegal drugs among minorities than among the white population. Rather, poor neighborhoods in the United States tend to be populated by minority groups; illegal drugs tend to be sold in street-level transactions in poor neighborhoods; and law enforcement can make arrests for street-dealing far more easily than it can for discreet illegal drug transactions in private homes or offices.

This reality had broken up families in minority communities. Large numbers of men were incarcerated. Less obviously (because the absolute numbers were considerably smaller), the number of women in prison in New York rose by an even larger factor than the overall six-fold national increase. Women in the illicit drug trade frequently operated at too low a level to have information to trade for effective plea bargains. In 1987 drug offenses accounted for 32 percent of the men sentenced under New York's Second Felony Offender Law, rising to 42 percent in 1991. The percentage of women sentenced for drug offenses rose much more quickly: from 42 percent of women inmates in 1987 to 72 percent in 1991. In the context of a rising prison population overall, this meant a huge increase in the imprisonment of women. A generation of children would grow up seeing their mothers only on visiting day.

More subtly, this kind of enforcement criminalized a portion of the population that would not otherwise fit the criminal profile, making a stay in prison relatively normal, and blurring the line between the truly criminal population and the rest. A thought experiment is in order. Alcohol abuse has been correlated with violence at least as reliably as the abuse of various illegal drugs. Imagine the political response if law enforcement efforts were directed effectively and vigorously at the sale and possession of alcohol in white middle-class neighborhoods, with imprisonment resulting for a large fraction of the population of those neighborhoods.

The world's economy increasingly rewards nations that educated their populations to perform highly technical jobs and punishes nations that failed to do so. However, the United States in the later portion of the twentieth century placed increasing numbers of its citizens behind bars, where they could not pay taxes, and paid for this by cutting support for higher education. With two million inmates in 2001, the United States had the world's highest incarceration rate, with almost one percent of its population in prison. The Justice Policy Institute in Washington D.C. found that in New York in 1998, almost six thousand more African Americans and over four thousand more Latinos were serving time in prison than attending the State University. In California, almost twice as many African Americans were serving time in California's state prisons as were attending its public universities.

The Rockefeller Drug Laws. The Rockefeller Drug laws arose after what came to be regarded as a failed rehabilitative strategy. Nelson Rockefeller's approach in the early 1960's was to treat addicts as "unfortunate victims" of a "dread disease." Under the Metcalf-Volker Law, passed in 1962, as an alternative to prison they were offered the option of a three-year-long rehabilitative program in dedicated facilities in state mental health hospitals. In 1966, noting that most who entered rehabilitation absconded or were rearrested, and that many addicts opted for short-term prison stays over rehabilitation, Rockefeller achieved enactment of mandatory treatment under a newly created agency, the Narcotics Addiction Control Commission. (At the same time, sentences for those convicted of selling drugs were lengthened.)

Treatment techniques available at the time proved largely unsuccessful; heroin addicts who had been through treatment continued to commit crimes. Prosecutors, judges, and the press called for stronger measures as the crime rate rose. At the national level, Richard Nixon and Spiro Agnew led the charge for "law-and-order" after the "permissive" 1960s, both reflecting and reinforcing the nation's more punitive mood. Rockefeller, who wanted to be president and had to get the GOP nomination to do so, could not afford to appear "soft on crime."

Rather than leave sentencing discretion to "soft" judges, Rockefeller asked the New York State Legislature in 1973 to enact long mandatory sentences for illegal drug offenders, and it did. Also in 1973, the Legislature enacted the Second Felony Offender law, forbidding judges to allow probation in such cases. Second Felony Offender, along with the other new drug laws, affected New York's imprisonment policies so powerfully that many or most consider it part of the Rockefeller drug laws, although the Legislature actually enacted it separately.

In 1975, 1977, and 1979 the Legislature ameliorated certain aspects of the Rockefeller drug laws, respectively permitting the use of the previously prohibited drug methadone for drug abuse treatment, reducing penalties for marijuana, and restoring a little more discretion to judges as to the minimum length of certain sentences for which the maximum was life. Overall, however, the laws continued to operate harshly.

The New Chair of the New Assembly Correction Committee

Throughout the winter of 1987 I put myself through a crash course in prison administration and penology, working till 1 A.M. in my Albany office at least once a week trying to learn all I could. Although it didn't take long for me to carve out an exception for drug crime policy in my generally prosecutor-oriented philosophy of criminal justice, it was hardly possible at that time for me to develop the picture of that policy reflected in the preceding pages.

Drug abuse treatment in prisons: Using the Budget Process. Still, some things became clear right away. Everyone knew that most inmates had substance abuse problems. In my personal visits to New York's prisons, I saw a few outstanding substance-abuse treatment programs, but I also saw a good many prisons with no substance abuse programs at all. (Two of the good ones were in medium security prisons, one at Arthurkill Correctional on Staten Island, run by Ron Williams, and another at Mt. McGregor Correctional about forty minutes north of Albany, run by Father Peter Young.)

As my first crusade as Corrections Chair, I sought to convince my colleagues in the Democratic conference, and thus Speaker Miller, to include in his budget negotiations the insistence that every New York State prison have a drug abuse treatment program available to inmates. In this effort I was joined by Mike McNulty, a colleague from Green Island (in the Albany area) and later a genuinely honorable Member of Congress, who had introduced me to Father Young.

No one in the Democratic Conference seriously objected to mandating drug addiction treatment programs in State prisons. I didn't get much resistance outside the Democratic Conference either. Tom Coughlin, the shrewd Corrections Commissioner appointed by Governor Hugh Carey and kept on by Mario Cuomo, happily supported the initiative. The State Senate Majority Leader Warren Anderson, a courtly, highly civilized Republican attorney from Binghamton, New York, a State University town in the southern tier, had no objection. He regularly adopted progressive measures whenever he could slip them past the more conservative members of his conference without their notice.

The treatment program mandate was linked to the budget process. After the Governor offered his budget proposals to the Legislature at the end of January, the Assembly and Senate negotiated with each other, and sometimes with the Governor, over additions and deletions. During Fink's and Miller's reigns, committee chairs like me were expected to identify specific budgetary needs and, if possible, areas warranting budget cuts. Speakers begged for recommendations for cuts—usually unsuccessfully—to balance committee chairs' (and individual Members') infinite demands for "adds."

My Committee had jurisdiction over a State program with a budget of over a billion dollars a year, the largest of any after Education and Health. The Codes Committee considered far more bills, but Corrections considered far more money. As committee chair I had ongoing relationships with particular constituencies: correction officers (otherwise known as prison guards), Commissioner Coughlin and his staff, inmates who wrote to me and met me at prisons, and inmate advocacy and support groups. All these constantly made their needs known to me. Had I not developed a bias in favor of their needs for more money for additional officers and security devices, nurses and medical care, instructors and educational programs, I would not have been human.

Years later, in the 1990s, Speaker Sheldon Silver and Majority Leader Joe Bruno established joint budget negotiating committees in subject matter areas (criminal justice, transportation, health, etcetera) led by committee chairs. But ultimate negotiating power still had to revert to the leaders, as Fink explained a decade earlier: "I do the budget," he told the Assembly chairs. "You do everything else." Only the leaders got inputs from all the different subject matter areas, were subject to pressure from every constituency statewide, and therefore could make the necessary trade-offs *among* subject matter areas to come up with a reasonable result within the available resources.

My mandate for drug abuse treatment programs in every prison appeared in what was then a semi-official part of the budget, the "Green Book language." (In those days, the agreed-upon two-house document that included this narrative had a green cover. In later years, it got a white cover, but we did not change the name.) Green Book language imposed programmatic requirements that became part of the legislative history, even though it was not included in the budget bills that the Houses actually enacted. A State agency ignored Green Book language at its peril, for doing so would anger both Houses and might jeopardize its ability to extract money from the Legislature the next time around. In 1987 the Green Book required the Department of Corrections to use part of its budget to make drug abuse treatment available at every State prison. By the beginning of 1988, Commissioner Coughlin reported that this effort resulted in a net increase of 60 percent in the system's drug abuse treatment capacity.

In 2001 Governor George Pataki took on and eliminated the till-then effective power of the Green Book process, by insisting upon the state executive's primacy over any conditions that might be placed on budget allocations. In a case that produced three distinct written opinions from the seven sitting judges, a majority of the Court of Appeals accepted the core of his argument (*Pataki v. Assembly*, 4 N.Y. 3d 75, 2004). Many observers found that this decision adhered to the language of the state constitution on budgeting but not to its intent, and in doing so dangerously unbalanced the relationship between the Governor and the Legislature. In response, the Legislature sought constitutional change, an approach that at once would override the high court and was not subject to gubernatorial veto. But its proposal was rejected by voters at the polls as undermining the executive budgeting system; that is, as creating a remedy worse than the disease. The Legislature responded by giving first passage to a revised constitutional amendment on budgeting. Language returning the executive/legislative relationship to the pre-*Pataki v Assembly* status quo, included in Lieutenant Governor Richard Ravitch's 2010 Plan for bringing the state budget into long term balance, was widely regarded as required to win Speaker Silver's support. The Legislature's deep dissatisfaction with the Court of Appeals ruling virtually guarantees that it will persist in seeking to redress the executive/legislative balance in budgeting in New York State.

Building More Prisons . . . and Developing Alternatives. In 1987, motivated by the flow of new inmates mostly from New York City resulting from the Rockefeller drug laws and his desire to buy peace and cooperation with the Senate Republicans, Governor Mario Cuomo insisted on authorizing three new prisons with 500 beds each. As the new Corrections Chair, I had neither the stature nor the confidence to resist. My tours of the prisons, often including meetings with corrections officers, made me realize that we could not assure the safety of officers or inmates at high levels of prison overcrowding. Under pressure from the Speaker to act pragmatically, and with my own sense of the need for more room, I reluctantly agreed to support capital budget authorizations for building three new prisons.

Late in the 1987 session Cuomo, Coughlin and Larry Kurlander (Cuomo's Criminal Justice Coordinator) sweetened the deal with two proposals to get inmates out faster and reduce recidivism: shock incarceration and earned eligibility. I signed on, as did the chair of the Senate Crime and Corrections Committee, Chris Mega, who became a good friend. (The Senate, unlike the Assembly, had had such a committee for a long time.)

"Shock incarceration" would enable young new drug offenders, who volunteered and met physical and mental criteria, to satisfy their entire felony sentence if they successfully completed a six-month army-like boot-camp regimen. Designed to build self-discipline and self-esteem, this program sought to help ensure success in breaking drug addiction.

Upon graduation from "Shock," inmates were supposed to enter an intensively supervised parole program. The State failed at first to keep its promise of sufficient support for this latter element of the program, compromising its success. The program never produced recidivism reductions much better than the levels of those who completed ordinary prison terms. Of course, the shock graduates who did not do any worse, on average, than ordinary inmates, served much less time.

We also cobbled together "earned eligibility." This was a program designed to entitle older inmates to earlier parole on the basis of their completion of education and rehabilitation programs. Again we sought to reduce the likelihood of recidivism, and thus to free up as many as 1500 prison cells.

On the Assembly floor, I had to defend shock incarceration and earned eligibility against some standard "soft-on-crime" attacks from Republicans. They needed a record upon which to attack Democrats in swing districts, where Republicans had some chance to win. However, they were aware that I personally had no vulnerability whatsoever, in my overwhelmingly Democratic district. In addition, they recognized my generally pro-law-enforcement history, so they didn't give me too hard a time.

With 95 Democrats in the House and only 76 needed to pass a bill, Mel Miller often encouraged vulnerable Democrats to vote "no." In this case, since the bill included new prisons, and the Republican Senate would pass it too, Miller could forego that sort of vote management, since the political price for a "yes" vote was not very high.

Taking the Issue Public and the Race for Brooklyn D.A.

With my own complicity in authorizing more prisons, the dimensions of the big picture increasingly alarmed me. I began talking with my colleagues about scaling back the Rockefeller drug laws. With virtual unanimity, from the black urban ghettos of Brooklyn to the ultra-liberal precincts of Greenwich Village and the Upper West Side, they turned me down. A few Assembly colleagues acknowledged, very privately, that it would be the right thing to do, but they couldn't say so publicly, for fear of massive political damage. One Democratic Senator from the Bronx, Joseph Galiber, began to make similar arguments, but Democratic state senators commanded about as much attention as Assembly Republicans: very little.

I could afford to question some of New York's "lock 'em up" policies publicly when many of my colleagues could not. Knowing that I had supported the death penalty, written the Organized Crime Control Act, fought for use immunity, and enacted other laws credited by New York City police with enabling them to catch major criminals, political opponents would have some trouble attacking me as "soft on crime." Besides, my legislative successes that benefited tenants, homeowners, drivers, and subway riders would have made me hard to beat in any case.

Frustrated, I wrote an "Op Ed" article published in the *New York Times*, explaining that the lengthy sentences meted out for many offenders would not solve our street crime problem. After years of tough sentencing, we not only had the highest incarceration rate in the world but also one of the highest rates of violent crime.

Although I didn't spell it out, I was beginning to understand that excessive incarceration of nonviolent felons could actually lead to decreased safety. No matter how fast we built prisons, we couldn't keep up. As a result, from time to time we released violent inmates sooner than we should have, in order to make room for the nonviolent ones. The latter's long sentences were mandated by law, even though their judges, if they were left with the discretion, would surely have imposed appropriately shorter sentences.

The *Times* ran the op-ed in October 1987. The newspaper chose to entitle the piece "Longer Sentences Do Not Deter Crime." At the time a number of my friends, who were familiar with my writing style, pointed out that the *Times* editors, having dealt with my essay, were sending me a message. (I hope readers of this book feel that I took the headline's advice to heart.)

After the end of the 1987 session, I thought I had acquitted myself well enough as a brand-new Corrections Chair. Miller, astonished at my transformation in at least one area of criminal justice, kept exclaiming throughout the session, "I can't believe it! Feldman's a liberal!" Although I had just begun to understand the problem, I had taken some modest steps in the right direction. Also in that year, my

Parking Violations Bureau bill, empowering beleaguered drivers to impose what was in effect a fine on the Bureau for its egregious behavior, had finally become law after my five-year battle. This made me ridiculously happy.

The 1988 session, however, proved to be another story. Sheldon Silver, chair of the Codes Committee, reacted to continuing public pressure for "tougher" sentences by introducing legislation to impose much harsher penalties for the sale of crack cocaine, used more in poorer neighborhoods, than for comparable weights of traditional, less-concentrated cocaine, the drug of choice of-the upper-middle-class. Widely accepted claims made at the time that crack use correlated with violent crime far more than the use of traditional cocaine would later be refuted, but the Legislature enacted Silver's bill. Much to my subsequent regret, I voted for it, based on the violent crime argument.

The conjunction of the Second Felony Offender law's impact with Silver's crack crack-down began to produce the results Coughlin reported, with addicted and addled crack dealers getting convicted for their second felony an average of nine days after getting convicted for their first, with mandatory prison time following. New York City's Tactical Narcotics Team, or TNT, began neighborhood drug arrest "sweeps," expanding and speeding up the relocation of residents of urban ghettos to rural upstate New York.

As a consequence, again in 1989 I had to negotiate legislation expanding New York's prison capacity, this time by 6,000 regular prison beds. The legislation also provided for over 2,000 beds for intensive alcohol and substance abuse treatment and for aftercare upon parole release, allowing Father Young and others to provide needed treatment. Essentially, however, we were deepening the bad public policy hole into which New York had dug itself.

Prison reform advocates began to intone the line from the movie "Field of Dreams" with dark irony: "If you build it, they will come." Logic dictated cutting off the flow of inmates at its source by changing the Rockefeller drug laws, rather than refusing to build prisons after the inmates were already en route. I was not making much progress in the Legislature. Since those laws took discretion away from judges, and gave it to prosecutors, it seemed that only by being a prosecutor could I make change happen. As the District Attorney in Brooklyn, the most populous county in New York State, I could single-handedly reduce the flow of drug offenders into state prisons by saving felony prosecutions for the real "players" in the drug trade and other dangerous criminals, while pushing into treatment most of the low-level infinitely replace-able drones, the addicted nonviolent street dealers.

The Race For Brooklyn D.A. So I ran for Brooklyn District Attorney, a job that does not often come open. The incumbent, Elizabeth Holtz-man, had become the Brooklyn D.A after losing her race for the United States Senate. She served for eight years, and was leaving the job to run for New York City Comptroller. Her predecessor was Eugene Gold, who served for thirteen years until 1981, when he was caught up in scandal and emigrated to Israel.

As in my Assembly race, whoever won the Democratic primary for District Attorney in Brooklyn would be assured of victory in the general election. This was, in a way, a free ride. I was committed to a career in public service. My Assembly seat, hard-earned and strongly-held, was my base. Lyndon Johnson ran for Senator and Vice President from Texas in 1960; Joe Lieberman did the same from Connecticut in 2000. Politi-cians from New York cannot run for two offices at the same time. But New York State legislators run in even-numbered years; district attorneys from the five boroughs of New York City run in odd-numbered years. So I did not need to give up my Assembly seat to run for D.A. in 1989.

In the three-way contest my opponents were Charles ("Joe") Hynes, and Assistant District Attorney Norman Rosen. Hynes, famous for his successful 1987 prosecution of a notorious hate crime in Howard Beach, Queens, was more formidable.

Late in the evening on December 19, 1986 four young black men—Cedric Sandiford, Curtis Sylvester, Michael Griffith and Timothy Grimes—were driving though a desolate area on Cross Bay Boulevard in South Queens when their car broke down. They went on foot for help, stopping to eat shortly after midnight at the New Park Pizzeria in Ho-ward Beach, a white working-class neighborhood. When the four emerged they were set upon by a group of white men shouting racial epi-taphs. Sandiford and Griffen were beaten severely. In attempt to escape Griffen tried to run across the highway, and was killed by a passing car.

Black leaders demanded vigorous prosecution of the three white teenagers identified as the assailants—Jasone Langone, Jon Lester, and Scott Kern. They also questioned whether Queens District Attor-ney John Santucci, who had represented the area in the State Senate, would seek justice in the case. Meanwhile, white leaders in the neigh-borhood opposed prosecuting the assailants at all. They alleged that the young black men who were assaulted were coming into Howard Beach to steal a car.

Large racially-charged demonstrations ensued in Howard Beach in late December, led by Al Sharpton, who became significant in city-wide politics as a result of this case. Sandiford and the Griffen family were represented by Alton H. Maddox and C. Vernon Mason, two lawyers later involved in the Tawana Brawley hoax (involving an alleged sexual assault by a police officer on a black teenage girl in upstate Dutchess County). When prosecution witnesses refused to cooperate with Santucci, Governor Mario Cuomo acceded to demands that he appoint a special prosecutor. He chose Hynes, who had been similarly designated by Governor Hugh Carey years earlier to investigate nursing home fraud. Langone, Lester and Kern were convicted of second degree manslaughter; Hynes also won the conviction of six others in connection with the case

Although Hynes's successful prosecution in the Howard Beach case clearly won him support among black voters, my efforts in the Legislature, as well as endorsements from such black colleagues as Clarence Norman, Frank Boyland and Congressman Ed Towns gained me significant backing as well. The vote for me in overwhelmingly black Assembly districts in Brooklyn matched the usual turnout in those districts. Aside from personal appearances, of limited value in a constituency of three million people, my campaign relied almost entirely on mail to "prime voters," those who had voted in three of the four previous Democratic primaries in Brooklyn. I did not use radio or television because I did not know how much money I would be able to raise. With mail, I could adjust the number of mailings as the funds came in.

What I did not count on was an expansion of the African-American electorate. David Dinkins's successful primary campaign tripled the usual turnout among black voters. Most of the newly mobilized were not regular voters, and thus did not receive my mailings. But they had likely heard of Hynes, who relied heavily on radio advertising and emphasized his work on the Howard Beach case.

I campaigned throughout the length and breadth of Brooklyn, a constituency of almost three million people, speaking against the massive incarceration of nonviolent, low-level drug dealers as a waste of scarce prison space that should more appropriately be used for violent felons, and as a waste of taxpayer money that should more appropriately be used for education, housing, and health care. I regularly pointed out how non-prison-based drug addiction treatment cost half as much as prison, or less. I pointed to the strange choice we make when we provide 40,000 units of housing, three meals a day, and some version of education, medical care, and drug abuse treatment only to the particular subset of the poor who happen to have been convicted of crimes, while stingily withholding assistance from poor people who do not commit crimes.

Hynes did not initially address this subject, but quickly followed my lead. In the end, I won five of Brooklyn's Assembly districts and 34 percent of the vote, Joe won fourteen and 51 percent of the vote, and Norman won none, with 15 percent of the vote. Hynes outpolled me in African-American districts by a margin of two to one.

To his credit, when the voters of Brooklyn elected him, Joe Hynes made good on his pledge to seek a better way to deal with addicted street-dealers. By 1991, the Brooklyn D.A.'s office was operating the Drug Treatment Alternatives Program (DTAP), and in years to come a number of other district attorneys around the State adopted DTAP as well. Under its provisions, which varied somewhat from D.A. to D.A., if a defendant charged with a second drug felony pled guilty, the prosecutor did not seek and the judge did not enter a conviction. Instead, the defendant began a carefully selected and approved drug abuse treatment program. If he or she completed it successfully, the judge dismissed the case against him or her, or allowed a conviction on a lesser charge than the original felony plea. If the defendant failed to complete drug treatment successfully, the court accepted the initial guilty plea and sentenced him or her to prison in accord with the requirements for a second felony conviction.

Renewed Efforts in the Legislature: With continued incarceration of drug offenders at numbers several orders of magnitude higher than those entered into this program, DTAP could not by itself change New York's overall approach. But the program kept hundreds of addicted former drug felony defendants out of prison each year and apparently rehabilitated them. And its implementation and apparent success marked the beginning of a change in attitudes.

It is very painful to lose. But though defeated for District Attorney, I was still an Assembly member with a key committee chairmanship and a solid base in my district. There was still a lot to do and, slowly, the world was changing. Hynes's actions showed that I was no longer the only significant elected official willing to publicly question the value of indiscriminate incarceration of low-level addicted drug dealers. Another harbinger: On February 21, 1991, I wrote in a *Times* Op-Ed piece:

In New York State, we have almost five times as many inmates as we did 20 years ago, and the state now spends well over a billion dollars a year on them with no significant decrease in crime. As a result of criminal justice policies like New York's, the United States now incarcerates more people per capita than any other nation, and more black men per capita than South Africa. Money is too scarce for us to continue to spend it so foolishly.

Even under the awful headline: "Let the Small-Time Drug Peddlers Go," neither screams of outrage nor calls for my beheading ensued.

Speaking to the press at Governor Pataki's signing of New York's Megan's Law. From left to right, Attorney General Dennis Vacco, hidden, unidentified, unidentified, Maureen Kanka (mother of slain victim Megan Kanka), Senate Majority Leader Joe Bruno, Governor George Pataki, Mark Klaas (father of slain victim Polly Klaas), unidentified. *97-0380 5-16*

With Governor Mario Cuomo's Criminal Justice Coordinator Larry Kurlander and crime victim Dora Wilensky, a constituent, whose need for a security window gate (paid for, in her case, by a generous private donor) helped Feldman secure a 75 percent increase in state funding to help elderly crime victims in comparable need. *9/86*

Uncomfortable addressing rally behind a sign saying "We must build to keep our prisons safe," a view he publicly opposed, Feldman nevertheless won support from correction officers for his efforts to increase prison staffing levels.

With Governor Mario Cuomo, with whom he had an often rocky relationship.

Arrested for picketing against apartheid at the South African embassy in 1985, with, from left, unidentified, Assembly Member Helene Weinstein, Assembly Member Rhoda Jacobs, staff member David Eichenthal.

With Governor Hugh Carey in 1982, signing Feldman's Tax Assessment Small Claims Court bill into law, enabling middle-class homeowners to challenge unfair property tax assessment increases. *B260-A 20A*

Debating a bill at his seat in the Assembly Chamber, 1996.   *96-0265-34*

With former Mayor Ed Koch, endorsing Feldman for Congress in 1998 with the comment "I had big fights with Dan Feldman when he was in the Assembly, and he was right!," probably referring to Feldman's laws making the Parking Violations Bureau liable to drivers it harassed unjustly and unduly, and creating the Tax Assessment Small Claims Court where middle-class homeowners could challenge unfair property tax assessment increases, both of which Koch initially opposed.

Speaking at a rally in support of Megan's Law in June 1995 shortly after the murder of 4-year-old My Ly Nghiem, with two legislators from her home region in the Binghamton area, seated with Maureen Kanka (mother of slain crime victim Megan Kanka, after whom the law was named) and Reverend Joseph Hein. Directly behind Feldman was Assembly Member Jay Dinga and behind the Reverend was State Senator Thomas Libous. *95-0159 4-25*

Debating a bill at his seat in the Assembly in 1994, with his long-serving legislative director Mindy Bockstein at right, providing counsel and the late Assembly Member Audrey Hochberg seated at left.   *94-0484-11*

With his friend the late Thomas Coughlin, who served as Corrections Commissioner during most of Feldman's tenure as chair of the Assembly Committee on Correction. *93-0388 5-25A*

Advising homeowners of recourse available to them against unfair property tax assessments, sidewalk repair bills, water meter bills, and mortgage refinancing costs, at a forum sponsored by the Midwood Development Corporation at Edward R. Murrow High School in Brooklyn.   *95-0616-7A*

In 1982, with (left to right) Speaker Stanley Fink, Mrs. Violet Zatkin, and Henry A. Feldman (his father).   *82-403-23A*

With Governor George and Libby Pataki, with whom he enjoyed a cordial relationship.

Briefly presiding over a session of the Assembly as Speaker pro tempore.   *96-0494-18A*

Speaking at a rally of the Transit Workers Union, which had earlier supported his successful initiative to create the Transit Corps of Engineers, a unit that succeeded in raising morale and competence levels among Transit Authority engineers during a critical period. *98-0316 1-2A*

With then-Brooklyn District Attorney Elizabeth Holtzman, as a member of her Policy Advisory Council.

Inspecting the condition of Brighton Beach in his Assembly district with Brooklyn Borough President Howard Golden (center)   6/86

Discussing his new law to allow tow truck drivers to let motorists "off the hook" if they arrived at their cars in time to pay their fines before the tow truck drives off with them.   City of New York D.O.T. photo

to DAA — who obviously knows how
to continue attention!

With then-Member of Congress Stephen J. Solarz, sporting hideous eyeglasses and much hair.

Albany Public Library

Washington Ave Branch
161 Washington Avenue
Albany NY, 12210
518-427-4300

15/02/2017 3.41 PM

Tales from the sausage factory :

38116101242899

DUE DATE: 03-15-17 00:00AM

Reforming the Rockefeller Drug Laws

Late on December 13, 1991 a federal jury in the Eastern District of New York found Mel Miller guilty of federal mail fraud charges arising out of a real estate transaction he had handled in his private law practice. Under New York State law, any conviction for a felony results in the immediate loss of elective office. Although an appellate court later reversed Miller's conviction, this ended his tenure as Speaker, and his political career.

Outside pressure again disturbed the equilibrium in the Legislature. Again change in leadership; again risk; again opportunity.

Backing the Losing Side . . . Twice

I favored Jim Tallon for Speaker. Jim was a former teacher who had represented Binghamton in New York's southern tier in the Assembly since 1975. He became one of the top experts in health-care finance in the United States as chair of the Assembly Health Committee during the Fink era. (He is now president of the United Hospital Fund.)

Honoring Fink's precedent, Miller had selected Tallon, an upstater, as his Majority Leader. In this role Tallon won respect from every Member of the House for his firm but fair floor leadership in Assembly debate.

At first glance, selection of a Democratic speaker from an upstate district seemed most unlikely. Speakers of the Assembly from our side of the aisle had come from New York City since we recaptured power in 1974. (This was also true on all but one of the few occasions earlier in the century—1911, 1913, 1935, and 1965–68 when Democrats had the majority). But Tallon was that rare bird, an upstate liberal Democrat. His overwhelming decency and obvious intelligence gave him a real chance to beat the odds. However, he turned out to lack the requisite focused, take-no-prisoners single-mindedness that a leadership race required. Jim refused—based on loyalty to the Speaker who had appointed him—to seek the support of his colleagues for the speakership until Miller's trial had an outcome.

Although Saul Weprin was a kindly and genial man, he had no such compunctions. As noted, he had become Miller's Ways and Means chair after his entry into the race for speaker as a second Queens candidate in 1987 undid Alan Hevesi and assured Miller's victory. Saul presided over the "Assembly Finance Committee," a venerable card game, said to have originated in the nineteenth century, which at this time included such senior members as Roger Robach, Joe Lentol, Howard Lasher and Vito Lopez. Not insignificantly, Weprin had Sheldon Silver as one of his strongest backers.

Another of Weprin's backers was Michael Bragman from Syracuse. Bragman, elected to the Assembly in 1980, the same year as I became head of the Assembly Democratic Campaign Committee in 1986, and was owed political debts by a number of new members who had, in part, won their elections with the expertise and resources he provided. Others hoped for future Campaign Committee support, in the event that they faced tough reelection campaigns. Bragman's early backing, therefore, gave Weprin a big advantage.

Create the impression that your march to the speakership is unstoppable and it probably will be. Members have a large career stake in being with the winner; this builds enormous pressure on them. Because he was not from a large county in New York City, Jim Tallon lacked a "natural geographic base" within the Assembly Democratic conference that might wait for him to declare, with the hope of gaining local advantage by having the speaker from their home county. By the time he starting asking for votes, it was too late. Weprin became Speaker. Silver became chair of Ways and Means. Bragman became Majority Leader. Joe Lentol, another member of Weprin's inner circle, became Codes chair.

I stayed put.

With his change in chairmanships, Silver no longer directly controlled Second Felony Offender Reform. But neither did I. He had backed the new Speaker, while I had not. He had moved on to even greater power in the house. I had not.

As it turned out, Weprin's service as Speaker was brief. During 1993 his health worsened to the point at which he could no longer perform his duties. Sheldon Silver ascended to the speakership in January of

1994 in an unusual maneuver. A majority of Assembly Democrats agreed to allow him to become Interim Speaker while he also remained chair of the Ways and Means Committee. The Silver-Bragman alliance held against a feeble challenge by Fink's local successor in the Canarsie Assembly seat, Anthony Genovesi. Genovesi's short-lived rebellion included very few Members, but I was one of them. Silver quickly consolidated his power as Interim Speaker. When Weprin died the following month, he officially assumed the speakership.

Weprin's elevation, and then Silver's, marked the beginning of the end of my career in the Assembly. As previously detailed, they increasingly centralized power, constraining the ability of committee chairs to act independently in moving legislation. For some of my colleagues this did not pose much of a problem. With little in the way of strong policy commitments, they were content to bow to leadership. But for me, the joy of legislating lay in changing society, even if only a little, to be more like what my values told me it ought to be. If I couldn't expect an independent role in fighting for my vision of healthy change, I saw no point in elective office. Moreover, I kept finding myself on the opposite side of Sheldon Silver, and kept losing. This doubtlessly increased whatever antipathy Silver had toward me. The antipathy of the speaker is not an asset in the Assembly.

A Climate Shift on Second Felony Offender Reform

I had introduced the first bill to reform the Second Felony Offender Law in the 1991 session, when Miller was still Speaker. With input and support from a number of district attorneys around the State, I had drafted my bill narrowly to exclude only addicted nonviolent offenders from the effect of the existing law, and only if a judge certified their removal to a residential drug treatment facility. My bill also *increased* penalties for those who exercised control of an illegal drug-dealing organization. The idea was to shift prosecutorial resources to those participants in drug trafficking whose removal experts said would make more of a difference, since they could not be easily replaced.

Seeing from reactions to media coverage that the position I was taking was not radioactive, some of my Democratic colleagues in Albany began to come around. In 1991 the State Office of Court Administration released a study that, for the first time, clearly established that a large number of inmates had never been convicted of anything other than the sale and possession of drugs.

There were major fiscal implications that should have made my initiative attractive to the executive. State prisons were overcrowded; maintaining ever increasing numbers of new prisoners or building new prisons for them cost money the state didn't have. Governor Cuomo, reading the changing political environment, included a proposal to eliminate various nonviolent felonies from the Second Felony Offender Law in presenting his 1991 budget. He also offered a "Departmental" bill proposal from his Division of Criminal Justice Services offering a wider exemption from Second Felony Offender treatment, also including burglars, robbers, and rapists.

This executive initiative was either incompetence or a political ploy. Notwithstanding the fiscal savings that might attract executive-side support, I suspected the later. The inclusion of violent offenders in the executive's draft legislation for exemption from second felony mandates made the bill dead on arrival. I interpreted it as a feint in the direction of reform that the Governor must have known was doomed to fail. Possibly Cuomo thought his bill might even tarnish my effort to reform Second Felony Offender. Perhaps it did.

As I began to gather support from a number of district attorneys around the State for a more narrowly targeted Second Felony Offender reform bill than the Governor's, then-Codes Committee chair Sheldon Silver complained to Speaker Miller that any such effort was rightly within his jurisdiction. Knowing that I had started pressing this issue four years earlier, with virtually no support from any colleague, Miller signaled his disagreement to Silver with a standard two-word obscenity. It would, he said, be my bill and my issue.

In an effort to highlight the distinctions between my bill and the governor's, I publicized the support mine had received from the district attorneys of Rockland, Ulster, Erie, Monroe, and Kings counties, and from the probation director of Suffolk County. In a fourteen-page letter sent on April 10, 1991 to the chairs of the Senate Finance Committee and the Assembly Ways and Means Committee, Mathew Crosson, then Chief Administrator of New York's court system (and later head of the Long Island Association), offered support. He noted that a bill "more narrowly drawn" than the Governor's would effectively "lift the requirement of a mandatory prison sentence for truly 'low-level, nonviolent' offenders" and commended my bill as doing just that, presenting "a sensible alternative to Departmental Bill #390 that the Legislature might wish to consider." He added,

If Assemblyman Feldman's bill were enacted—together with *increases* in intensive supervision probation and drug treatment funding to deal with the population of second felons who need not be sent to prison—the State could likely save the cost of as many as 3255 prison beds [in the following fiscal year], and still provide adequate public protection and a realistic prospect that those second felons would receive some meaningful rehabilitation services.

Unlike those district attorneys who endorsed my approach, Kings County D.A. Joe Hynes, while describing my bill as "a step in the right direction," urged me to adopt legislation he proposed, because, he said, he believed his bill went "much further." Actually, the key distinction between Hynes's bill and mine was that his bill would have allowed prosecutors, not judges, to retain veto power over alternative sentencing.

Despite Speaker Miller's support, a procedural decision in which he had little choice made advancing it more difficult. The speaker and his counsel control the reference of legislation to committee. In ambiguous circumstances the choices they make at this very early stage may be critical to legislation's success. I made an effort to get Second Felony Offender Reform referred to my committee by making the first part of the bill a change in the Corrections Law. Really, however, it was a dramatic change in sentencing. Miller in this case had had no choice but to refer the bill to Codes, which properly handles sentencing legislation and where Silver was Chair.

In the end, no bill went anywhere in the 1991 session. Cuomo's bill obviously had no chance. No one introduced Hynes's bill. And Silver, chair of the Assembly Codes Committee, had no special interest in advancing my bill and thus calling more attention to it.

However, the outcome of the 1991 effort was not all negative. The press began to take an interest in Second Felony Offender Reform. *Newsday* editorialized in favor of my bill and the Governor's. WPIX-TV followed suit in 1992. Here and there around the country, a few other states began to respond to the evidence. Tennessee halved its sentences for low-level cocaine sales and increased sentences for violent sex offenses. North Carolina similarly revised its sentencing structure.

While New York State avoided any official change in policy, the New York City Police Department began to move away from the TNT patrol approach, focusing more on mid-level traffickers and making fewer of the easy, low-level, street-sweep arrests.

While support grew outside the Assembly, the inside politics remained difficult. In 1992 the new chair of Codes, Joe Lentol, refused to report my Second Felony Offender Reform Bill, as had Sheldon Silver before him. Silver may have had a role in this decision, inasmuch as Weprin had designated Silver as chair of an Assembly "crime task force," a new entity.

In 1993, *Newsday* ran an even stronger editorial than it had offered the previous year calling for repeal of the Rockefeller drug laws and for passage of Second Felony Offender Reform. Under a subhead reading "New York Must Stop Its Prison-Building Binge," the paper particularly noted that the $3.7 billion spent on New York's prison expansion in the 1980s had not made New Yorkers safer. Newspapers and magazines published several dozen letters to the editor and articles I wrote making the same case, as I introduced the same legislation, slightly modified, in every succeeding session of the Legislature.

Developments outside the Legislature—and within it, with the important exception of the legislative leadership—remained encouraging regarding changing views on the Rockefeller drug laws and their effect on the prison population explosion. As prison spending rose into the billion-dollar-plus range, state officials generally became more sensitive to the fact that such high cost made some other options, like tax reductions, less available. The higher education/prisons tradeoff became more important. Even Republicans in New York with prisons in their upstate districts really did not like to reduce support for higher education: apart from the social policy considerations, SUNY campuses were also in their districts. However, no other area of direct state spending was big enough, and no other constituency offered less political resistance, when additional funding for prisons had to be found.

As prison costs continued to rise to staggeringly high levels, legislators' discomfort increased. Things were not improved when Governor Mario Cuomo, always at risk for being labeled "soft on crime" for his anti-death penalty stand, climbed onto a national bandwagon promoting "three-strikes-and-you're-out" laws—mandated life imprisonment for three-time violent felons. As a counterweight to this in his first session as Speaker, Silver announced an Assembly "criminal justice plan" to lengthen sentences for more serious felons while giving judges more discretion to send nonviolent drug offenders to treatment. The "plan" went no further than the press conference at which it was introduced.

The Assembly did, however, undertake more practical, lower-profile efforts. As part of the 1992 budget we amended the Correction Law to add the Comprehensive Alcohol and Substance Abuse Treatment Program (CASAT). An addicted inmate in prison for a nonviolent offense could enter CASAT when he or she successfully completed one of the existing, non-intensive prison treatment programs for substance abuse, and had no more than two more years to serve before becoming eligible for parole. CASAT entailed intensive drug abuse treatment for six months in prison, six months more in a residential drug treatment facility outside of prison but still under the supervision of the Department of Corrections, and then, upon successful progress, continued drug abuse treatment as a parolee. This program was expanded in 1994. By the late 1990s, between seventeen and eighteen hundred inmates were participating in CASAT at any given time.

Enter George Pataki

Little-noticed, and overshadowed by George Pataki's pro-death penalty attacks on Mario Cuomo during the course of the campaign for governor in 1994, the Republican candidate more than once remarked that we "can't build our way out of the drug problem." Pataki certainly understood the issue. Although on opposite sides of the aisle, we had been reasonably friendly as Assembly colleagues, before he went over to the Senate. He had questioned me very intelligently on the subject at the time, and paid close attention to my explanations, although without commenting in any way that would signal a commitment to my position.

Upon taking office in 1995 Governor Pataki immediately said he thought the Rockefeller drug laws should be changed to divert about 4,000 nonviolent addicted drug dealers away from prison to treatment programs or job training. This would, the new governor said, enable New York to impose longer prison stays on violent criminals. A few newspapers published my comments—overoptimistic as ever—to the effect that after the governorship of a supposedly liberal Democrat, Cuomo, the advent of the Pataki administration created a Nixon-in-China possibility for drug law reform. In fact, 1995 saw the first explicit statutory exception to Second Felony Offender, the "Willard" program. Under this initiative nonviolent second felony drug offenders could be sentenced to three months at Willard, in rural central New York's Seneca County. Technically the Department of Corrections operates the Willard Drug Treatment Campus not as a prison but as a secure drug abuse treatment center. The Pataki administration assured the Legislature that every Willard "graduate" would be provided with several months of outpatient follow-up treatment.

Actually, the follow-up treatment was spotty, at best. But a more important problem was that the Willard legislation gave district attorneys the right to veto its use, either for newly sentenced offenders or for the "retro pool" cases (inmates previously convicted as nonviolent second felony drug offenders). They did so routinely. With little support from the DAs, the Pataki administration quickly began "violating" parolees at a higher rate to help fill Willard, just as it reduced the parole release rate to keep the ordinary prisons full. As a result, Willard's 750 beds went mostly to parole violators rather than to reducing the population of the targeted pool of inmates. In the end, the program had little of the intended effect.

Chris Mega's successor as Chair of the Senate Crime and Corrections Committee, Michael Nozzolio, represented Seneca County. Willard gave jobs to a great many of his constituents. Still, in creating Willard the Legislature engaged in the kind of hypocritical tribute that "vice pays to virtue." At least it recognized the political need to bow in the direction of Second Felony reform.

Bypassing the State Constitution to Build Prisons: Fiscal Chicanery

One way to pay for a building, a road, a bridge or a prison is to save for it, and then buy it when the money is entirely in hand. A second way is to increase taxes some for each year that a big project is being built, paying for it as you go. (Governor Tom Dewey made this method famous, but he had the benefit of lots of tax revenues piling up during World War II, when capital spending was impossible because of the preemptive claim of the war effort on resources.)

But deferring gratification is as hard for governments as it is for you and me, perhaps harder. Saving to build doesn't work well because costs tend to rise while you're waiting, pushing the project further into the future as you save. Paying as you go is challenging because the same amount of money is not needed year after year; more must be raised in some years than in others, while a project is being built. Both of these approaches are generally very hard to use in situations where priorities differ substantially and there are a far larger number of immediate needs than there is money to pay for them, drawing resources away from long-term needs. Additionally, if a project is paid for in these ways, the people who pay taxes for it are not necessarily those who will get to use the resulting facility after it is finally completed. They may move away; they may die.

A third way to finance a capital project is to borrow, and pay back the cost with taxes or fees collected from those who use the faculty for the twenty or thirty years after it is built. The cost is higher—you have to pay to borrow the money as well as the cost of the building, or road, or bridge—but borrowing does not require putting aside money right away, or at least as much money. Nor does it require the taxes or fees paid by current taxpayers to be raised as much—and current taxpayers are the ones who vote for current politicians. There is a ribbon-cutting now, with most payments later, sometimes much later, perhaps by people not even here now. This is a politically attractive solution.

When the Legislature put the prison construction bond issue on the ballot in 1981, it was obeying the letter and spirit of Article 7 Section 11 of the New York State Constitution. That provision, adopted in reaction to a fiscal crisis of the early 1840's arising from excessive issuance of debt by the Legislature for canal building, requires voter approval at referendum for any public borrowing backed by the full faith and credit of the state government. The constitution-writers envisioned a system under which Legislature could put the question of whether to borrow on the ballot, but only the voters themselves could choose to borrow money for a public purpose. This was to be a check on excessive borrowing. They did not want legislators to leave office, no longer accountable to voting taxpayers, having saddled those taxpayers and their progeny, without their explicit consent, with debts that it would take decades to repay.

Unlike many of its sister states, New York is not one in which laws are generally made by voter initiative and referendum. New York State voters, therefore, are relatively unfamiliar with referenda. Additionally, voter turnout in New York State tends to be low, and only a relatively small number of those who actually show up at the polls pull the lever on bond issues and other ballot questions. Over the recent history of New York, the minority that votes on ballot questions has sometimes been amenable to bond issues for environmental or transportation purposes, but not for social purposes. And as the century came to a close, and sensitivity to New York's relatively high taxes grew, anything that looked like an authorization to spend money became suspect to the voters. To make a long story short, the 1981 $500 million prison construction bond issue failed at the polls.

Because of the difficulty of obtaining public approval at referendum, the need for money for capital projects, and the desire to avoid tax increases to pay for these, the governor and Legislature in New York (and other states) developed means for borrowing that were within the letter of the constitution, but not within its spirit. One major technique was the creation of public authorities. The Legislature created the "independent" agencies and authorized them to incur debt to build revenue-generating projects—bridges on which tolls were to be collected, or college residence halls that charge room rents—with the tolls or rents collected used to pay back the debt. The courts have found that in doing this the Legislature was not encumbering the citizenry with debt in contravention of the state constitution, because the toll- or fee-payers will pay off the borrowing, not the general taxpayers.

Of course, the borrowing agency generally must pay bondholders a higher interest rate on these "revenue" bonds than the state pays on the "general obligation" bonds authorized at the polls. This is because lenders know that the state's entire taxing authority backs the kind of bond that voters authorize at the polls, and that under the law they have a first claim on tax revenues. In contrast, revenues from a particular project or group of projects might fall short, leaving the lenders pressed to get back their money.

Space precludes detailing here all the nuanced ways in which New York State has found around the constitution's intent that the state's borrowing be authorized by the voters, so money for capital projects would still flow. There are many. They involve giving voters or interest groups the pleasure of getting now what they want or say they want (facilities, jobs, public safety), while avoiding until later the pain (taxes) of paying for these. Almost all involve a financial relationship between the State government and a public authority it has created. Formally the debt obligation is the authority's, but actually it is the state's.

The cost to New York is greater than direct borrowing would be. But the real story is the resulting level of overall debt. According to the New York State Comptroller, in 2005 New York State had $3.2 billion in debt outstanding that was actually authorized by the voters, and $45 billion (more than fourteen times as much!) in state-backed public authority debt that bypassed constitutional limits. And this does not include another $80 billion in authority debt not supported by state revenues.

Here's how a small piece of this happened. After the voters said "No" to the prison bond in 1981, the Legislature and Governors Cuomo and Pataki turned to public authority bonds without a revenue stream to

pay for more prisons. This was done by increasing the bonding authority of an existing public authority created to build housing, the Urban
Development Corporation (UDC, later called the Empire State Development Corporation). Since these prisons would not generate revenue
to repay bondholders, tax revenues would subsidize the Development
Corporation's repayment of the bonds, at the higher, revenue-bond rate
of interest.

Technically, the State was not liable for repaying these bonds, but
everyone involved understood that if New York State permitted the
UDC to default on these bonds the financial markets would certainly
punish the State, and quickly. The State's credit rating would plummet,
thus significantly increasing the interest it would have to pay on its own
traditional general obligation bonds, if it could sell them at all. In fact,
the New York City and State fiscal crises of 1975, involving a UDC default, provided a relatively recent and painful lesson confirming this reality. How this lesson was forgotten so soon in New York is a testimo-
nial to the seductive attractiveness—to politicians serving relatively
short terms and eligible for reelection—of that great idea that drives the
American economy: "buy now, pay later."

Fiscal conservatives—in Change New York, a new organization that
had supported George Pataki for Governor, the Conservative Party,
which had also supported Pataki, and the Citizens Budget Commission,
a prominent non-partisan civic group—all had previously raised alarms
about New York's irresponsible off-budget borrowing through public
authorities, including the UDC. I thought I could mobilize them to oppose this latest abuse, and I was right. The leaders of the three organizations took a principled and courageous stand, joining me in an attack on
the tactic favored by two Governors of opposite parties and two Houses
of the Legislature, also led by opposite parties.

I had been right about principled fiscal conservatives. But I was
wrong in thinking that many of my conservative *or* liberal colleagues in
the Legislature would help. The upstate conservatives needed prisons
for their constituents and would take them any way they could get them.
The downstate liberals did not want to question a borrowing device they
had used, and hoped to use again, for "liberal" projects that also might
not generate revenue streams. One notable exception, John Faso, a conservative Republican from the small town of Kinderhook in Columbia
County, incurred tremendous wrath from his party by backing me. His
sterling personal qualities, and assiduous efforts, allowed him to win
enough forgiveness to later become Assembly Minority Leader, and

Republican candidate for New York State Comptroller (in 2002) and for Governor (in 2006). A lawsuit brought by anti-tax activists challenging the use of UDC borrowing for prison construction prevailed at the trial court level, but failed on appeal.

The Conservative Party and Change New York leaders made it clear that they supported hard line criminal justice policies and therefore prison construction. They simply sought to finance prison construction honestly, through another bond issue proposal on the ballot. Especially since the general public had now begun to rethink its support for massive incarceration, well ahead of most of the State government, I expected a new ballot proposal for prisons to do no better than the 1981 edition. But my conservative allies were willing to take that chance. Obtaining *The New York Times'* editorial support for my effort in May 1996 was the high water mark. Both houses of the Legislature and the governor systematically ignored it.

Drug Law Reform Gains Public Support

The Pataki administration kept prisons full by decreasing the parole release rate: parole boards denied parole to inmates whose prison record would have justified their release in earlier years. In 1987 New York was incarcerating 60 percent of its inmates for nonviolent crimes, as compared with 40 percent twenty years earlier. (The official figures claim that 50 percent were violent in 1987, but New York pads the figure for nonviolent crime by 10 percentage points. This results from the State's artificial categorization of virtually every residential burglary as violent even when the burglars do not use force or a weapon or encounter anyone.) By 1997, New York's crime rate had begun its dramatic downward trend, yet the State was still authorizing additional spending to construct new prisons.

The Pataki administration continued to play to both sides of the debate over drug enforcement policy. Shortly after returning to private practice in March 1997, Pataki's former director of criminal justice, Paul Shechtman, publicly floated the notion of a "deal" that would see the Assembly get Rockefeller drug law reform and the Senate get harsher youthful offender laws. Shechtman's closeness to Pataki signaled the Governor's potential support for such a deal. Nothing happened.

Across the nation, the ranks of skeptics grew to include former defenders of the policy of massive incarceration of drug dealers. John

DiIulio, a leading academic always sensitive to political winds, had infuriated me with arguments, prominently featured in the New York *Times* and prestigious journals, that casually lumped together "violent" and "repeat" offenders in his characterization of the prison population, and therefore justified the high levels of incarceration. DiIulio certainly should have known—and probably did know—that to the extent that "repeat offenders" were addicts, their "repeat" status meant nothing more than that they were caught again after a meaningless slap on the wrist in response to their first felony. This certainly provided no justification for blanket incarceration instead of treatment.

In 1992, opponents of the massive incarceration policy, including a number of former state prison commissioners and myself, created the national Campaign for Effective Crime Policy. Within a few years it included over a thousand mostly law-enforcement and corrections professionals. DiIulio scoffingly called us an "anti-incarceration penal reform elite" in the *Wall Street Journal* of May 13, 1992.

John Dunne, formerly a State Senator and Deputy U.S. Attorney General, and Warren Anderson, the former (and revered) Senate Majority Leader, had both voted for the Rockefeller Drug Laws. Dunne, Anderson, and David Rockefeller, the late Governor's brother, later all became outspoken anti-Rockefeller drug law converts on the basis of sincere changes of heart in response to the evidence. DiIulio switched sides too.

William F. Buckley, Jr., in the pages of the February 12, 1996 issue of *National Review*, the leading conservative journal, went further. He concluded that the failure of the "war on drugs," that effort's tendency toward the erosion of civil liberties, and the crime and suffering it caused [and the crime and suffering it exacerbated in original} all justified steps toward legalization. In 2000, 61 percent of California voters enacted a ballot initiative to substitute drug treatment for prison for nonviolent drug users. California was also among ten states that decriminalized possession of small quantities of marijuana. In 2002 New Mexico changed its laws to increase judicial discretion in sentencing drug offenders. With state budgets facing more serious shortfalls in the early 2000s than in the 1990s, officials in Washington, California, Oregon, Ohio, Michigan, and Illinois either closed prisons or explored legislation to reduce prison population pressures and thus permit prison closings in the future.

New York remained unmoved. In 1998, Speaker Silver once again went through the motions of offering to trade reform of the Rockefeller drug laws for a law-and-order proposal, this time a Pataki initiative to end parole for first-time violent felons. However, ultimately the Pataki initiative was enacted without any Rockefeller drug law reform.

The most draconian of the Rockefeller drug laws, the A-I felony law, produced notorious decisions. It forced unwilling judges to sentence minimally culpable first-offender relatives or girlfriends of dealers to minimum prison terms of fifteen years, based solely on the weight of the illegal drugs found in their possession. Rockefeller Drug Law reform advocates often used the emotional value of the A-I cases for dramatic effect in their lobbying, but the A-I's constituted a very small percentage of the numbers of inmates serving drug offense sentences—in the late 1990s, perhaps four or five hundred out of 23,000. Silver's Rockefeller drug law reform proposal had included among its elements a great increase in judicial sentencing discretion for the A-I's. The reform advocacy community understood that A-I reform alone would take away its most powerful emotional issue without addressing the bulk of the problem.

Early in 1999, Chief Judge Judith Kaye targeted reform of the A-I law as needed to remedy injustice, cautiously proposing that appellate judges be permitted to modify downward the long sentences that the trial judges would still be forced to impose. No doubt recognizing the limited impact of this approach, her chief administrative judge, Jonathan Lippman (later her successor as Chief Judge) likely at her suggestion, a few months later published a prominent special Law Day feature in the New York *Law Journal.* In it he explained the Kaye administration's view that judges should very narrowly limit the degree to which their comments could be interpreted as participation in the debate over the substance of legislation. He justified Kaye's specific proposals as growing out of the unhappiness of the judges in her administration with having to implement the A-I law. Through this essay Judge Lippman may have reinforced the perception that notwithstanding Kaye's limited recommendation, her personal views on Rockefeller drug reform went further.

With Kaye's proposal as cover, Pataki called for similar A-I reform. While Kaye would have let the appellate judges reduce mandatory minimum sentences from fifteen years to five, Pataki would only have allowed sentence reductions down to ten years in return for the elimination of parole for nonviolent felonies. Once again, the session ended without any serious negotiation.

The Pataki-Silver Drug Reform Dance

As noted in Chapter 5, Mike Bragman's alliance with Silver ended in 2000, when the Majority Leader attempted a coup. While Bragman generally associated himself with the right wing of the Democratic party, he picked up some support from the left by including in his criticism of Silver the Speaker's failure to achieve, or even to press hard for, Rockefeller drug law reform. Indeed, most legislators thought Silver feared being thought "soft on crime," and therefore refrained from more strenuous efforts.

Silver's energetic efforts to shore up support for himself seem to have included a commitment, particularly to black and Latino legislators, to press harder for Rockefeller drug law reform. But from a public relations point of view, Pataki scooped Silver. Early in the 2001 session the Governor issued a strong and well-publicized statement of support for reform.

Pataki received some rhetorical backing from Senate Republican Majority Leader Joe Bruno, who talked about unfair mandatory minimum sentences and the need to focus more on treatment. Heretofore, the Senate's traditional need to keep building and filling prisons in Senate Republican heartland districts seemed to require protection of the Rockefeller drug laws, with their production of a steady stream of inmates. To those who understood the politics of prison building, Bruno's apparent conversion therefore seemed a watershed more notable than Pataki's proposal.

Responding to the newly empowered constituency for Rockefeller drug law reform within his Democratic caucus in the Assembly, Silver had virtually no choice but to go further than Pataki when he issued the Assembly plan in March, two months later. Both proposals would have reduced sentences for nonviolent drug offenses, except for managerial-level participants, but they differed in other important respects. Pataki's plan still required prosecutor consent for all B felony drugs offenders, the largest single category supplying the bulk of the drug offender population in prison, and for the C, D, or E drug *sale* offenders. It permitted untrammeled judicial discretion only for the much smaller population of *possession* offenders. Silver's plan provided judicial sentencing discretion for all of those groups. One advocacy group calculated that the Silver plan would have allowed for judicial discretion in fourteen times as many cases as the Pataki plan, not counting the cases in which the prosecutor agreed.

Pataki's plan also actually increased sentences for marijuana offenses. When Silver translated his proposal into legislation in May, his bill earmarked $55 million for additional drug abuse treatment slots; Pataki's bill provided, much more vaguely, that added treatment costs would come out of prison savings. Silver's plan also allowed judges to sentence some drug offenders to shock incarceration, while existing law allowed only the Corrections Commissioner to place eligible inmates into the shock program.

Pataki's spokespersons regularly told the press that they were prepared to negotiate with the Assembly, despite the serious differences between the bills. Pataki revived press attention to his "commitment" to reform with a late July proposal, possible only because the session ran well past its June deadline. In this version he included sale offenses as well as possession offenses, and expanded the treatment option, which he called Court Approved Drug Abuse Treatment (CADAT), to include 2800 defendants a year. However, B-level offenders would still go to prison for nine months and would be released to community residential treatment only if they had dealt successfully with their prison treatment program. The Governor's proposal also continued to include harsher marijuana penalties. The exchanges seemed more serious and more focused, but the session ended without any more movement on either side.

Apparently distracted by the events of September 11, 2001, Pataki and Silver do not seem to have talked about Rockefeller drug laws again until March 2002, after several hundred protesters endured steady rain while gathered on the steps of the State Capitol to hear Albany Roman Catholic Bishop Howard Hubbard and others call for "long overdue" reform.

As his 2002 reelection race approached, political observers overwhelmingly believed that Pataki had more incentive than did the Assembly to press for Rockefeller drug law reform, so as to take the issue away from either of his potential Democratic rivals. Throughout the spring of 2002, the Governor talked about but did not advance a new reform proposal. In June, in the week that Pataki's new criminal justice coordinator Chauncey G. Parker announced that he planned to release the Governor's new bill, the Assembly offered revisions to its earlier bill. Silver claimed that the timing of the release of the new Assembly bill had nothing to do with any effort to upstage the Governor. The Governor denied that the presentation of his proposal, and subsequently his legislation, had any political motivation. No sensible person believed either of them.

With the two sides closer to agreement than ever before, newspaper editorial pages around the State pressed them hard for compromise. The Senate passed the Governor's bill, which the Assembly again characterized as inadequate, and the Assembly passed its own bill.

After Governor Pataki's overwhelming reelection in 2002, he no longer needed to curry favor with supporters of Rockefeller drug law reform, and Silver had less incentive to attack Pataki on the issue. Still, the Governor had charged Chauncey Parker with the task of working to enact the reform in 2002, and Parker's efforts continued. Jeff Aubry, my successor as Chair of the Assembly Corrections Committee, continued to press Silver for reform. Outside forces also tried to hold both sides to their earlier expressions of commitment. Early in June 2003, virtually simultaneously, the staid and respectable New York State Bar Association proposed a compromise between the Assembly's bill and the Governor's proposal, and Russell Simmons, a popular hip-hop artist and impresario, successfully urged the Governor to move still closer to the Assembly position.

Randy Credico, the founder of New York Mothers of the Disappeared, a Rockefeller Drug Law reform group of families of inmates, had demonstrated impressive skill in building and publicizing a coalition with Andrew Cuomo, the former Governor's son (elected Attorney General in 2006), Simmons and others. Simmons relied for guidance on Deborah Small, a drug reform expert from liberal billionaire George Soros's Lindensmith Center. Although Simmons's solo foray into Pataki's parlor irritated his allies, the work of the alliance apparently gave him entrée to and influence with the Governor.

Simmons, Small, Pataki, Bruno, and Silver negotiated for more than seven hours on Thursday night, June 19, 2003, but failed to reach agreement.

The Assembly and the Governor, at the end of the 2003 session, would both have:

- permitted judges to send defendants into drug abuse treatment programs in lieu of incarceration notwithstanding prosecutors' objections;
- excluded from treatment anyone convicted of a violent crime in the past or of selling drugs on school grounds;
- reduced the minimum possible sentence for the A-I's from 15 years to about 8 years;
- reduced sentences for B offenders, including repeat offenders;

- doubled the weight thresholds for A-I and A-II drug possession offenses; and
- made inmates currently in prison eligible for re-sentencing under the new milder laws.

According to news reports, the group could not close the gaps between their positions on the precise degree of discretion available to judges to use drug treatment as an alternative to prison, on how to release current inmates whose sentences would be reduced under the new law, and on the details of sentence increases for "kingpins" and for those who used guns in the course of their drug dealing businesses. It sounded very much as if the remaining differences could have been surmounted by parties committed to a meaningful compromise.

Silver's efforts probably reflected his political commitment to black and Latino legislators in return for their continued support of his speakership. But most of those legislators failed to press Silver strongly on the matter. A few, like Jeff Aubry, felt strongly. Many others made a show of support, no doubt out of an unwillingness to contest liberal opinion or challenge their more committed colleagues. However, aware that significant elements of their own communities distrusted Rockefeller reform out of fury with the devastation that drug dealers had wreaked on their neighborhoods, they fell short of heartfelt commitment to the effort. Russell Simmons' hip-hop followers had not yet demonstrated any clout at the polls; politicians questioned whether many of them voted at all. So what limited political pressure Silver felt on the issue really came only from a handful of legislators and liberal newspaper editorial boards, like the *Times*.

As soon as discussions appeared to move beyond reforming the A-I law, the District Attorneys Association fought back efficiently and skillfully. The D.A.s had their strongest allies in the Senate. A highly influential Republican, Senator Dale Volker, kept reassuring them that whatever was said publicly, nothing they regarded as terrible would happen. Volker's enormous influence in the Senate, and thus on Joe Bruno, allowed him to provide such reassurance with great credibility. And indeed, nothing much did happen. Every year the debate seemed to be between Pataki and Silver, but at the end they could not produce a law without Bruno, and they did not have him.

Pataki showed true mastery of political choreography in the 2002 election-year version of the dance. He publicized his support of Rockefeller reform so energetically and thoroughly that the average person interested in that debate could not see the lackluster quality of his commitment to the actual negotiations. The general outline of his proposals evolved as the public debate evolved: when reform of the A-I sentences sufficed to garner him publicity as committed to Rockefeller drug law reform, he proposed very little more than that. When he could still get favorable press coverage for proposing judicial discretion for possession offenses alone, he did that. When the press caught wind of the limits of that approach, he added the sale offenses—but always sufficiently short of what the Assembly could accept so that no agreement would emerge. With no agreement, he would avoid fatally antagonizing the prosecutors or his core Republican support among unreconstructed law-and-order advocates.

Pataki maneuvered similarly on replenishing New York's bankrupt toxic cleanup fund and raising the minimum wage. He "supported" both; neither happened. In reaction Michael Long, the chair of New York's Conservative Party and a Pataki supporter, said "I think clearly he's sticking to his core beliefs, which on a lot of issues are conservative," and added, "I think he's positioning himself to win this election." The headline of Richard Perez-Pena's astute article on the front page of the Metro Section of the *Times* on June 27, 2002 said it all: "In Election Year, Thorny Bills Aren't Reaching Pataki's Desk."

Laboring to Produce a Mouse—the 2004 Reforms

The winds of change blew just a little more vigorously late in 2004, a legislative election year. Nothing much happened on any front throughout most of that year's session, except the twentieth consecutive year of late New York State budgets. Failure, again, to resolve the Rockefeller drug law issue or to raise the State's minimum wage seemed to bring disgust with the Legislature to higher levels than ever before. The Brennan Center's conclusion that New York's was the "most dysfunctional" legislature in the nation hit a chord that reverberated in the press throughout the State.

Outside the Legislature, events sent interesting signals on Rockefeller drug law reform. A plea bargain gave an NYU student only a sentence of drug treatment despite her fairly vigorous drug-selling activities on campus. By this time, only the *New York Post* of the four major daily newspapers in New York City continued to support the Rockefeller drug laws. Recognizing now that the sentence for the white, middle-class student gave credence to the argument that the laws worked on a double standard based on "race, class and other subjective factors," the *Post* editorialized, "So why continue the charade? Scrap the Rockefeller laws," and continued, with in its characteristic style, "Little Miss Tokehead's slap on the wrist is a little too much to bear, if equal justice before the law is to mean anything in New York." While it was unclear that the *Post* would firmly maintain this stance, the fact that it took it even temporarily signaled a significant change.

Less than a month later, the sitting District Attorney in Albany, an outspoken defender of the Rockefeller drug laws, lost a Democratic primary to David Soares, the current Albany County District Attorney. Soares chose to make opposition to those laws the centerpiece of his campaign. And in December, the dean of District Attorneys, Robert Morgenthau of Manhattan, at age 85 facing a potentially serious primary the next year, called publicly for reforms that would exclude "less serious drug felonies" from the reach of the Second Felony Offender Law.

After weeks of uncharacteristically quiet negotiations, on December 7, 2004 the Assembly and Senate passed legislation to end life sentences for some Class A drug felons; to reduce sentences slightly for B's; to increase access to the CASAT program; to double merit time taken off sentences for A's and B's, both for inmates already serving time and for future inmates; to double the weight thresholds for AI and AII possession offenses; and to provide for re-sentencing, likely reducing sentences, for about 400 inmates already serving sentences for A felonies. On December 14, 2004, Governor Pataki signed the bill into law.

Critics among reform advocates noted that judges still lacked discretion to award drug treatment to second felons instead of prison, that AI defendants still faced sentences of up to twenty years, that the quantity of drugs in possession rather than the defendant's role in the hierarchy still drove the sentence (so impoverished drug "mules" working out of desperation would more likely get the long sentences than "kingpins," who rarely carry drugs at all), and that the legislation included no additional funding for treatment. Prosecutors complained that the legislation lacked enhanced penalties for kingpins, and that the reduced sentences also reduce the incentive to undergo what may be for some the more difficult alternative of treatment. In response to the complaint that even under the new law New York would still have some of the most draconian sentences in the United States, Senator Volker said, "I think they should be."

Since the new law provided neither for fuller judicial discretion and treatment as an alternative to incarceration on one side, nor enhanced punishment for kingpins on the other, both reform advocates and prosecutors had unfulfilled goals.

Victory 2009

The mid-term elections of 2008 put Democrats narrowly in control of the Senate. As a result this party controlled the governorship, the Assembly, and the Senate for the first time since 1965. Democrats, especially in the Senate, had consistently argued that the Republicans who formerly controlled the body were largely responsible for failure to repeal the Rockefeller Drug Laws. Now they had to deliver. And they did.

On April 24, 2009, Governor David Paterson announced that he had signed into law, as part of the 2009–2010 budget, repeal of the Rockefeller Drug Laws. He said, "With a stroke of the pen, the regime of the Rockefeller Drug Laws will end." Apparently, he had actually signed the changes into law weeks earlier, on April 7, as a small part of Chapter 56 of the Laws of 2009, formerly Assembly Bill 156, Senate bill 56-B.

The core of the reform restored judges' power to send addicted drug offenders to treatment instead of prison. A new part of the Criminal Procedure Law, § 216.00 and § 216.05, permits judges to allow even repeat drug offenders to submit to drug abuse treatment in lieu of prison time, if the offender so chose and met eligibility requirements. These included an evaluation that determines that the offender is indeed addicted, an agreement by the offender to enter a plea of guilty (except under unusual circumstances, particularly when such a plea might trigger deportation) and to abide by the conditions of the program, and a record absent of violent felony offenses. If the offender successfully completed the treatment program, the court might permit the guilty plea to be withdrawn and dismiss the indictment.

While the *Times* reported that the law gave "judges the authority to send first-time non-violent offenders to treatment instead of prison," in fact judges had only been forced to sentence a relatively small number of first-time B-felony offenders to prison under the prior law. The real significance of the changes lay in the discretion they gave judges to deal with repeat offenders. The law also offered potential early release to a number of incarcerated drug offenders estimated at about 2000, three percent of the 60,000 inmates serving time in New York State prisons in

2009. These, too, were mostly second-felony offenders. Though designated "hard-core criminals" by the New York *Post*, they were more likely drug addicts who continued to support their addiction by selling drugs even after their first felony conviction.

The new law drew fierce criticism from both the right and the left. The president of the District Attorneys Association, Staten Island D.A. Daniel Donovan Jr., argued that the pull of addiction needs to be counterbalanced by strong penalties, or else treatment will not work. New York City Police Commissioner Ray Kelly criticized the way the law would work to hide prior convictions from prospective employers. And a *Daily News* editorial quoted an inmate, whose remarks had been taped without his knowledge, as saying

even if you have three or four, no, four or five convictions, you're still eligible for a program, and you know me, I got no sales on my records. All is possessions, so they got to give me a program . . . You know what that means? I'm burnin' the streets up when I go home . . .

For those who believe that the most harmful consequences derive from the criminalization of recreational drug use itself, of course the 2009 revisions did not go far enough. Bob Gangi, executive director of the Correctional Association, noted that judges remain without discretion, even in appropriate circumstances, to ameliorate long sentences for low-level non-violent offenders who are not addicted, and pledged to continue fighting for "full repeal" of the laws requiring such "long and hard prison terms." Randy Credico, as usual, had the most colorful comment, unfair though it might be: "They came up with an agreement to get people to stop complaining. It's not sweeping. It's misleading advertising. These guys may as well be selling used cars."

In fact, well before these drug law changes were passed, and contrary to national trends, crime and incarceration rates in New York had dropped dramatically. The Pew Research Center's "One in 31" report released in 2009, noted:

Between 1997 and 2007, New York experienced both the greatest decrease in violent crime and, simultaneously, the greatest decrease in prison population and incarceration rate of any state in the country. During that decade, the national prison population grew by more than 350,000 inmates, a 28 percent jump that corresponded to a 14 percent increase in the national incarceration rate. Over the same time period, New York's prison population declined by almost 6,500 inmates, a 9.4 percent dip that amounted to a 15 percent drop in the incarceration rate. [Citation omitted.] To the surprise of many at the time, New York's violent crime rate fell a remarkable 40 percent during the decade, while the national violent crime rate dropped by a much smaller measure, 24 percent. In terms of crime and prison contraction, New York led all regions of the country and every individual state. [Citation omitted.]

Suggesting that no further changes were necessary, speaking for the State's District Attorneys, Staten Island D.A. Donovan attributed these changes to the amendments of 2004. "There has been a 43% decrease in the number of felony drug offenders sent to state prison in the past decade," Donovan said, "and a 23% decline in drug felons imprisoned in the past four years."

But the findings of the Pew report, impressive though they were, did not actually demonstrate that Donovan was right that the law at that point had reached the proper balance between fairness and security. Even news sources upstate, where the prison industry was strongest, noted this. The *PressRepublican.com*, billing itself as "the online community and news source for Clinton, Essex, and Franklin Counties of Northeastern New York," counties at the very top of the list for the number of state prisons within them, editorialized that "The State Legislature has decided that Gov. Nelson Rockefeller's oppressive sentencing laws for drug possession were oppressive indeed," and *MPNnow.com*, "the leading news source in suburban Rochester and the Finger Lakes," wrote "Sadly, prisons have been an easy way for legislators to provide well-paying jobs to struggling communities that have watched their factories depart for more business-friendly environs. But it's no real substitute for economic development. Keeping prisons open amid a declining jail population just adds to the cost of state and local governments that already spend and tax too much."

Values in Legislating — No Permanent Friends, No Permanent Adversaries

Senator Dale Volker. Senator Dale Volker was an ally of mine on many of the same issues as the D.A.s, but had strong and principled views in opposition to mine — again in alliance with the D.A.s — on Rockefeller Drug Law Reform. Dale, who had been a police officer before his election to the Legislature, actually voted against the Rockefeller drug laws as a young legislator. He thought that they would be ineffective. But he later became their most vigorous defender. Dale's Senate district, near Buffalo in western New York, included eight big prisons. He typified the low-density rural Republican heartland representative. His constituents wanted new prisons built for the construction jobs and existing prisons full for corrections officer and non-uniformed prison employee jobs, and a continuing stream of prison visitors spending money in local stores and restaurants.

Though Volker is very smart, he was not immune from the subtle process through which people persuade themselves to accept as true what is in their interest to believe. Dale Volker's constituents wanted prisons. The Rockefeller drug laws produced inmates in numbers that continued for many years to justify the creation of prisons. Dale Volker came to believe in the Rockefeller drug laws.

The leading advocate for the restoration of the death penalty in New York, Dale stood more generally for conservative principles, and did so with forceful logic. Regarding the drug laws he argued that reform advocates seriously overestimated their ability to predict that any given drug-offense defendant will remain nonviolent, or indeed, to determine that he or she had been nonviolent.

A conviction of sale-and-possession offenses only in no way guarantees that a person has not in fact committed violent offenses or will not commit them in the future. This view was confirmed for Volker by corrections officers, with many of whom he maintained close relationships, who saw many drug-dealing and/or addicted inmates engaged in sickening violence against officers or other inmates even while in prison. This led Volker to argue that every drug-dealing inmate behind bars reduces the likelihood that an innocent person will suffer victimization by violence, in addition to whatever reduction in the proliferation of illegal drugs such incarceration might achieve.

A *reductio ad absurdum* response to Volker would be that we could reduce the likelihood of violence on the streets still further by incarcerating everyone. But going beyond this, the absence of reliable statistics about how many or what percentage of drug dealers do in fact engage in violent crime at some point in their careers made the argument more difficult. The bottom line was that Dale and I differed in our willingness to use incarceration to reduce risk. For me, the social destruction attributable to excessive incarceration outweighed the benefit of a marginal decrease in violent victimization.

Of course, this conclusion depended on my assessment of the degree of risk. A couple of exaggerated examples illustrate the point. If Dale thought that breaking up thousands of poor black and Latino families and imposing an annual aggregate half-billion dollars of extra tax burden on other citizens prevented just three muggings, he would have opposed the Rockefeller drug laws too. Likewise, if I thought that breaking up a few hundred families and imposing an annual aggregate one hundred thousand dollars of extra tax burden on other citizens prevented a few thousand murders, obviously I would have supported the Rockefeller drug laws. So a difference in our estimation of the facts, not a complete difference in values, underlay our disagreement.

Still, since our appreciation of the facts did not differ so much as these grossly exaggerated illustrations suggest, it is clear that some difference in underlying values contributed to our disagreement as well. Although Dale might disagree with my interpretation of his position, I think that while we both highly value liberty and security, I would sacrifice a little more security for liberty, while he would sacrifice a little more liberty for security. His society might be more orderly, with more people in prison. Mine might have more disorder, but more diversity and freedom—even though all else being equal, I would much prefer an orderly society.

The D.A.s. The District Attorneys' Association fought at my side as my most important ally in many battles, big and small: for use immunity; for the Organized Crime Control Act; for a more effective money-laundering law; for fingerprinting more of the serious juvenile felony offenders; for the Oral Search Warrant Law; and for the Juror Identity Shield Law. Our history of close alliance enabled us to maintain our friendships despite our profound disagreement over the Rockefeller drug laws.

My differences with the district attorneys had complicated roots. Although I came in to the Legislature sharing the general public's attitudes on drug-related crime and punishment, my perceptions began to change in the mid-1980s (as detailed above) under the force of evidence about the invidious consequences of our policies. The prosecutors never conceded that the policies they followed then were wrong. But in fact they changed their policies.

The police ended TNT. Along with the prosecutors, they tried to go after the mid-level dealers more than they did the street crowd. Charles Hynes began DTAP, and other prosecutors followed suit, sending those dealers they thought suitable off to treatment instead of prison (within the limits set not by them, but by the availability of treatment slots). Earned eligibility and shock incarceration, and later CASAT, further reduced prison time served by the less violent, lower-level, apparently corrigible defendants. The Office of Court Administration established "drug courts" specifically intended to direct as many defendants as possible to treatment, rather than prison, subject, of course, to prosecutors' wishes.

By the twenty-first century, prosecutors could argue more plausibly that they already sent anyone appropriate to treatment instead of prison. Furthermore, they used the NACC experience (Rockefeller's Narcotics Addiction Control Commission) and statistical studies to support their argument that drug treatment programs produced much better results, far more completion and far less relapse, when the defendant faced no alternative but prison. The "stick" of a lengthy prison sentence, they argued, gave them immensely valuable leverage in persuading defendants to enter treatment instead.

As did Volker, the prosecutors sincerely believed the arguments they made against Rockefeller reform—and some of their arguments had validity. But self-interest has great persuasive power for everyone. Prosecutors seemed to have two interests in this matter. First, no one likes to give up power. To return discretion to judges meant taking it away from prosecutors. Second, the "need" to prosecute large numbers of drug defendants helps to justify having large numbers of prosecutors. Especially with crime rates falling, a further reduction in the number of defendants to be sent to prison might well start editorial boards, if not legislators, thinking about reducing prosecutorial budgets—and in 2003, the State and New York City did indeed reduce their budgets anyway.

According to the prosecutors, judges historically demonstrated their tendency to let too many offenders evade prison, and the Office of Court Administration, the central authority for New York judges, exacerbated the situation by pressing judges to reduce caseloads. Only they themselves, the prosecutors, faced the right set of pressures to ensure public safety. First and most important, elected District Attorneys had to face voters who would punish them if they let dangerous criminals escape punishment. But also, the workloads prosecutors faced would suffice to dissuade them from seeking unduly harsh sentences for those defendants who did not deserve them. They had enough to do to get appropriate sentences for those who needed them, they claimed; they had no time to waste seeking unnecessarily harsh sentences.

Arguments matter. Certainly these had merit. Had they been less persuasive, prosecutors' political clout alone might not have made their lobbying as effective as it was for years against any significant changes in the Rockefeller drug laws.

Nonetheless, for me the problem with the case the prosecutors made was in its premise. In our Anglo-American legal system, prosecutors argue for one side, defense attorneys for the other. We assign to judges the ultimate decision-making role. For their part, lawmakers should not legislate on the premise that any participants in the process will do their jobs badly. If a judge makes poor decisions, replace the judge; don't change the law to take decision-making away from judges.

We expect independence of judges. That is why we provide unlimited tenure to appointed federal judges, and lengthy terms of office to most state judges, elected or appointed. The greater responsiveness to the electorate expected of prosecutors provides precisely the reason that they should not act as ultimate decision-makers.

These considerations all concern matters of degree. Of course, prosecutors must exercise considerable control over the process. The decision to prosecute or not itself carries enormous significance for the life of the defendant. So do the decisions on whether to charge a mere misdemeanor or a felony, and/or the degree of felony charged. No one denies the propriety of the prosecutor's control over those decisions.

But judges are supposed to judge: to take into account the individual facts and considerations special to each case. Legislators cannot anticipate every circumstance that may be relevant to the appropriate disposition of a case. Mandatory sentencing removes an important part of this core judicial function.

A sentence—prison, or an alternative such as drug abuse treatment—settles an allocation of society's resources, as well as a balance between one individual's freedom and the safety of the public. Anglo-American jurisprudence generally counsels that such settlement power be left to the judiciary. In a way, my value conflict with the prosecutors repeated my conflict with Dale Volker, as a clash between liberty and security. In another sense, though, one could characterize this conflict more accurately as between fairness (due process) on my side, and representativeness—pursuing the perceived interests of the majority—on the prosecutors' side.

Americans designed our judicial system to maximize fairness, not representativeness. My disagreement with the District Attorneys Association rested largely on my perception that the Rockefeller drug laws skew the judicial system the wrong way.

In rebuttal, the prosecutors often pointed out that no one particularly complained that the Second Felony Offender Law prevented judges from letting repeat felony murderers or robbers evade a prison term. The very lack of controversy on that score, however, reflected the fact that the Second Felony Offender Law imposes no serious limitation on what judges might want to do in *those* cases anyway, even if in principle judicial discretion should not be limited there either. By contrast, judges often complained about unfair sentences they were forced to impose by the Rockefeller drug laws. Although they usually complained only about the A-I's, unfairness imposed by other aspects of those laws most likely simply flew below the radar—that is, were too common and too low-level to merit comment.

Logic and Experience. Oliver Wendell Holmes, Jr. famously observed, in a far different context, that the life of the law is experience, not logic. As the new century began, prosecutors were sending 7,000 defendants to treatment every year rather than to prison. The Department of Corrections, under many of the laws we had helped to institute, was releasing many more into treatment after shortened prison stays in Shock or CASAT. Despite the Pataki administration's increase in parole revocation rates and decrease in parole release rate, New York's prison population, at long last, finally began to drop. By July 2006, the State prison population was down to 63,493 from its peak of about 72,000 at the beginning of the year 2000. (By January 1, 2008, at the beginning of the second year of the Spitzer administration, the population had dropped further, to 62,599.)

The State's budget troubles, the emergence of Islamic terrorists as a new external enemy to replace the Communists, or any number of factors were chosen by partisans of one theory or another to explain the decrease in crime. An article in the *Quarterly Journal of Economics* in 2002 even attributed the decline in crime to the legalization of abortion in the early 1970s, reducing the population of 18-to-20-year-olds, those most prone to violent crime.

Maybe the fever just broke. Physicians sometimes say that they can cure 10 percent of patients, another 10 percent cannot be cured, and the remaining 80 percent will get better by themselves. But I'd like to think our efforts had some role in ameliorating the problems that enabled New York's addiction to prison building.

While we battled unsuccessfully for the headline issue, "Rockefeller drug law reform," our quiet, un-dramatic, low-profile changes in police, prosecution, and prison procedures freed through the back door many of the low-level nonviolent addicted defendants the Rockefeller laws would otherwise have incarcerated through the front door. When in 2004 the Legislature enacted some degree of front-door reform, and the headline came, even the Senate and Assembly called the result "Partial Reform" in their press releases, and the contents satisfied few.

"Life is what happens while you are making other plans." Maybe reform is too. But those who call the 2009 "reform" legislation "repeal" have a much stronger argument than those who so designated the earlier legislation. The 2009 law will mean no prison time for some and less prison time for others. Although sometimes that will probably be a bad thing, on balance it will almost certainly result in less social disruption. Even if its enactment were merely symbolic, however, by sealing the long effort with a heralded victory, it brought important hope and encouragement to every other long and weary march on behalf of major policy change in New York.

Beating the Leadership, Winning in the Courts: Sex Offenders and Megan's Law

In my office, the basic criminal justice legislation came from me—bills giving police and prosecutors stronger legal tools, or bills designed to ensure fairer treatment for defendants. Likewise, I initiated our First Amendment-related bills, our education bills, and our bills for tenants, homeowners, drivers, and subway riders.

But when it came to crime victims' issues, environmental issues, information privacy issues, consumer issues generally, Mindy Bockstein spearheaded the effort. The law required us to introduce them in my name, but I thought of them as Mindy's bills, and they were.

Mindy Bockstein: The Importance of Staff.

Done well, the job of a state legislator is really the equivalent of several full-time jobs. Maintaining the visibility necessary for re-election requires presence in the home district every week—sometimes, every day. Diligent attention to constituent demands requires long hours on the telephone with government officials. Creative legislating takes research and careful drafting. Responsible voting requires the review of thousands of bills each year. Only if supported by good staff work may a member begin to meet all these responsibilities.

I judged my staff's performance in accord with the expectations I had of myself when I was a staffer, first for Elizabeth Holtzman when she was in Congress and later for (then) Assemblyman Charles Schumer.

My responsibility, I thought, was to get the job done perfectly, no matter what it took. When I uncovered the Summer Food Program scandal for Holtzman in 1976—me and two other staff members against hundreds of canny thieves stealing tens of millions of dollars—my usual 9:00 A.M. to 11 P.M. workdays were supplemented by a weekly allnighter throughout the summer. (I found that a 6-mile run at 7 A.M. would allow me to work through the next day without sleeping. I was 27 years old. This would not work now.) When I worked for Schumer, the one time I thought I had slipped up (in fact, I had not) Schumer was more alarmed by my suddenly-green complexion than by the possibility of error.

Some of my Assembly staff worked hard and effectively. No one met or exceeded my benchmark, though, until a professor at Brooklyn College I knew sent over one of his graduate students, Mindy Bockstein, for a semester internship in my Brooklyn neighborhood office.

At first I was oblivious. A year after she joined us, Mindy was still interning. She seemed good, so we had asked her to extend her stay. On the other hand, my legislative director in Albany confused me. She seemed to handle some matters superbly and others so abominably that I found it hard to believe the same person was at work. In fact, the same person wasn't. Anything she did well Mindy (still an intern) had told her how to do over the phone from Brooklyn. The rest she did herself.

Mindy didn't breathe a word of this. When I finally figured it out, I asked Mindy to take over as legislative director. Mindy's staff work wasn't just good, it was phenomenal. Years later, after I gave a talk on Megan's Law at a professional conference in Seattle, a member of the audience approached me. ""You're from New York, right?" he asked. "Do you know Mindy Bockstein?" I allowed as how I did. "Well," he said, "I've been in this field for more than twenty-five years, and she knows more about it than I do!" Showing mercy, I refrained from explaining to him that experts in a dozen different fields had conveyed essentially the same message to me over the years.

Mindy's thoroughness and tenacity became legendary in the Albany world of legislation. Her regular ninety-hour work weeks combined with her extraordinary intelligence to produce an amazing work product. Although my schedule took me to innumerable meetings of community organizations in Brooklyn and of lobbying groups in Albany, we were together during our three-to-four hour drives or car-service-and-train rides from Brooklyn to Albany and back each week. During these we would brainstorm on policy and legislation nonstop, unless I was sleeping. (I slept only on the train, not when I drove; Mindy didn't drive.) After the first few years our ability to read each other's minds and finish each other's sentences on the basis of very few clues or words stopped surprising us.

Mindy first got us involved in crime victim issues after meeting with the families of victims of drunk drivers. Later she personally established the first chapter of Mothers Against Drunk Driving (MADD) in Brooklyn. Gradually, as the years progressed and we earned the confidence of crime victim advocates, we broadened our participation in the field to include legislation sought by victims of gun, domestic, and sexual violence.

Inside Politics Yields to Outside Politics: Sex Offenders and the Press Explosion

By 1994 Mindy Bockstein had established relationships with the National Center for Missing and Exploited Children as well as with the parents of some children who had been murdered by sexual predators. They urged her to consider legislation requiring that after serving their prison sentences, or in some cases if they had served sentences of probation only, sex offenders' names and addresses be kept in registries accessible to local police departments.

Mindy agreed. The evidence they presented convinced her that access to such registries significantly aided police in solving sex crimes more quickly by apprehending perpetrators whose localities and patterns of criminal behavior were known to them. If the police caught them more quickly, the perpetrators would have less opportunity to commit additional crimes.

The precedent of creating, in essence, a class of permanent suspects made me uncomfortable. The furor that sex offenses generated made me nervous that public hysteria could result in some unjust and oppressive use of a registry of sex offenders.

Mindy and I argued it out over a long car ride back to Brooklyn. She won.

The Speaker and the Agenda: Control, Opportunity and Opportunism. Throughout 1994 Mindy argued with Codes Committee staff, attempting to overcome their objections the way she had overcome mine. But with them, superior arguments on the merits did not assure success.

The Speaker of the Assembly likes to shape the legislative agenda for the year. He has a notion of the general picture he wants to present to the world. When he must, he will bow to political necessity and make alterations in that picture. For Stanley Fink and Mel Miller, the will of the Democratic Conference constituted political necessity. Fink usually controlled that will; Miller usually anticipated it. But Sheldon Silver tended to prevent the Conference from articulating its will, often announcing Assembly initiatives to the press prior even to briefing the Conference.

Under Silver, the will of the Speaker *became* the will of the Conference.

Silver had no intention of enacting a sex offender registration law in 1994. Moreover, if he were to choose to do so it would be under conditions *he* chose: time, manner, and sponsorship. The fact that Dan Feldman thought such a bill should be enacted in 1994 hardly mattered.

Here, again, earlier speakers operated somewhat differently. Speakers Fink and Miller rarely put their names on bills. While from time to time they conferred attractive bills on members who they thought needed some political help, they tended generally to respect initiatives members had personally cultivated. So if they intended that a bill would actually become law, they wouldn't steal the idea for the bill from the legislator who had initiated it, for the benefit of another legislator.

Fink especially, and Miller to an extent, understood that creative legislators would be difficult to control legislators. Miller had not forgotten our pitched public battles, but he made me Corrections Chair anyway because he knew I would bring energy and imagination to the job.

An alternative approach was to appoint committee chairs who could be relied upon to do the Speaker's bidding. Under this paradigm, the less independence a legislator displayed, the more eligible he or she was for a key committee chairmanship. I made more than enough trouble as Corrections chair; surely I would not be rewarded with an even more powerful committee.

Joe Lentol read the signals in a way that would justify Silver's confidence in him as Codes chair. He received no signal from the Speaker to report the bill, so it fell to Codes staff to invent any excuse they could, preferably plausible, in response to Mindy's queries. So despite her entreaties, and ultimately mine as well, sex offender registration never emerged from the Codes Committee in 1994.

But then something happened that pulled the cork from the bottle.

A Defining Event Resets the Agenda. During the summer of 1994, a sex offender named Jesse Timmendequas sexually abused and murdered a seven-year-old New Jersey girl named Megan Kanka. The press had highlighted earlier cases, but with the Kanka case the issue reached critical mass. The issue now generated intense nationwide coverage, and the nation exploded with outrage. New Jersey quickly enacted not just a sex offender registration statute but one that included in it a community notification provision as well.

We had considered community notification. The Codes staff had encouraged us to keep tinkering with registry provisions, dangling before us the possibility that some formulation might eventually satisfy them. But these would merely create a record for the use of the police. Such a provision would be helpful in rapidly identifying likely suspects, but it was crystal clear from staff that community notification, a measure that goes much further to expedite identification of likely suspects, but exposed sex offenders to wider hostility, would take the bill completely off the radar screen, absolutely killing any chance of approval by the Codes Committee.

Then in response to the Megan Kanka case, Speaker Silver told the press that he, for one, was committed to the enactment of a sex offender community notification bill. With avoidance and delay no longer options, via a single public statement he sought to take ownership of the issue.

Dean Skelos, the Senate Republican (later the Majority Leader) with whom I had sponsored a number of bills to protect children, reacted with fury, and so did I. After handing us excuse after excuse to avoid enacting our much milder bill, Silver was now claiming to support the stronger bill we had not dared to introduce. We resented this self-protective but disingenuous effort to ride the "new" issue, and take it away from us.

I sent a letter to the *Times* applauding Silver's commitment but questioning, in view of his apparent support, why he had failed to enact the Feldman/Skelos bill during the previous session.

Silver, whom I have never heard raise his deep bass voice or otherwise engage in an outward show of anger, must have been very angry. No matter what provocation I had, he must have felt that nothing could justify this public attack on the leader of my own party in my own House. In his next public comment on the subject, he let it be known that he would enact a sex offender registry with community notification, but it would be "a better bill" than mine.

Community Notification

Meanwhile, the stakes had been raised. Now I had to commit myself to community notification as well as to a registry.

Americans laughed at Claude Rains's quick shift of allegiances or priorities when he protected Humphrey Bogart by ordering his police staff to "round up the usual suspects" in *Casablanca*. But notification laws create a permanent class of usual suspects not only for police purposes, but for the public as well. This conflicts with a very deep-seated American commitment to the notion of rehabilitation, based (perhaps) on fundamental religious beliefs in redemption. The belief that a person can be cleansed or renewed generated passionate support for at least five different arguments against notification laws:

1. sex offenders can be cured using appropriate treatment, so we do not need to warn the public;
2. sex offenders do not have particularly high recidivism rates, therefore, the danger they pose to neighbors is exaggerated, as is the cost of withholding notification;
3. notification does not enhance community safety, so there is no reason to sacrifice equality for what is merely the illusion of enhanced security;
4. strangers rarely commit sex offenses, therefore notification does not warn likely victims of the real sources of danger; and
5. offenders will either refuse to register or else flee to another jurisdiction to avoid registration.

In sum, critics claimed that community notification neither aided police nor inhibited potential recidivists, instead fueling out-of-control harassment by self-appointed vigilantes and scaring offenders into avoiding registration altogether.

These arguments appeared to be inconsistent with statistical evidence available at the time. Certainly in 1995, despite self-serving claims by various treatment providers, and wishful thinking by those who hoped to avoid the values conflict, the overwhelming weight of credible evidence supported the conclusion that no treatment program then available provided statistically reliable assurance of results. Others offended by notification laws tried to downplay the likelihood of recidivism. But unlike other criminals, sex offenders are not less likely to repeat their crimes as they age. The mere passage of time does not render sex offenders less dangerous.

Those who claimed notification had no useful impact also ignored the results of experience. By 1995, Washington State had had enough experience with its notification laws (enacted in 1990) to demonstrate that such laws provide some protection for communities against previously convicted sex offenders. The laws enabled Washington police to apprehend sex offenders after their first new offense, rather than following the sixth or seventh offense subsequent to release. Citizens alerted to an offender's presence can help shorten the time it takes police to identify a suspect after a new offense occurs. This can cut days or weeks off of an investigation, thereby preventing the offender from completing what might otherwise have been a series of attacks.

In some cases, when neighbors recognized a known offender loitering around a schoolyard or in a basement laundry room of an apartment house, they were able to notify police early enough to avert any new offense. Washington State also found that released sex offenders subject to the notification law tended to be arrested for less serious new offenses, such as "communicating with a minor for immoral purposes" rather than rape. Thus the Washington data showed clearly that while sex offenders generally continue to commit new crimes, the notification law reduced both the number and the seriousness of new offenses.

California began to use a 900 telephone number information line on registered sex offenders in July 1995. Before 1996, almost 300 of the more than 3,500 calls made to it produced positive identifications of registered child molesters. Those identifications included a non-teaching employee at a school, a man looking for a job photographing children, the coach of a "12 and under" girls volleyball team, a day-care center employee, and many other persons in positions that placed children at risk.

Perhaps the most important criticism of our proposed law complained that since relatives and "friends" commit between three-quarters and nine-tenths of child sexual abuse, Megan's Law focused on the wrong population. However, to the extent that Megan's Law reduced the risk of such abuse by the one-tenth to one-quarter of the perpetrators who are strangers, it performed a valuable function. Furthermore, when relatives and "friends" are caught and convicted, community awareness that their names are on the list will also have some salutary effect.

And Megan's Law applies to sex offenders who attack adults as well as children. Washington State statistics showed that "dangerous strangers" accounted for 30 percent of sex offenders as a group, and had almost twice the recidivism rate of those who committed crimes against relatives or others known to them. A 1994 federal Justice Department study found that strangers attacked 44 percent of females over the age of eleven who were victims of rape or attempted rape.

Those critics who based their opposition on the contention that notification requirements encouraged flight or refusal to comply had little evidentiary support. Studies showed that community pressure provided by notification actually reinforces the offender's own efforts at restraint. While the professional testimony I heard to this effect was a bit denatured, the message was vividly brought home by the sex offender who called in to a talk show I was doing. He said on the air that he personally would find Megan's Law helpful in attempting to curb his own dangerous impulses. In any event, flight would become a non-issue as soon as Congress acted on its intention to encourage national notification. Finally, Washington State statistics showed the mythical nature of the "noncompliance" argument. There compliance rates, as opposed to flight, exceeded 70 percent even when Washington was the *only* state with such a law.

The Legislator's Need to Be Consistent. Largely on the basis of Mindy's work, I had become the leading legislator in Albany during the early days of the information privacy movement. With my legislation, New York became the first state to ban carbon copies of credit card receipts, filched by thieves to steal identity information and then to make extensive purchases in the true cardholder's name. We prohibited merchants from requiring customers to provide social security numbers and other personal information on checks or for credit card transactions. Most merchants wanted the personal information to sell to telemarketers or database companies or use for further marketing themselves, not for financial protection. When the credit card issuer authorized the transaction, the merchant obtained all the financial protection he or she needed. I had a lot more information privacy bills in the pipeline, including the statewide do-not-call registry, which became law under other legislators' names in 2001, and evolved into the national do-not-call registry in 2003.

Sexual offender registration and community notification opened us up to charges of inconsistency. We were, it was alleged, dramatically attacking the privacy of a category of persons who had "already paid for their crimes." This charge raised a fundamental difference between advocates and legislators. Advocates can be purists advancing a single dominant value, following it wherever it takes them. Legislators must balance equities.

Here a reasonable balance of values justified our position. Privacy, as people usually use the word, means many things: freedom from observation or publication of one's more embarrassing behavior or characteristics; freedom from intrusive or annoying communications via telephone, mail, or computer; security against crimes such as blackmail, identity fraud, or larceny by fraud on the basis of what one expects to be private and/or personal information.

But privacy, arising out of fundamental commitment to liberty and security, is not an absolute value. When courts convict people of crimes in public session those convicted have no traditional legally cognizable expectation of privacy with respect to the facts on which their convictions were based. The public has always had access to records of criminal convictions. Those convicted of crimes pay a penalty that includes some degree of sacrifice of privacy; we were incrementally altering the balance of values by making this information more available. American society ideally attempts to enhance security fairly, depriving citizens who have done crimes of their privacy and other goods only constitutionally, through the due process of law.

Making Megan's Law Constitutionally Sound, or, You Have to Know the Law to Write the Law

In writing Megan's law we were entering into a constitutional thicket. Questions of constitutionality gave me serious concern. When assuming public office, politicians take oaths to support the Constitution of the United States and (if it is a state post) the state constitution as well. While some legislators felt that they could properly leave questions of constitutionality to the courts, to me my oath to support the Constitution meant that I could not in good conscience vote for, much less introduce, legislation that I thought unconstitutional. This became a challenge in addressing sex offender registration and community notification.

The most serious objection to sex offender registration and notification statutes (Megan's Laws) arises from the U.S. Constitution's Ex Post Facto prohibition. The public wanted protection against convicted sex offenders, those who committed their offenses before the new statute would take effect or even before its enactment, and who had already been released. Under the Ex Post Facto prohibition, no statute enacted after a person has been convicted can impose a new punishment on him or her.

In addition to raising the Ex Post Facto prohibition, challengers to Megan's Law alleged actual or potential violations of constitutional prohibitions against:

- unreasonable search and seizure of fingerprints and photographs;
- denial of equal protection of the law;
- cruel and unusual punishment;
- double jeopardy;
- bills of attainder;
- invasion of privacy (by virtue of government disclosure of certain types of information to the public); and
- violations of procedural due process.

Regarding the Ex Post Facto concern, the question turned upon whether a Megan's Law constituted punishment. Under the Constitution, legislatures may impose burdens on citizens so long as those burdens do not newly punish previously sentenced criminals. If these burdens were not to be classified as punishment, they must do no more than necessary to achieve legitimate, non-punitive social goals.

Once the Ex Post Facto hurdle was passed, most of the other constitutional challenges to registration requirements were easily met. For example, courts typically ruled that a statutory requirement for sex offenders to provide fingerprints and a photograph in the registration process was not a "search." This is true even if the class of persons to whom the law applies is broad. Because registration and notification are not "punishment," arguments failed as well when based upon prohibitions against cruel and unusual punishment, double jeopardy, or bills of attainder.

There was a relatively small issue with privacy. If community notification constitutes an invasion of privacy, it may implicate a liberty interest, which justifies an inquiry as to whether the statute provides adequate procedural due process. After our bill became law, the courts found that we had failed to provide adequate procedures to safeguard the rights of those defendants who did not receive prison time. The courts simply and easily imposed a remedy for that minor deficiency, an inadvertent error on our part, adding judicial review of the determination by the Board we had established to ascertain the defendant's degree of dangerousness and thus his or her registration and notification level. But overall, the courts generally found favor with our inclusion of the offender's right to a court hearing prior to any final order of classification, of the attendant right to counsel, right to subsequent appeal, and limits on notification enforced by criminal and civil sanctions.

The Ex Post Facto Question: The Precedents. The courts have used a variety of tests to determine whether the burdens imposed by a statute constitute punishment. They ask whether the burden has an alternative purpose rationally assigned to it, other than as a criminal penalty, and seek to determine whether the burden is excessive relative to that alternative purpose. A long line of decisions now establishes the government's right to place burdens on citizens when such burdens are incidental to legitimate regulatory goals, independent of punishment. Such burdens can be as heavy as, for example, preventive detention. But the guidance provided for lawmakers by judicial precedent based upon vastly different statutes and explicit factual conditions is rarely perfectly clear.

Serious analysis of how to weigh the burden usually begins with *De Veau v. Braisted*, 363 U.S. 144, a 1960 Supreme Court decision upholding a New York law barring convicted felons from serving as officers or agents of unions, on penalty of prohibiting the collection of dues by the unions who employed them. One felon, who had been convicted prior to the enactment of the statute, argued that his consequent suspension as an officer of a union was an additional, *ex post facto* punishment. The Supreme Court rejected this claim because the Legislature's goal had been to regulate the waterfront, not to impose further punishment on already-convicted felons. Any additional burdens it placed on them were merely incidental to the statute's real purpose.

Our bill easily met the *De Veau* test. Its purpose was not to punish sex offenders, but to enhance community safety.

In 1989, in *United States v. Halper*, 490 U.S. 435, the Supreme Court expanded its inquiry beyond the question of the statute's purpose to look at the statute's actual effect. This case concerned a defendant previously convicted of false Medicare claims that netted him an overpayment of $585. After his conviction, the United States sued him for $130,000, or $2,000 for each of the sixty-five counts on which he was convicted. The government claimed that its remedial purpose for the statute was to compensate the government for its costs.

The amount for which the government sued, however, exceeded more than 220 times the government's damages. Thus it could not "fairly be said solely to serve a remedial purpose, but rather can only be explained as also serving either retributive or deterrent purposes." On that basis, the Court agreed with the defendant that the excess part of the sanction constituted impermissible double jeopardy. The Court did not convey the idea that if any sanction served any purpose in addition to a remedial one, such a sanction must therefore be deemed punishment. Rather, the Court merely rejected the government's allegation that the fine imposed was "*solely* to serve a remedial purpose." (Later, after the governor signed New York's bill into law and the Legal Aid Society challenged its constitutionality, the trial judge based his decision in part on a gross misinterpretation of this language from *Halper*, as will be related below.)

Another line of cases examined the historical role of the sanction applied in determining whether a statute imposes punishment. In the leading case of that kind, *Austin v. United States*, 509 U.S. 602, the Supreme Court in 1993 refused to permit the government to seize, in forfeiture, the mobile home and automobile repair shop of a defendant as compensation for the government's investigative expenses in connection with his prosecution and conviction for a drug offense. Based on the historical role of forfeiture in law enforcement, the Supreme Court held it was punishment.

Nonetheless, in two subsequent cases the Supreme Court appeared to move away from, or at least to complicate, its application of a sanction's history to the question. In 1994, in *Department of Revenue v. Kurth Ranch*, 511 U.S. 767, the Court held that imposing a tax on the sale of illegal drugs levied subsequent to a defendant's conviction for such sales constituted punishment under the Double Jeopardy Clause. Taxes were not historically viewed as punishment, but the Supreme Court saw the levy of this tax on illegal drugs as pure punishment.

The following year, a California statute made certain inmates ineligible for annual parole suitability hearings. Historically, deprivation of a degree of eligibility for parole has been considered a form of punishment. The Supreme Court, in *California Department of Corrections v. Morales*, 514 U.S. 499, however, rejected an Ex Post Facto challenge to the statute, since the plaintiff-inmate's chance of winning parole was slim.

Finally, in *United States v. Ursery*, 518 U.S. 267, the Supreme Court in 1996 effectively did away with the *historical* role of the burden as a criterion for determining whether it was punishment.

Concomitantly, in *W.P. v. Poritz*, 931 F. Supp. 1139, the New Jersey Federal District Court that same year met the historical argument head-on and rejected the efforts of Megan's Law opponents to attack it by equating it with older "scarlet letter" laws. First, the court noted that the colonial branding or letter laws themselves had the remedial purpose of warning communities of the danger posed by offenders likely to recidivate. In rejecting the comparison of Megan's Law with the older laws, the court noted that while public shaming, opprobrium, ostracism, and punishment were intended and inevitable parts of the colonial sanctions, they were neither intended nor inevitable under Megan's Law. There was certainly no historical counterpart for the procedural due process afforded to offenders by the New Jersey Supreme Court and thus by judicial ruling incorporated into the New Jersey law.

In any case, the New Jersey District Court noted that it could not very well invalidate as unconstitutional all efforts to warn communities about dangerous offenders, or it would have to throw out wanted posters, television's "America's Most Wanted" show, and the statutorily required notification of victims upon offenders' "possible parole, escape, furlough, or any other form of release" under New Jersey law. Thus, the historical approach reinforced the conclusion that Megan's Law did not impose "punishment" for purposes of the Ex Post Facto prohibition.

Our Draft. While some of these decisions did not emerge until 1996, they reflected legal principles already clear enough as Mindy and I were writing our version of Megan's Law. Mindy did most of the drafting herself, but we spent some late nights rewriting and revising together. (Senator Skelos's able aides Tracy Lloyd and John Conway contributed as well.)

We paid particular attention to the New Jersey State courts' criticism of that State's Megan's Law, which had already been enacted. Those courts essentially rewrote the New Jersey Legislature's bill in order to impose judicial review of "dangerousness" classifications, which determined the level of community notification, if any, prior to such notification. We wanted to ensure that our bill would meet any constitutional test, first because I imposed that standard on myself; second, to take the "unconstitutional" argument away from opponents in my own House; and third, so that our bill, should it become law, would not be invalidated by the courts.

The New Jersey Legislature had drafted its statute in such a way that police could believe they had a responsibility to leaflet and poster communities with pictures of offenders. Although at the time we drafted the New York statute the courts had not yet thrown out those New Jersey provisions, they were under challenge. I thought that if they were not unconstitutional, they should be. We therefore drafted the New York statute to make such activity an unauthorized use of information, punishable as a misdemeanor. Thus, what was arguably mandated in New Jersey was prohibited in New York, illustrating again a great strength of our federal system, learning in one state from the experience of another.

The basic provisions of the New York law would require most types of sex offenders, upon release or upon sentencing to probation, to register periodically and report changes in their home address to the State Division of Criminal Justice Services (DCJS), or be liable for a misdemeanor for a first offence. It would permit public officials to alert individuals and communities to the presence of certain sex offenders in those communities. The bill categorized offenses either as sex offenses or as sexually violent offenses, depending on the degree of violence. The registry at DCJS would keep on file the offender's name, aliases if any, address, date of birth, gender, height, weight, race, eye color, driver's license number if any, photograph, fingerprints, description of the offense of conviction and date of conviction, and sentence imposed. A Board of Examiners of Sex Offenders would attempt to assess dangerousness, defined as the individual's likelihood of recidivism and the likely degree of harm if such re-offense were to take place, using factors including the nature of the current offense and previous offenses, post-offense behavior, and post-release plans including supervision, work, and home.

The offender would be assigned to one of three classification levels, depending on the dangerousness assessment. The higher the level, the more information the system would make available about the offender in question. Offenders could challenge their classifications in court before and after the fact, appear and be heard, and have counsel appointed, if necessary. Every offender could petition the court for relief from any or all of the statute's requirements, upon a showing of good cause. We explicitly imposed civil penalties, in addition to existing criminal penalties, on those who abuse offenders, utilizing information acquired under the statute. We were guided by the principle that the statute should provide *access* to information; it should not call for the *mandatory* dissemination of information.

Under our law, designees at levels one and two must register annually for ten years. For level one designees (the least serious sex offender classification), DCJS notifies the police department in the community in which the offender resides but neither the police nor DCJS may permit further access to the information. (Note, however, that the most minor sex offenses, like public lewdness, do not fall under Megan's Law at all.)

For level two designees, law enforcement may choose to alert local institutions of the presence of an offender to whom their populations might be particularly vulnerable. Thus, a day care center could be alerted to the presence of a child molester, or a senior citizen center to the presence of one who tends to prey on the elderly. The institution may choose to further disseminate the information to its clients or, if appropriate, to their guardians. Actually, with regard to this provision, the statute constrained rather than expanded existing practices. Prior to the enactment of the law, parole officials in New York supplied information about sex offenders to local school boards. These boards could then give the information to the public in any manner they saw fit. DCJS must make information concerning level three designees, "sexually violent predators," available through a subdirectory arranged by county and zip code, to be provided to police departments throughout the State. Individuals may inspect the directory upon written request, after supplying reasons. The subdirectory includes much of the file information, including addresses and photographs. Level three designees must register quarterly for life, in person, unless a court grants a petition for relief.

Callers to the 900 telephone number may obtain information about designees at any level. However, callers are told only that a level one designee appears in the registry. Callers must first provide information to identify the offender, have the caller's own telephone number, name and address recorded, and be assessed a fee for the call. Citizens who obtained such information might publicize it as they saw fit, unless they harass offenders, or otherwise abuse the information obtained under the statute's aegis.

Therefore, from a theoretical legal perspective, our statute would impose little or no negative impact on offenders. Conviction records of adults (the statute would only apply to adults) have always been open to the public through the courts. In 1995, at the time of our drafting efforts, any citizen for a fee of $16 could get from New York's Office of Court Administration a computerized criminal history of any other citizen living in the state's thirteen most populous counties, including sentences, fines, and any other case dispositions. Citizens making the application needed to supply only the subject citizen's name and date of birth. They could obtain the latter from the State Department of Motor Vehicles as part of the record available from that Department merely upon submission of the name and five dollars. On that meager basis, neighbors could learn the color and make of the local sex offender's car, his date of birth, eye color, restrictions on driver's license, whether the license had been revoked or suspended, a list of the offender's accidents and traffic convictions during the prior three years, the nature of the penalties imposed, and whether the offenses constituted felonies, misdemeanors, or violations.

Moreover, anyone could—and still can—attend a trial, sketch the defendant and take notes about the most inflammatory charges, print the sketch, the notes, the color and make of the offender's car, and his address on a poster, and then exhibit the poster all over town. Citizens could do all of this prior to—and without any need for—Megan's Law.

The new statute would save citizens the trouble of attending trials, spending hundreds of hours searching through court records to compile lists of offenders, and paying the Department of Motor Vehicles and the Office of Court Administration for requested information. Still, even in the absence of the law, businesses had paid database information companies to perform such services (and still do), conceivably raising the possibility of an equal protection claim against the state by impoverished citizens were a state to *refuse* to enact a notification law.

Inside Politics/Outside Politics: Battling the Speaker

While we were carefully drafting the bill to meet constitutional standards, we had an altogether different battle to win: overcoming the Speaker's antipathy to *any* sex offender registration and notification bill we might put forward, no matter what the content.

Normally, people assume that reality creates perception: something happens, so people see it. In politics, perception often creates reality: people see something, so it happens. Thus, people *see* a politician as having power, or they imagine it, so they contribute campaign money or in other ways help that person, hoping to curry favor. As a result of their help, and with lots of other people ready and willing to do that politician's bidding, now that politician really does have power.

Getting the Media's Attention. Statewide or citywide public officials automatically attract significant amounts of press attention. Upstate legislators are major figures in their communities; few seemed to have much trouble getting their activities covered by their local media. In New York City it is different. The city is a world capital of business, commerce, sport, education, entertainment, and culture. There is just too much going on, and too many celebrities in every field of endeavor competing for coverage, for there to be much media space left for any one of the City's (then) 65 Assembly members, 26 state senators, or even its 13 Members of Congress. New York City politicians, therefore, must constantly struggle for press coverage.

Getting media attention is essential both for moving legislation, and for advancing in political life. Publicity can move a particular proposal front and center, even if it has significant opposition. Contributors give money to those they see on television and read about. Those that they see from media coverage are on the rise. People are far more likely to vote for persons whose names they know. The question, again, is one of balance. Politicians, like others, have only a finite amount of time at their disposal. You hope for synergy, great publicity generated from advancing good policy.

With the speaker opposed, we had to get attention for our draft of Megan's law. We had to give it visibility, to make it the focus of attention and expectations in the capital and across the state. To have any chance of passage, we had to create a perception of desirability and inevitability. If the bill merely languished in the Codes Committee, crime victim advocates, fellow legislators, and editorial writers would assume it was going nowhere. Either they would turn their attention to other matters, or they might look for another vehicle to create sex offender registration and notification.

Our first effort to do so, my letter to *The New York Times*, appeared at the end of August 1994, two months after the legislative session ended and right after the massive press coverage of Megan Kanka's murder. I wrote, "we are puzzled why our bill did not pass the Assembly during the last session in light of the murders of Polly Klaas and Amanda Weigert," two other young victims whose deaths had also received considerable publicity, although not nearly so much as Megan Kanka's.

This first effort had mixed results, coming as it did after Speaker Silver's comments, quoted in the press, that he supported sex offender registration and notification. Within a week, the *Times* reported Silver's response: that Silver planned to introduce his own bill, "stronger legislation" than the Skelos-Feldman bill. The article also quoted me, though, noting that "my leadership"—Silver's henchmen—"gave me a clear message that my bill was too strong and I should work on a compromise." This further attack on Silver's credibility surely did nothing to soften his feelings.

Note that we were using the media not only to build support in the public but to talk with each other. The Speaker was telling me that I was going to be cut out of the action in this important, high-visibility area after I had worked long and hard on it. I was telling him that I was not going to go down without a fight. And we were speaking in public, telling others in the majority and in the know that the stakes were elevating, that this was not only about what was going to be enacted and by whom, but how the Assembly was being run.

After session began in January 1995, Silver had his staff quickly draft a very rudimentary version of sex offender registration and notification. Instead of introducing it himself, which would have been obvious and awkward, the Speaker had it introduced by Naomi Matusow, then a junior legislator much indebted to Silver for helping her win a close election victory over her Republican opponent. Since I had a "safe" Democratic district and Matusow was a "marginal," (that is, possibly vulnerable to a Republican opponent), Silver had at least some conventionally acceptable basis for gifting her with a popular bill. Then in response to a press question about the likely fate of Skelos-Feldman, Silver was quoted as commenting that he "preferred the Matusow bill."

We needed serious visibility to keep our draft alive, so Skelos and I did a little old-fashioned media management. We countered with a Sunday afternoon press conference on the steps of the State Supreme Court building near City Hall in downtown Manhattan. The presence of Megan Kanka's parents guaranteed us coverage.

By 1995, Dean Skelos safely represented his Senate district in Nassau County, although he initially won his seat in 1984 in a hard-fought battle with a Democratic incumbent, Carol Berman. A very good-looking man, he was close to the Republican political organization at home and a "player" in the Senate—Deputy Majority Leader—despite his relative lack of seniority there. The Senate had passed the 1994 version of our bill. This was not surprising, given the Senate's "law-and-order" proclivities and relative lack of responsiveness to civil liberties concerns in the face of very popular legislation. We both knew that the Assembly posed the problem, not the Senate, but we had an equal interest in making this a "two-house" bill, one that could really become law, not just a "one-house" bill useful just for posturing, political credit, and grandstanding.

New York City politicians have traditionally scheduled Sunday press conferences on the steps of City Hall or at other visually appealing locations. My suburban friend Dean was happy to join in that tradition. There is a risk. Television stations have fewer crews and newspapers have fewer photographers and reporters available on the weekend than during the week, so if a bigger news event breaks, you may get nothing. An airplane crash or the capture of a notorious criminal will commandeer the press coverage you thought you had coming. But if the press does cover your Sunday event, you'll do much better than you would on a weekday, because there won't be much competition. Monday's newspapers tend to be thin, but they get good readership, and a good story from Sunday may snare the front page. Sunday night television news follows comparable logic.

The *Times-Union*, Albany's major newspaper, ran the Associated Press story from New York City on its front page, guaranteeing at least that Albany legislators would take our efforts seriously. The lead paragraph noted our event and summarized the bill, with particular emphasis on its provision for a 900 telephone number citizens could call to get information about sex offenders in the most dangerous category. The story quoted me saying "We need to provide a safeguard against the sexual abuse of innocent victims, a safeguard that our current system of law simply cannot provide and does not provide."

Another key group, besides legislators, looks carefully at the *Times-Union*: reporters working for the Albany bureaus of other news outlets. Two days later in Albany, Skelos and I did it again, this time with additional family members of sex crime victims and two leaders of the victims movement who happened to be clergy in collars. Now news outlets throughout the State covered the story as well.

As far as I can tell, no one outside Albany ever sees the *Legislative Gazette,* published in the capital by SUNY New Paltz. College interns write this newspaper, but it covers the Legislature in greater detail than any other publication. Legislators and reporters for the Albany bureaus of other news sources read it probably more thoroughly than they read the *Times-Union*. A smart student reporter asked Mindy Bockstein whether Skelos-Feldman actually had any chance of enactment, given Silver's attitude. Someone from Silver's entourage might conceivably have given the reporter a hint to this effect, in an effort to deflate the bill's credibility. Mindy responded diplomatically. As the *Gazette* reported, "Feldman's spokesperson, Mindy Bockstein, said that Speaker

Sheldon Silver will support the bill because it has a good balance of due process protection, it is fair and it protects citizens." After unleashing our salvos, we told the Speaker this way through the *Gazette* that we wanted to remain on talking terms.

Jurisdictional and Process Choices. We had carefully planned the next step in our strategy as well. Like my Second Felony Offender reform bill, we led off the bill with an amendment to the Corrections Law, presumptively flagging it for reference to the Corrections Committee. But unlike Second Felony Offender, which anyone could see was primarily intended to change sentences, and thus could plausibly be referenced to the Codes Committee, this bill explicitly argued that changes in punishment were not its intention, and we had a constitutional concern as the basis for this argument. The Corrections Law covered such non-punitive matters as provisions for work release intended to rehabilitate inmates while protecting the public. If the Speaker overrode the presumptive reference to Corrections signaled by the Skelos-Feldman bill, that move alone could generate negative publicity for him. I got jurisdiction.

As previously discussed, a committee chair that wants a bill out of his or her committee can almost always get it out. And Speaker Silver certainly recognized the futility of any efforts on his part to discourage a favorable report on the bill by this particular committee chair. On March 18 we were able to announce that the bill had been favorably reported out of its Assembly committee of origin, Corrections: the bill was *moving*! Of course, anyone who paid close attention to the politics of the matter would hardly have been impressed, given that I chaired the Committee. Nonetheless, we were beginning to create the perception of inevitability, a perception that would (we hoped) generate the reality.

The Assembly Steering Committee mostly does nothing besides rubber-stamp the Speaker's wishes, or in more democratic times, when the two can be distinguished, the wishes of the Democratic majority. Its chairmanship—with an attendant "lulu" (payment in lieu of expenses)—is another place the Speaker can put a senior member who for one reason or another has not been given a real committee to chair. At the time, the Steering Committee was chaired by Ivan Lafayette.

In April 1995, the Speaker seemed to feel the need to take the temperature of his colleagues on sex offender registration and community notification. He turned to this available venue. By then, two other Assembly members, besides Matusow and me, had introduced bills on the subject, so the Steering Committee met to consider all of them. Sam Colman from Rockland County, Fran Pordum from Buffalo, Gary

Pretlow from Westchester County, and Brian Murtaugh and Richard Gottfried from Manhattan all spoke against the bills. The comments of the civil libertarians from Manhattan genuinely reflected their own concerns. Those who performed mostly to please Silver probably shared civil-liberties qualms to some extent as well.

The sponsors of the bills—Robin Schimminger from the suburbs of Buffalo, Joe Morelle from Rochester, Matusow, and I—of course each supported our own bills. Helene Weinstein, who represented the district just east of mine, tried to take a middle position. Given that we represented similar communities, with the same local press that had been extremely supportive of my efforts, she might have upset some constituents had she opposed the bill. On the other hand, she tried hard to please Silver and had some sensitivity to civil liberties concerns as well.

The Steering Committee came out with no clear position. Silver could conclude that at least within his Democratic Conference, he could get away with stonewalling the legislation if he wanted. But his options were narrowing. On May 24, the Senate passed the Skelos bill. It was hardly about to pass versions of the Schimminger, Morelle, or Matusow bills. Silver could no longer talk about "preferring" some other bill to mine. Perhaps he could take the heat for not enacting sex offender registration and notification at all. But if he was talking about enactment, Skelos-Feldman was now the only game in town.

More Pressure From Events, and the Media. In early June, a sex offender murdered four-year-old My Ly Nghiem in the Binghamton area in New York's Southern Tier. The pressure on Silver increased as the Republican legislators from that region suggested publicly that enactment of Megan's Law could have prevented her death. "It sickens me personally when legislation that could help keep something like this from happening again just sits in committee," said Binghamton Republican State Senator Tom Libous, as quoted in the June 14 edition of the Binghamton *Press Sun Bulletin*. The big New York City dailies, the *Post* and the *Daily News*, along with smaller newspapers around the State, ran editorials pressing Silver to enact Megan's Law.

The same day Libous was quoted, Silver had some crime victim leaders friendly to him, including one he had placed on the Assembly payroll, join him in a press conference in the Capitol to highlight anti-crime bills he was supporting. From the audience, Marc Klaas, father of the 12-year old California girl Polly Klaas murdered two years earlier, interrupted: "How many more of these murders do we have to take?" he asked Silver. "If it was your daughter, my judgment is that it would be passed yesterday and it would be law tomorrow, sir." Silver tried to tell Klaas that he had concerns about constitutionality. But even some of Silver's pet crime victim advocates could not remain unmoved. The Associated Press quoted Ellen Levin, whose daughter had been killed in the well-publicized "preppy" murder by Robert Chambers as saying: "I got upset myself because I fully understand the urgency about having a bill like this passed."

With Klaas were the Kankas and Pastor Robert Wood, whose 13-year-old daughter had been killed in 1993. Silver wouldn't guarantee that the Assembly would pass the bill before the end of the 1995 session. Klaas and Maureen Kanka protested. Silver invited them to continue the discussion in private. With Wood and others, they waited for Silver for thirty-five minutes while he kept another commitment, then met with him for ten minutes in his office. When he emerged, Klaas told the press, "I'll be satisfied with what he had to say to me if this bill gets out on the floor and a vote is taken on it. That's the only thing that will satisfy me."

The *Times* story on the controversy reported my belief that we had addressed the constitutional problems flagged by the New Jersey courts when they reviewed their Megan's Law. Taking a note from Mindy's playbook, I also said that I expected the bill to pass in the Assembly.

Silver now had no real options left. In the context of tragic events, we had raised the political price of stonewalling so high that no matter how angry he might have been with me, he had no choice but to pass my bill. The solidly liberal but almost always accurate *Newsday* supported us in a June 26 editorial headlined "Down the Middle," commending us for avoiding the kind of "[l]egislating in a climate of hysteria [that] often makes for bad law," and calling Skelos-Feldman "a carefully crafted version of New Jersey's 'Megan's Law.'" The next day, the *Times* demurred. Disappointed that Silver seemed to back down from his stated concerns about the constitutionality of the bill's application of registration and notification provisions "to sex offenders already in prison or on parole," it claimed, inaccurately, that it was "precisely that application that has been struck down by a trial judge as unconstitutional extra punishment in the original 'Megan's Law' in New Jersey." The *Times* seemed unaware that we had learned from the New Jersey experience, and avoided inclusion of numerous constitutionally questionable provisions in our bill.

But events had moved the issue even beyond the influence of the *Times*. On Monday, June 26, two months after my Corrections Committee had reported the bill to Codes, Codes reported it to Ways and Means. On Tuesday, Ways and Means reported it to Rules. On Wednesday, Rules let it out on the Floor as Assembly Calendar Number 739. I made the necessary motion to substitute the Senate bill, because it had passed first, and debate began.

Floor Debate and the Constitution

The exceptions to passage once a bill reaches the floor in New York State Assembly are so few that it is fair to say that the outcome of floor debate is preordained. Nonetheless, this particular debate promised to be significant. The criminal defense bar and the Civil Liberties Union would surely challenge Megan's Law in court. Its legislative history— including the record of the floor debate—could affect the courts' view. Also, as a civil libertarian myself, I was anxious to refute the inaccurate but plausible accusation, reinforced by the *Times's* editorial and others, that I had pandered to public hysteria by introducing legislation that trampled offenders' rights to no useful purpose. I therefore approached this debate with particular care and concern.

Assemblyman Ed Sullivan from Manhattan's Upper West Side led off: "Madame Speaker" (the actual Speaker rarely presides; the usual acting Speaker in those days was Staten Island's gracious and dignified Betty Connelly), "the bill before us is one that has received a great deal of publicity. However, it is one that is essentially fraudulent. . . ." He continued with the usual arguments that it would promote vigilante activity while failing to provide any significant protection to victims because sex offenders would fail to register, if not at first then later, after suffering harassment; would hide; would have no helpful or rehabilitative human contact; and would strike again.

This, of course, reinforced precisely the misperception I needed to combat. But I started from a different tack, as had been recommended by Dan Tubridy, a long-time friend from Broad Channel in the borough of Queens, near where I had grown up, a savvy restaurant owner and political activist. "This bill allows the people of New York to know what the State of New York already knows," I said. "I operate on the premise that we can have some confidence in the people of New York"—a proposition, I assumed, that my colleagues might feel some discomfort rejecting. I noted that individuals rarely responded to Megan's Law information with vigilante harassment, although such responses had received highly disproportionate publicity. Knowing that Silver had been bashed ferociously by the Republicans on this issue and would be again, I then defended Silver's "cautious, deliberative approach to this legislation." I had two reasons. First, I wanted to be gracious in victory. Second, I intended to remain in the Legislature for a while and didn't plan to switch my party affiliation. Finally, I got to the main point, explaining that "[w]hat the bill will do, at the very least, is assure that in a number of cases the police will be able to apprehend an offender after the first new offense after release rather than after the sixth or seventh, and the scars on children's lives and people's lives that that will avoid, and indeed, the lives that will be saved as a result, I think, have to be balanced against whatever unhappy results of the bill may also be a reality."

Susan John, Democrat of Rochester, acknowledged my good intentions but repeated the usual constitutional concerns. Jim Tedisco, Republican of Schenectady, urged support for the bill by stressing the need to protect children against child molesters who entice children to accompany them. My friend Pete Grannis, a Democrat from Manhattan's Upper East Side, who sat right in front of me and disliked the bill, asked me a long series of technical questions intended to elicit answers that would strengthen his argument. Although my answers did not strengthen his argument, Pete forged ahead, undeterred, as was his style:

"Can I ask what your intent—this bill lists a warn-the-public approach, this public 'Scarlet Letter' approach. Do you view this as—" I interrupted, "—You mean, 'When have I stopped beating my wife?'" Pete ignored me, continuing, "—part of a program of rehabilitation or punishment?"

Had I said punishment, I might well have sabotaged the subsequent court case for the bill's constitutionality. But of course punishment never had been the intent. I answered "Neither. This is a program to promote public safety."

Pete had done some homework. He cited a decision by New York State's highest court fifteen days earlier for the proposition that "these kinds of public 'Scarlet Letter' laws, particularly in the format that you have, are universally viewed as punishment." He had not done quite enough homework, however. The decision, *People v. Letterlough*, 655 N.E. 2d 156 (N.Y. 1995), held that New York's probation law precluded requiring a drunk driver to post a "convicted dwi" (driving while intoxicated) sign on his license plate as a condition of probation. However, the Court explicitly noted that the Legislature could change the law, allowing courts to impose such a condition "as a measure to protect the public through warnings," and even used Megan's Law as an illustrative example.

So I told Pete that the decision was "clearly, obviously, and utterly inapposite to this discussion. It is in the context of probation. It specifically refers to a Megan's Law as the kind of thing a state can do by legislative determination. I looked carefully at that quotation; it has nothing to do with the legislation." Actually, I understated the point. The decision really gave strong support to the argument in *favor* of the bill's constitutionality. But Pete wasn't convinced. He proceeded to the heart of the matter, the question at the heart of the bill's constitutionality, and he did it well.

He said, "People who have been sentenced and served their terms or whatever part of their terms, and they have been paroled, they are out on parole and all of a sudden this bill passes, or whatever the effective date is, they are kicked in and there's a very real concern, Dan, and maybe you can address it for us. Why isn't this kind of added punishment, after the fact, after the trial, after the conviction, after the sentence has been imposed, why isn't that unconstitutional?"

I recognized the quality of his question but knew it was one for which I had a wholly sufficient answer: "Mr. Grannis, that is an excellent question to which I have a rather lengthy answer. I can provide it now if you'd like, or I can provide it in my closing statement." "Recognizing you are well-versed in the Constitution," Pete responded that later would be fine (when my answer would not come out of *his* speaking time), and he concluded his remarks, repeating his constitutional argument.

Mike Spano, a Republican from Yonkers, had himself been the victim of a child molester in early adolescence and spoke movingly about his experience and in support of the bill. Carmen Arroyo, Democrat of the Bronx, was the first member of my party to speak in support. Deborah Glick, Democrat of Manhattan, spoke against it, repeating earlier arguments.

Phil Healey, an earnest older Republican from Nassau County, supported the bill in a way that began to make me nervous when he concluded by saying to our colleagues, "Vote for this bill, take a chance regardless what it may be, the Constitution, the apprehension." (Phil wasn't always the most articulate presenter of his point of view.) "Don't give protection to the animals, don't give it to the people exploiting children, protect the children."

This did not set the tone I was looking for. Fortunately, next to speak was another good friend of mine, Jules Polonetsky, a thoughtful young Orthodox Jewish Democrat from Coney Island and those parts of Brighton Beach I didn't represent, immediately to the west of my district. And Jules supported the bill from the same point of view I did, protection of the community, without vindictiveness toward the offenders. The remaining speakers, all in support, did likewise: Jay Dinga, Republican of Broome County, in New York's Southern Tier; Roann Destito, Democrat of Utica; Joe Robach, then a Democratic Assemblyman and later a Republican Senator from Rochester.

So I closed—with some sense of relief that vindictive and punitive statements had not set the tone—with my promised answer to Pete's earlier question. I explained that the Federal District Court judge in New Jersey had stricken down the retroactive provisions of their statute because the overall statutory scheme was, "on balance, more punitive than regulatory." By regulatory in this context, the judge means safety enhancing or safety promoting. Twenty-six states have community notification and registration schemes. The majority of those schemes have been upheld against constitutional challenge because the court found that their legislative schemes were predominantly regulatory, not predominantly punitive.

"The hundreds of hours of effort that my staff and Senator Skelos's staff put into this legislation were mostly directed toward building on the experience of New Jersey and other states, to assure that our scheme would, indeed, be considered more regulatory than punitive.

"If you put the various states on a spectrum, if New Jersey is at the punitive end of the spectrum and those states whose schemes have been upheld are in the middle of the spectrum, ours is, if anything, at the regulatory end of the spectrum. So, for a court to declare this scheme unconstitutional it would have to ignore all the legal opinions in this area."

I finished by "thanking the Speaker, again, by thanking those crime victim advocates who were tremendously committed to this effort, by thanking members and staff of both Houses and, in particular, although she will be very upset with me for doing this, Mindy Bockstein, without whom this absolutely would not have taken place."

My relief had proved premature. In addition to two fifteen-minute periods allowed to members for debate or statements before the vote, members may, if they wish, make statements of up to two minutes to "explain" their votes. Members usually use the two minutes to make short arguments, not explanations. The first few were fine: Jeff Klein,

Democrat of the Bronx; Harvey Weisenberg, Democrat of Nassau County; Sandra Wirth, Republican of West Seneca.

But then, my friend Pat Manning, the ranking Republican on my Corrections Committee from Hopewell Junction, concluded his comment by saying, "I will tell you personally, I think these people have no rights, especially when they touch the body of a young girl or boy." Pat and I always had a great relationship based on mutual respect, despite the fact that his views were thousands of miles to the right of mine, but I feared what floodgates that comment might open. Sure enough, the next speaker, Tom Kirwan, Republican of Newburgh, was much worse: "The usual defenders of the depraved, once again, we are worried about the constitutional rights of the criminals." The next few speakers kept to the appropriate points, but then Jim Tedisco, who had spoken reasonably during debate, called repeat sexual predators "the human equivalent of toxic waste." A few more speakers, and it was over. New York Assembly members vote by pressing buttons on their desks. Betty Connelly instructed the Clerk to announce the results: Ayes 140, Nays 9. In the negative, all Democrats: Arthur Eve of Buffalo, David Gantt and Susan John of Rochester, Glick, Gottfried, Grannis, Stringer and Sullivan of Manhattan, and Greg Meeks of Far Rockaway.

A month later, Governor Pataki signed the bill into law as Chapter 192 of the Laws of 1995, at a nice ceremony with the victim advocates, Dean Skelos, myself, Senate Majority Leader Joe Bruno, and other legislators. But it was not over.

In January, Governor Pataki scheduled a special ceremony to herald the date our Megan's Law would take effect in New York. Only a statute that had generated such extraordinarily widespread support and publicity could have prompted him to take this unusual step. Although Silver had obviously cut his losses by finally allowing the Assembly to pass the bill, his residual vulnerability on the issue may have heightened the Governor's motivation. Pataki and Silver held each other in contempt, and the governor was looking for a chance to take a shot at the Speaker.

After noting that Silver's spokesperson called Silver a strong supporter of the legislation, the Associated Press story on January 22, 1996 reported that Pataki said "he did not invite Silver to attend the ceremony because he felt the speaker had to be prodded into moving the legislation through the Assembly last year, after an emotional news conference by the parents of murdered children."

Silver issued an edict that no Democratic member of his House was to attend a Pataki event until and unless Pataki invited Silver as well.

Fred Dicker, the political gossip columnist *par excellence* at the *Post*, found out and wrote that I was the chief victim of this policy, given my role in enacting Megan's Law.

The Governor had earlier been kind enough to have me stand right next to him at the actual moment of signature, so the photo, front-paged in many newspapers, had featured us together. Since the press had already covered my Megan's Law work extensively, I would be making no great sacrifice by obeying Shelly's order, and I had no desire to antagonize him further. Dicker's column made him look petty enough anyway. I stayed home.

The Southern District Strikes it Down

The Legal Aid Society filed the lawsuit we expected, challenging the constitutionality of Megan's Law on behalf of anonymous sex offenders John Doe, Richard Roe, and Samuel Poe, and seeking a preliminary injunction blocking the statute from taking effect. Governor's ceremony or no, Megan's Law would not be enforced quite yet.

My first problem was to figure out how to be heard on the matter. The New York State Attorney General had the legal obligation to defend the statute. The plaintiff named as defendants the Governor and various other executive officials of the State, not me or any other legislator. I had never actually practiced in federal court, where the suit was brought, and had therefore never bothered to seek admission to the bar of any federal court. (Passing the bar examination in New York, as I had over two decades earlier, gives an attorney automatic admission only to State courts.)

While the federal courts often admit attorneys *pro hac vice* — "for this occasion" — to argue a particular matter, in the circumstance I could only enter the case as *amicus curiae*, friend of the court, and federal courts did not generally admit *amicus* counsel *pro hac vice*. Also, the case would come up too quickly for a regular admission application to be processed in time. So I wrote the brief, but my friend Roger Stavis, an excellent and prominent criminal defense attorney, edited it and filed it under his name as attorney, representing me as the *amicus*, on March 15, 1996.

In a suit for a preliminary injunction, the plaintiffs have the burden of proving that the potential harm from implementing the statute clearly outweighed the potential harm from delaying its implementation.

It seemed to me that the statute's potential for reducing sex offense victimization clearly outweighed its potential for subjecting sex offenders to harassment, particularly in view of its stringent provisions deterring vigilantism. In addition, the public already had a legal right to offenders' conviction records; the statute merely made such records much more accessible. "Only an odd perception of the right to privacy," I argued, "includes a right to keep out of the public record the fact that one has been convicted of committing a criminal offence." The law conferred no such right.

The plaintiffs also had to prove, and the defendants to disprove, that the plaintiffs' constitutional challenge was ultimately likely to succeed, should the court grant the immediate plea for an injunction. I argued again, as I had in the Assembly floor debate, that a court "would virtually have to ignore all the existing judicial analysis of various state statutes in this field in order to find ours unconstitutional."

Judge Denny Chin, of the Southern District of New York, did just that in his September 26, 2006 decision in *Doe v. Pataki*, 919 F. Supp. 691 (S.D.N.Y. 1996). In my naiveté, the opinion actually shocked me. I complained to friends more experienced in federal litigation than I that Judge Chin had clearly reached his conclusion first and backfilled with unpersuasive legal arguments later. I could have written a decision against my own position, I said, more coherent and more persuasive than his. More cynical, my friends assured me that his approach was by no means as unusual as I seemed to think.

Some of the vote "explanations" offered on the floor at the end of the Assembly debate on Megan's Law had made me nervous at the time. This was not so much because I thought they would give the courts reason to overturn the law as a punitive violation of the Ex Post Facto Clause, as because they reinforced its image as mean-spirited. Had the overwhelming majority of my colleagues revealed vindictive motivation for supporting the legislation, of course, a court might have had good reason to dismiss my own non-punitive rationale as an implausible effort to disguise the bill's "real" intent. But only a few colleagues expressed such sentiments.

Moreover, having taught the use of legislative history in statutory interpretation in law school, I knew that judges were advised to not give weight to floor debate comments by legislators who had nothing to do with a statute's drafting. Courts are supposed to give deference to floor statements by sponsors of legislation because they know that, within the legislature, others defer to them as most knowledgeable. Legislators are less likely to be influenced by the comments of colleagues who know as little about the bill as they do. And they expect similar deference on their own bills.

Nevertheless, I would have been happier had some legislators not tempted the courts to do the wrong thing with their remarks.

Judge Chin succumbed to the temptation.

He wrote, "Although the legislature's stated intent in passing the Act was to protect, it is clear that the legislature also intended to punish sex offenders. In approving the Act, members of the New York State legislature referred to sex offenders as 'depraved,' 'the lowest of the low,' 'animals,' and 'the human equivalent of toxic waste.'"

Clearly, the trial judge had marshaled testimony from the Senate and Assembly debate records in a selective manner. He ignored my floor statements and those of Senator Skelos, which demonstrated only regulatory, remedial, and non-punitive intent. Instead, and contrary to accepted best practice, he relied solely on the statements of legislators who had had no input in the shaping of the legislation.

It takes quite a stretch to excuse the judge's "error." To have cited the comments of a handful of minority party legislators in the Assembly and uninvolved majority party members of the Senate, while ignoring the comments of the chief sponsors of the legislation, verges on willful misrepresentation.

One defining dimension of modern American government is the extraordinary growth of the role of courts in making public policy. This may be justified when the legislature fails for political or other reasons to do its policy-making job, or as a majoritarian institution, is insufficiently attentive to the needs, claims, and interests of minority groups. But when the legislature does act, it is a long-established principle that courts should honor the presumption that its enactments are constitutional. In New York's Megan's Law, the preamble to the statute itself "evinces an unmistakable intent to promote public safety and enhance law enforcement efforts," as the New York State Supreme Court in Monroe County noted in *People v. Afrika,* 648 N.Y.S. 2d 645 in 1996.

The Southern District's other errors could more easily be forgiven, were Judge Chin's overall attitude not illuminated by the glare of his misuse of legislative history.

The U.S. Supreme Court's in the *Halper* case, noted earlier, rejected the imposition of a heavy fine because it could not "fairly be said solely to serve a remedial purpose." This language did on its face appear to support the judge's conclusion in *Doe v. Pataki,* and therefore his decision to issue a preliminary injunction to stop implementation of New York's Megan's Law. But in taking this action Judge Chin ignored the argument we made in defense of the law—and by the New Jersey Supreme Court on that state's Megan's Law—that the *Halper* decision and other similar cases had to be read more closely.

In *Halper*, the U.S. Supreme Court rejected the prosecution's argument that it had sought imposition of the massive fine "*solely* to serve a remedial purpose." It did not say that any sanction that served any purpose in addition to a remedial one must be deemed punishment.

In *Doe v. Pataki* Judge Chin essentially ruled that even a small punitive impact in proportion to the remedial impact would render a burden "punitive." This reading of the law violated both precedent and common sense. It would mean that the Legislature could never take any action to safeguard the public from those known, by virtue of their previous criminal convictions, to pose special risks. The courts have repeatedly rejected this ridiculous proposition. For example, doctors who defrauded Medicare before a new statute was enacted can indeed be kept out of Medicare practice. Mafia associates convicted before a new statute was enacted can be kept away from a waterfront union. Felons convicted before a new statute was enacted can be prohibited from disbursing controlled substances. A merely incidental and minimal punitive impact does not render a statute "punishment."

In granting its preliminary injunction the Southern District also too casually dismissed the illumination of the actual meaning of the *Halper* decision offered in the Seventh Circuit's decision in 1995 in *Bae v. Shalala*, 44 F. 3d 489. The *Bae* case concerned a defendant who was convicted of bribing Federal Drug Administration officials to obtain approval to manufacture drugs. Congress later barred persons convicted of crimes relating to drug product regulation from further participation in drug approval applications. The defendant challenged his debarment as a violation of the *Ex Post Facto* Clause of the U.S. Constitution. The court rejected this challenge. It noted that a "civil sanction that can fairly be said solely to serve remedial goals will not fail under *Ex Post Facto* scrutiny merely because it is consistent with punitive goals as well." The *Bae* court also noted that the Supreme Court "has consistently required 'unmistakable evidence of punitive intent' to characterize a sanction as punishment."

In its following decision, *Doe v. Pataki*, 940 F. Supp. 603 (S.D.N.Y. 1996), this time permanently barring implementation of Megan's Law, the Southern District assumed a more sophisticated stance. Here Judge

Chin conceded that the presence of some deterrent impact does not make a statute punitive. He argued, however, that the presence of some remedial impact does not necessarily render a statute regulatory, and that the excessively punitive impact of the statute overcame whatever regulatory purpose it might serve, violating the *Ex Post Facto Clause.*

The judge simply misunderstood or ignored the need for the law we had drafted and passed to assure public safety, our attention in writing Megan's Law to precedent in New York and elsewhere, and the care we had taken to include procedural safeguards in this law in accord with U.S. Constitutional requirements. Moreover, in considering the potential impact of the law, he gave little attention to expert testimony, systematically gathered social science evidence, and the actual experience in other states with the implementation of similar laws. In doing so he ignored Justice Felix Frankfurter's advice, given in a 1958 dissent in *Trop v. Dulles*, 356 U.S. 86, that:

It is not the business of this Court to pronounce policy. It must observe a fastidious regard for limitations on its own power, and this precludes the Court's giving effect to its own notions of what is wise or politic. That self-restraint is of the essence in the observance of the judicial oath, for the Constitution has not authorized judges to sit in judgment on the wisdom of what Congress and the Executive Branch do.

As a result, as of September 26, 1996, the community notification provisions of Megan's Law could not be implemented in New York with respect to any offender whose crime had occurred prior to January 21, 1996, the date called for by the statute for Megan's Law to take effect. We had to appeal to the Second Circuit.

Politics and Law: Winning on Appeal

Politics in Court. Although my friends had assured me that the Second Circuit would not indulge in the kind of decision-making reflected in the Southern District opinion, I could not help being nervous. It makes a difference who the judges are. For this case, I thought, I needed more conservative judges who would defend society's need to protect itself against the false arguments that the Southern District had accepted and/ or concocted. As I reviewed the history of the judges assigned to the panel, I took some comfort in the presence of Wilfred Feinberg, known as fairly conservative. I admired Joseph McLaughlin, a moderate whose captivating wit and brilliance had made the parts of my bar exam review course that he had presented actually enjoyable. But Jonathan Newman, an outspoken liberal, worried me. Far more senior than McLaughlin, he might, through his considerable intellect and greater experience, sway the newer judge. When I learned that Newman would preside, my trepidation increased.

I remained completely confident that I had by far the better of the argument on the merits. But the court did not permit me to present oral argument, just my brief, and I was worried about whether the state would be ably represented. Attorney General Dennis Vacco, a Republican narrowly elected and seeking to build his political base, had contributed nothing to Megan's Law. He did however, barge into the first press conference Dean Skelos and I called on the subject, and grabbed press coverage at every possible opportunity thereafter to associate himself with the issue. Vacco's arrival in office was followed by the replacement of many accomplished and experienced senior attorneys in the Attorney General's Office and their replacement with political appointees, many of them marginally competent.

Neither Vacco nor one of these political appointees appeared for the State. The Assistant Attorney General who did, Christine Morrison, a very able advocate, had joined the Office of the Attorney General well before Vacco arrived and managed to survive there. The case was argued on January 6, 1997. I was there. Judge Newman questioned Morrison most skeptically, reinforcing my gloomy perception of his likely predisposition on this matter. I had a long wait: The Second Circuit issued its unanimous decision, written by Judge Newman, nearly eight months later, on August 22, 1997.

The Second Circuit's Decision: It turned out that my fears came out of an overreaction to the Southern District's decision. In the end, neither politics nor ideology influenced the result. Judge Newman's decision for a unanimous Second Circuit court in *Doe v. Pataki*, 120 F. 3d 1263 (2d Cir. 1997) reversed the Southern District politely but decisively, making short shrift of Judge Chin's problematic reading of legislative intent.

To my delight the Circuit quoted my arguments in support of the legislation three times. It mentioned the joint Skelos-Feldman Introducer's Memorandum, describing the motivation for the bill as "[p]rotecting the public, especially children, from sex offenders" and its character as "predominantly regulatory." It then quoted my argument for the legislation in my letter to the Governor contained in the law's Bill Jacket, that community notification would likely "advanc[e] the protection of the public" by enabling the community to serve as the "eyes and ears" of law enforcement, and "enable the authorities to intervene when a releasee's behavior begins to pose a threat to community safety." Finally, with respect to the Ex Post Facto issue itself, it quoted my comment that unless applied retroactively, "the Act would "leave[] the majority of sexual offenders cloaked in anonymity," in the context of our stated desire to (in the court's words) "protect the public from potentially dangerous persons."

Regarding legislative intent, the Second Circuit wrote that "[t]he views of a law's sponsors, though not conclusive, are entitled to considerable weight," and utterly rejected the Southern District's effort to divine legislative intent from the "isolated statements" of "some legislators."

Most important, the Circuit held that "the Act's text and core structural features reasonably bear out its stated non-punitive goals of protecting the public and facilitating future law enforcement efforts." For the court, Judge Newman strongly rejected the notion that:

all of the unfortunate incidents that occurred in the aftermath of notification must be considered effects of [Megan's Law] for purposes of overcoming the Act's regulatory purpose . . . The incidents (1) are wholly dependent on acts by private third parties, (2) result from information most of which was publicly available prior to [Megan's Law], and (3) flow essentially from the fact of the underlying conviction.

He wrote that *"illegal* actions by members of the public, such as physical attacks against the offender, are not consequences that the operation of [Megan's Law] contemplates or condones."

The Circuit Court remanded the case to the Southern District to deal with additional legal issues. As noted, the Southern District then actually improved upon our work by providing for judicial review of dangerousness classifications of offenders who had not been sentenced to prison.

The Aftermath. Given my own initial doubts about Megan's Law, I would never have championed the legislation unless I had been able to assure myself fully that I could write it in such a way that it would not violate the constitutional values that I cherish. Although neither our legislative opponents, nor the *Times* editorial board, nor the Civil Liberties Union, nor the Southern District judge had been willing to admit it, we had taken our constitutional responsibilities seriously and effectively when we drafted the statute. Once the Second Circuit had spoken, at long last, our critics had no more to say.

We had never claimed panacea status for the legislation. Megan's Law assisted law enforcement, as we predicted, but the heartache of victimization and the hard work of prevention and apprehension continued. We continued to press forward in the effort to combat sexual and other forms of victimization. We won grant money for preventive education and expanded State funding for the effort to locate missing children. Congress conditioned financial assistance to states on strengthened Megan's Law provisions, requiring a variety of amendments, mostly minor. But in terms of the self-righteousness, political aggrandizement, and vituperation that had characterized the debate on both sides over the community notification core of Megan's Law, the war was over.

The States and Incubators: New York as a Model (or Sadly, Not)

In their rush to adopt Megan's Laws, not all states were as careful as was New York. Alaska and Connecticut, for example, did not design systems that made dissemination of information proportional to the level of dangerousness of the offender. They made no attempt to limit its easy availability to the narrowest audience consistent with public safety. Under their statutes, every registered sex offender's name, address, photograph, crime, and other identifying information was published on the Internet. They also found themselves in federal court.

In 2001, in *Doe v. Otte*, 259 F.3d 979, the Federal Court of Appeals for the Ninth Circuit held that Alaska's law imposed burdens on sex offenders so onerous as to qualify as punishment, despite non-punitive legislative intent. Thus the court said, the statute violated the Ex Post Facto Clause of the Constitution with respect to those who had been convicted of their sex offenses prior to its enactment. The Ninth Circuit contrasted the Alaska approach with that taken by New York, which ". . . permitted such disclosure only on the basis of an individualized assessment of the risk of recidivism." Also unlike the New York and other state statutes, the Alaska statute did not even allow for the possibility of rehabilitation: once convicted, the defendant would continue forever to be portrayed on the Internet as a threat to society even if judges and prosecutors all ultimately felt otherwise.

In the same year, in *Doe v. Dep't of Pub. Safety ex rel. Lee*, the Second Circuit considered Connecticut's Megan's Law, which more directly than Alaska's required the State to post sex offenders' names, addresses, photographs, and descriptions on the Internet. Again unlike the New York case, the statute did not provide a mechanism to ascertain whether an individual offender currently posed a threat to society. The very court that had upheld the New York statute against an Ex Post Facto Clause challenge said that it would not permit Connecticut to disseminate information about sex offenders unless its Legislature designed a process to determine individual dangerousness, and conditioned dissemination of information on such determinations. Its explicit finding of unconstitutionality of the Connecticut law was based not upon the Ex Post Facto Clause, however, but on a violation of due process. It said that the plaintiffs were deprived of liberty by being stigmatized as dangerous and forced to meet onerous registration requirements without benefit of a hearing to ascertain that they were indeed dangerous.

In *Conn. Dep't of Public Safety v. Doe*, 538 U.S. 1 (2003), every member of the Supreme Court concurred in rejecting the Second Circuit's decision. Connecticut's statute did not require a showing of dangerousness before placing a convicted sex offender's name on the list to be published. Therefore, the court said, the statute's failure to include a procedure verifying offenders' dangerousness could not constitute a procedural violation.

With respect to the Alaska statute, Justice Kennedy writing for the majority in *Smith v. Doe*, 538 U.S. 84 (2003), reversed the Ninth Circuit and held that the statute did not violate the Ex Post Facto Clause. The majority found that the Alaska Legislature had intended the statute to promote public safety, not to "humiliate the offender," and the statute, for the most part, achieved its purpose. Since sex offenders, like anyone else in today's world, can enjoy substantial geographical mobility, next month they may live far away from where they live this month. For that reason, explained Kennedy, publication on the Internet or in other far-reaching media may provide a necessarily broad reach for the warning information. Besides, he wrote, the statute did not have to devise a narrow remedy to be found non-punitive. To be constitutional, Alaska's statutory choice to make information about sex offenders widely available need only be "reasonable," not "the best choice available."

Justice Ginsburg, in dissent along with Justices Breyer and Stevens, conceded the "legitimate civil purpose" of the statute in "promot[ing] public safety." But for her, the statute's "excessiveness" in imposing humiliation beyond the degree necessary for public safety, and its failure to account at all for "the possibility of rehabilitation," placed it irredeemably in the category of punishment, not regulation.

After the Supreme Court announced its decisions in these cases, Pete Grannis called to congratulate me. It was of course kind of him, and consistent with his usual graciousness. Nonetheless I was not pleased with the Court's decisions. The Alaska and Connecticut statutes did not strike the balance I had sought, and had thought best.

I'm not sure that Justice Ginsburg's dissent was right on the law. For the state to publish accurate information might not constitute punishment no matter how widely the state disseminated it. Requiring onerous registration requirements based on the statistical likelihood that sex offenders, as a category, are likely to re-offend, might lead to more irrational discrimination than mandating a less lazy, individualized appraisal process. But Kennedy might still be right that constitutionality does not depend on the state making "the best choice available"; the sloppy, lazy choice might still pass muster. The absence of any provision for rehabilitation, an even more draconian choice, again might not require invalidation on constitutional grounds.

But what is constitutional and what is right might be very different things. Statutes like Alaska's and Connecticut's realized the fears I had had at the very beginning, before I had agreed to sponsor Megan's Law in New York, about creating a permanent class of suspects. Americans have enacted mean-spirited laws before my time and will do so after me. But I hope I still have the right to disown them as my personal legacy.

CHAPTER IX

Guns—The Struggle in the Legislature and Courts

Americans love their guns. We revere the heroic Minuteman, laying down his plow and taking up his muzzle-loader to defend hearth and home. We cheer for the lawman, outdrawing the bad guy and shooting him dead. We know the pistol as "the great equalizer," democratically erasing the advantage of the big man over the little man. We remember the Winchester "repeating" rifle as an instrument of proud national expansion westward. All of these associations help keep our attachment to our firearms close to our hearts, at the center of our culture.

Most deeply engrained is the idea of the gun over the mantelpiece as a protection against an oppressive government. No less a figure than the father of our country, George Washington, believed and said that a free people ought to be armed. His fellow Virginian Thomas Jefferson wrote "The strongest reason for the people to retain the right to keep and bear arms is, as a last resort, to protect themselves against tyranny in government."

Some decades later Supreme Court Justice Joseph Story—the author of some of the most influential treatises on American law ever written—asserted that an armed citizenry could best resist oppressive rulers. Later in the nineteenth century the great constitutional scholar Thomas Cooley, in his *General Principles of Constitutional Law,* traced the development of the second amendment in significant part to the English Bill of Rights of 1688, as "a necessary and efficient means of regaining rights when temporarily overturned by usurpation."

This idea that gun ownership by private citizens' helps to protect liberty remains mainstream, often expressed in unexpected quarters. For example, former Vice President and U.S. Senator Hubert Humphrey of

Minnesota remarked: "The right of citizens to bear arms is just one guarantee against arbitrary government, one more safeguard against the tyranny which now appears remote in America, but which historically has proved to be always possible." More recently, in 2003, Federal Circuit judge Stephen Reinhardt warned that "tyranny thrives best where government need not fear the wrath of an armed people," *Silveira v. Lockyer*, 328 F.3d 567, 596 (9th Cir. 2003).

I don't participate in this American love affair, but I don't hate guns either. I learned to shoot a rifle as a Boy Scout, liked it, and was not bad at it. Although I'm not a hunter, for over thirty years I've had hiking and backpacking friends who hunt and enjoy it.

At some point in the 1970s, when like other middle-class people in New York City I began to feel threatened by violent crime, I did spend several hours one night wrestling with the idea of carrying a handgun for self-protection. I decided against it because I knew something about myself. It was likely, I figured, that if I found myself in a tight place I would approach the question of whether or not to shoot deliberatively and judiciously. Using my usual *modus operandi*, I concluded, I would no doubt be shot dead by my assailant long before I decided that it was O.K. to pull the trigger.

This judgment was probably right. A decade later I was invited to try out the "shoot/don't shoot" training exercise at the New York State Police Academy. My virtual "bullet" missed the image screen entirely, and well after the "bad guy" had killed me.

With Americans' devotion to guns came widespread ownership and use. There followed a record of gun violence notorious throughout the world that reached a peak in the midst of my time of service in the New York State Legislature.

We considered in a previous chapter why this likely happened. To re-summarize: harsh sentences for drug dealers caused them to recruit teenagers to do the low-level work on the street. Like their adult predecessors, these teenage couriers carried guns to protect their valuable goods and cash. Their greater willingness to take risks resulted in their using those guns far more than the adults had.

Moreover, in the late 1970s and early 1980s some entrepreneurial teenage drug couriers entered into the lucrative side business of gun sales. Eventually, inner-city youths without guns who were not dealing came to feel isolated and vulnerable. Many gave in to the pressure to arm themselves as well.

Thus, the dispute that might once have been settled with a punch in the nose now was resolved with a bullet, or several, in the chest. Inner-city homicide rates rose steadily.

Pistols: Demand, Supply, Effect, and Regulation

The handgun industry played an essential role in responding to this market demand. Throughout the 1950s, shotguns and rifles for hunting made up three quarters of civilian gun sales in the United States, with the rest mostly accounted for by revolvers. In the 1980s and 1990s, all of those three sectors showed major declines, but total gun sales increased, based entirely on huge increases in a fourth sector, pistols.

By 1987 semiautomatic pistols outnumbered revolvers in their use in crimes. Between 1980 and 1994, U.S. domestic production of nine millimeter semiautomatic pistols increased at least ninefold. Handgun imports from Austria (the Glock company's base) increased from 668 guns in 1983 to 213,837 in 1996. And Austria was just one of many foreign sources.

Owners load semiautomatic pistols with magazines, or "clips." Before limited by law, these could hold thirty rounds of ammunition each. In tests at a firing range in San Jose, California, police found that an Uzi pistol set on fully automatic could fire its thirty-round magazine in less than two seconds. On semiautomatic it took five seconds. I used to make a not-very-funny joke to illustrate the weakness of the National Rifle Association position in defending such weapons: You need them only if you want to do your hunting and food processing at the same time — to make hamburger.

Between 1985 and 1992, while the manufacture of pistols in the United States almost doubled, handgun deaths in the United States rose from about 9,000 to about 13,000. In the same period, gun-related homicides among inner-city non-white youth more than doubled, while non-gun homicides did not show any significant increase.

Also during this period, the cost of treating victims of firearms violence reached gigantic proportions. Researchers concluded that total firearms violence in 1992 cost the United States over $100 billion, counting direct medical costs, lost productivity, and lost quality of life.

In Great Britain, when the horrible consequences that might arise from the easy availability of guns became dramatically apparent, a strong governmental response ensued. Within seven months of the Dunblane elementary school massacre in March 1996, when an assailant shot to death sixteen schoolchildren and their teacher, high-caliber handguns were banned there. Shortly thereafter, when the Labor party came into power under Tony Blair, the ban was expanded to *all* handguns (with trivial exceptions) in response to the public's continued outrage.

We in the United States do not always shy away from regulating potentially dangerous machines and behaviors, and holding those who use them liable for negative consequences to others. For example, in 2005 about two-thirds as many people were killed by guns as by cars in the United States. We test and license drivers, register vehicles, and require insurance to provide some reasonable scheme of control, accountability and compensation.

Cigarettes also harm substantial numbers of people. We regulate where they may be consumed, and their manufacturers have incurred tort liability (albeit initially *de facto* by way of settlements).

Places serving alcoholic beverages are licensed. Both courts and legislatures have imposed liability to third parties on those who sell alcohol by the drink.

But when it comes to guns action has been sporadic and sparing, both in legislatures and in courts.

Public policy arises and changes from a complex interaction of institutions and circumstances. In presenting the story of the drafting, adoption, and successful defense in the courts of New York's Megan's law in the previous chapter, I strongly argued for judicial deference to the will of the Legislature. With regard to gun control, I summarize less successful efforts at legislating, followed by an attempt to win in the courts what could not be gained in the political arena. Questions naturally arise: "Am I being inconsistent?" "What is the proper relationship between the legislative and judicial branches?" "Are some sorts of matters better addressed in legislatures and others in courts, and *vice versa*?" "If so, are there principles by which these may be distinguished?" This chapter seeks to address these questions.

Additionally it takes up a core issue of federalism. It is at the state and local levels in the United States that matters of crime and punishment have traditionally been decided. This is purposeful: decentralization of police and prosecutorial power has long been seen as an additional protection against a strong central government's potential intrusions upon personal liberty.

We have already seen examples of how state legislation must be carefully crafted in anticipation of constitutional objections raised in one of the three federal branches, the judiciary. As our federal system has evolved and developed, and the national government has grown, responsibility for key areas of domestic policy, never really fully demarcated, increasingly became shared. Criminal justice was no exception: increasingly over the 20th century, often in response to "crime waves," there was greater involvement of the national government in matters of crime and punishment. Congressional and national executive branch involvement in criminal justice decision making offer additional arenas for reform, but also—as we shall see from the stories that follow about efforts to achieve greater control over firearms sales—additional venues in which state and local reform efforts may be blocked.

There is one national government. There are fifty states. There are literally thousands of local governments. For the advocate of change, choosing *where* to proceed—not only in which institution, but at what level—becomes a key choice, a choice as important as deciding on the substantive focus of action.

New York City Comptroller Liz Holtzman and the Unlikely Origin of a State Assembly Gun Control Bill

Liz Holtzman was no ordinary City Comptroller when she won the job in 1989. The youngest woman to be elected to the United States Congress, Holtzman was outspoken, incisive, and courageous as a second-term Member of Congress on the House Judiciary Committee when it investigated Watergate. Later the first woman District Attorney in Brooklyn, she habitually enraged powerful institutions and politicians with her blunt and undiplomatic honesty. Her take-no-prisoners approach ultimately contributed to Holtzman's defeat by less than one percent of the vote in a three-way election to the United States Senate in 1980. (Republican Alfonse D'Amato won, after defeating incumbent Jacob Javits for that party's nomination, leaving Javits to run on the Liberal line.) Liz served as City Comptroller until defeated by Alan Hevesi 1993, and left a legacy of honorable and creative governance.

Internalizing Externalities. Elizabeth Holtzman knew that by the 1990s policymakers had become accustomed to "internalizing externalities," particularly as an instrument of environmental policy. An externality is a cost arising from economic activity that is borne by a third party. For example, a manufacturer might increase dry-cleaning costs for citizens who have to get their clothes cleaned more often because of the air pollution generated from a factory. Or the particulate pollution caused by the factory might increase medical costs and result in lost wages from illness of citizens affected by it. But any single individual would have a hard time trying to prove in court that the polluter caused his or her particular damages.

By requiring manufacturers to add such devices as smokestack "scrubbers" or otherwise reduce harmful pollutants in plant emissions, government provided them an incentive to reduce the costs they imposed indirectly upon others or, if not, forced them to incur monetary costs closer to the previous total direct and indirect costs of their activities. Meanwhile, indirect costs imposed on third-party citizens not directly engaged in the economic transaction between manufacturer and customer were reduced.

Holtzman sought to internalize the externalities of the gun business—the criminal justice, social and medical costs of gun violence. Her approach was not through a regulatory scheme, but by harnessing liability law.

Liability law is used to settle disputes between private parties. If you fall and injure yourself in my house, you may sue me, and courts might determine that I have to compensate you. The prospect of being sued provides me an incentive to reduce your risk of injury while in my house, and also to avoid the relatively heavy costs that might occur in the uncertain future from the outcome of a suit by buying insurance now at a relatively moderate cost.

Absolute Liability. Elizabeth Holtzman called in June of 1991 for the imposition of "absolute liability" on the manufacturers of and dealers in handguns and assault rifles (rifles equipped for semi-automatic firing) when the person using the gun did not hold a valid gun license, so long as the victim had not been committing a crime when he or she was shot. That is, she wanted gun manufacturers and dealers to be legally responsibility for the injuries that arose from the use of their products under these broad conditions, even though they were not at fault or negligent in a particular situation.

Critics complained that the analogy Holtzman made with environmental policy did not work, because no intervening action imposed the pollution costs on citizens, while "guns don't kill people, people do." In reality, however, limiting liability to the perpetrator neither diminished the number of guns in circulation nor allowed recovery by the victim.

Under this approach, the price of guns in the market remained unchanged. Moreover a handgun crime victim could rarely recover damages from a criminal; most criminals had no assets. In almost every case therefore, if no one in the chain of commerce (manufacturer, wholesaler, retailer) could be held liable for the crime victim's suffering, the innocent victim would bear the burden.

Guns are a special kind of product. One of their major purposes is to injure or kill others. The manufacturer and seller make profits from the sale of handguns. The victim and the society bear the costs. An absolute liability law, by effectively making sellers insurers of victims against harm from their products by internalizing some or all of the costs in the economic transaction, sought to force gun makers to add enough to the price of each weapon to create a pool of insurance. The purchaser of a weapon would then pay a price that included recompense for the cost to society of the occasional misuse of such weapons. And at the higher price, to the degree that demand was elastic, there would be somewhat fewer guns sold, in the aggregate potentially reducing the likelihood of gun violence.

As important or more important, absolute liability would create an economic incentive for gun sellers to invest, or to invest more, in an effort to keep guns out of the hands of potential criminals. For example, wholesalers would want to keep track of retailers whose guns tend disproportionately to end up in criminals' hands, and would want to require such retailers to impose stricter sales controls at the risk of losing their wholesale supply.

Of course, implementation of this policy might raise gun prices beyond what purchasers would be willing to pay. For advocates, this would be as effective as a total legal ban on sales, arising out of a demonstration that the true cost of handguns renders them unmarketable. Despite some protestations by the gun community, no one ever offered convincing evidence that absolute liability would indeed raise gun prices beyond the willingness of consumers to pay in the market.

My bill implementing Holtzman's suggestions was introduced in the New York State Assembly too late in 1991 for serious consideration by the Judiciary Committee (even if it had not earned the deep enmity of the National Rifle Association). In addition, as a bill that affected all handguns, not just assault weapons, it made very nervous my moderate colleagues from upstate districts where hunting was popular. They might conceivably make a case to their constituents that assault weapons or "Saturday night specials" (cheaply made handguns often used in crimes in urban areas) deserved this kind of treatment in the law; but the shotgun stood up there with motherhood and apple pie, and to the minds of many of their constituents, the ordinary handgun did not lag far behind.

As the success of federal legislation to ban assault weapons later demonstrated, those weapons enjoyed less solid popular support. The United States has long banned fully automatic weapons—machine guns—from civilian use. Many semiautomatic versions of such guns, however, may easily be converted to fully automatic. Some assault pistols have threaded barrels for the easy attachment of silencers. The Cox newspaper chain completed a controversial study in 1999 of 43,000 guns traced to criminal activity. It claimed that although they represented less than one percent of the total guns in circulation, each assault weapon on average accounted for twenty times as much crime as any other type of gun.

Given their particularly hazardous nature, logic as well as politics suggested limiting our absolute liability approach to sellers of assault weapons, as opposed to handguns in general. A few days after a February 1, 1992, *New York Times* editorial urged support for a "measure before the New York State Legislature" (without further identifying it) imposing absolute liability on gun manufacturers, I introduced a new version of the bill, so restricted.

Later in February, a Brooklyn student shot and killed two of his fellow students inside Thomas Jefferson High School. Again it seemed a tragic event was giving a boost to needed legislation; I seemed to be in the right place at the right time. In a front-page follow-up story on March 2 reporting Mayor David Dinkins's plan to install metal detectors at school entrances, the *Times* acknowledged the existence of my bill. The paper credited me and Roger Green. Roger was the Assembly Member representing the district in which Thomas Jefferson High School is located. I had invited him to cosponsor the legislation, and he had invited me to join him a press conference at the school announcing it.

The same day, *Newsday*'s Jim Dwyer wrote a column vividly describing the way in which some irresponsible gun manufacturers got rich selling firearms that seemed to be designed to end up in the hands of urban ghetto teenagers. Dwyer praised our bill as "the first signs of a movement to hold gun manufacturers responsible for the damage caused by their weapons."

Both the *Daily News* and the *Times* ran editorials in March. The *Times* again supported the concept while again refraining from acknowledging the actual existence of my bills. The *News* more properly and usefully explained that of my two bills, both of which they supported, the more limited one was "an easier political sell."

A Friendly Committee Chair, Skittish Leadership: Absolute Liability Fails

Oliver Koppell was a superb state legislator, first elected in 1969 and fully devoted to the public interest. The 280 laws he wrote included the Utility Consumers Bill of Rights, the Returnable Bottle Law, and the Automobile "Lemon" Law. While a Member of the Assembly, the handsome, six-foot-four-inch Koppell, a Harvard College and Law School graduate twenty-odd years into his political career, once wrestled a shotgun away from a mugger on the street. (The press, as it habitually does in New York City, respected his innate sense of modesty by virtually ignoring the incident.) In 1994, the Legislature elected Koppell to fill the position of State Attorney General when Robert Abrams left that post prior to the expiration of his term.

In a relatively small district, most voters could see up-close and in-person Koppell's impressive personal qualities. In elections in larger constituencies—the entire borough of the Bronx, a statewide Democratic primary for Attorney General—Koppell lacked the penchant for self-promotion or the capacity to connect through the media that was essential to win. Oliver Koppell lost two campaigns for Bronx Borough President to Stanley Simon, an unimpressive man who later resigned in disgrace prior to his imprisonment for corruption. After failing to gain the nomination for Attorney General in both 1994 and 1998, Koppell was elected to the New York City Council in 2001. He was reelected by a 3 to 1 margin in 2005.

In 1992, Koppell chaired the Assembly Judiciary Committee. Given his approach to public service, I knew I could rely on him to secure a favorable report on the tort liability bill from the Committee. With Koppell's help, on March 24 I was able to announce in a press release that "the concept of holding manufacturers and sellers of assault weapons financially responsible for the cost of bloodshed . . . advanced today with a favorable report by the Assembly Judiciary Committee."

Still trying to generate publicity and pressure from the outside, I did whatever I could to get the bill out of Codes, the next committee whose approval I needed to get it to the Assembly floor for a vote on passage. In one memorable moment, a radio show caller asked whether, under

my absolute liability logic, I would impose liability on a salami manufacturer for the customer who eats a salami, raises his cholesterol level,
has a heart attack, and dies. After all, the heightened cholesterol level
and consequent risk are imposed on society by the salami business. I
noted that assault weapons have no legitimate non-military use; that sa-
lamis contribute much more social utility; and that Anglo-American
legal tradition has long imposed absolute liability—without the need
for a showing of fault or negligence—for inherently dangerous activities, and sometimes for inherently dangerous products. Besides, the
voluntary eater of salami may have assumed the risk; I was not aware of
evidence that salami-eating had endangered innocent bystanders.

Then I won another moral victory. The lobbyist for the National Rifle
Association (NRA) circulated to the Legislature a memorandum in opposition to my bill citing an article in the *NYU Law Review*, "Closing the
American Products Liability Frontier: The Rejection of Liability Without Defect." It was written by two of the nation's leading tort law experts, James A. Henderson of Cornell Law School and Aaron D. Twerski of Brooklyn Law School. The NRA presented Henderson and
Twerski as opposing the extension of absolute product liability in the
manner I proposed in my bill. In fact, the two law professors had been
arguing against the further expansion of strict product liability by *courts,*
not by legislatures. As it happened, I had been teaching at Brooklyn Law
School and had a good relationship with Professor Twerski. He therefore
supplied me with a letter from himself and Henderson that set the record
straight. They wrote to me, in part, that they were:

. . . convinced that our analysis of 'product category liability' should not provide any basis for objecting to your proposal. As we tried to make clear, legislatures are capable of imposing defect-free liability on carefully delineated categories of products, such as assault weaponry. Your Bill appears to be
carefully and precisely worded to identify a category of products which the
state has a clear and convincing interest in regulating . . . [We] believe that it is
important that our analysis not be misused to oppose measures of the sort you
have advanced.

With the professors' approval, I circulated the letter to colleagues.
But it didn't help.

The Assembly Democratic majority is often characterized as dominated by members from New York City, and we did comprise the preponderance of the conference. But the party's large majority in the

Assembly then, as now, depended in significant degree on the Members from upstate districts, where the National Rifle Association exerted powerful force. In the mid-1990's about thirty of my Democratic colleagues were from outside New York City, most from suburban areas or other cities, six or eight from truly rural areas. (As earlier noted, in 2009, 44 of 109 Assembly Democrats were from outside New York City.) Even in those districts, most of the constituents would have supported gun control. But it was a matter of intensity. The NRA could persuade its most zealous adherents to oppose my bill fanatically. Thus, if the bill went to the floor, those Members would face a dilemma. If they voted "No," they would annoy most of their constituents. If they voted "Yes," they would so infuriate a certain small number of constituents that their next Republican opponent would have two dozen or so around-the-clock, devoted volunteers deeply committed to defeating them. So, as was the case for me on "Baby AIDs," they did not want to vote at all.

Downstate Members might face similar dilemmas on other issues (not on this one: downstate constituencies too overwhelmingly supported gun control), but if challenged and defeated, it would be in a primary, by other Democrats. The Assembly leadership could risk downstaters in "safe" Democratic districts, but not upstaters in "marginal" districts. That is why this bill would *never* advance to the floor.

The irony is that if it had gotten to the floor, it would surely have passed. With the votes of urban and suburban legislators, as well as those rural legislators who would finally have opted to vote with the majority of their constituents, we would have had a majority in the Assembly with just the support I could gather from my Democratic party colleagues. We would have had some support, too, from across the aisle.

One can only speculate as to whether we could then have generated enough pressure to get the bill to the Senate floor, and what would have happened there. Unlike for other initiatives, I was hard pressed to find a Republican Senate sponsor for this measure. For reasons of history, as explained in Chapter One, including the much larger districts and the way their boundary lines were drawn, the mathematics of constituent interests did not necessarily affect the Senate, with a Republican majority, in the same way that it affected the Assembly, with a Democratic majority.

The National Rifle Association regularly took more extreme positions than its membership—attempting, for example, to defend armor-piercing bullets, a type of ammunition apparently sold on the civilian market to persons primarily interested in shooting police officers through their Kevlar vests. NRA members might be embarrassed by such stances, but the manufacturers of guns and ammunition provide the organization with most of its funding. As the old saw goes, the NRA follows the golden rule: whoever gives the gold, makes the rules.

Absolute liability put fear in the hearts of the NRA leadership in a way that a statewide ban on assault weapons, later passed, never could. That is because it posed a direct threat to the weapons manufacturers' margins of profit. Even Senator (then-Representative) Charles Schumer's well-publicized efforts to enact the federal Brady law, making purchasers wait for their criminal background checks to clear before they could receive their weapons, apparently engendered less hostility than absolute liability: while Schumer touted the "F" rating the NRA had awarded him in our very pro-gun control part of New York City, my absolute liability crusade allowed me to trumpet my better grade: "F-minus."

In 1995, the *Times* reported on the New York City Council's consideration of an absolute liability approach to assault weapon control, and finally even mentioned Holtzman's connection with it (now that she was safely out of elective office). In covering the Council's deliberations, the *Times* quoted Anthony Weiner's opposition to the bill. Yet in 1998, when I ran in a Democratic primary for Congress with Weiner as one of my opponents (he won), I could obtain neither endorsements nor campaign contributions from the gun control lobby in Washington. (Giving me an edge over my two other opponents was not a factor; they had no significant role in any part of the gun control debate.)

While the gun control lobby surely wanted to avoid annoying Schumer, who endorsed the ultimate victor in the primary, its failure to support me illustrates the basis for the widespread disdain for such "good government" groups among professional politicians. I worked hard for an issue they gave the highest priority; they were not there when I needed them. Both politicians and issue groups are cross-pressured and do what they think they must to advance their political agendas, but the latter often seemed to us in the trenches to claim higher moral ground than they earned or, sometimes, deserved.

As it turned out, the Assembly "marginals"—those Democrats who beat Republican opponents by narrow margins in closely contested campaigns—could afford to vote either for or against legislation to ban assault weapons. The Assembly voted to ban assault weapons altogether in 1993, 1995, 1996, and 1997. In 2000, the Senate voted the ban too, and the bill became law.

In the end a simple ban presented a concept far more understandable to most people than "absolute liability." Moreover, legislation to ban assault weapons at the state level benefited from the New York *Times's* vigorous support for a ban at the federal level. In 1993, prior to the passage of the federal ban, an assault weapons ban in New York had little meaning: the guns mostly came illegally up Route I-95, the "iron pipeline," from Florida, Georgia, South Carolina, North Carolina, and Virginia. After the federal ban, the NRA did not feel or generate the same degree of passion in opposing the state legislation, which, all told, posed relatively little threat to the gun industry.

Attacking the Problem a Different Way: A Domestic Violence Gun Control Win

The crime victim groups that helped in the battle for gun control included many of the leaders of the effort against domestic violence. It took a long time and a lot of effort for advocates to bring this issue to the top of the political agenda. Like many Americans, I had a limited awareness of the subject.

One big problem was that most politicians found it far easier to ride the public's hostility to criminals perceived as strangers, likely with different skin color, than to point to the serious damage inflicted by criminals who were not strangers at all, but often in fact were intimates of their victims. Additionally, most people, myself included, thought of domestic violence as "hitting." Indeed, that is bad enough. But shockingly, the reality of domestic violence often escalated to shooting. Of adult female victims of homicide in the United States in the early 1990s, about 40 percent were killed by husbands or boyfriends.

When the United States busily increased its incarceration rate several-fold in the 1970s-and 80s, largely by increasing sentences and prosecutions of drug offenders, violence among family members affected approximately half of American households. Domestic violence resulted in more injuries than auto accidents, muggings, and rapes combined, claiming over a million women as victims each year. Credible sources estimated that abusers used a weapon in at least one out of three reported domestic violence assaults. In most weapons cases, the abusers shot the victim, inflicting at least serious bodily injury.

Furthermore, domestic abusers tended not to stop. Victims of domestic assault were three times more likely than other assault victims to be assaulted again by the abuser within six months—not altogether surprisingly, since they usually lived with their abuser.

Moreover, prevailing norms discouraged acknowledgment of the seriousness of domestic abuse as a crime. Those norms carried over to the police and the judiciary.

As a result, when courts issued orders requiring abusers to keep away from their victims under various penalties of law, abusers violated these "orders of protection" with impunity. In New York State in 1991, abusers violated over four thousand such family court orders.

Early in 1993, Mindy Bockstein and I developed and I introduced legislation in response to these realities. Because certain abusers—those who were ordered by courts to refrain from further threats or violence and nonetheless threatened their victims with firearms—were statistically likely to carry out those threats or other serious violence, the bill required incarceration for these violations of court orders of protection. At least as important, it also authorized judges to revoke firearms licenses held by the batterers and to confiscate their guns.

My legislative colleagues initially reacted with skepticism to this later provision: they doubted that many of the abusers had licenses for their weapons and that judges would therefore be able to locate the weapons to seize them.

Their notion of abusers was lodged in class-based prejudice. Domestic violence spans the entire social spectrum. "Respectable" middle-class and wealthy people engage in domestic violence at rates similar to those at the economic bottom. When they owned guns, they tended to have gun licenses too. This picture discomfited many; people have some difficulty accepting facts that do not fit their preconceptions.

On gun-linked domestic violence I had some strong allies. Politicians trifled at their peril with an alliance comprised of NOW (the National Organization of Women) and the crime victims' movement. (An occasional female abuser shot a male victim—and an occasional female victim shot a male abuser—but the vast bulk of domestic violence shootings involve men abusing women.) Even the NRA did not dare oppose this one.

In addition, now that Sheldon Silver had become Speaker, Helene Weinstein, the Assembly Member representing my immediate neighbors to the east, had succeeded Oliver Koppell as chair of the Judiciary Committee. Helene felt a strong commitment to the cause of battered women.

My colleague in the State Senate, Dean Skelos, who later joined me in our battle to enact Megan's Law, also allied himself with me in this effort to save women's lives. But Dean ran into a problem in his House, because under the original version of the bill even police officers who violated orders of protection could be compelled to relinquish their service weapons. Police organizations lobbied vociferously in opposition. They argued that a criminal with a grudge against a police officer who learned of the officer's loss of weapon might well take advantage of the opportunity to shoot the now-unarmed officer.

It took us until June to work out a version of the bill that both houses could accept; it excluded police officers. It then flew through. The bill was reported out of Judiciary on June 2, 1993, out of Codes on June 8, given additional technical amendments in Rules on June 15, reported to the floor on June 21, passed by the Assembly on July 1, substituted for the Senate bill and passed by the Senate on July 3, delivered to the Governor on July 16, and signed into law on July 26.

It turned out that the scourge of domestic violence does not particularly spare police spouses. A *Gannett Suburban* editorial published on November 5, 1993, after the bill was signed into law, cited the case of a police officer whose gun was taken from him temporarily by the New York City Police Department after he had destroyed his estranged wife's furniture and threatened her. He got the gun back. When he happened to see his wife in the waiting room of the Westchester County Family Court, he pulled it out. She struggled with him, the gun went off, and another woman, struck while waiting for a hearing on the support payments owed to her by her ex-husband, died later of the gunshot injury.

The editorial complained that our law failed to give a judge the power to take the police officer's gun after his initial threat. It urged that the Legislature amend it to restore the section applying to police, who, it said, "should be held to the same standards as others." Policy opportunities are fleeting. It never happened. Still, our law has no doubt saved lives.

In marked contrast with the absolute liability bill, the history of the gun license revocation law shows how quickly the Legislature can enact a useful bill when the stars, the timing, and the politics are properly aligned.

The Importance of Facts: Where Criminals' Guns Come From

For a long time, the gun lobby prevented collection of the data necessary to show where most crime guns actually came from. In 1978 the

Carter administration attempted to computerize the mandated task of the Federal Bureau of Alcohol, Tobacco and Firearms (ATF) to trace crime guns. In response to a furious lobbying effort by the NRA, Congress first rejected the funding request for computerization and then made sure ATF could not do it anyway by cutting other funds the agency might have used for that purpose.

In the 1990s, the most pervasive media effort the world had ever seen, covering new excesses of American gun violence, aroused American public opinion and diminished the NRA's influence. One result in 1993 was enactment of the Brady Law, requiring a background check and waiting period for the purchase of handguns. Even before the Columbine high school shootings in 1999, the Clinton White House was emboldened, at long last, to have ATF systematically analyze crime gun trace data in order to determine the origin of these weapons.

The conventional view, long promulgated by the NRA, held that most criminals steal the guns they use from the enormous existing stock—more than two hundred million, by most accounts—already in the homes of American citizens. If this were really so, the ways that manufacturers marketed and distributed their new handguns would have made little difference in crime control.

In 1998, however, a Northeastern University study based on records maintained by ATF demonstrated that the conventional wisdom was wrong: more criminals were shown to buy their guns new than to steal them. Based on firearms trafficking investigations performed between July 1996 and December 1998 around the United States, ATF determined that while over 11,000 of the weapons traced were stolen from Federal Firearms Licensees' (FFLs, or licensed gun dealers), residences, or common carriers transporting the guns, almost four times as many, or over 40,000, were trafficked by licensed dealers. Of guns trafficked to youth and juveniles, ATF found that only about 14 percent "involved firearms stolen from a residence," while half "involved firearms trafficked by straw purchasers" (persons who bought them on behalf of another), and a fifth involved firearms "stolen from a Federally licensed firearms dealer."

In summary, in mid-1999 the public learned for sure for the first time that a small and identifiable percentage of wholesale and retail gun sellers were responsible for the overwhelming bulk of sales to criminals. Moreover, manufacturers stamp a unique serial number on each gun they produce, enabling ATF to identify the source of the weapon. ATF trace data now could be used to show that manufacturer "A" received, say, an average of thirty telephone calls a month over a period of years from ATF inquiring about the purchasers of particular weapons it had produced that were traced to crimes. Manufacturer A's records then could be used to show that it sold twelve a month to Distributor B, five a month to distributor C, and so forth. The distributors receive comparable follow-up calls from ATF with respect to their retailers, and their records could be used to show which retailers received their guns that later were used in crime.

Since, as it turns out, a small and identifiable group of retailers is responsible for the vast bulk of the sales into the criminal market, distributors know precisely which retailers' sales foreseeably resulted in criminal use, and manufacturers know which distributors sold disproportionately to such retailers. If litigants have access to this information, they will be able to identify with precision the manufacturers and distributors who knew that sales to particular business customers resulted in criminal use but nonetheless continued to supply those customers. If most crime guns are bought, not stolen, sellers of guns can greatly influence the degree to which guns flow to the crime market. Through their records of responses to ATF, manufacturers can, if they wish, stop dealing with distributors who keep dealing with retailers who continue to leak inventory into the hands of criminals.

The vast majority of retailers manage to avoid selling any guns at all into the criminal market by techniques that are not secret, and most of the rest only very rarely get fooled into selling guns to "straw purchasers," persons who buy illegally on behalf of felons or minors. Straw purchasers tend to buy multiple firearms in a single transaction. Retailers who sell to straw purchasers enhance the risk to the public resulting from criminal use. Criminal activity by the ultimate purchaser should not constitute intervening cause under these circumstances, or, in other words, should not provide an adequate excuse for the sellers.

Even with the best of efforts and intentions by sellers, some criminals will buy guns. Even if manufacturers insist that distributors sell only to legitimate storefront retailers, some people will buy guns to commit crimes. Danger to the public inheres, then, in the sale of guns. But successful plaintiffs must prove that it makes a great deal of difference *how* guns are sold: without the best of efforts and intentions by sellers, far more criminals will buy guns.

Lawsuits Against the Gun Industry, Round I

In a horrifying incident on December 7, 1993 Colin Ferguson murdered six people and injured nineteen others on the Long Island Railroad in Nassau County. The next year survivors of those injured, including Carolyn McCarthy (now a U.S. Representative), sued Sturm, Ruger & Company, the manufacturer of the semiautomatic weapon, and the Olin Corporation, the maker of the hollow-point expanding Black Talon bullets that Ferguson used. ·

McCarthy argued that Olin was negligent and had strict liability for the design, manufacture, marketing, and sale of the Black Talon ammunition, which has exceptionally ferocious wounding power. The federal trial court, which must follow the substantive law of the state in which its sits, noted that New York courts separate issues of duty and foreseeablity in considering negligence, unlike the Michigan court upon whose ruling McCarthy had attempted to rely. In the context of its consideration of Olin's motion to dismiss McCarthy's claim, the New York court accepted her allegation that criminal use of Black Talon bullets to injure innocent victims was foreseeable. However, the court said that the company owed no duty of care to victims of such use, and therefore was not liable. Writing for the Second Circuit, affirming the Southern District's decision against McCarthy, Judge Thomas Meskill said, "New York courts do not impose a legal duty on manufacturers to control the distribution of potentially dangerous products such as ammunition." Judge Guido Calabrese dissented.

The lawsuit set a terrible precedent for subsequent plaintiffs to overcome, but it helped propel McCarthy, the lead plaintiff, to a seat in Congress in 1996.

Also in 1994, families and victims of a shooter in San Francisco sued the gun manufacturer Navegar, which notoriously advertised its best-known semiautomatic as "fingerprint-resistant." With a gun that could fire dozens of bullets very quickly, the perpetrator had killed eight and wounded six people in one brief incident. The plaintiffs based their lawsuit on the theory that the manufacture and sale of that kind of weapon constituted "ultra-hazardous" activity and therefore incurred absolute liability. The perpetrator purchased the weapon in Nevada; it could not have been sold legally in California.

Courts rarely allowed such absolute liability to be imposed on manufacturers of products unless they were defective. However, in April

1995, the California court issued a ruling refusing to dismiss the suit. I tried to use the temporary victory, a rare success in the effort to hold a gun manufacturer liable for the criminal use of a product, to confer legitimacy on and plausibility for my bill. But I failed even to enlist a sponsor for the absolute liability bill in the State Senate.

In March 1996, almost a year after the California ruling, Judge Jack Weinstein of the Federal Court for the Eastern District of New York in Brooklyn allowed yet another lawsuit against gun manufacturers to proceed to discovery in the case of *Hamilton v. Accu-tek*. This was an action in which relatives of victims of handgun violence sought to recover damages and, in the future, halt the injury and death of victims of armed youthful criminals. The district court dismissed plaintiffs' product liability and fraud claims, but Judge Weinstein did give the case to the jury in a way that allowed it to assess damages against three gun manufacturers for negligence. The jury found that several manufacturers had not exercised reasonable care in their marketing and distribution so as to keep their handguns from falling into the hands of criminals and minors. Because the actual guns in most instances were not recovered, and their manufacturers therefore were not known, the damages assessed were apportioned in accord with the market share held by the manufacturers.

The gun manufacturers appealed to the federal Court of Appeals for the Second Circuit, raising questions about interpretations in the Federal District Court of New York State's negligence law, and challenging the manner in which damages were apportioned. The highest authority on any state's law is that state's high court. Before rendering its decision, the Federal Second Circuit therefore looked to New York's highest court, its Court of Appeals, for definitive guidance on these matters. On the basis of the opinion given it by the New York Court of Appeals, the Federal Circuit Court in 2001 vacated the Federal District Court's judgment.

The Center to Prevent Handgun Violence, chaired by Sarah Brady, which had provided representation for the California lawsuit, greeted the Brooklyn suit as perhaps the first to try "to hold the industry collectively liable." But it would not be the last. As we shall see below, over the next few years, the Center and other gun control groups aided and encouraged first New Orleans, and then dozens of other cities around the United States to launch their own lawsuits against manufacturers constituting the vast bulk of the industry.

Lawsuits Against the Gun Industry, Round II

Although dozens of cities joined New Orleans in suing gun manufacturers, arguing that they sold guns with far from the best of efforts and intentions, no state could be enticed to step forward. State involvement was critical. Here again federalism comes into play. Under the law, states are sovereigns in the American federal system, while localities—their creatures—are not. States as sovereigns might not face certain "standing to sue" problems that plagued the municipal plaintiffs that brought the early lawsuits. For example, the State could proceed by seeking to recoup Medicaid payments for the treatment of gunshot injuries, a direct cost they incurred as a result of gun violence.

The barrier to state involvement was the same kind of politics that operated in my legislative effort. While big city residents overwhelmingly supported almost any gun control measure, no state in the Union lacks a rural component, and there the NRA holds sway. Any Attorney General who dared sue the gun industry risked incurring its wrath.

One Attorney General would soon take that risk.

Eliot Spitzer: When Eliot Spitzer announced his candidacy for Attorney General in 1994 it made me unhappy for several reasons.

First, the sitting Attorney General was my good friend and colleague Oliver Koppell. I thought it was amazing that a thoroughly decent fellow like Koppell had managed to gain a statewide office. Very rarely does an Attorney General or State Comptroller leave office before the expiration of the term. Bob Abrams stepped down as Attorney General in 1994. In this circumstance the Legislature elects a replacement to serve until the term expires. It chose one of its own, and Koppell got the job. Given this opportunity for Koppell to acquire the publicity and prominence he would need to retain this post through a brief incumbency, I resented anyone who challenged him. (When Alan Hevesi stepped down as Comptroller very early in 2007, another good friend and colleague, Tom DiNapoli, became Comptroller through the same process. (See chapter XI) Once again his colleagues elected a colleague with extraordinary decency, intelligence, and integrity. DiNapoli, however, had the advantage of starting early enough to serve for virtually an entire term. He hired me as Special Counsel for Law and Policy in the fall of 2007.)

Circumstances made Spitzer's entrance into the race even more damaging for Koppell, because two other candidates joined the fray. One was Joe Hynes, who had defeated me in the primary for Brooklyn District Attorney and had previously made an unsuccessful run for the governorship. Although I liked Joe's innovative program to avoid incarcerating low-level drug offenders, he was a "real" politician, more image than substance, and would surely take votes away from Oliver. And there was Karen Burstein, an outspoken former state senator and head of the State Civil Service Department. In a four-way race she would have the advantage of facing an electorate split by three male candidates. Karen was very smart and accomplished but openly gay, in a decade far less tolerant than the present one. If nominated she would almost surely hand the general election to the Republican-Conservative candidate, Dennis Vacco, a former U.S. Attorney from the Northern District of New York. Vacco's performance as U.S. Attorney had not been outstanding, and he was not particularly admired by his fellow prosecutors.

Moreover, Spitzer's public service record consisted of his work as an Assistant District Attorney in Robert Morgenthau's office in Manhattan. At any given time, New York employs about two thousand assistant district attorneys. Had Eliot Spitzer's father not been extremely wealthy and willing to finance his son's campaign, he would not have come close to a viable candidacy.

I don't have lot of prejudices, but as a politician with no money, I had a big one against candidates born to wealth who spent it on winning elective office.

Spitzer came in dead last in the primary. As I had feared, however, Hynes and Spitzer took enough votes from Koppell for him to lose narrowly to Burstein. Vacco then clobbered Burstein in the general election.

Over the next four years, Vacco performed so pathetically that he actually managed to lose as an incumbent after one full four-year term. (Koppell had served only for about a year.)

Between the 1994 and 1998 Democratic primaries, Spitzer did his homework. He courted elected officials assiduously—even those, like me, who had opposed him. Most significantly for me, he submitted an *amicus* brief in support of Megan's Law on behalf of a public policy group he founded, the Center for the Community Interest. In fact, he had his assistants seek my input on the brief, and impressed me with his seriousness of purpose. It was clear that Eliot Spitzer's next campaign for Attorney General would leave no stone unturned, no upstate county Democratic organization uncosseted.

On reflection, I have to admit it: wealth can enable an otherwise meritorious candidate to avoid the Hobson's choice I previously described, the necessity to choose whether to spend time on substantive efforts or on self-promotion. Politicians need enough press attention to win political credibility, which in turn is essential to enlarge a political base and build a donor base. Spitzer, like some other successful New York politicians before him—Averell Harriman and Nelson Rockefeller come to mind—could leap to statewide office without holding local office first because he and his family could afford to finance a big campaign mostly on their own.

In the course of Eliot Spitzer's 1998 Democratic primary campaign for Attorney General and mine for Congress, we found ourselves at the same Democratic club in Queens on a night when we were the only candidates there, and we had little enough on our respective schedules to stay a long time. As I heard him speak and respond to questions, I realized that my prejudice had blinded me to his considerable talent and ability. You don't make Law Review at Harvard because your daddy has money. You don't lead the successful prosecution of the Gambino Mafia family for their illicit control of New York City garment center trucking based on your personal wealth. You don't become a star, impressing all your colleagues with hard work and incisive intelligence, at the high-powered law firms you join because of your position in society.

Apparently Spitzer liked what I had to say too. After he won his primary and I lost mine, I ran into him at a political breakfast. At that point, he was trailing Vacco by about ten percentage points in the polls. I told him, "I want to work for you, but you have to win!" (I learned later that he doubted at that point that he would—but knowing what I know now about his grit and determination, I'm sure that if he had not prevailed in 1998 he would have run a third time.) He said, "Even if I don't win, I want to keep in touch."

Going After Guns From the Attorney General's Offices: After Eliot Spitzer won the general election, I sent a résumé to the Attorney General's transition team. The Attorney General-elect and two of his colleagues interviewed me. He knew enough about my interests and how they fit with his to make a very welcome comment: "I assume you'll want to work on the gun case." I knew that he intended, as the next Attorney General, to make New York State the first in the country to sue the gun manufacturers. I had a new job.

In Chapter XI, you will read my co-author's description and assessment of the end of Eliot Spitzer's political career nine years later, in March of 2008, only a few months into his second year as Governor. I cannot join or concur in that assessment. The experience of working for Spitzer left me with a dramatically different impression of the man, apparently, from the impression left on those who know him only from what they have read in newspapers or seen on television. I had hundreds of encounters with Spitzer in the course of my work for him, and they were invariably a pleasure. Whenever he was physically present, he made the job more fun with humor, insight, brilliance, and collegiality. I remain mystified by some of his actions as Governor—especially his response to Tom DiNapoli's candidacy for Comptroller—and I have no hope of understanding whatever personal demons led to the prostitution scandal. I do have some hope that history will look very kindly on Spitzer's record as Attorney General, and even on the few victories he had time to win as Governor. My overwhelmingly positive personal experience with Spitzer, though, makes it impossible for me to withhold my continued affection and admiration for the man, and I feel that his good qualities vastly outweigh his faults. Obviously others have come to different conclusions. However, most of us who have participated personally in matters that made the news would agree that the news reports can never transmit the whole story. Perhaps the "whole story" is different for each participant.

I will always remember the gun case as a glorious crusade, one of the most compelling projects I pursued in Spitzer's office.

Design Defect: A Rejected Option. In the first few months of our work, we explored the various legal concepts upon which we might build a case against gun makers: fraud, deceptive acts, false advertising, duty to warn, design defect, negligent marketing, public nuisance, and negligent entrustment. I sent an intern, Hillel Deutsch, to the Washington, D.C., office of the Violence Policy Center, which keeps an extraordinarily fine library of gun catalogs and magazines. Using those sources, he compiled the only existing comprehensive summary of handgun design defects, model by model. Those problems caused many unintended deaths and injuries among children and teenagers who played with pistols that they thought were unloaded.

Magazine clips removed from pistols often leave a round in the weapons' chambers. Devices costing manufacturers a dollar or two can prevent the weapon from firing at all when the clip has been removed ("magazine safety disconnects"); and other inexpensive devices signal the user that a round is indeed in the chamber ("chamber-loaded indicators"). Many popular models produced by Colt's, Browning, Ruger, Glock, and Sigarms lacked these devices, as well as models produced by the less reputable Bryco, Davis, Lorcin, HiPoint, Intratec, Phoenix, and Sundance.

Smith & Wesson discontinued its "child-proof" "lemon squeeze" grip safety in 1937. Without such a device, children under eight could fire the company's guns.

Between 1953 and 1972, more than one and one half million Sturm Ruger "Old Models" were sold before a "transfer bar safety" was added to the gun's design. Without that addition, the model tended to fire when dropped. More than 600 people were killed or injured in consequent accidents. Ruger never recalled the gun, but instead began to offer retrofitting in 1982 (fewer than one-tenth were in fact retrofitted by 1993). As of 1999, Ruger continued to distribute flyers offering the free retrofitting.

In 1983, the New York Court of Appeals set forth seven key factors plaintiffs needed to assess and find in proper balance to win a suit for design defect: the product's social utility, utility to the individual user, likelihood that it will cause injury, availability of a safer design, practicability of a safer design in terms of functionality level and reasonable cost, the at-risk victim's likely level of awareness of the product's dangerousness, and the manufacturer's ability to pass the cost of design change onto new purchasers. This seven-factor test remains good law. We noted the preference of the U.S. Army and some law enforcement groups for guns without some of the safety features we sought. Our arguments would therefore not have gone unchallenged. Nevertheless, based on the factor analysis, we would have made a strong case had we chosen to focus our lawsuit on the manufacturers of those guns used in the majority of unintended shootings because of the absence of the safety features noted above or because of other defects we identified.

Negligence: Too Risky. We chose to pursue the manufacturers on the basis of the guns that entered the criminal market and were used in shootings that were all too intentional, rather than focusing on the defects that contributed to death and injury for unintended shootings. Here the range of theories we had examined yielded two choices as our final "contestants." I wanted to advance a negligence-based theory, but we all had deep qualms about the negligence claims in *Hamilton*. Out of a large number of guns even carefully sold, a small percentage may find its way to criminals. Based on anecdotal evidence, the *Hamilton* plaintiffs, jury, trial judge, and others believed that negligence, not volume, accounted for the leaks. But without sales figures, dealer by dealer, to match against crime gun traces, plaintiffs had no proof that the negligence of dealers, or the distributors and manufacturers who continued to supply them, caused their harm or enhanced their risk of harm. The manufacturers' respective market shares, or perhaps better, their respective shares of the guns traced to crimes in New York by ATF, might provide an adequate proxy for such figures, but we could not be sure. Moreover, we had to decide on a course of action without the luxury of knowing how the negligence claims in *Hamilton* would ultimately fare: the appellate courts might reject them so forcefully as to discredit any further negligent distribution lawsuits against gun manufacturers.

Public Nuisance: Our Approach. Another attorney in the Office, Peter Pope, argued that a public nuisance action gave us a better chance of success. For a negligence case to succeed, we would have to prove that the manufacturers owed a duty of care to the public and had breached that duty of care. We would also have to show that their breach of that duty—that is, their negligence—had caused the gunshot injuries to New Yorkers we would adduce.

A public nuisance case, in contrast, would not require us to establish a duty of care on the part of the manufacturers. Nor would it require proof that the manufacturers' behavior had caused the injuries. We would merely have to show that the nuisance existed and that the manufacturers created, maintained, or contributed to it. Rather than using all the information ATF had provided to us, the mere list of handguns found in crimes in New York, broken down by manufacturer, with each manufacturer having produced hundreds or even thousands on the list, might well suffice. On the other hand, we ran the risk that courts would reject a nuisance claim on the basis that too many kinds of injury could be attributed to "nuisance" in the way we would have to use the concept to place reasonable limitations on litigation so framed.

We asked ATF for computer tapes reflecting the "crime gun trace request" records it keeps on handguns found at crime scenes. Based on make and serial number, ATF asked manufacturers to look up the gun to determine which distributor bought it, and then asked the distributor which retailer bought it. With these records we could easily see how many manufacturers allowed distributors to keep selling over the years to the small percentage of retailers responsible for the overwhelming bulk of leakage into the crime gun market.

Trying to Talk to the Manufacturers: Now, six months after we had started, I thought we were nearly ready to sue. Spitzer, though, argued that an effort to negotiate with the gun manufacturers would be more responsible. We might or might not win a lawsuit, which could in any case take years. A negotiation could win concessions by the manufacturers resulting in more careful distribution that could keep guns out of the hands of criminals and save lives within months. Also, this way we could put design-defect issues on the table as well, also with great life-saving potential.

Spitzer was persuasive, and he was also the boss. Based on the knowledge we had acquired in six months of frenetic preparation for a lawsuit, we enlisted most of the cities around the country whose lawsuits were already underway, as well as a number of the leading gun manufacturers, and entered negotiation.

In mid-July Andrew Cuomo, then Secretary of Housing and Urban Development (HUD) in the Clinton administration, announced that he too was suing the gun manufacturers, for deaths and injuries to the inhabitants of the federal housing projects under HUD jurisdiction. Then he called Spitzer, asking to join in our negotiating process.

The possibility that a settlement with governments might encourage more private lawsuits already gave the manufacturers a disincentive to sit down with us. The Cuomo request put us in an even more uncomfortable position. This was not because Cuomo was already rumored to be eyeing the 2002 race for governor in New York, when Spitzer felt an obligation to support Carl McCall, the State Comptroller who had earned the nomination. And it was not because as a contemporary, Cuomo might pose a future threat to Spitzer's own political future. It had to do with national politics.

Andrew Cuomo was part of the administration that was setting up the 2000 presidential candidacy of Al Gore. The gun manufacturers—the financial base of the NRA—did not want a national Democratic win, and would certainly shy away from a negotiated outcome likely to be seen as a victory (through Cuomo) for the Democrats in Washington.

On the other hand, we could not very well tell the Clinton administration that its cabinet member was unwelcome in our effort. Cuomo joined our parlay.

The negotiations began to drift. Feedback from the individual gun manufacturers participating got more and more negative. Eventually, the companies walked away, as we had feared they would.

Cuomo called to seek reassurances that we were all on one team, and that we would not sign an agreement independently or with the cities as our allies, leaving him on the sidelines. Of course we obliged.

Then in March 2000, one of Spitzer's deputies received a late-night telephone call. Cuomo would be signing an agreement with Smith & Wesson early the next morning. Spitzer joined Cuomo and Smith &

Wesson's chief executive, Ed Schulz, in announcing the agreement in Washington on March 17.

At first, we thought that other gunmakers might follow Smith & Wesson's lead. Instead, the NRA and others led a boycott of Smith & Wesson, ultimately resulting in its sale to new ownership.

The Public Nuisance Lawsuit: In June 2000, we filed *Spitzer v. Sturm Ruger et al.*, a public nuisance case, in New York State Supreme Court (the State's major trial-level court) with Peter Pope, the attorney who had urged that theory, at the helm.

In August 2001 New York County Supreme Court Judge Louis York issued an opinion in *Sturm Ruger* granting defendants' motion to dismiss before trial. He said that we had failed to show in our pleadings that defendants could possibly have a sufficient connection to the nuisance. To render this kind of decision before trial seemed unreasonable to us. It did not give us an opportunity to present the evidence that would establish defendants' connection, much of which we already had in the printouts of guns traced to crimes in New York, listed by manufacturer.

We made this point and others in the appellate brief we filed in mid-February 2002. On Friday, May 10, Eliot Spitzer himself argued the appeal before the Appellate Division of the New York State Supreme Court's First Department. Never before had Spitzer argued a case personally for our Office. He did so brilliantly.

But it was all in vain. Almost two years later, in June 2003, the First Department entered its decision. The majority affirmed the lower-court ruling over a dissent by Judge Ernst Rosenberg, who noted that that to reach their conclusion his colleagues had given little regard to well established procedural rules for consideration of motions to dismiss. These required it to accept as true the plaintiff's allegations and reasonable inferences derived from them. This is because if dismissal is granted the opportunity is lost to prove the truth of such allegations.

If two judges had dissented, the highest court in the State would have been required to hear our further appeal. But there was only one. In October 2003, the New York Court of Appeals declined to hear our appeal.

Negligence: A Final Try. While we were at a relatively early stage in our own suit, we hoped that the New York Court of Appeals would rule on the request of the Federal District Court in the Brooklyn gun case discussed above in way that would strengthen our argument. A key issue was whether the gun manufacturers had a "duty of care," and obligation in law that arose from their manufacture and marketing of a product that might be used to harm others. The issue turned on whether the gun makers had the ability and authority to exercise control over the person who injured the victim of gun violence, or over the victim him or herself.

In a "friend of the court" brief we submitted in that case, we discounted precedent in light of newly discovered facts. We said that because we now knew that most guns used by criminals were purchased, not stolen, and because manufacturers could know from ATF data which sellers were the source of many of these guns, gun makers could more effectively exercise greater authority and control in product distribution than had the courts earlier realized, and therefore were obligated to do so. Defendants argued that whether they could do so notwithstanding, manufacturers still did not have the kind of relationship with sellers that the New York precedents required.

The New York Court of Appeals decision, written by my former Assembly colleague Richard Wesley (now on the Second Circuit), did not reject our argument on principle. But it demurred on the facts. There was, after all, only one gun in evidence, and its manufacturer could not even be identified. This was insufficient basis upon which to say, the Court concluded, that the industry had acted in a way that triggered a "duty of care." But the language of its decision invited future plaintiffs to pursue a negligence cause of action if they could show that manufacturers knowingly supply guns to wholesalers who regularly leak them into the criminal market.

We had lost in the Federal courts with our public nuisance approach. Private litigants, whom we supported, lost in the Federal and state courts with their negligence approach. Not total losses, perhaps, but nevertheless tough ones. And our opponents were relentless.

Federal and State Legislative Responses to Lawsuits: Forum Shifting

In many states the NRA and its supporters do not merely stonewall legislative efforts they oppose: they win enactment of legislation they support. In response to the lawsuits against gun manufacturers by dozens of cities, thirty states enacted legislation substantially immunizing gun manufacturers against such suits.

And when the NRA does not have the power to win in the state legislature, it seeks preemption by a supportive Congress. In April 2003, the U.S. House of Representatives passed a bill that would prohibit third-party tort liability or public nuisance lawsuits against gun manufacturers or sellers. The Senate version of the bill, introduced in that chamber by Senator Larry Craig (R-Idaho), later notorious for other reasons, garnered fifty-four sponsors. When faced with a potential Democratic filibuster to block enactment, 75 senators—fifteen more than the 60 required—voted in February 2004 to end the debate.

Before the Senate could approve the Craig bill, however, two amendments that led to its ultimate failure were added by narrow margins. Senator John McCain's proposal to close the "gun-show loophole" to the law requiring a waiting period to check to see if a purchaser has a criminal record, won a 53-to-46 vote. Senator Diane Feinstein's amendment providing for a ten-year extension of the ban on assault weapons (which in fact ultimately expired, without extension, in September 2004) passed 52-to-47. Those amendments caused the National Rifle Association to reverse course. It e-mailed each Senator a message expressing opposition to the Craig bill in its amended form. When the amended bill came to a vote on March 2, 2004, Senator Craig and his allies were among the 90 votes against it.

Still, the measure continued to enjoy impressive support. The 2004 elections saw an increase in GOP strength in the Congress. In July of 2005 the Senate passed the "Protection of Lawful Commerce in Arms Act"—an even worse version of the bill they had considered and rejected in the previous year. It barred lawsuits alleging that the manufacturer continued to supply weapons to a dealer whose stock it knew was regularly traced to crimes, as well as mass tort claims brought by municipalities and public interest groups. In addition to immunity against lawsuits for negligence, this version included additional provisions to immunize gun dealers against such administrative sanctions by ATF as loss of license. Sponsors accepted only one amendment—permitting lawsuits in which weapons lacked child safety-locks (already an industry standard). An attempt to include in the measure an extension of the assault weapon ban failed. The bill passed the House on October 20, 2005, and was signed into law by President George W. Bush six days later.

In response, on April 25, 2006 New York City's Mayor Mike Bloomberg and Mayor Thomas Menino of Boston invited thirteen of their colleagues to a meeting at Gracie Mansion to discuss strategies for stopping the flow of illegal guns into America's cities. This marked the founding of Mayors Against Illegal Guns, a group that grew to include more than 230 mayors from 40 states. Among its founding principles was " . . . oppos[ition to] . . . all federal efforts to restrict cities' right to access, use, and share trace data that is so essential to effective enforcement." The US Conference of Mayors and the National Conference of Black Mayors backed the effort. Support came too from national and state organizations of police officers. But the gun lobby in Washington continued to prevail.

In September and October of 2002, sixteen people were killed and a number of others wounded in Virginia and the Washington D.C. Metropolitan area by a sniper. Bull's Eye Shooters, a gun dealer that had "lost" 300 weapons used in crimes and that supplied one of the weapons used by the sniper in 2002, paid about $2 million to settle a suit against it by surviving victims and families of victims, *Johnson v. Bulls Eye Shooter Supply*, 2003 WL 21639244 (Wash. Super. 2003). The next year, the manufacturer of an assault rifle used by the sniper agreed to pay $550,000 to surviving victims and families of victims to settle their lawsuit. The 2004 version of the Craig bill would have barred plaintiffs like Johnson from suing. The 2005 version now does so, and even prevents ATF from taking the dealer's license: they can just keep on trafficking. Moreover, if there is no successful challenge, the law will now supersede and invalidate all contrary state and local law.

There might be some hope for gun control advocates seeking to challenge the Federal immunization statute in Justice White's dissent from the Supreme Court's rejection of Due Process and Equal Protection challenges to caps on damages in medical malpractice cases. He noted that the Court had not determined whether the Due Process Clause requires that when legislation ends or limits a plaintiff's common-law remedy, it must also provide a reasonable substitute remedy. The gun law immunization statutes even more clearly shortchange plaintiffs: they provide for no private remedy at all for most injured plaintiffs, while at least medical malpractice plaintiffs can get damages up to the amount of the statutory cap.

Also, however implausible the argument that the malpractice insurance industry needs caps to protect its continued existence, at least the argument can be made that malpractice plaintiffs benefit from the protection of that industry, inasmuch as the plaintiffs need the industry to improve their chances of recovering damages. Immunizing the gun industry, however, cannot even arguably help plaintiff victims. Therefore, gun control advocates will posit that statutes depriving plaintiffs of their rights to sue as third-party victims of gun manufacturers' negligence may violate the Due Process Clause, or even the Seventh Amendment, which guarantees the right to a jury trial in "Suits at common law, where the value in controversy shall exceed twenty dollars."

Legislators swear to uphold the Constitution. They should not vote for legislation they think violates it. However, legislators may be understood to have varying opinions on the constitutional issues raised here. No obvious principle bars legislative consideration of the gun manufacturer immunization statutes enacted by many states and the national government. Just as clearly, however, litigants may bring constitutional challenges to these statutes.

Federalism's Opportunities: States and Localities Persist. As the story of ongoing efforts to achieve gun control dramatically demonstrates, in a country as large and diverse as the United States, policy in important contentious areas does not develop in a clear, coherent, linear, sequential manner when the stakes are high and values strongly conflict. The policy environment is constantly shifting: old leaders depart, new one are elected or appointed. Partisan majorities change. Public opinion shifts in response to events and altered demographics and social and economic conditions.

One great virtue of the federal system for advocates of change is that it provides multiple points of entry. Ideas that may be tried and tested in one place are adopted in another. Lessons are learned in defeat. Legislation provokes litigation. The outcome of a lawsuit results in further legislation. A promising law in one jurisdiction is tried in another. Victories in a locality may be undone by state-level action. Similar state action may be overcome in the Congress, or in the federal courts. It is one step forward, two steps back, until (perhaps) a breakthrough is reached. Regarding gun control, at the state and local levels steps continued to be taken.

In 2002, the California State Legislature repealed an older statute prohibiting product liability suits against gun manufacturers. The repeal reflected disgust with a decision by California's highest court rejecting a previously successful negligence claim against Navegar, the notorious gun manufacturer mentioned earlier. The court alleged that the lawsuit was merely a disguised version of a product liability/design defect claim.

Although California includes about an eighth of the population of the United States, clearly its Legislature was bucking the national trend. Elsewhere gun control advocates achieved very limited success in challenging state immunization laws in court. A Michigan court rejected the retroactive aspects of that State's immunization law as an unconstitutional interference with a pending case, violating the separation of powers requirement. A Georgia court upheld retroactive application of its State's immunization law in the face of the same argument. A Louisiana court rejected arguments that retroactive application to an ongoing lawsuit by the City of New Orleans would violate its due process rights under the Fourteenth Amendment, "the federal Equal Protection Clause, the Contract Clause, and the prohibition against bills of attainder," and its home rule powers. But it limited its conclusion to "the City, as a political subdivision of the state," leaving open the possibility that the court would treat differently a suit by a private party.

Meanwhile in New York City, on January 18, 2005 Mayor Michael Bloomberg signed into law City Council Member David Yassky's bill imposing liability on gun manufacturers and dealers for deaths and injuries resulting from crimes in which their guns were used, if: the manufacturer or dealer allowed sales or sold guns at gun shows, from the back of a truck, or from a kitchen table; or if they allowed sales of or sold more than one gun a month per customer. Elizabeth Holtzman joined the lawmakers at the bill-signing ceremony.

Patrick Brophy, a director of the New York State Rifle and Pistol Association, threatened to challenge the new law in court. Laurence G. Keane, as general counsel for the National Shooting Sports Foundation, had previously argued vehemently against Spitzer and the *Hamilton* plaintiffs that the legislative process, not the judicial arena, was the appropriate forum for the issue of gun maker tort liability. Now he attacked the new law as unconstitutional. For Brophy, where he stood did very much depend upon where he sat.

Drawing upon ATF data, early in 2006 New York City initiated a sting operation against forty gun dealers in Georgia, Ohio Pennsylvania, South Carolina and Virginia who had sold guns linked to more than 500 crimes that occurred in the city between 1994 and 2001. Using the evidence it gathered from this effort, the city sued fifteen of these dealers for violation of federal laws on gun sales. Though Congress had barred the use of federal data for this purpose the previous fall, Judge Jack Weinstein allowed it in this case because the city had obtained the information upon which it had initiated its action prior to the federal law's passage. By the end of 2006 New York City had reached settlements with six gun dealers. For a period of three years, they agreed to allow a special master appointed by Judge Weinstein to review their records, place video recorders in their stores and provide special training to their employees. They also agreed to allow the city to send undercover agents into their stores at any time, to assure compliance with gun sales laws.

Encouraged by this success, the City initiated action against an additional twelve gun sellers. Some counter-sued, among them Larry Mickalis in the Mickalis Pawn Shop of Summerville, South Carolina. But even he opined that under the pressure of the city's aggressive efforts: "No one in their right mind is going to sell someone from New York a gun."

However, in March 2009 the Supreme Court refused to reconsider the reversal of Judge Weinstein's decision by the Second Circuit Court of Appeals, holding that the Protection of Lawful Commerce in Arms Act did retroactively bar New York City's lawsuit, ending that struggle.

Law and Values: Court, Legislatures, or Both?

We intend our courts to maximize fairness to individuals. Inherent in our idea of fairness is the protection of "rights," which do not change when conditions change. The process is structured to be adversarial, a "fair fight" between genuinely opposing parties. Procedures are highly specified. Information is gathered to inform decisions in accord with strictly defined rules. Judges, neutral third parties, are expected to justify their decisions with logical reasoning that most people will find persuasive. They are not ordinarily required to think about the implications of their decision beyond the equities being weighed in the immediate matter.

In contrast, the value we seek to maximize in legislatures is not fairness but representativeness. Legislatures act primarily in response to aggregated interests. We accept as legitimate (and even protect constitutionally) the idea that organized groups will and should be able to influence legislators with the votes and other support they can deliver (workers, money) at election time. In the making of budgets, the central legislative function, the nature of that political support, as well as their ability to collect information from the widest range of interests by way of hearings and the importuning of lobbyists, brings legislators to allocate resources in some approximate proportion to perceived needs, and to collect taxes in some approximate proportion to perceived ability to pay. These decisions are based on a great array of factors—among them ideology, partisanship, influence, even the pure provision of information—but only marginally on the "rights" of interested parties. Therefore, they may be changed from year to year as conditions change.

In the 1970s and 1980s, judges may have ventured too far into the core legislative function. In institutional litigation, courts required legislatures to allocate hundreds of millions of dollars for the rehabilitation and construction of prisons, hospitals for the mentally ill and developmentally disabled, and schools, skewing and altering the overall direction of some state budgets. Constitutional claims powered those lawsuits. To the extent that courts granted claims to stated levels of material support as of right, they infringed on the legislative budgetary power, whether or not some legislatures may have covertly signaled their desire for such decisions, or invited them by failing to meet their responsibilities to make hard choices.

A landmark example is federal Judge Frank Johnson's requirement [*Wyatt v. Stickney*, 344 F. Supp. 1341 (M.D. Ala. 1971), mod. *sub. nom. Wyatt v. Aderholt*, 503 F.2d 1305 (5th Cir. 1974)] that the State of Alabama provide Bryce Hospital with sufficient resources to bring its treatment of mentally impaired residents up to levels specifically set forth by a special master. In his judicial role, Judge Johnson could not properly take into account the interests of all the indirectly affected parties to whom resources would not flow as a result of this order: e.g., patients in hospitals treating the physically ill, children in the public schools of Alabama, potential victims of crime on streets with less police on patrol. The judge could only consider the arguments brought to him by parties to the lawsuit, and decide on the basis of the "rights" of those parties. In fact, obeying the judge's order would have taken more than half of Alabama's annual operating budget, stripping the resources for serving other worthy social purposes. Johnson proved himself a great and courageous judge in his long history on the bench. The heart goes out to those he tried to help in his Bryce Hospital ruling. But the head should resist such conclusions.

In general, courts are far less good at deciding controversies that affect numerous and varied interests in numerous and varied ways. To the extent that Judge Johnson's decision usurped the budget-making function of the Legislature, it illustrated the comparative institutional incompetence of courts in the pursuit of distributive justice. Legislators operate in an environment in which public needs, the economy, tax revenues, and other conditions change. We do not expect them to be neutral, but to assign benefits and burdens in accord with to their own views and loyalties, and the character and intensity of the desires of the constituencies they represent. Outcomes arise out of a process of contained conflict among a multiplicity of parties, informed (at its best) by deliberation and reasoned argument. Tradeoffs across numerous matters and parties, as in the case of budgeting, are at the center of what legislatures do. There are rules, but they are far less constraining than those used in courts. Nor do we hold legislatures to the same standard of fairness as we do courts, in the sense of requiring from them a logical defense of their decisions, although we prefer logic to its absence.

This is not to say that courts should always refrain from disputes with large policy implications. For better or for worse, rights-based court decisions have long shaped policy as forcefully as have legislative decisions. In *Lochner v. New York*, 198 U.S. 45 (1905) the U.S. Supreme Court threw out as unconstitutional a New York statute attempting to limit the number of hours bakeries could make their employees work. The New Deal decisions reversed *Lochner*, opening the door to widespread legislative limits on business behavior. Other major breakthroughs in the law, whether in the Supreme Court's 1954 school desegregation decision, *Brown v. Board of Education*, 347 U.S. 483, or in *Roe v. Wade*, 410 U.S. 113 (1972), the abortion-rights case, dramatically altered the course of public policy.

The truth is that if courts do their job some policy impact of their decisions is inescapable. For example, and as we have seen, others are often affected by the outcomes of disputes over tort liability to third parties that arise in the context of a battle between two opposing parties, each seeking justice on the basis of rights. Resolving such disputes involves complex policy analysis. Only with great difficulty can courts determine whether tort liability will reallocate risk in a manner likely to result in its reduction, will burden or destroy commercial activity, or will approximate justice in its effect. And when courts take action, they set precedent.

Judges should decide fairly, within the constraints of the law, between two parties, and ordinarily should only consider matters brought to their attention by the parties. Yet in cases like those against gun manufacturers, where courts *must* decide whether to find a duty to third parties in tort, judges *are* expected to apply public policy considerations, even when the parties have failed to raise such issues. In a leading case on duty to third parties in tort in 1994, the New York Court of Appeals said that relevant public policy factors should include "reasonable expectations of parties and society generally, the proliferation of claims, the likelihood of unlimited or insurer-like liability, disproportionate risk and reparation allocation, and public policies affecting the expansion or limitation of new channels of liability."

In other words, the matter of who should do what is not black and white, but very, very gray. The place and process in and through which the interests of the individual are likely best served conflicts with the place and process in and through which the interests of the community are likely best served. This tension is at the root of the dispute about the legitimacy of our efforts to harness liability law to achieve gun control. One ideal, justice (and fairness) requires that tort liability disputes be left to courts. Another ideal, representativeness (liberty, equality) requires that tort liability disputes to be left to legislatures.

With regard to gun control, courts are hampered because no one has yet been able to show precisely how gun manufacturers' negligence in the aggregate has caused gun victims' injuries. Ultimately, if courts are to act, plaintiffs must demonstrate the causal relationship clearly enough for them to meet their responsibility to ensure particularized fairness to individual parties. Otherwise, only legislatures may legitimately rearrange burdens and benefits to reach the broader version of fairness I sought with my proposed law by forcing gun manufacturers to internalize the costs of their economic behavior.

That is, we expect even more of legislatures than we do of courts. As early as the 1970s, gun industry experts were concerned that product liability suits could end their business entirely. They have not provided convincing evidence that this draconian outcome would occur. But if it were so, absolute liability legislation poses an even greater threat. Putting gun manufacturers out of business would surely impinge on the ability of Americans to defend themselves by acquiring guns. While probably not unconstitutional as a violation of the Second Amendment (even in the eyes of its most fervent scholarly supporters), laws that had this effect would undermine liberty as many Americans understand it. More obviously there would be a drastic effect on the property rights of gun manufacturers.

Legislatures must balance these values—liberty and property—against equality (by remedying the inequitable burden on victims of gun violence) and security (by reducing the risk of gun violence). If they find that the former two values outweigh the latter, they will reject the imposition of tort liability.

In this ambiguous environment it is natural, even inevitable, that committed advocates will seek out the decision arenas in which they are most likely to succeed. If courts find that plaintiffs meet the appropriate evidentiary burdens, nothing in the theory of tort liability makes it an inappropriate subject for adjudication. And if legislatures find that advocates can muster sufficient political support around the values of equality and security, nothing in the theory of tort liability makes it an inappropriate subject for legislation.

Consider another reality. Processes impose costs, whatever their outcome. As legal scholar Timothy Lytton has pointed out, unlike private plaintiffs, city and state governments attempting to recoup enormous public costs, say for health care, can justify reaching far into their relatively deep pockets to finance litigation. The cost of defending against the multiplicity of municipal lawsuits may itself have altered the marketing practices of some gun manufacturers and forced others out of business. Increased product prices may have even, at the margin, diminished the availability of guns in the marketplace.

Unfortunately, it seems impossible to keep out of court lawsuits brought on the basis of ill-advised legal theories without blocking suits whose novel legal bases, which at first blush may appear unsound, ultimately strengthen and advance American jurisprudence. More to the point, discomfort that arises from municipal lawsuits that stretch the use of the judicial process to seek a remedy for gun violence, no more justifies closing the courts to tort liability—as Congress has sought to do—than do analogous distortions of the legislative process justify denying access to the political process to seeking remedies for this problem.

In most of Europe political parties offer candidates for legislative office primarily on the basis of their views on national policy, not on the basis of their connection or responsiveness to the local constituency. In contrast, the American political process, for both structural and cultural reasons, produces legislators who must be far more responsive to their constituents than to their political parties.

This provides one part of the explanation for the inaction or weak action of the New York State Assembly on gun control when overwhelming majorities in almost every Assembly district supported it. To protect its "marginal" members from serious challenges, the Assembly leadership kept tough gun control bills off the floor, even though a majority in the constituencies of even those members might have supported this legislation. The point was to avoid the risk of adding intensely committed NRA partisans to the campaigns of the opposition.

When it comes to gun control and other similar issues, what matters is not numbers but intensity. The overwhelming majority of the population would benefit from real gun control. But the vast majority of people will never personally experience gun violence. To each individual, therefore, the benefit from strong gun control legislation seems very small. In contrast, the gun manufacturers, relatively small in number, have a direct and enormous stake in combating the kind of gun control measures I was urging. Small, intensely interested groups mobilize far more quickly, easily, and energetically than do big, amorphous ones, and are far better sources of campaign cash.

Closely related is the "free rider" problem identified by political scientist Mancur Olsen. A gun-control advocate—remember, with relatively little at stake—may reasonably decline to pay dues to a gun control group, even though he or she will still enjoy safer streets if the group wins. In contrast, gun makers who believe that their entire business is at stake cannot afford to be free riders. The business owner who decides to let his competitors bear the whole lobbying burden may even find that the resulting legislation somehow targets his particular product model for regulation or taxation, and not theirs. This is why small, intensely focused interest groups win a bigger share of their legislative battles than their size and numbers otherwise seem to justify.

The free-rider problem distorts the legislative process, if we assume that representative democracy should be majoritarian. Municipalities entering the courts may generate unfortunate financial pressures by imposing litigation costs on private defendants. But one can no more keep the resulting distortion out of the courts than one can keep free-rider problems out of legislatures, and still have these institutions do their jobs. In both cases, the cure would be worse than the disease.

In the end, Aristotle's distinction between corrective justice and distributional justice provides guidance but not bright line rules for society's allocation of policy decisions between courts and legislatures. Courts have the comparative institutional advantage in seeking corrective justice, legislatures in seeking distributive justice. When courts have to resolve tort liability problems that invoke issues of distributional justice, they should respect some limits beyond which they truly intrude onto territory that properly belongs to legislatures. But at the margins overlap is inevitable, and even necessary. Public policy in the United States emerges from complex interchanges among all the branches of government, as citizens respond to decisions by one arm of government by petitioning another.

CHAPTER X

Life in the Legislature: Politics and Lawmaking

It is said that in 1972 China's brilliant Premier Zhou En-Lai was asked by the U.S. Secretary of State Henry Kissinger, "What was the effect of the French Revolution on humanity?" Zhou was reportedly silent for a moment, and then famously replied: "It's too soon to tell."

In looking back at 25 years experience from less than a decade's distance, with the wisdom of Zhou's (possibly apochryphal) observation in mind, it seems at first presumptuous to reach any firm conclusions on the nature and effect of public safety lawmaking in general, or even just in New York. I am keenly aware of the problem of generalizing from specific experience, in a specific policy area, with a singular perspective. Moreover, I know it is hard for me, as it is for any participant in events, to achieve analytic distance. Deep commitments to people and ideas get in the way. So do strong enmities. On any given day the record of experience supports both cynicism and optimism, a glass half full, or half empty.

Nevertheless I think that the events and experiences chronicled here add to the body of available evidence on how and why legislatures act, and what they can or cannot be expected to do. The following observations are offered with awareness that legislating not only produces concrete results—including failures; also, in their way, results. It also involves what noted American political scientist Murray Edelman called "the symbolic uses of politics." For surely, while making policy, politicians are also self-consciously and importantly sending psychological messages to voters, signaling empathy, reassurance, or inclusion.

Legislating is Slow and Hard

Walk into any legislator's office. Take a look at the trophies on the wall. They are not moose heads. They are rarely diplomas. They are most often the framed first pages of bills sponsored and passed, accompanied by the pens governors used to sign them.

Bills are the currency of the legislature, and passing bills into law is the primary measure of a legislator's achievement. (Any doubts? Check the achievements claimed in the biographies legislators write about themselves.) So there is significant potential benefit to a member for identifying and taking ownership of an issue, and offering a solution. But in truth it takes time to simply recognize that a problem exists, and more time to decide that it is a problem that you want to address. This involves some complex thinking—about such things as what you believe and stand for, who you represent, the nature of your ambitions, and your job within the legislature.

Bills are not only put in with serious intent to solve problems, but to please a constituent or an interest group, or to stake a claim. If an issue gets hot, having introduced a bill to address it allows you to say that you were there first, and that therefore it is yours. In a way also, the very act of introducing a bill is an outcome, a result both substantive and symbolic that a member may turn to if asked: "What have you done about this?"

Unlike a number of other states, New York has no limitation on the number of bills a legislator may submit during a session (nor should it). There are about 10,000 bills entered in the Assembly during an average two-year legislative session, and 6,000 in the Senate. Few have serious prospects of passage. It takes more time, much more, to convince leaders and colleagues that the problem you think important is worthy of *their* attention, and of any legislative remedy.

American state and federal constitutions, featuring separation of powers and bicameral legislatures (except in Nebraska), intentionally make it relatively difficult for government to act and relatively easy to prevent government action, even when one party controls the executive and both legislative houses. In modern New York, an additional impediment to action was, until 2009, the institutionalization of divided partisan control of the Legislature. Apart from the structure of government, and partisan dynamics, decision processes in socially and economically complex polities develop many informal stopping points for legislation. The result: it is far easier to resist policy change than to produce it.

Slow going is thus the norm. Since government can do more to hurt people than to help them (maybe government can give people wealth, but it can also kill them), such constitutional constraints probably operate for the best. Not uncommonly, by the time the officials have responded, the nature of the problem has changed. Worse, since government action often has unintended consequences, the official response may well engender a new problem. The solution to that problem, when it comes, may be too late, and may create yet another problem.

Thus for example, observers might well conclude the New York lurched from overly lenient sentencing for criminal acts in the 1960s to overly harsh sentencing in the 1980s. Sometimes it seems that the *only* policy response that state government can't find is the appropriate one. Control of policy by the extreme wing of one political party or another sometimes exacerbates this perception, or perhaps, from time to time, this reality. But this cannot be said of the Organized Crime Control Act (OCCA).

The OCCA Worked: The Organized Crime Control Act probably holds up better against historical scrutiny than any other major public policy-making effort in which I was involved. However, OCCA took severe criticism immediately after enactment. It was called a product of compromises that made it too weak to be useful.

At least since the 1970s American society has been fascinated by La Cosa Nostra (LCN) the traditional Italian-American mafia. (We remained fascinated into the twenty-first century, if the enthusiastic public response to the cable television show, *The Sopranos,* was any guide.) Most legislators who supported the enactment of the OCCA probably thought of it at the time as a tool needed to combat this mafia. Yet by 1986, when OCCA became law in New York, LCN was well on its way to second-class status in organized crime. But the Asian and Russian mafias rose in power as the Italian fell, and OCCA retained its value. New York prosecutors continue to use OCCA effectively against those groups that have supplanted La Cosa Nostra as the dominant force in organized crime, and of course LCN continues to offer some attractive targets for prosecution, as well.

Drug Reform Laws: Symbolism over Substance. The Rockefeller drug laws notoriously failed to curb drug abuse or even raise the street price of illegal drugs over a sustained period, either of which would have provided inferential evidence of effective enforcement. In light of the analogous and disastrous constitutional experiment with the Prohibition of the manufacture and use of alcohol in the 1920s, the "War on

Drugs" of the last quarter of the twentieth century is a clear example of the triumph of hope over experience, however brief and transitory such hope may have been in this instance.

The history of the movement to reform the Rockefeller drug laws in New York engenders cynicism at various levels. Most superficially, the failure for years of both New York State Assembly Speaker Silver and Governor George Pataki to reach obvious compromises may be attributed to gross political self-interest. Both needed an issue more than a result. Pataki simultaneously sought to avoid annoying his political core, the right-wing opponents of reform, while softening opposition to his reelection from the supporters of reform with trumpeted proposals that he never pushed hard. For his part, Silver simply needed differences over drug law reform to remain unresolved so that the failure to act might be used against the Republicans in the campaigns.

But there were deeper currents running, as well. Support for reforms of the Rockefeller drug laws increased dramatically in numbers and in noise level just as the need for these reforms declined. This was because thoughtfully selective enforcement and quieter reforms rendered the Rockefeller Drug Laws relatively innocuous.

In 1987, 1988, and 1989, the big-city district attorneys—primarily the five elected from the counties of New York City—were sending thousands upon thousands of low-level non-violent drug dealers to prison upstate. These were replaced on the streets within hours. In those years few voices criticized this counterproductive strategy or called for appropriate changes in the law. But by 2002, having come to understand its inefficiency, the big-city D.A.s had largely abandoned that strategy, reserving most upstate sentences for serious offenders whose incarceration might make a useful difference. Low-visibility changes in sentencing laws also substantially reduced the length and cost of incarceration for low-level non-violent drug offenders.

Thus policy changed in practice, if not in form. One reason for this is that once legislators put "tough-on-crime" laws on the books, they have trouble taking them off for fear of sending the wrong message, of looking "soft on crime." Since the D.A.s had never acknowledged their previous misjudgments, however, the reformers—by then much more popular—could continue to engage in the same rhetoric that the reform pioneers used in 1987. The symbolic legislative politics continued the play out in the public arena after the practical policy had been changed by other means.

The Rockefeller drug laws were modified in 2004, with some fanfare. Simultaneously New York prosecutors were hearing from the

State Police, and talking more among themselves, about the frightening new epidemic of methamphetamine use in New York's rural areas. Facing a similar development, other states responded variously. Missouri's harsh penalties for distribution had little apparent effect. Oklahoma did better by attacking the production process by regulating the sale of pseudo ephedrine, a key methamphetamine ingredient.

The New York State Law Enforcement Council consists of representatives of the District Attorneys Association, the Chiefs of Police, and the Sheriffs, as well as the Attorney General, the New York City Criminal Justice Coordinator, and Tom Reppetto of the Citizens Crime Commission. At a January 2005 meeting the Council decided to support legislation to criminalize methamphetamine production and increasing penalties for those who produce it in the presence of children. They also agreed to study proposals to limit access to pseudo ephedrine.

Hope and experience confronted each other once again. This time, however, the United States Congress intervened, to its credit, on the side of experience, before New York could embark on yet another costly and ineffective version of the "experiment" that had so often failed before. The enactment of Public Law 109–177, Title VII, as of March 9, 2006 adopted the restricted-access approach.

In 2009, with the new Democratic majority in the State Senate, New York finally enacted the kind of substantial reform of the Rockefeller drug laws that advocates had sought, "reform" that could, with some justification, be called "repeal." Notwithstanding the quiet reforms that made that victory less urgent, its editorial celebration, along with what appears to be its general popularity, may serve usefully to delay the next cycle of punitive prohibition.

Methamphetamine, for example, could still become the new bogeyman to justify the next wave of drug incarceration. New York could still impose harsh sentences on methamphetamine offenders, again increase its prison population, again push the capacity limits of its prisons. But with the rational federal approach and the "repeal" of the Rockefeller drug laws, such an outcome seems less likely.

Megan's Law: An Achievement, but . . . Statistics available in the 1990s showed that sex offenders recidivated at far higher rates than other offenders. This evidence, and the clear absence of proven treatment programs at that time, justified my support for Megan's Law.

However, in the years following the mid-1990s, when most states' Megan's laws were enacted, treatment programs for sex offenders began to show more promise. Statistics showing far greater recidivism among sex offenders than among other types of offenders became more controversial and less authoritative. In 2003, a federal study by the Bureau of Justice Statistics found that sex offenders actually recidivated *less* than other types of offenders, undermining some of the original rationale for the legislation.

The fact that Megan's Laws were now on the books may itself have influenced those findings. Moreover, it remained undisputed that recidivism among sex offenders did not decrease with age, in contrast with other offenders. It also remained undisputed that community notification enables law enforcement to apprehend sex offenders more quickly after the first re-offense, thus often preventing subsequent offenses, which are usually more serious.

The apparent ineffectiveness of the treatment programs and the apparently authoritative statistics had persuaded me and many others at the time to press for the registration and notification statutes. Later doubts on those points shook our confidence that we had done the right thing, particularly in view of the Rehnquist court's decision to uphold varieties of Megan's law whose constitutionality I had earlier questioned. The New York version still seems on balance a positive contribution to public safety, but by a smaller margin than we imagined when we advanced it.

The lesson? The lawmaking process never reaches a final conclusion. When making law you are acting in a specific context, at a specific time in history. You must rely upon the best evidence you can get at the time you act. And you have to stand ready to change again, if circumstances demand it, or convincing contravening evidence arises.

Guns: An Ongoing Struggle. The law enabling courts to seize the guns and revoke the gun licenses of spouse abusers has saved lives, probably between ten and twenty a year. Neither those spared nor I know whose lives have been saved. But there is deep satisfaction in knowing the statistical facts of the matter. When tempted to discount this achievement as modest, the eighteenth-century English poet Thomas Grey's wise advice given in *Elegy in a Country Churchyard* is, I think, an apt reminder: "Let not ambition mock thy useful toil."

We fared less well on the more ambitious battle to impose tort liability on gun manufacturers. The legislation failed entirely. The lawsuit, and more particularly the amicus brief in *Hamilton v. Beretta USA Corp.*, 750 NE 2d 1055 (N.Y. 2001), did change New York law somewhat. After *Forni v. Ferguson*, 232 A.D.2d 176 (N.Y. App. Div. 1996) and *McCarthy v. Olin Corp.*, 119 F.3d 148 (2d Cir. 1997), New York law seemed to give manufacturers of non-defective legal products a free pass no matter how negligently they peddled their wares, thus allowing their products to fall into criminal hands. *Hamilton* at least removed the official imprimatur from the free pass.

The fall 2004 settlement of *Johnson v. Bull's Eye Shooter Supply*, 2003 WL 21639244 (Wash. Super. 2003) under which the gun manufacturer and the dealer each paid damages to victims of the Washington area snipers on the basis of negligent distribution, probably resulted in part from the rationale of *Hamilton*, even though *Bulls' Eye* was brought in a different jurisdiction. Again, a small victory.

Nationally, Democratic Presidential candidates Al Gore in 2000 and John Kerry in 2004 both took strong pro-gun control stances. Both were assaulted by the NRA; both lost crucial states and demographic groups. Congress enacted the federal immunization statute in 2005. This result suggests that efforts to win mass-tort lawsuits against gun manufacturers might be blamed for the ultimate doom of future *Bulls' Eye*-type individual lawsuits as well, at least until and unless someone brings a successful constitutional challenge to the federal statute.

One of my uncles taught me an important lesson when I was about twelve years old. It suddenly occurred to me that his job, teaching deaf children, was especially difficult with respect to children who had been born without any ability to hear. He confirmed this, and told me that it could take six months to teach such a child a single word. "How frustrating that must be," I said. "No," he responded, "you don't understand. When the child learns that word, you feel pretty good." Drawing upon this insight, I often advised junior legislators that—since achieving any worthwhile legislative goal required enormous effort—they had best learn to take satisfaction in whatever small victories they did achieve.

Symbolic Politics

Legislatures are not simply arenas for rational problem solving. They are places in which society's emotional and psychological needs are manifested, manipulated and addressed. On this point the classic Greek drama by Aeschylus, *The Eumenides*, is instructive. In it tragedy and chaos pursued the citizens of Athens until they established a place of honor, an altar of sorts, for the Furies. The lesson: A society cannot with impunity banish the Furies from the public sphere.

Symbolic appeals to emotion are an inescapable element of public life. Even when the substantive effects of legislation are small, as with gun control or sentencing reform, the symbolic benefits should not be discounted. Lawmaking with barely marginal impact on gun violence or excessive incarceration may nonetheless give hope and comfort to victims. We can easily see the worthiness of such psychological benefits. Sometimes—as we saw with the debate over reform of the Rockefeller Drug laws—the symbolic largely displaced the substantive, taking on a life of its own.

Giving the Law a Name, and a Face: Non-rational appeals are not solely the province of demagogues. Symbolic politics may be used to advance as well as impede reformers' objectives. Megan's law was the first of several to be given a human face. Naming a bill for the victim of a terrible crime or policy lapse both personalizes and dramatizes the initiative. It also draws upon the emotional energy brought to the debate by involved families and others affected, many of whom had never before even thought to visit the state capital. Distraught parents channeled their energies into lawmaking efforts, whether for Megan's Law or for other laws and proposed laws subsequently named for children, such New York's VaSean's Law (facilitating vehicular manslaughter prosecutions against drunk drivers, named for an 11-year-old victim), Timothy's Law (mandating the availability of insurance coverage for mental health treatment for children), and the federal Hillory J. Farias and Samantha Reid Date Rape Drug Prohibition Act of 2000.

Kendra's Law: In January 1999, Kendra Webdale, a 32-year old editor and aspiring writer was pushed to her death onto the subway tracks in Manhattan by a schizophrenic outpatient, Andrew Goldstein, who had stopped taking his medication. Four months later, Edgar Rivera, was pushed onto the subway tracks by Julio Perez, a homeless untreated schizophrenic. This father of three lost both legs.

In response New York adopted Kendra's law, harnessing the great emotional energy generated by these tragic events to produce smart policy. Social policy advocates in the Democratic party are often faulted for being "bleeding hearts," "soft on crime." In Kendra's law we found a way to take a symbolically "tough" approach to involuntary treatment of seriously mental ill people, while also generally enhancing the availability of services for New York's mentally ill.

Arguably, these two incidents—and the desperate lives endured by mentally ill outpatients themselves—resulted from the deinstitutionalization movement of the 1970s. In 1975 the Supreme Court ruled in

O'Connor v. Donaldson, 422 U.S. 563, that the state could only institutionalize people against their will if they were found dangerous to themselves or others. Earlier, Geraldo Rivera's reporting on the horrifying treatment of the developmentally disabled (a different group, of course) at the Willowbrook School on Staten Island galvanized opinion against "warehousing" people in massive state institutions. Judge Frank Johnson's decisions in *Wyatt v. Stickney*, previously mentioned, were based on similar conditions at Bryce Hospital in Alabama that same year.

In New York alone, the deinstitutionalization policy resulted in a massive reduction of the population of psychiatric hospitals, which dropped from close to 100,000 in the 1960s to under 10,000 by the mid-1990s. This statistic should have warmed the hearts of the reformers who saved the mentally ill from institutions unable to provide decent treatment. However, despite the promises of state government, funds for medication and support for local facilities did not follow those who were deinstitutionalized into the communities.

Former patients, many seriously ill, could now exercise their individual right to be let alone. One result was reinstitutionalization, in state prisons and local jails. The Mental Health Association in New York State estimated that in 2002 about 15,000 mentally ill individuals were incarcerated. In late 2004 the State prison system alone housed over three thousand inmates with the most serious kinds of mental illness, according to a reputable estimate. Another consequence was burgeoning homelessness. Advocates for the homeless commonly estimate that the mentally ill comprised between a fifth and a third of the homeless population, which grew exponentially in the 1980s. Especially in big city neighborhoods, the visible presence of mentally ill homeless people on the streets generated serious public safety fears and quality of life concerns.

Powerful symbols of the failure of long-standing state policy, the Kendra Webdale and Edgar Rivera tragedies were triggers for action. In 1999, Attorney General Eliot Spitzer's office responded by drafting legislation to provide that, under carefully delimited conditions, a mentally ill outpatient could have appropriate medication imposed on him or her. According to psychiatrist Jonathan Stanley, Director of the National Treatment Advocacy Center in Arlington, Virginia, this law reduced homelessness among mentally ill outpatients in New York by 74%, psychiatric re-hospitalization by 77%, arrests by 83% and jailing by 87%.

When as Attorney General Spitzer's representatives we in his office lobbied for, negotiated, and succeeded in winning enactment for Kendra's Law, we anticipated that mental health advocates would sharply criticize the effort as a mean-spirited attack on the rights of the mentally ill. (The popularity of this legislative effort with the editorial page of the New York *Post* lent credibility to this reading.) But it was clear to Spitzer's office from the first that Kendra's Law could not be implemented without a solid support system to identify those mental patients whose conditions might actually deteriorate without adherence to a treatment program. This would provide the overwhelming majority of patients with some version of the support the political system had implicitly promised—and failed to deliver—since the 1970s. With such a system in place, only a tiny percentage of these would ever need to have medication involuntarily administered.

When Governor George Pataki announced his budget proposals for the following year, he included $125 million in additional funding for mental health services. Counting aid to localities, the Governor claimed that the total budget increase for community-based mental health services was more than $420 million. (As not unusual in Albany, this total was disputed; others used different counting rules.) Notably, this package followed several years of cuts in the funding of mental health services.

An interesting ends-versus-means question is embedded in the story of Kendra's Law. We in the Attorney General's office linked a "mean-spirited" approach to a few mental health patients to successful advocacy for enhanced services and support for many, an approach that was both Machiavellian and altruistic. In contrast, the reform wins in the "enlightened" *Donaldson* decision and the reformist *Wyatt v. Stickney* and *Willowbrook* decisions did a good deal to transform resident mental patients into inmates and the homeless. These outcomes suggest that successful legislating requires willingness to engage in the hurly-burly of actual politics, to accept the occasional necessity for less palatable tactics to gain strongly desired outcomes.

Symbolism and Legitimacy: Interestingly, even laws that express irrational hostility might play a useful role, perhaps as an alternative to violence. Megan's Law was triggered by abduction and sexual abuse of a child by a stranger. Abuse by strangers, though less common than that within a family or by a trusted adult (a priest, for example), is more likely to be accompanied by murder. Just the idea terrifies parents. When a spate of such incidents comes to the attention of the public, government *must* respond in some official way in order to avoid jeopardizing its legitimacy.

Of course, police will arrest and prosecutors will bring charges against the perpetrators. But when the perpetrators are released sex offenders, often new to their post-incarceration communities, the public needs an additional official response to the more particularized fear. If government does not appear to do all it can to promote public safety, public confidence in government diminishes.

By mandating the availability of information about released sex offenders, Megan's Law has been accused, perhaps to some extent correctly, of encouraging vigilantism. (The accusation may rest on firmer ground in states, unlike New York, whose Megan's Laws mandate the publication of such information, not merely the release.) However, one must consider the scope and nature of vigilantism that might result if the state government failed to respond as it did to the perceived need for increased public safety measures.

Similar symbolic arguments may be made for a wide variety of draconian measures ostensibly set forth to promote public safety. Legislators have the opportunity and responsibility to channel those responses within the most reasonable possible boundaries. At least the New York version of Megan's Law incorporated serious attention to the rights of the offender, as well as to the perceived and real needs of the public. New York's "Little RICO," the Organized Crime Control Act, likewise responded to a felt public need, but the Assembly side of the negotiation specifically addressed the fairness and civil liberties criticisms directed at the federal law, the original RICO Act.

Public concern over drug addiction-based crime resulted in the Rockefeller drug laws in 1973. With the hindsight available to some by 1987, and to many more in later years, that response did not appear to have been channeled within the most reasonable possible boundaries. Efforts to change the laws—the bills introduced to reform the Rockefeller laws, and the widely publicized arguments by politicians who supported them—did constitute a kind of "official" response. The fact that some part of the government—the legislators advancing reform ideas—was "trying to make things better" brought some limited satisfaction to those in the public who were outraged by the injustice they perceived as resulting from those laws.

Of course, however, as we have seen with the corrosive effects of New York State's persistently late budgets, efforts without outcomes over many years are ultimately not legitimizing but delegitimizing. A regularly demonstrated incapacity to reach a result inevitably undermines public confidence in government.

The assault weapons "ban" enacted by Congress operated from 1994 until September 2004. Both this law's enactment and its expiration generated enormous publicity, yet it did not effectively block acquisition of assault weapons. That is, neither the practical effect of this law nor its expiration warranted the degree of excitement it generated among both supporters and opponents. But the symbolic effect was enormous. It is not just a matter of winning or losing. Defeats, victories, and even efforts on this and other issues bind one or another constituency closer to the social fabric through the legitimacy-conferring properties of official action.

Participants in a representative democracy need hope to continue to feel bound to the political institutions of their country. They do not have to win every time, or even most of the time. But they do need to see that government can and will act. This keeps them engaged.

Succeeding with Peers, Succeeding with the Public

Different skills are needed to succeed with peers in relatively small groups than to win popular election. Some politicians are better at one, some at the other. Peer-oriented skills help legislators win passage of laws and, with an added dash of Machiavellian ruthlessness, they also help in gaining legislative leadership posts.

Inside Skills: In this account we saw that a paragon of achievement inside the Legislature, Oliver Koppell, could get elected and reelected from an Assembly District because it was small enough for voters to know the character of his work. He could get selected by the Assembly to succeed a retiring Attorney General, Robert Abrams, because legislative colleagues knew him so well and respected him so highly for his intellect and character that he simply overwhelmed his opponents. But he lost in four attempts to win popular election from a larger jurisdiction.

Winning a leadership role in the Legislature also requires inside skills, but of a different sort. New York State Assembly Speaker Stanley Fink, and New York State Senate Majority Leader Warren Anderson, rose to command their respective institutions in ways that resemble Oliver Koppell's achievement with his colleagues. Each of them had exhibited great skill in the legislative process, but neither was likely to have achieved success in the wider arena of elective politics beyond their home districts.

But the approbation of peers is not enough to win legislative leadership. It helps if your elevation seems somehow "natural," up from an institutional base in the body, a chairmanship that is significant and in which that you are seen to have done well. You need to achieve a certain gravitas, but without appearing to be inaccessible, stuffy, or academic. You have to demonstrate that you really want it, to go for it hard, knowing that if you fail your career in the body is almost certainly over. It helps also to have a geographic base, or some other base (ethnic, ideological) that you may call upon. Jim Tallon was greatly admired internally, but lost his chance for becoming Speaker because he just could not put enough of these elements together. It was especially significant that he did not seem to want it badly enough to be willing to bruise the feelings of the then-current Speaker.

Fink's wit and verbal agility might have counterbalanced his bluntness and honesty enough to get him over that hurdle, but his pugnacious Canarsie Brooklyn style, almost a caricature of the New York City stereotype, would most likely not have played well statewide. Nor would Warren Anderson's courtly and gentle demeanor have "played well" in a statewide New York campaign brawl.

And those were the best. For a more typical example of elective politics internal to legislatures, look to the campaign between James Emery and Dominick DiCarlo for leadership of the Republican minority in the New York State Assembly in 1978. Only DiCarlo could stand up to Stanley Fink in legislative debate—sometimes. Even legislators who did not share DiCarlo's deeply conservative views could not help recognizing his brilliance. Emery did not shine at all. But Emery begged his colleagues to elect him. DiCarlo assumed they would vote for him on the merits. Emery defeated DiCarlo resoundingly.

As Fink often reminded us, "Politics is not a merit system. None of you took civil service tests to get here."

Public Support: The Cost of Getting It. The DiCarlo-Emery lesson applies to street politics as well. The appropriate attitude is "Please please please please please vote for me." Former U.S. Senator Al D'Amato, it is said, once rang a doorbell to ask for a vote in one of his campaigns for Hempstead Town Supervisor, an important local office. He was told by the voter that she could not leave her kitchen to vote because she was in the middle of basting a turkey. D'Amato did what was necessary. While she voted, he basted the turkey. He won the election.

When I ran for Congress, aware as I was that my record as an Assembly member amply demonstrated my ability to provide better representation in Congress than my opponents, I asked voters to examine the record and choose rationally on that basis. What I didn't say, but perhaps tacitly communicated, was, "If you want to be an idiot, vote for someone else." I came in last. "Please please please please please vote for me" would have been much better.

Adlai Stevenson, campaigning for the presidency in 1956 at a factory gate, met a worker who told him, "Mr. Stevenson, you will have the vote of every intelligent American." "That's not enough," replied Stevenson. "I want to win."

The foregoing may present the situation somewhat unfairly. It's not that voters are stupid. Rather, they cannot be expected to follow the issues, or the candidates' credentials, with the care and attention that political professionals devote to them. Further, they respond emotionally, as humans must. They want reassurance, inspiration, pride, confidence, and maybe a little entertainment. Supplying those needs must be a higher priority for a successful electoral politician—most of the time, anyway—than presenting an accurate portrayal of the complexity of the issues of the day.

Alliances with other politicians count too. I have observed that many people in positions of power like deference. Showing deference—sucking up, in the common parlance—generally wins favor. More powerful politicians especially like deference from less powerful politicians: it reaffirms their confidence that even other elected officials must kowtow to them.

Fundraising requires the ability to show deference, and more. Politicians may ask for money from people they know, people they don't know, people who think the politician's political position can produce practical benefits for them, and people who don't think the politician can help them. Which of these groups would *you* enjoy soliciting for contributions?

As to that matter of providing practical benefits, I learned a lesson when I asked the relatively new leader of Brooklyn's Democratic party organization to find a judge willing to employ a talented local campaign worker of mine, a young lawyer, as a law clerk. My campaign worker had pressed me to consider his outstanding academic and practical qualifications for the job. I had no good reason to refuse to take his request to the County Leader, except that I had never used the political system to seek a court job for anyone. But this once, I did.

I had strongly supported the County Leader when he was seeking the position, but I sensed that he was not planning to help my campaign worker, and I knew why. I told him that I knew the demands on him from his supporters would greatly outnumber the rewards he had the ability to provide, probably by a factor of twenty to one. I explained that I therefore understood that he had needed, during his ambitious effort, to imply that he would later give his friends more help than the conditions of his position would actually allow. But understanding this, I warned him also that he should not treat me as one whose demand could be sloughed off. I didn't say it, but he must have understood that otherwise I would reveal his over-promises to others.

This made me recognize that politicians tend to promise more than they can deliver. It might astonish readers that it took me twenty-five years in politics to learn this, but I learned it in a much more concrete and specific sense, I think, than most people do. In terms of personal, practical favors, as well as in broader social policy terms, politicians have a mere fraction of the resources necessary to satisfy the broad range of support they need to attract in order to win initial election to office. What they try to provide, instead, is hope. They may create unrealistic hopes, but maybe, ten years later than expected, one supporter may actually get the favor sought, or a bill may actually become law.

When such a debt to one supporter is paid, or a campaign promise fulfilled, the politician may keep other supporters' hopes alive. On the other hand, sometimes it may be as an earlier leader of the Brooklyn Democratic organization, Meade Esposito, once said, that every time you do someone a favor, you make "one ingrate and nine enemies."

Among my many deficiencies as a participant in electoral politics, then, was my refusal to promise anything to anyone, ever. Since I knew that I did not truly know what I would be able to produce, I could not make promises sincerely. This limited my ability to create hope. In retrospect, I have come to believe that a politician should not shrink from creating hope. This not only improves the politician's own electoral prospects, it also, in the long sweep of history, provides the germ of progress. My stubborn insistence on "honesty and sincerity" may have been too expensive an extravagance, at the cost of limiting my political productivity. The shrewd English political scientist Bernard Crick showed great insight when he noted forty years ago that liberals tend to place "excessive trust" in those two virtues.

Many of the politicians I have named previously in this book are certainly honest and sincere (and many I have not mentioned). In general, however, prospects for electoral success are dismal for politicians unable or unwilling occasionally and selectively to mislead the public in order to inspire hope and confidence, to show deference to people they may not genuinely respect, and yes, . . . to beg everyone for money.

And yet, the alternatives are worse. Politics may require insincerity, chicanery, and self-aggrandizement, but the alternatives to politics are violence and dictatorship.

Why Inside Politics Is More Honest than Outside Politics: Stanley Fink once described us in the Assembly as crabs in a bottle, crawling over each other's backs in our attempts to get to the top and out into higher office. Yet I found the politics of the legislative process far more congenial than electoral politics. A legislator cannot base sound working relations with his or her colleagues on deceit. Merit and substance, character and intellect will over time win the trust and confidence of fellow legislators. Those who too obviously seek the limelight at others' expense incur a significant measure of resentment and distrust.

The legislative process actually improves participants' behavior in some respects. Since legislators must negotiate to win enactment of bills, they learn to consider viewpoints quite different from their own. Some of my ultra-Orthodox Jewish constituents vehemently objected to my refusal to support legislation that I thought was unconstitutional banning pornography. Fred Schmidt, probably the most conservative Democratic member of our House, and among the most conservative of either party, sat next to me for twelve years. Responding to his own very conservative and mostly Roman Catholic constituents, Fred had a bill prohibiting the public display of racy magazines that I thought I could revise into constitutionally acceptable form. I could, I did, and the Schmidt-Feldman bill became law, of course with conservative Republican sponsorship in the Senate.

Since I knew and liked the immensely personable Schmidt even before I took office, and since his wild sense of humor kept me laughing throughout our tenure together, perhaps he's not a good example. But legislative coalitions often open minds to the reality that people can differ dramatically on what kind of society we should have (within some limits: I don't think any of us were totalitarians) and still respect the intelligence and integrity with which they hold their views. I never had much trouble respecting and working with people whose vision of society differed from mine. As noted in Chapter Five, Republican-Conservative Senator Dale Volker would probably trade away some degree of freedom for more security, while I would trade away some degree of security for more freedom; and we hold opposing views on many, if not most, major policy issues. But I continue to hold Dale in the highest regard.

I had, and have, more trouble respecting those legislators who have no particular vision for society but who seem to be in politics for the ride, for the status, for the perquisites, for self-advancement, in sum for any reason but the ones for which we have a legislature at all. Even so, time servers and political "fixers" must inevitably be counted among the representatives of an imperfect humanity and indeed may play an important role in organizing and leading political institutions.

Notwithstanding the publicity and notoriety given the exceptions, few legislators engage in actual corruption. Still, the views of an early twentieth-century Tammany Hall political leader, Boss Croker, in response to criticism by a literary English liberal, may still be instructive in understanding the role of the versions of "honest graft" more operative today. (George Washington Plunkitt, the nineteenth century New York Tammany Hall politician, coined the phrase.) Croker noted that the Englishman's American counterparts, "cultured" citizens with high principles, will not "take more than a fitful interest in an occasional election . . . Why, then, when mugwump principles won't even make mugwumps work, do you expect the same lofty motives to be sufficient to interest the masses in politics? . . . And so," Croker continued, "we need to bribe them with spoils . . . you must have an incentive to interest men in the hard daily work of politics, and when you have our crowd you have got to do it one way, the only way that appeals to them . . ."

As I said earlier, I learned to respect the late Angelo Del Toro, a corrupt politician who nonetheless transcended the genre: he also held his own vision of the better society and did so with sensitivity, generosity, grace, and courage. As (I am told) Plutarch said of the Roman general Belisarius, his faults were those of his generation, his virtues his own.

At the simplest level, as Stanley Fink also taught us, even those who entered legislative life as racial, religious, ethnic, or gender bigots rarely remained so. In a diverse society, most legislators who need to learn tolerance are forced to do so by the need to appeal to a variety of constituencies. Moreover, the Legislature is a great equalizer. Whatever his or her credentials, wisdom, grace, style, or background, each member has one vote; for whatever you wish to accomplish you must get one more than half of these votes.

Perhaps by some chance a legislator, once elected, managed to remain a bigot. Then, the legislative experience, in which success depends on enlisting the support of a different subset of diverse colleagues for every given legislative effort, and in which long-term success depends on winning their trust and respect, will encourage a greater openness of mind and heart to those of different background.

Writing many years ago (and unduly negatively, I thought and still think) about national politics, H. Mark Roelofs, a political science professor at New York University, provided an unusually insightful description of relationships among "players" in Washington that is especially applicable to legislators in Albany:

. . . the Washington law of reciprocity means much more than simply honor among thieves. More fundamentally, it means that Washington politics can only proceed on the basis of very large measures of mutual respect . . . [U]nder a constitutional system that radically fragments and disperses power . . . each [political actor has] a place, an office, a position from which they can say "yea" or"nay" to what comes across their desks. That demands respect. . . . This is not to say that the law of reciprocity is unfailingly observed. It often is not, sometimes deliberately. "Civility," as it is called, can be lost, sometimes for months on end. Sometimes the only way to overcome an opposition is to ignore it, run by it, or crush it. But Washington's law of reciprocity is rooted in some of the most fundamental realities of the nation's political system. Violating it will always bring a cost.

The mutual respect Roelofs described would seem to foster tolerance. In the years since he wrote, bitter partisanship has greatly lessened cooperation, mutual respect, and even civility "across the aisle" in Washington, Albany, and from all evidence, in government at every level across the nation. This makes it even more important that politics within the legislature require at least a bare minimum of the kinds of relationships that Roelofs described, providing the basis for a more general return to earlier standards.

Casework: On the Legislator as "Social Glue"

In a widely read analysis, political scientist David Mayhew wrote that citizens don't give individual members of Congress credit for institutional accomplishments. They refused to believe that any one legislator deserved plaudits for the product of so complex an institution as Congress, with so many individuals commanding crucial checkpoints. Rather, Mayhew said, citizens voted for legislators who pleased them by their stated positions and votes on prominent issues.

But this is true only at first. Incumbents are strong for a reason. Over time, legislators who do their jobs right build their autonomy, and therefore their ability to act with enormous discretion on policy, by connecting directly and personally with individual voters at all those church suppers and community board meetings. One by one each voter comes to vote loyally for Feldman time after time because a personal connection has been forged.

Thus the importance of legislative casework. Citizens connect with, remember, and vote for the politician who can: nudge the bureaucracy to get their garbage picked up; obtain a "green card" for an immigrant cousin; find or replace the Social Security check that got lost in the mail; or get an extra crossing guard or stop sign at the street intersection near their children's school.

The Brighton Baths. Of course, the home district role can involve bigger issues, casework writ large. My district included the Brighton Baths, an extremely well known and important institution to many of my constituents. For ninety years, between 1907, when it was founded, and 1997, when it was torn down and replaced by luxury apartment buildings, the Baths occupied a full city block right on Brighton Beach. While the ordinary folks went to the public beach in Brighton, the elite "kept a locker" at the Brighton Baths beach club.

My father-in-law used to sneak into the Baths as a young teenage boy in the 1920s. There he found fresh water swimming pools and handball courts. Sixty years later, the fifteen thousand "members" of the Baths—his age group now grown older—made use of the mahjong tables and steam rooms.

I use "elite" here in a narrow sense"—these were the elite among immigrant Brooklyn Jews, those who had "made it" financially. In the classic Mel Brooks-Carl Reiner comedy record, *The 2000-Year-Old Man*, issued in 1961, Reiner, the straight man, asks Brooks what he liked to do for vacation. "I like Europe," Brooks said. With an intonation reeking of false modesty, he added, "I keep a locker in Europe." I didn't grasp the full meaning of that line until I learned the story of the Baths. If you had truly made it—maybe you owned your own home and ran a small business—in 1930s Jewish Brooklyn, you "kept a locker" at the Brighton Baths.

My constituents—those from New York's 45th Assembly district, in the middle of southern Brooklyn—made up a majority of the membership of the Baths. Every New York politician of significance—and many lesser politicians too—made the mandatory campaign stop to visit them there from the 1950s through the 1970s: New York City mayors Robert F. Wagner, John Lindsay, Abe Beame; Governors Nelson Rockefeller and Hugh Carey; Senators Jacob Javits, Kenneth Keating, Robert Kennedy. When I first ran for the Assembly in 1980, I didn't just have a mandatory *day* at the Baths: I spent the summer campaigning there. With 15,000 elderly, mostly Jewish Brooklynites to meet, in a good mood but a little bored, that was really all I needed.

In the 1970s New York imposed a tax on membership fees in private clubs. On the six hundred dollars annual fee for the Baths, this came to maybe $35 a year. In 1982 a constituent of mine pointed out that the tax was supposed to be levied on memberships in clubs whose members owned or controlled them, not on institutions like the Baths owned and operated by a private company whose "members" were really just customers. Throughout the July Fourth weekend of 1982 I stood at the entrance to the Baths in the broiling sun for four and five hours a day, handing out four thousand applications for sales tax refunds along with an explanatory pamphlet from me. Over the next few months, my office sent out another four thousand in response to requests.

The average refund recipient got back a check from New York State for three years worth of sales tax, or about $100. Eight thousand people received these refunds. Had I solved the crime problem, elevated the education level in the schools, and rendered the streets of Brooklyn permanently and sparklingly clean, I might not have assured my re-election—for years to come—as thoroughly.

Seven or eight years later, a pornographic movie theater opened on Avenue U, a major shopping street in my district, just half a block from a Catholic elementary school and a synagogue. Its huge marquee made the nature of its offerings evident. My constituents had long tolerated a small pornographic movie theater discretely tucked into a quiet corner of Kings Highway, only a few blocks northwest. The Avenue U theater, though, slapped them in the face. For several weeks, I led a contingent of picketers, armed with cameras, exercising our First Amendment right to protest the theater. (Those of my fellow ACLU members who think first of the First Amendment rights of the theater owners should bear in mind that the picketers equally legitimately exercised such rights.) Ultimately, we prevailed—the theater closed its doors for good. But in the most memorable episode of the effort, the wizened elderly woman in the ticket-seller booth furtively beckoned me over. After cautiously scanning the scene to make sure no one from management was watching her, she whispered to me, "I'm on your side—you got me my Brighton Baths tax refund back."

Meetings and Legitimacy. I came to understand another aspect of my role in the seemingly unending string of evenings and weekends dropping in on meetings: the East 22nd Street Block Association (or any of dozens of other block associations); the Sheepshead Bay Kiwanis Club; the Plumb Beach Civic Association; the St. Edmund's Home School Association; the Beth El Synagogue Men's Club; the Midwood Development Corporation; the Meyer Levin Post of the Jewish War Veterans; the P.S. 195 Parent-Teacher Association, et cetera, et cetera, et cetera.

Sometimes the participants actually asked me to help them solve a problem. Far more often, though, I could cover five or six meetings a night (or Sunday morning) because they really wanted me just to drop in and greet them. I struggled to understand whether this effort had any rational purpose beyond getting my name and face known to voters. In my part of Brooklyn, members of these groups got very angry at politicians who did not pay these courtesy calls. At last, I came to understand why.

These groups engage in volunteer work that greatly benefits their communities. Thanks to their efforts, schools perform better, public safety is enhanced and crime deterred (because criminals who invade get spotted and arrested more often), parks stay cleaner, and the poor benefit from charity. My presence brought the State to them. Even more, it conferred the imprimatur of the State, the dignity of the State, on them and legitimized their work. By visiting the various organizations, I served the function of a sort of social glue: I cemented all these groups into the polity, into the political fabric that makes up the State. This dignity, this acceptance, was for them a significant psychological reward for their past efforts and incentive for their future efforts on behalf of their communities.

Perception is Reality

From time to time, my constituents saw me on television. When they told me they saw me, I'd ask, "What was I saying?" More often than not, they'd reply, "I don't know. But I saw you!" This enhanced and strengthened my ability to confer dignity and inclusion into the greater world. Since they could see that I held citizenship in TV-land, not only was I part of the State, I was an important enough part to join in the world of Jay Leno, Derek Jeter, Roseanne, Mickey Mouse, the President, and Oprah Winfrey. Anyone who lives in that little box shares in the world of the people who really matter, so that my corporeal presence in their own actual living rooms or shabby meeting halls gave them a bridge to that "important" world too.

Many, many people understood this function earlier and better than I did. After I rewrote Fred Schmidt's bill into the Schmidt-Feldman law, the publisher of *Screw* magazine, Al Goldstein, debated me on a local New York City TV station. Wearing a t-shirt imprinted with pictures of tiny sperm, he scoffed at our legislation, which he maintained—incorrectly—would suppress the display of his tee shirt. He challenged my legislative and ethical priorities, along the lines of "instead of fighting violence and poverty, you're trying to suppress freedom of speech!" After the show, as we were unclipping our microphones, he leaned over and assured me that we had written a sound and sensible piece of legislation, "but I couldn't say so—that wouldn't make good TV." Though I hadn't known it, I had participated in a fictional debate, but its political value to him and to me, and perhaps even its educational value to the audience, would have been no greater had he been sincere.

The power of image, regardless of substance, emerged in an odd way out of a story made possible by one of my first achievements in government, long before I reached the Legislature. As related earlier, in 1969 I helped design what became the New York City Parking Violations Bureau. While, as also recounted, it fell prey to a variety of political predators for a while, the Bureau did succeed in curbing the exercise of one of the classic political favors: the fixing of parking tickets. When judges who had emerged out of the political clubhouse heard parking ticket cases, someone with enough clout—perhaps the local Democratic district leader—might be able to "reach" the judge. But who could reach the anonymous computers and bureaucrats my system had substituted to process the tickets now?

All the more impressed, then, were the members of a Democratic club in Brooklyn when a newcomer, only a few months after making his initial appearance, announced to one and all that from then on, he could "take care of" parking tickets for anyone who wanted this service. Over the next two years, club members who handed them their tickets found that their trouble was over. No dunning notices arrived, no arrears statements appeared. Whatever he had done, had worked. Clearly, this was a man who wielded major clout. He so impressed his compatriots with this political legerdemain that they finally chose him as their club president, from which post he rose to "district leader"—leader of the local Democratic party organization in his Assembly district. Years later, when asked how he had managed those parking tickets, he finally confessed: he had simply paid them. Had they known that, his buddies would never have elevated him to the giddying heights above them.

Utilitarianism Again: Balancing Values

Just as a dollop of yogurt culture starts the next batch of yogurt, a dollop of older law comes in as an ingredient of the next product of lawmaking. Law emerges as complex derivative of balanced values in response to societal needs.

Balancing Values. The fight for New York's Organized Crime Control Act rode on the resolution of difficult legal issues necessary to the balance between fairness at trial and prosecutorial efficiency. Negotiators had to find a way for prosecutors to show the larger scope of the crimes and thus the greater damage inflicted by members of criminal organizations, while avoiding prejudice to individual defendants with minor roles and tenuous connections to such organizations.

The fight for reform of the Rockefeller drug laws rode more on the conflict between established interests of economics and power. Still, even there the argument between fairness at trial and prosecutorial efficiency played an important role. Prosecutorial efficiency benefited from mandated sentencing. However, mandated sentencing also meant sentences that did not fit individuals' personal circumstances and were therefore not fair.

In the Megan's Law debate, the legal issue would more properly be posed as society's fairness to the defendant who has already been convicted, versus community safety.

In the tort liability fight, a variety of legal issues emerged. In the legislative forum, proponents and opponents battled primarily over the extent of constitutional rights and the balance among them: the right to bear arms and the right to property on one side of the issue, society's interest in community safety and fairness to the innocent victim of gun crime on the other. In the judicial arena, additional legal issues were brought to bear: the extent to which a gun manufacturer owes a duty to a crime victim with no connection whatsoever to the manufacturer except through a criminal the manufacturer does not know; and how to define causation in the law to determine whether the manufacturer's action or inaction could in some way be said to have caused the victim's injury.

Politics and Lawmaking: Are There General Lessons?

Outside Politics. Successful lawmaking on serious questions of policy always requires harnessing the force of outside politics. Mobilizing systematic effort takes skill. Local prosecutors in New York needed a racketeering statute to pursue criminal organizations more effectively. Editorial pages, properly cultivated and encouraged, kept pressure on the Assembly to enact the Organized Crime Control Act. Exploiting opportunities of the moment also takes skill. Rudy Giuliani's use of the federal statute as a U.S. Attorney convinced the Assembly leadership of the dangers of a federal monopoly on such statutory powers, thus softening their opposition. This served as a second vector of outside politics in producing the eventual law.

The drumbeat of news accounts of horrible offenses against children, combined with the highly effective lobbying of parents like Mark Klaas and the Kankas, unquestionably supplied the force of outside politics necessary to propel Megan's Law into enactment in New York.

The Police Benevolent Association's opposition to the use immunity bill broke the law enforcement coalition and drove the final nail into the bill's coffin. With the law enforcement community split, political pressure from the defense attorneys and the Civil Liberties Union prevailed.

The NRA won its battle in Washington to immunize gun manufacturers and dealers against tort liability suits, and pushed its advantage further. It defeated the earlier legislative effort to impose tort liability on handgun manufacturers. But even this powerful lobby didn't dare oppose the legislation empowering judges to take guns away from abusers when such legislation had the strong support of groups opposing domestic violence, like the National Organization of Women's Legal Defense Fund or the Coalition Against Domestic Violence. That victory, though small, carries an important lesson. The "free-rider problem" can be overcome. Sustained passion for change, harnessed and focused, can overcome the ordinary tendency of those with shared beliefs in an issue to leave the work to others, and can prevail against more easily mobilized economic interests.

Repeal of the Rockefeller Drug Laws meant job losses for rural communities. Also, prosecutors stood to lose staff as well as power, because repeal would lessen the justification for funding large units to prosecute drug crimes. (The prosecutors would take offense at this characterization, believing themselves motivated solely by the public interest, but Demosthenes' warning bears repeating: people have infinite capacity to believe what is in their own interest to believe.) Here the free rider model seems to work better: for a very long time, a focused economic interest held a more diffuse public interest constituency at bay. As important or more important, Rockefeller drug law protagonists were defending the status quo on an issue of great emotional power in the larger society. In lawmaking, achieving change is far harder than defending the status quo. And as we have seen, lawmaking has very important non-rational dimensions.

At the same time, quiet reforms between 1987 and 1998 reduced the length of sentences actually served for drug crimes and the number of inmates actually incarcerated for such crimes. Those quiet changes did not undermine the public justification for large prosecutorial staffs, and thus did not energize the prosecutors in opposition. Nor did they challenge the public justification for prisons, and thus did not energize the rural state senators in opposition. This suggests that for some matters around which positions are hardened and major change through legislation is blocked, a less visible incremental strategy—perhaps through executive action, with supportive budgeting—may be a smart way to lay the groundwork for later larger scale reform through legislation.

Inside Politics. Outside politics ultimately exercises irresistible force over major public controversies played out in legislatures. However, "ultimately" is a long time. Inside politics can greatly retard progress in the context of public controversies and can determine the outcome entirely when the issue has not entered public consciousness.

The pace of outside politics set the preconditions for enactment of the New York State Organized Crime Control Act. I first introduced the bill in 1983, but the Assembly leadership would not even consider adopting it until they reacted to Giuliani's prosecutions in 1986. Without the right inside politics, however, the Assembly still would not have passed the bill in 1986. My good personal relationship with Miller, my willingness to work with Yates, the leadership's correct assumption that I would accept with alacrity when Miller asked to go on the bill as the second lead prime, my insistence on and the leadership's acceptance of my personal role in the negotiations—all of these contributed to the successful effort to reach an acceptable compromise between the prosecutors and the Assembly leadership.

My considerably cooler relationship with Silver in the 1990s may have hurt the progress of Rockefeller drug law reform. Given polling results starting in the early 1990s suggesting public willingness to substitute treatment for incarceration of drug addicts, the Assembly could have highlighted the issue at that time by enacting one-house legislation without excessive political cost, instead of waiting until the early 2000s. The Senate would of course have rejected the legislation, as they did later anyway, but the Assembly's action could have hastened a statewide organizing effort that, with sufficient momentum, might have overcome the Senate's opposition by 2000 or so.

Outside politics limited Silver's options in resisting Megan's Law, notwithstanding his indifference toward me, but missteps in the inside politics of that controversy could have been costly nonetheless. First, without the superb working relationship between Senator Skelos and me and our respective staffs, Silver could easily have played a divide-and-conquer game. As with my Parking Violations Bureau reform bill earlier, or Rockefeller drug reform later, leadership of the two Houses has many variations on the ploy of claiming support by passing bills that don't match and therefore don't become law. Since Skelos and I never fought each other for primacy but insisted on amending our bill in tandem, we made it clear early on that once the Senate passed the Skelos bill, no other Assembly bill but mine—identical to the Skelos bill—would be viable.

Then, on the more speculative side, a number of my Democratic colleagues in the Assembly told me that they would have less trepidation about voting for the bill because I was the author. They knew me well enough, they said, to assure themselves that I would have written it with as much sensitivity to civil liberties concerns as possible. But for the "inside politics" of my personal relationships with those colleagues, perhaps enough Democrats in the Assembly would have objected to the legislation to stiffen Silver's opposition, despite the outside pressure.

On the gun liability bill, inside politics accounts for the different treatment the bill got from Koppell's Judiciary Committee and Lentol's Codes Committee. Silver simply could not expect the level of deference from Koppell that he had from Lentol. I could count on Koppell to act on the merits of the bill: his motion to report the bill out of Judiciary carried, of course. Lentol kept the bill bottled up in Codes. Lentol could certainly argue that Koppell made Lentol's life harder: Koppell got credit among the Democrats' natural constituents, the gun control forces, for approving the bill, while Lentol, whose committee stood between Judiciary and the floor, had to protect the Democrat Conference by keeping the bill from the floor. Still, if Koppell had chaired Codes, I believe the bill would have been reported.

The "little" gun bill, calling for revocation of gun licenses from domestic violence abusers, came out of Judiciary later, after Helene

Weinstein became chair. Although reasonably friendly to me, Weinstein remained very responsive to the Speaker's wishes. All relationships are at least somewhat bilateral, so the Speaker understood and respected Weinstein's commitment to what were perceived as "women's issues," including protection of victims against domestic violence. Outside politics would have sufficed to assure enactment of that bill, but inside politics might have done the job had the outside pressures been somewhat weaker.

Values, Politics and Law

One thing is certain: no one will ever be able to devise a how-to guide with sure-fire steps to the mastery of the legislative process. As we have shown, this process too closely resembles an ever-changing kaleidoscope of issues, outside pressures, inside relationships, and personalities to identify systematically those characteristics that hold true for authoritative, legitimate lawmaking over time, everywhere, in all kinds of organizational structures and under all political conditions.

By now, repetition alone should have made obvious the constant impact on lawmaking of pressures from voters, the press, lobbyists and anyone else outside the lawmaking body; friendships, relationships in the hierarchy, and favors owed or awaited within the body; ethical values deeply held; and commitments to principles of law.

Less explicitly addressed, but also very important, is the matter of personal character, though this factor is hard to fit under the heading of "values." Courage, self-sacrifice, loyalty, and honesty—and their absence—also transcend time, place, and issues as perpetual factors in lawmaking. The role of personal character makes the process fascinating, infuriating, loathsome, engaging, and even more difficult to organize into a deductive system of logical precepts.

The present volume, nevertheless, has offered a degree of guidance. Its stories convey some broad direction to the would-be lawmaker, some instruction as to the essential elements that must be assembled and brought to bear, and some warnings of pitfalls to avoid. The public safety or criminal justice scholar has now seen how policy emerges from the "sausage factory" of government, the legislature, often with help from the courts. The historian and political scientist have looked at the factory through the same window to see what really happened in Albany at the end of the twentieth century and the beginning of the twenty-first. The student with a purely academic interest in the legislative process should understand that lawmaking is far more an art than a science.

Nonetheless, we have seen many illustrations that can be expressed syllogistically: "if A, then B"; or, at least, "if not A, then not B." In the absence of outside pressures, inside politics will prevail. The most strongly held values will trump everything else. Some issues truly should belong to courts, or legislatures, though most will find their way into more than one of our branches of government. Policymakers, as humans, will respond to normal human relationships among themselves: friendship influences policy.

But none of these deductions have as much value as the lessons that cannot be summarized, but that the astute student draws by induction, not deduction. The stories convey the textures, the rhythms, the *feel* of lawmaking life, and thus should impart confidence that lawmaking is an accessible human process that its students can understand and even use to impose, in some measure, their own visions of a better society. Like any history, they can only have value within the constraints of circumstance and our own personal limitations. We can do no more.

History is all we have.

CHAPTER XI

The New York State Legislature— On Balance

Gerald Benjamin

New York State Comptroller Alan Hevesi threw in the towel just six and a half weeks after his reelection in November of 2006. His campaign was predicted to be a cakewalk. Instead it became a nightmare, dominated by charges—first made by his Republican opponent J. Christopher Callaghan and later substantiated by investigators—that the Comptroller had regularly violated the law by using state employees to chauffeur his wife and attend to her personal needs.

Comptroller Hevesi could not convince anyone that he had all along intended to reimburse the state for these services. Political support eroded as the campaign unfolded. The Democratic candidate for governor, Eliot Spitzer, running on a government reform platform ("On Day One Everything Changes"), walked away from his statewide running mate in mid-campaign. A public apology and offer of restitution, later determined to be insufficient, saw Hevesi through election; he won against his under-funded opponent with 57% of the vote. But a large part of the Comptroller's job was to assure probity and integrity in state and local government, and Hevesi's reputation—and therefore his ability to be effective as Comptroller—was irreparably damaged. Facing a grand jury indictment, the recently reelected Comptroller pled guilty to a class E felony and resigned.

Speaker Sheldon Silver

This unexpected unfolding provided Assembly Speaker Sheldon Silver with both an opportunity and a problem.

Sheldon Silver, the winner in a five-way lower East Side primary, entered the New York State Legislature in 1974. Looking back, some of his friends said that Silver might have aspired to be president if he was not an Orthodox Jew. In fact the future speaker represented portions of the district on Manhattan's lower East Side that had sent the legendary Alfred E. Smith to Albany. Smith, regarded by many as the greatest New York state governor of the 20th century, was of course the first Catholic to be nominated for the presidency of the United States.

When Silver took up the reins of leadership the Assembly majority was about one and a half times as large (94 members) as the entire Senate (61 members). Because of the impact of U.S. Supreme Court one-person-one-vote decisions and the Voting Rights Act, this majority was very diverse—racially, ethnically, geographically, and ideologically. A big difference between the Assembly and the Senate was that in the former body racial and ethnic minority group members were in the majority party, and thus were situated to share power, while in the latter they were in the minority party, and had no expectation of having real consequence in policy making.

From the first, Silver had to balance and manage these expectations. Dan Feldman—who did not support him for Speaker—was not happy about how Silver did this. As a consequence, Dan defined his electoral goals outside the Assembly, and left elective politics when he failed to become the Brooklyn District Attorney or a member of Congress. Growing unhappiness among others about Speaker Silver's continued centralization of institution power, personal inaccessibility, and lack of responsiveness to members led to a revolt in the year 2000 spearheaded by his Majority Leader, Michael Bragman. But Silver survived. Enough members remained loyal, or fearful of the consequences of failure, or obligated to the Speaker for the support that he provided or promised for their election and/or reelection (through the Democratic Assembly Campaign Committee), or hopeful—for benefits for their districts, or for themselves.

The Speaker is reputed to have become far more responsive to the members of his conference since this abortive revolt. "There are really two Shellys," one old friend, Heshey Jacob, said, "There's a pre-Bragman Shelly and a post-Bragman Shelly." For example, Silver attributed lack of support in the Assembly Democratic conference for his failure to support Mayor Michael Bloomberg's congestion pricing proposal to diminish traffic (and air pollution) in Manhattan. Silver did not even permit the matter come to a vote in his house, a move characterized by Bloomberg as ". . . a special kind of cowardice."

But for the Speaker this was simply a way of using his "big shoulders" to protect some of "his" members from having to go on the record on a no-win matter and by doing so preserve "his" Democratic majority, and confirm his leadership of it. Silver summarizes: "I'm almost in the position of the union leader who listens to people, tries to get the best possible deal from the bosses, and then comes back and says, 'Look we may not be able to get you better health insurance, but I can get you a better pension." Dan Feldman's experiences reported in this volume were entirely with the pre-Bragman Silver, a man with whom he had a very checkered history, and whom he had not supported for the leadership post.

Upon becoming Speaker in 1994 Sheldon Silver was confronted almost immediately with both an entrenched Republican Senate majority and a newly elected Republican governor, George Pataki. For twelve years thereafter, with the Democratic party insurgent in state government, it was Silver's job to "play defense." He became famous for his willingness to use time as his friend, stalling even in the face of great pressure and criticism to get the tradeoffs he demanded to effect Assembly priorities in such areas as social and educational policy. Silver appeared dispositionally well suited to this role. Former Governor Eliot Spitzer, with whom—as we shall see—the Speaker butted heads early on, called Silver ". . . an enigma, the grandmaster of the chess game of Albany maneuvers."

Silver's success is measured not only by his tenacity in gaining Democratic Assembly objectives in a Republican-dominated state government, but also by his ability to grow his majority as he did so. As noted, when he became Speaker there were 94 Democrats in the Assembly. At the beginning of the 2009 session, Assembly Democrats number 109, a very veto-proof majority.

Silver's Opportunity. The New York constitution gives the state Legislature responsibility for filling vacancies in the office of state Comptroller. The Legislature, in turn, long ago determined that this would be done by joint ballot of the Senate and Assembly. The combined membership of the two houses totals 212. Because there were, as noted, 108 Assembly Democrats when the session convened in January of 2007 (just half of both houses sitting together), the effective choice for filling the vacancy created by Hevesi's resignation fell to the Assembly majority. And because of the way (as we have seen in this book) that the Assembly works, this meant the choice was the Speaker's.

This was Silver's opportunity.

Silver's Problem: Governmentally, the selection of Comptroller was very important because of the duties of the office. The Comptroller is the auditor of all of state and local government in New York, and serves as sole trustee of pension funds for state and local workers then totaling over $140 billion.

Politically the decision was crucial, too. This is because the comptroller's office is one of the few proven statewide bases from which to launch a gubernatorial run.

Moreover, this selection was for almost a full four years of service. This was because the New York state constitution also provides that "No election of a comptroller or attorney general shall be had except at the time of electing a governor." Hevesi was newly elected; his resignation therefore created a vacancy in what was only the second month of a four year term. Whoever was appointed to fill it would therefore have almost an entire term to do the good work of holding government accountable and advocating reform, taking credit and, in general, deeply entrenching him- or herself. He or she would then seek election with all the advantages of an incumbent.

In sum, the value of the Comptrollership, both governmentally and politically, made it very attractive to a lot of ambitious players in the state political system, several of them senior members of the Assembly.

This was part of Silver's problem: one job, lots of aspirants. But it was also the kind of problem Speaker Silver was used to handling; he had been doing it for years.

Governor Eliot Spitzer

There was, however, another part of Speaker Silver's problem: the new Democratic governor-elect, Eliot Spitzer.

Eliot Spitzer will forever be remembered for his resignation in disgrace on March 17, 2008 under threat of impeachment. He was undone when the public came to know of his assignations as "Client #9" with Ashley Alexandra Dupre, a high priced hooker in the employ of Emperor's Club VIP.

Earlier the Spitzer administration was racked with controversy over the use of the state police to track the movements of Republican Majority Leader Joe Bruno. (This first "Trooper-gate," anteceded the controversy of the same name, but far different facts, involving Governor and Republican Vice Presidential candidate Sarah Palin during the 2008 presidential contest.) Governor Spitzer's involvement in New York's Trooper-gate was initially denied, and later (inadequately, it proved) covered-up This was an excessive, foolish use of executive power in an attempt to get the goods on a political adversary—ironically employing state resources improperly and in a partisan manner to try to prove the improper, partisan use of state resources by another.

Piling irony upon irony, there was no need for Spitzer to make a special effort to discredit Bruno. For the Senate Majority Leader was already under federal investigation for influence-peddling. With the federal investigation still unresolved, Bruno announced in June of 2008 that he would not seek reelection, stepped down from his leadership position on June 24 and resigned his Senate seat on July 18, 2008, thus ending one of the longest terms as Senate leader in New York State history. He was later convicted for corruption on two Federal felony counts. The matter was on appeal at this writing.

Perhaps the most damning dimension of both these episodes was the hypocritical contrast between the manner in which Spitzer actually lived his personal life and did his job and the posture of extreme moral rectitude he espoused in the public arena. This was a governor whose first official act was to issue a strict code of ethics for all his appointees. In retrospect, Spitzer admirers, if they carefully read his biographer Brooke A. Master's *Spoiling for a Fight*, could have found ample warning of the aggressive, explosive, confrontational, self-righteous take-no-prisoners style of which critics (and targets of Spitzer's investigations) warned, and that led to his downfall so few months after he took office.

Hindsight is 20–20. Knowing of the Spitzer implosion, it is hard to remember that the Governor was lionized—indeed named "Crusader of the Year" by *Time* Magazine and "Public Official of the Year" by *Governing* Magazine—for his aggressive prosecution of the Wall Street moguls who his unprecedented investigations found were victimizing "the little guy." Or that he gave great hope, after seeming decades in the wilderness, to New York's good government reformers, fully embracing their agenda to transform the troubled state and local government system in New York. Or that he was elected to the governorship by a landslide 69% of the vote in 2006, both on his record and his promise.

Though given no formal role by constitution or state law in filling vacancies in statewide office, Eliot Spitzer nevertheless sought to insert himself into the choice of Comptroller. In truth, his intervention was expected. As noted, Spitzer received more than two-thirds of the vote for governor in November; with this mandate, citizens would have been puzzled if he stood apart from such an important decision. Moreover, when vacancies in statewide office had previously arisen earlier governors had not been hands-off. Mario Cuomo, to cite one example, had pressed hard and successfully to have the Assembly elect Carl McCall as State Comptroller after the resignation of Ned Regan from the post in 1993.

The governor-elect had no candidate (at least overtly). What he did have, and what he convinced Silver to accept in the name of reform, was a screening process to "ensure the appointment of a highly qualified individual."

Speaker Silver had just completed twelve years of warfare against George Pataki, a Republican governor whom he genuinely disliked. He had no desire to get off on the wrong foot with Eliot Spitzer, a new and popular Democratic chief executive just entering his "honeymoon period." Moreover, Silver probably calculated that the screening process to which he finally agreed would satisfy the governor while also allowing the Assembly majority (that is, Silver himself) to control the actual selection of the Comptroller.

On January 17, 2007 Spitzer, Silver, and Senate Majority Leader Joseph L. Bruno (a Republican whose support was almost always crucial, but who had little power in this situation), announced an "Independent Screening Panel" for Comptroller candidates, comprised of former New York City Comptroller Harrison J. Goldin and former State Comptrollers Edward V. Regan and H. Carl McCall. There was a certain partisan symmetry in this approach. Goldin and McCall, both Democrats, had been state legislators (albeit in the Senate). Regan was a Republican.

The panel was to solicit applications from interested parties. Aspirants would then be interviewed by it and the Legislature's fiscal committees in public, televised proceedings. Thereafter the panel would, the Legislature's press release said, ". . . submit five candidates to the Legislature for their consideration." Not insignificantly in light of later events, the release was also very careful to note the Legislature's ". . . ultimate responsibility for the selection of the Comptroller."

On January 26, 2007 the Independent panel recommended not five but three finalists for the comptroller's position. They were New York City Finance Commissioner Martha Stark; Bill Mulrow, an investment banker and Spitzer supporter who made an unsuccessful bid for Comptroller in 2002; and Nassau County Comptroller Howard Weitzman. An Assembly member, Pete Grannis, said to have been favored for inclusion by the panel, removed himself from consideration when he agreed to accept Governor Spitzer's unexpected (and perhaps calculated) nomination to head the state's Department of Environmental Conservation. None of the remaining four Assembly members who aspired to the position and appeared before the panel were on the list: Thomas DiNapoli of Long Island, Richard Brodsky of Westchester, Joseph Morelle of Rochester, and Felix Ortiz of Brooklyn.

Assembly Democrats were enraged at an outcome that found none of their members qualified. They believed that the panel members— dubbed (somewhat sarcastically) "The Wise Men"—all of whom had progressed in their careers through the political process, were insufficiently considerate of the value of public policy-making experience in legislative office. Legislators also believed that panel members were hypocritical in their application of ill-defined professional criteria for the comptrollership. (This seemed especially true of Carl McCall, who first became Comptroller by virtue of election by the Legislature.)

As the Assembly's Democratic Conference considered its options, the governor put on the pressure. In an open letter to legislators he wrote: "If you choose not to select one of the three designated candidates for Comptroller, you will be sending a clear message that the three individuals found most qualified for the position are being rejected for one reason only—because they are not sitting members of the Legislature. Stated differently, you are telling the public that only legislators are eligible to serve as Comptroller, and that merit, independence and qualifications do not matter."

Now the Speaker found himself between his Conference and the governor. So he backed away from the selection process, denouncing it as "flawed." For one thing, Silver said, it had given the Legislature only three recommendations, not the expected five. (Governor Spitzer insisted that the agreement was that "up to five" nominees would be advanced.)

On February 7, 2007, by a vote of 150 to 56 (for Martha Stark) the state Legislature meeting in joint session elected Thomas DiNapoli as Comptroller. DiNapoli was a twenty year veteran of legislative service, and before that a manager for AT&T and a member of the Mineola School Board on Long Island. The vote was not partisan; it is better understood as an act of assertion of legislative prerogative, and institutional equality. Remember, the Legislature was still smarting as having only recently come out on the losing end of a bruising fight with the previous governor over the budgetary power.

All but three of the Democratic majority members in the Assembly (104 of 107) supported DiNapoli. Of the Republican majority members in the Senate, 29 of 33 voted for him. The exceptions among Assembly Democrats were Paul Tonko, who soon accepted an appointment in the Spitzer administration, and Joan Millman, for whom Stark was a constituent. Pete Grannis, also—as noted—shortly to become a Spitzer appointee, was absent for the vote.

Martha Stark drew unanimous support from Democrats in the Senate and most Assembly Republicans (a corporal's guard). Some few Republican Senators joined them. (Without any real say, there was no need for the Senate majority to demand discipline on this matter.) Because she was a very capable professional, an African American and a woman, Stark's candidacy was attractive to many downstate Democratic Senators. Moreover, Senate Democrats had a special reason to want to please the new Governor. Spitzer had overtly embraced the goal of helping them to gain a majority in the Senate, and had in fact just helped create a vacancy and then backed an effort that added a Democratic senator in a special election on Long Island.

The Legislature—Wrong When It's Wrong, Wrong When It's Right

Predictably, Governor Spitzer reacted with an attack on the Legislature. "We have just witnessed an insiders' game of self-dealing," he said, "that unfortunately confirms every New Yorker's worst fears and imaginings of all that goes on in the Legislature of this state." Also predictably, the editorial writers followed. In two separate comments the New York *Post* condemned the legislative leaders for "Their Worthless Word," and proclaimed "Cronyism Triumphant." "Shame on You," The Syracuse *Post Standard* wrote. The Buffalo *News* condemned ". . . the most dysfunctional legislature in the country, apparently more interested in sticking it to New Yorkers than bending to reform." *The New York Times,* more measured, critically commented that the ". . . Legislature failed to select the best candidate for the job," and instead "chose a person who had been ". . . a member of Albany's inbred club for two decades." A rare demurrer was filed by *Newsday* on Long Island, the daily that knew Tom DiNapoli best. It too did not like the process, but hailed the selection of a "Mr. Clean and Mr. Consensus" with deep experience and ". . . keen insights into how state and local governments work."

One aspect of the New York *Post* and Buffalo *News* editorials was particularly revealing. The *Post* wrote: "Silver and Bruno, through member items and extra salary, have bought the legislature. They own it, lock stock and members—and they'll do with it what they please. The *News* wrote ". . . lawmakers did the bidding of leaders who have helped make a wreck of this state." In fact, this was a decision in which Senate Majority Leader Bruno had no real say (and did not deliver a majority of the Senate). And in fact, this was a matter on which the members of the Democratic Conference in the Assembly asserted themselves, just as critics—and we in this book—have been calling upon them to do. They did not simply do the Speaker's bidding. They held the Speaker accountable, requiring him to abrogate an agreement that did not allow them to effect their preference.

In other words, for these editorialists the Governor was a reformer and therefore right. The Legislature was dysfunctional, and therefore wrong. As for the facts of the matter at hand, well these were beside the point.

Yet the Governor had none of the formal power to fill a vacancy in the Comptrollership: no nominating authority; no veto power. And for good reason. A big part of the Comptroller's job is to audit the executive branch. That's why the state constitution carefully defined the job as independent of the executive, and specified that the Legislature ". . . assign him no administrative duties . . ." beyond those directly required for performing the office's assigned functions.

And remember, the Comptroller is elected. By keeping the job elective even after many formerly elected statewide offices in New York were made appointed, state constitution makers confirmed that it required not just fiscal but political skills. These were summarized by Speaker Silver in describing Tom DiNapoli as having the ". . . demeanor, integrity and ability to get along with people. . . ." We like to think a strong résumé counts in seeking statewide elected office; but as we've seen from the accounts in earlier chapters of this book, it's far from all that counts.

Filling a four-year-long vacancy in any elective office by legislative election is not a good idea; a special election would be better. But there is a rationale for legislative election to fill shorter term vacancies: this is election by those who are themselves chosen by the people when a popular election cannot be held in timely manner. Indeed, there is a hoary debate in American politics, with good arguments on both sides, about the relative merits of a peer process—selection by those who have long worked with and know the aspirants well in a proverbial "smoke filled room"—as opposed to a popular process, selection through primary election, for nomination to the highest office in the land.

In appearances around the state Spitzer continued his assault, debunking Tom DiNapoli's qualifications and attacking in their home districts legislators who had supported him. A flood of calls, e-mails, and letters ensued—both to media outlets and to legislative offices—condemning the legislative leaders, individual members and the Legislature generally. Interestingly, even with all this *sturm und drang*, most New Yorkers contacted by the Qunnipiac University poll were uninformed on the subject. But of those that did know about it, almost twice as many condemned the Legislature as supported it.

Unloved

Quinnipiac regularly polls New Yorkers' attitudes toward "the way the state legislature is handling its job," and regularly finds—urban, suburban, or rural, male or female, upstate or down—that less than a third approve. The high point, over the three-year period between the summer of 2004 and the summer of 2007, 34% approval, was achieved on April 4, 2007; the low point, 26% approval, was recorded on August 11, 2004. It appears that the Legislature is the Rodney Dangerfield of New York politics. It just "don't get no respect."

Part of this, of course, is the low regard for legislatures that prevails generally in the contemporary United States. The term limits movement of the 1990s was a clear expression of general skepticism about (if not hostility toward) legislatures. Recently, Congress has regularly been ranked at or near the bottom when Americans are asked about their trust in institutions. When it comes to performance, the Quinnipiac poll most recently found that about a quarter of citizens approved the work Congress does (April, 2007), with the percent approval no higher than 39% during the 2004–2007 period. Results from other major polls were quite similar.

With regard to other states, Karl Kurtz, the respected director of the Trust for Representative Democracy of the National Conference of State Legislatures, wrote in May of 2006 on that organization's blog that "the hard fact is that legislative institutions do not rate well in the public's eye." Kurtz cited in particular polls in California, where the Legislature's ratings have dropped into the teens, and Pennsylvania, where the word most frequently associated with the state Legislature by poll respondents was "greedy."

Scholars argue that legislatures are critically perceived by the general public because they are complex, hard to understand organizations whose compromise resolution of difficult problems is never fully acceptable to particular individuals or interests. It does not help, they add, when individual legislators—who are often strongly supported in their districts—"run against the institution." In particular, the New York Legislature is especially vulnerable because the state has almost all the attributes that correlate most strongly with low citizen confidence in legislatures: higher taxes, questionable fiscal health, divided government (until 2009), higher unemployment (in some regions) and greater legislator professionalism.

We've detailed at length the many problematic dimensions of the operation of the New York state Legislature in general, and the Assembly in particular. Districts are gerrymandered; this diminished competitiveness and accountability and cemented divided partisan control continuous until 2009. Internal democracy is largely absent. The rules empower and serve the leadership. The leadership controls all institutional and most political resources. Competition is further diminished, and leadership further empowered, by the flow of campaign funds, minimally regulated, to those in power. Minority party members count for little. Committee chairs dominate committees. They in turn are dominated by the leaders, who can make or break their careers. Those same leaders hold direct sway over the members, and even, with rare exceptions, dominate the party conferences to which they are ostensibly accountable.

The resulting reality is that the Legislature's record of performance on highly visible matters of public policy has been dismal in recent years. For most recent years, too, timely passage of the state budget has been the metaphoric example. Another is New York's dead last finish among the states in complying with the requirements of the Help America Vote Act (HAVA). Here some in the state have even tried to make nonperformance a virtue, arguing that missing federal deadlines allowed it to learn from and avoid the mistakes of other jurisdictions in implementing new voting technologies.

"Most Things We Do Well"

And yet the Legislature retains its advocates. Syracuse University Political Scientist Jeffrey Stonecash has called the idea that the New York State Legislature is dysfunctional a "myth. . . . [W]hat takes place in Albany," he said, "is just normal haggling over policy." Long-time Assemblyman Richard Brodsky, who himself had sought the job, asserted in *The New York Times,* in response to the criticism of Tom DiNapoli's election as Comptroller: "Although in the last few years there have been things the Legislature has had to improve, most things we do well." Brodsky went on to attribute the New York State Legislature's problematic reputation to bad public relations. "We've been very effectively Swift-boated as dysfunctional, ineffective and corrupt," he said. "And it's our fault. We have never gotten the message out in a coherent way of what we do well and right."

Stonecash and Brodsky overstate the case. But this book demonstrates that they have a point in at least four areas: district representation, representation of New York's diversity, protection of institutional interests, and the development of public policy.

REPRESENTING THE DISTRICT

One thing legislators and the Legislature are good at is representing home districts.

Each Assembly and Senate District in New York has a unique character and feel. Part of this has to do with what political scientist Dan Elazar has called political culture. Visit the Rochester area and you'll feel as if you are somewhere in the Midwest, Wisconsin perhaps. A "politics as public service" ethos prevails. In contrast, about an hour's drive to the west, in the Buffalo area, entering political life for personal advancement is seen as perfectly legitimate.

Though they are not particularly small in population—125,500 in the Assembly, 306,000 in the Senate—districts have defining characteristics. It may be that one or two racial, ethnic or religious groups are locally dominant. White, Black, Hispanic or (now) . . . Asian. Italian-American, Irish-American, English or Central European. Protestant, Catholic or Jewish. Or the district may be defined by a dominant economic activity: dairy farming, nuclear power generation, higher education, finance, tourism. Each district is urban, suburban or rural; affluent, middling or poor. Some remain work-where-we-live local. Others accept, or even embrace, their "bedroom" status. Most often, a district's definition arises from a particular mix of these demographic, social, and economic elements.

Legislative districts do not emerge, of course, fully formed like Athena from the head of Zeus. They are designed in the legislature to assure first that partisan majorities in each house persist and thrive, and second that most (but as we have seen, not all) sitting majority members thrive as well. District design was formerly governed by rules in the state constitution written to assure that New York State was "constitutionally Republican," as Governor Alfred E. Smith once put it. As a result of national constitutional litigation, few of these state constitutional requirements remain in force. Most parameters that govern districting are now drawn from two sources: the one-person-one-vote standard established by the U.S. Supreme Court in *Baker v. Carr* and following cases, and the requirements of the Federal Voting Rights Act designed to assure that members of minority groups, especially in some specified jurisdictions, have an effective say in choosing their representatives. If anything, the applications of these federal standards work to assure that legislative districts are more demographically homogeneous. (More about this, below.)

The state legislature may not be the major leagues of American politics, but it is certainly Triple-A. Few legislators get to call a state legislative district their own without playing in the A, Double-A or the rookie leagues; few get to Albany without significant experience in public life. This means that they have spent a lot of time getting to know the district they represent, or at least a part of it, before they ever get elected to the state Legislature.

Dan Feldman's experience was not in elective office but as a staffer for Elizabeth Holtzman and Chuck Schumer. He was later elected to Schumer's Assembly seat. This is not uncommon in New York City. Atypically, local elected offices in New York City—in the City Council, for example—are seen as equal or better jobs and career stepping stones as are state legislative seats. The pay and perks are as good or better for City Council members; there is far less time on the road or away from home, and there is more-or-less equal visibility in the media. Thus until the advent of term limits for the Council in 1993, the political career path was at least as likely to be from Albany back to New York City than the other way around.

Outside the City, experience for Assembly aspirants is far more likely to be in local elective office: in the county legislature, or on a town or village board or as a member of a city council. That is, most of those who run for state legislative office have already represented at least some part of the district they are seeking to represent in Albany. Also, with the primary exception of county executive posts, state legislative seats are more visible, more prestigious, and even better paying than elected jobs in local government.

In sum, state legislators representing districts outside New York City are big fish in small ponds. New York City-based legislators (the Speaker of the Assembly excepted, of course) are small fish in big ponds.

Most legislative districts in the state are dominated by one of the two major parties, more these days by Democrats than Republicans. Incumbent reelection rates that approach 100% discourage challenges to seated members. Shots at open seats are rare opportunities. So even with one party dominant, access to the Assembly or Senate is likely to be contested. Dan Feldman had to cultivate party support and win a primary to gain his nomination; winning a contested election to gain his seat provided him a fundamental shared experience with those he joined in the Assembly. And the prospect of having to defend his seat in two years, by keeping local party leaders happy, discouraging ambitious potential challengers, and building support in the district to assure victory if a challenge occurred, gave him a shared goal with virtually all of his colleagues—and a basis for understanding their priorities and motivations.

The state constitution requires that a member of the Senate or Assembly be resident in his or her district for ". . . the twelve months immediately preceding his or her election. . . ." The political reality is far more demanding. To gain an Assembly seat a person has to be deeply rooted in the district, knowledgeable about its politics, and credible as a candidate. This means that the member is likely to share the demographic and social characteristics of one of the dominant groups in the district (though he or she may be far better educated, that is, have "risen" from that group, and have become an "exemplar" or "role model"). It is also likely that the member knows and shares the core values and priorities of the people and major institutions and industries in his or her district.

Legislators get to know their districts even better as they work to keep their jobs. In *Home Style*, his ground-breaking book on Congressmen in their districts, Richard Fenno described how incumbents gained electoral security by building support outward from an inner circle, thus establishing a network of personal and service relationships in the district. Dan Feldman was similar to all his colleagues in the emphasis he placed upon performing service for individual constituents: answering their inquiries, intervening and advocating for them with state and city agencies. After several election cycles passed, he achieved a shift of the loyalty of voters in his district on election day from "the Democratic candidate" to "Feldman." More and more constituents could say, "I shook his hand," "I heard him speak at my church," "He gave my son an award," "He knows me."

This, of course, discouraged potential challengers. Another key result of re-grounding support in the district was greater autonomy in leading with controversial positions on such matters of public policy as reform of the Rockefeller Drug laws. Like virtually all legislators from NYC, Feldman knew that rent control was an issue on which he had to be "right" or risk challenge and defeat. But this, he says, was truly exceptional. Certainly, Dan's liberal positions on dealing more flexibly and less punitively with low level, non-violent drug law offenders were not the mainstream views in his district. But even when he was far out in front of other legislators on this issue, writing editorials for *The New York Times*, he was never punished for his views at the polls.

Other members enjoyed this same autonomy. But interestingly, most did not feel it, or if they did, they did not act upon it. Support had to be painstakingly gathered for years outside the Legislature—in editorial boards, among interest groups—before other members began to sign on to Rockefeller Drug Law Reform. (Senator Joseph Galiber was an exception.)

This behavior by most Assembly members offers an explanation for one apparent paradox in the working of the state Legislature. Literally thousands of bills are introduced during a biannual session, each presumably seeking some sort of change. Members report in their newsletters to the district, as a measure of performance, the number of bills they introduce. Legislators measure their success by the number that they "pass"—though no one, of course, passes a bill on his or her own. In fact, we have seen in this book that many claim patrimony for laws that later prove popular but in support of which, when it counted, they did little or nothing. In fact, the aggregate effect of risk aversion by members, who are not really at all at risk, makes the legislative institution profoundly change resistant, profoundly conservative on most controversial matters of public policy.

Like other legislators, Dan Feldman introduced legislation or took actions that directly benefited his district when he could, for example with regard to abuses at the New York City Parking Violations Bureau. Like other legislators, he sought to "bring home the bacon" by obtaining member items, for example for pre-kindergarten and senior citizen programs in his district. Unlike colleagues outside New York City, his efforts gained relatively little publicity, and his performance appeared to be less measured by the results of these efforts.

Dan Feldman was one of 65 Assembly members and 26 Senators from New York City (and one of a somewhat larger delegation from New York City when he was first elected). The City has an extensive legislative agenda for each session, and a lobbying office in Albany to advance it. Members from the city are usually disposed to support the City government's requests. (Though not always, not for example when there are partisan or arcane intra-party differences involved, or when the City's goals are in conflict with those of public employee labor unions.) But these members are not so directly seen as representative of the City government as are members from the rest of the state outside the City seen as representative of local governments in their districts.

Localities often need some special action by the state Legislature to do what they want to do. Ulster County, seeking to avoid a heavy property tax increase on local homeowners, wanted state authorization to levy a real estate transfer tax. Potter, New York, in the Finger Lakes, needed state legislation to allow the continued local sale of beer while it undid the unintended results of a local referendum that, much to its chagrin, left the town dry. The state constitution provides a process through which localities may request this assistance through special law. Each house of the Legislature relies on advice from the member or members from whose district such a request emanates. If he or she supports it, it almost always goes; if not, it almost always doesn't. Most often, citing "home rule," the state legislators defer in turn to the wishes of local government leaders in their districts, and advance this kind of initiative. But if a state legislator disagrees with the locals about the proposed special legislation, for example the aforementioned mortgage tax, a bruising local political battle might ensue.

To serve his constituents, and (not insignificantly) cement his incumbency, Dan Feldman spent hundreds of mornings greeting citizens at subway stops and attended thousands of meetings in his district. After entering office he was constantly on the move between the district and Albany. Legislators outside New York City keep similar schedules, though often with even more travel because of the geographic expanse of their districts. After a member becomes entrenched, the time and energy needed to keep the job might slacken. But whether out of commitment, habit or insecurity (justified or not), most legislators feel the necessity or obligation to keep up the pace. It takes high energy to get and keep the job, another shared characteristic.

With this in mind, it is understandable why most members don't accept that their longevity in office is due entirely or even substantially to rigged district design. Unlike Groucho Marx, who declared that he would never join any club that would have him as a member, legislators work hard to get and stay in "the club."

Honoring and Protecting the Institution

Once elected, legislators have another shared experience: the experience of being legislators. They enter a several-hundred-year-old institution, assuming in some small way, as they do so, trusteeship for a founding place for representative democracy in America, and the world. The grandeur of their meeting place reminds them each time they enter it of the importance of their work, and that they may there create for themselves a place in history. This and other special spaces are reserved for their use; others enter only at their deference. In recognition of their status, upon assuming their seats newly elected legislators become "honorables," and (at least formally) receive a degree of respect in the political world. That title, that status, stays with them as "formers," as does the right of access to the floor in the house in which they served. All current and former members who have been elected to at least five legislative terms in the Assembly are members of the Legislative Pilots Association. These "pilots of the ship of state" meet annually for a dinner in May.

Almost from the first day, members are subject to the Legislature's rituals, like the one Dan Feldman described on the passage of his first bill. They are socialized and come to know and value the "way things are done"—as did Speaker Stanley Fink when he sought to "get the Chapter" for the Organized Crime Control Act by passing it in his house before it passed in the Senate. (Or if norms are violated, as we see from Dan Feldman's view about others who did not hold themselves to Fink's standard, they have a point of view about it.) They see important differences between the two houses in small matters of procedure and institutional practice. "In the Assembly we do it this way, while in the Senate they do it that way." They join subgroups based upon race, gender, shared interest—the Black, Puerto Rican, Hispanic, and Asian American Caucus, the Women's Caucus—that have importance insofar as they may affect the performance of the entire body.

As we have seen, citizens are already quite skeptical of state legislatures. Because they have a shared title, a shared status, each legislator has a stake—acknowledged or not—in what other legislators might do to affect the legislative institution's already shaky reputation. All benefit when one acts in a way that brings credit to the institution. All are in some small measure diminished when one acts dishonorably.

As we have also seen, some deal with this by distinguishing themselves from the institution and its leadership, an especially easy task for minority members in each house who are denied any substantial say in policy making. Others behave or communicate differently at home than in Albany; they are "lions in the district, lambs in the Legislature." But this dichotomy, though it may serve in the short term, has a cost. It puts members who behave in this way at risk of being seen as less than "standup" by their legislative colleagues. For most know or come to know that their own influence and status rises or falls with that of the legislative institution.

Ultimately, almost all legislators come to understand their personal stake in the institutional power of the Legislature within the separation of powers system. They are powerful only insofar as it is powerful. It is when an issue comes to be defined as primarily involving the power of the legislative institution that the Republican Senate and Democratic Assembly are most likely to come strongly together. This was the case regarding the Legislature's insistence upon dealing with smoking in public places by law, not regulation, described in this book. It was the case in the confrontations between the Governor Pataki and the Legislature over the budgetary powers. And it was the case, of course, in the election of Tom DiNapoli as Comptroller.

Opposition to controversial initiatives like the state RICO statute or Megan's Law does not go away once legislation passes. Especially on matters that implicate civil liberties, litigation to test federal or state constitutionality is almost inevitable. One lesson of this book is that the Legislature protects its institutional power, its capacity to be the place where the final decision on policy is made, by preparing for potential challenges in the courts. This requires anticipation and thorough advanced study of the constitutional dimensions of the issue at hand, careful drafting, and the creation of a defensible record of the Legislature's intentions.

Another lesson, this one arising form the gun control case, is that inaction by the Legislature carries with it the risk of lost institutional power. This is the case even when inaction is an outcome, that is, when change has been pushed but its proponents lack the political force to overcome defenders of the status quo. The absence of an action by the Legislature invites efforts to bypass it by changing venues. Wearing a different hat, that of the State's Deputy Attorney General, Dan Feldman sought to limit the availability of handguns in New York through litigation, when that objective could not be achieved through law. He failed, and other efforts to use the courts provoked pro-gun interests to seek another venue shift—into the national Congress, where they achieved supportive legislation for their cause.

DIVERSITY AND REPRESENTATIVENESS.

A third thing the Legislature is good at is representing the diversity of New York.

One difference between the legislative "club" and other exclusive clubs is that current club members do not select new ones. There is no review of credentials for entry into the Legislature; (again) as Stanley Fink was fond of saying to his members, "None of you got here by passing a Civil Service test." New members are sent by their districts, and once elected enter the body legitimately, as a matter of right. Each house is the judge of the qualification of its own members, the state constitution tells us (Article III, section 9); therefore individuals may be barred, or expelled. But such actions are very rare, and as we saw in 2010 in the case of former Senator Hiram Monserrate, undertaken with great hesitation, and angst.

Collectively, new and old members together create a diverse environment in which all must function and seek their goals, personal and legislative. Not all see the world as does a white, male, middle-class, Jewish Ivy–League-educated lawyer from Brooklyn with a penchant for political philosophy. There is fundamental equality. Whatever their race, ethnicity, brains, brawn, pedigree, experience or education, legislators each have one vote.

But there is inequality, too. Not all are members of a majority party conference, with a shot at becoming a committee chairman or otherwise rising to a leadership position in the Senate or Assembly.

Legislators take each others' measure in formal and informal settings: in conference, in committee, on the floor, over the chessboard, at the dinner table or the card table, in the gym. They reach points of view about who has formal power, who has influence, and who has both; who's serious and who's not; who may be trusted to keep his or her word, who not; whose ambitions are inside and whose outside the body. And of course, each member gets to know and appreciate perspectives and priorities that they never previously had to consider, and comes to realize (sometimes) that taking these seriously is essential to getting the body to do what he or she most wants done.

The New York State Legislature has fewer voting "citizens" than all but the smallest of New York State's villages. It should not be surprising, therefore, that it is a place in which relationships matter. We offer Dan Feldman's points of view over the course of this book (mostly positive, sometimes not) about the character, capacity and commitment of numerous of his former colleagues, but none are given in greater detail than those concerning the leaders with which he served. Again, not surprising; the greatest focus is upon the most important relationship.

It is well understood that this relationship is most important because the leader controls the resources members need to succeed and advance. Among these are: appointments to committees and committee chairmanships; budget for district offices, staff and operations; and access of bills to the floor. Another that has become very important, but not touched upon earlier in this book (because Feldman, as a non-marginal, never received any assistance from the Democratic Assembly Campaign Committee, although he occasionally raised relatively small amounts of money for it), is control over campaign funds through the operations of chamber-based campaign committees. The consolidation in the hands of leadership of both governmental and political power within each of the legislative houses in New York is a signal transformation of the late twentieth century.

The tendency in reportage about all politics is to emphasize personalities; the subtleties of institutional dynamics are elusive and—for most people—boring. It is not the Assembly as an institution or the Senate as an institution that makes headlines; it is Speaker Silver or Majority Leader Bruno. For good or for ill, therefore, the legislative institution is reified in the leader.

This focus has two consequences. It further empowers leaders relative to their members. And it makes the reputation of the institution in which members have a stake dependent upon the reputation and performance of the leaders.

It is another apparent paradox of legislative life that the members choose the leaders, and must reelect them every two years, yet leaders seem to hold such absolute sway over them once they are elected. The first thing to say about this is that the sway is not so absolute. We show how leadership opposition was overcome to pass Megan's Law in the form and with the character that it ultimately took. Admittedly, however, this result was exceptional. It was achieved in a very special context, by a member who had skill at exploiting interest group and extraordinary media attention and who was willing to confront and overcome leadership opposition.

Most often, the costs—marginalization within the house and diminished career prospects outside it—are simply too high. The group chooses the leader, but thereafter the relationship is between that leader and each individual member. In this one-on-one relationship, as noted, the leader holds almost all the cards. Just as being on the right side in a leadership selection fight may accelerate a career, a wrong choice may stall or even end one. And even if there is considerable discontent with a leader, as the experience of Michael Bragman's challenge to Sheldon Silver shows, effectively organizing against a sitting leader is near impossible. Joe Bruno did it in the Republican Senate in 1994, but this was with the help of a newly elected governor of his party, George Pataki (a former Senator with a real ax to grind with Ralph Marino, the incumbent leader).

We make the case that shared values make compromise possible in controversial areas of policy. But this compromise comes in a Legislature that is ideologically diverse, reflecting the diversity of points of view in the state on criminal justice and social policy. The "ideological center" of the Democratic majority in the Assembly was more to the left, more liberal, and that of the Republican majority of the Senate more to the right, more conservative, on most issues. But there is great ideological diversity within the Democratic membership of the Assembly; witness the division there on the death penalty, the baby AIDS issue, and the civil liberties implications of Megan's Law.

There is also great demographic diversity. Though each legislator is sent to Albany by a district that has a certain homogeneity, because of the diversity of New York's population the collective outcome is an institution that is enormously heterogeneous. The New York State Legislature is one of the most demographically diverse — though still not fully demographically representative — in the nation. In 2007 there were 45 legislators who were members of the Black, Puerto Rican, Hispanic and Asian Legislative Caucus. New York had more African-American state legislators than all but seven states (all these in the south) when the last comparative count was made in 2003, and more legislators from Puerto Rican and other Hispanic backgrounds than all but four states. In 2006, according to the National Conference of State Legislators, 48 New York legislators were women (22.6%), equal to the mean percentage for the nation.

This record and requirements of the Federal Voting Rights Act notwithstanding, demographic change in the Legislature is slower than in the state at large. Though Asian Americans comprised 6.9% of New Yorkers in 2006, for example, there was still in 2008 only a single Asian American in the state Legislature. The strength of incumbents at the polls, and the majorities' predisposition to protect sitting members, slows the rate at which the Legislature achieves demographic representation of New York's people.

The Assembly Speaker is elected from a district, and then elected again by colleagues to his leadership post. His elevation requires him thereafter to consider the views of all the members of his conference in setting priorities and making choices; in fact it requires him to develop a statewide perspective. Something similar happens to legislators as they become more senior. As they gain more formal responsibility, for example as committee chairs, and informal influence, as seasoned members, their ideas about representation shift and broaden.

Dan Feldman was from Brooklyn. So was Speaker Stanley Fink. Fink supported Feldman with very good early committee assignments. The young assemblyman's star rose further when he backed Mel Miller's successful bid for to succeed Fink as Speaker. Miller actually created a committee, the Corrections Committee, for Feldman to head.

Feldman was serious. He studied. He visited prisons. He realized that the relationships between lock-'em-up, tough-on-crime laws, and prosecutorial and sentencing practices, and the upstate demand for the jobs that prison construction brought, were synergistic, and massively costly. Most people who were sent to state prison were African American and Hispanic. Feldman saw the devastating social consequences upon urban minority communities of jailing non-violent drug offenders, many of these in Brooklyn.

Feldman's views developed and changed as he became the go-to guy on corrections policy in the Assembly and active on corrections issues in the National Conference of State Legislatures. He found himself negotiating on criminal justice and corrections policy with the Corrections Commissioner, with gubernatorial aides, with Senators, with prosecutors, with other Assembly members, with prisoner advocacy and prison reform groups, and with correction officer associations.

As he functioned as Correction Committee chair, Feldman's constituency changed too. He developed new relationships, relationships with different kinds of people than those in his district. In sum, he came to number among those he represented a broader and more geographically and racially diverse group of New Yorkers.

Ambition is the engine of political life. Deaths or resignations provide rare open-seat opportunities that many are likely to seek to exploit. Each time he or she seeks to advance to higher office, an incumbent has to roll the dice, calculating the risk—losing his or her current job—against the potential reward—gaining a better one. Dan Feldman was no exception.

Lots of African American and Hispanic people lived in Brooklyn. Many of their lives were touched by the effect of draconian drug laws.

Feldman thought that his work on corrections policy and Rockefeller Drug Law reform might gain him support in this broader constituency, and help him advance. In 1989 the candidacy for mayor of David Dinkins, an African American, vastly boosted Black voter turnout. Feldman ran and lost for Kings County District Attorney, against a white opponent whose work as a prosecutor on a racially charged issue was more visible and dramatically responsive to sentiments among Black voters than were his efforts in Albany.

Because the contest for this local office was in an odd numbered year, Feldman did not have to sacrifice his Assembly seat to make the D.A. race. It was a "free ride." Later, blocked from further career development in the Assembly because of a bad relationship with Speaker Silver, Feldman rolled the dice again. The term for both the New York Assembly and U.S. Congress is two years, and election to these offices is simultaneous. Feldman's failure to win the Congressional nomination ended his career in elective office.

Public Policy Incubator

The public policy agenda in state government is driven by the governor. He enters office with policy commitments made during his campaign for office. His state of the state message in the first year and thereafter, informed by a systematic survey of executive departments, launches the annual legislative session. A few weeks later his budget concretizes his priorities; it provides focus for the policy debate for much of each year. Annual media assessments of outcomes are framed primarily in terms of the governor's "wins" and "losses." Prognosticators assess prospects for the chief executive's future success based upon past performance in getting his legislative agenda enacted.

All this notwithstanding, we've organized much of this book around "sex, guns, drugs, crime and punishment" to drive home this point: much of legislative life, much more than usually acknowledged, is about serious efforts at public policy making. Many incentives drive in this direction. Members need formed policy positions to credibly contest for office. Moreover, as noted, they cannot have won their seats without becoming intimately aware of their constituents' concerns. Introducing legislation addressing promises they've made and concerns they have identified is an obvious way to demonstrate that they are doing something about what they say they care about, and what people in their districts care about.

The sources of ideas are various. Expert staff like Mindy Bockstein generate many. Organizations like the National Conference of State Legislatures have issue-focused efforts that identify best practices. As earlier noted, the process identified by scholars as "diffusion of policy innovation" through the federal system operates. Initiatives in other states provide models. Interest groups—providers of financial and political support during the election season—expect legislators to sponsor or co-sponsor legislation they favor. Members themselves are always on the lookout to take ownership of a blockbuster issue that will build their reputations and advance their careers.

The attention span of the legislative institution is limited. Only a few major matters may be addressed in each session. Some of these—the budget is the biggest and best example—must be considered in each session. Others, like HAVA, are placed on the agenda by external deadlines. Where discretion remains, the governor primarily, and the leaders and other statewide elected officials secondarily, are far better situated than individual members to choose which subjects of the hundreds vying for priority will get serious consideration in a particular year. But policy important to many is made through lesser actions as well as those of massive statewide consequence. And on both big and small matters, all legislators all the time can and do introduce ingredients to the "primal stew" of legislation always kept simmering in Albany.

It is clear from the accounts in this book, and many elsewhere, that legislators "keep score," and encourage others to do so, on the basis of the number of bills they introduce, and the number that they "pass." Some regard the relatively low ratio of bills passed to bills introduced in each session of the New York State Legislature as evidence of inefficiency. Critics argue, rightly, that time, energy, and money are wasted when members, acting in response to constituent expectations or "pressure," introduce bills that they have no serious intention of supporting further. The Legislature would be a better run place, they conclude, if limits are placed on the number of bills a member may introduce in New York, as is the case in some other states.

This is a bad idea. Legislatures act by legislating. Drafting legislation places policy ideas into precise, actionable form. Often there are a number of draft bills addressing a single subject. The precision required for drafting and the availability of drafts taking alternative approaches makes policy differences clear and identifiable, and focuses debate.

One clear lesson of this book is that making policy takes time. Support has to be gathered, public opinion mobilized, opposition overcome or accommodated. For years, sometimes, the stars may not be aligned, the timing never quite right. And yet the caldron simmers. And when the time finally is right, state policy makers are more likely to be informed and ready to act intelligently if draft legislation has been previously available for consideration and debate. This requires that legislators, as entrepreneurs of policy, retain the right to introduce legislation freely.

Much of the detailed work of legislating is done by highly trained staff expert in the law, policy analysis, and (less evident from this book) public finance. The New York State Legislature is one of the most generously staffed in the nation. Dan Feldman's experience reinforces that the support provided by skilled, expert staff (and enthusiastic interns, given initial access to careers in public life in this way) is essential to a legislator's success.

But there are also tensions. During Dan Feldman's tenure, control of committee staff in the Assembly was increasingly centralized in the hands of the speaker. This led to serious differences between Feldman and some other committee chairs and the Assembly leadership. (Things were different in the Senate, where chairs retained control of committee staff.) Central control of staff gave the Speaker still another tool for controlling the working of the Assembly, and diminished chairs' sway in policy making.

Perhaps because of his training in the law and prior experience as a staffer, Feldman inserted himself more fully into negotiations about specific legislative language than is common in the Legislature. The resistance he sometimes encountered from staff is illustrative of an underlying tension in legislative life in the Assembly. Those elected legislators who care about policy making think they should be "in charge," and chafe when they feel that they are (in fact, if not in form) subordinated to staff in key roles working directly for the leaders.

Their lesser involvement in the details of drafting does not necessarily mean that Dan Feldman's colleagues who relied more than he did on the Legislative Bill Drafting Commission, or even on central or committee staffers, were uninterested in policy—though admittedly more than a few surely were. Rather, it meant that they were less prepared by education and experience than was Feldman for this task, less confident in their skills to reach the exact outcomes they sought, or simply more willing to delegate.

Finally, it is striking that much important legislative policy making that occurred during Dan Feldman's time in the Assembly is not discussed in this book. There is little here about budgeting, or higher education. There is little here about Medicaid, or banking regulation, or workers compensation. This list could go on and on. Legislators must vote on everything. However, no legislator, not even the leaders, can be deeply informed on all that the New York State Legislature does. Specialization is inevitable. And therefore, no account of legislative life from a single perspective can ever really be complete.

Perhaps that is why the legislative institution in New York is so fascinating and yet so illusive as we seek to understand both its shortcomings and its strengths. Our Legislature in New York, like—we suspect—all legislatures in democratic societies, will always remain a little bit mysterious. For those who care about government and policy making in representative democracy, that mystery is part of the attraction.

Sources

Prologue: The Senate Scandal of 2009

The New York Legislature's top rating from the Citizens Conference on State Legislatures was noted in Thomas H. Little and David B. Ogle, *The Legislative Branch of State Governments*, ABC-CLIO, Santa Barbara, California 2006, at page 67; and in Alan Rosenthal, The "Good" Legislature, *The Book of the States 2005*, Council of State Governments, 103, http://www.csg.org/pubs/Documents/BOS2005-Good Legislature.pdf.

The Citizens Conference report itself is Citizens Conference on State Legislatures, *State Legislatures: an evaluation of their effectiveness*, Praeger, New York 1971. Although Little, Ogle, and Rosenthal all—more than thirty years later—question the usefulness of the Citizens Conference model, its ratings certainly reflected the consensus of opinion at the time.

The praise for Stanley Fink from Mario Cuomo and Warren Anderson was quoted in Obituary, Stanley Fink, Assembly Speaker, 61, Is Dead, *The New York Times*, 3/6/97, http://www.nytimes.com/1997/03/06/nyregion/stanley-fink-assembly-speaker-61-is-dead.html. For acknowledgement of Anderson's role in the fiscal crisis, see Hugh Carey, The Transition, Gerald Benjamin and T. Norman Hurd (eds.) *Making Experience County: Managing Modern New York in the Carey Era* (Albany: Rockefeller Institute of Government, 1985) p. 15.

Chapter Four explains in more detail the demographic and political changes resulting in the shrinking of the Republican caucus in the State Senate.

For background on ethnic succession through politics and government in New York see, for example, Theodore Lowi, *At the Pleasure of the Mayor: Patronage and Power in New York City, 1898–1958* (New York: Free Press, 1964); Daniel Elazar is famous for his exploration of the idea of state political culture in his *American Federalism: A View From the States* (New York: Thomas Y. Crowell, 1972). For a brief discussion of the growing diversity in state legislative leadership and membership see http://www.ncsl.org/default.aspx?tabid=17917. The National Conference of State Legislatures also offers up-to-date information on this website regarding the racial, ethnic, and gender composition of American state legislatures.

Azi Paybarah, The Bruno-Kruger Connection, *The New York Observer*, 2/28/07, http://www.observer.com/node/31597; and Elizabeth Benjamin, "Bruno Names Democratic Committee Chair," Albany *Times-Union*, 2/28/07, http://blog://blog.timesunion.com/capitol/archives/3888/bruno-names-democratic-committee-chair/, among others, reported Democratic State Senator Carl Kruger's pre-2009 cozy relationship with the Republicans.

Editorial, The Senate's Bitter Pill, *Times-Union*, 7/10/09, http://www.timesunion.com/AspStories/storyprint.asp?StoryID=818560; James Odato, "Espada profits, firm owes," *TimesUnion.com*, 6/25/09, http://www.timesunion.com/ASPStories/story/print.asp?StoryID=813737; Suzanne Sataline, New York Standoff Sharpens Focus on

Lawmaker, *The Wall Street Journal*, 6/22/09, http://online.wsj.com/article/SB 1245625; Nicholas Confessore, "Before Defecting, Espada Sought $2 Million for Bronx Groups," *The New York Times*, 6/9/09, http://cityroom.blogs.nytimes.com/2009/06/09/ before-defecting-espada-sought-2-million-for-bronx-groups/, set forth Senator Espada's legal and ethical issues.

For descriptions of the domestic violence charges brought against Senator Monserrate, see, e.g., Danny Hakim, "In the New York Senate, Order is Restored, but Decorum Isn't," *The New York Times*, 7/18/09, http://nyregion/18notebook.html?_r=1&ref=ny region&pag; Editorial, "Grand jury fodder: Rotten pay deal for domestic abuser Monserrate demands investigation," *New York Daily News*, 7/16/09, http://www.nydaily news.com/opinions/2009/07/16/2009-07-16_grand_jury_fodder_rotten . . . Senator Monserrate's misdemeanor conviction and subsequent expulsion from the Senate were reported, respectively, in Ralph Blumenthal, Monserrate Cleared of Felonies, *New York Times*, 10/15/09, http://www.nytimes.com/2009/10/16/nyregion/16monserrate.html and Glenn Blain and Kenneth Lovett, State Senate Votes to Boot Sen. Hiram Monserrate, citing his misdemeanor assault conviction, *New York Daily News*, 2/9/10, http:// www.nydailynews.com/news/2010/02/09/2010-02-09_state_senate_to_vote_to_expel _sen_hiram_monserrate_over_misdemeanor_assault _conv.html.

Senator Diaz's opposition to gay rights, and other aspects of his legislative record, are mentioned in, e.g., Danny Hakim and Jeremy W. Peters, "Paterson Says State Senate Can't Put Off Its Return," *The New York Times*, 6/23/09, A21, c5-c6. Jeremy W. Peters, New York State Senate Votes Down Gay Marriage Bill, NY Times, 12/2/09, http://www.nytimes.com/2009/12/03/nyregion/03marriage.html reported the defeat of the gay marriage bill.

Danny Hakim, in "Democrats Reach Pact to Lead the Senate," *The New York Times*, 1/6/09, http://www.nytimes.com/2009/01/07/nyregion/07albany.html_r=1, described the various rewards Malcolm Smith bestowed on the "four amigos" in return for their support for his candidacy as Majority Leader.

Elizabeth Moore, Experts: Political circus has serious stakes for GOP, *Newsday.com*, 6/11/09, http://www.newsday.com/news/region-state/experts. . .-gop-1.124 3284?printerfriendly=true; Sewell Chan, City Room Blog: "Population Shifts in Democrats' Favor," *NYTimes.com*, 6/29/09, http://cityroom.blogs.nytimes.com/2009/ 06/29/population. . .-favor/?pagemode=print; and Danny Hakim, "Blame Panic in G.O.P. for Standoff in Albany," *The New York Times*, 7/1/09, A25, c6, described what was at stake, politically, for the Senate Republicans, in the battle for control of their Chamber. Senator Bruno's felony conviction is reported at, e.g., Nicholas Confessore and Danny Hakim, Bruno, Former State Leader, Guilty of Corruption, *The New York Times,* 12/7/09, http://www.nytimes.com/2009/12/08/nyregion/08bruno.html.

James M. Odato, "Bold coup upsets Senate," *timesunion.com*, 6/14/09, http:// www.timesunion.com/AspStories/storyprint.asp?StoryID=810055, described the June 8, 2009 coup that temporarily handed control of the Senate to the Republicans. Elizabeth Benjamin, The Daily Politics: "The Hiram Monserrate Project," *Daily News Blogs*, 6/9/09, http://www.nydailynews.com/blogs/dailypolitics/2009/06/the-hiram-monserrate -project.html, discussed the political pressures on Monserrate that ultimately forced his return to the Democrats. Rudolph W. Giuliani, among others, urged a constitutional convention to address the structural flaws that contributed to the crisis, in "Putting New York Back Together," Op Ed Page, *The New York Times*, 6/24/09, http://www.ny times.com/2009/06/24/opinion/24giuliani.html.

New York State Constitution, Amended to January 1, 1976, Office of the Secretary of State of New York State, Albany, N.Y. 1976, 85 lists the 1953 amendment that provided for the joint election of governor and lieutenant governor. For a summary of efforts to change the constitution regarding vacancies in the lieutenant governorship, see Peter Galie, "Naming of Lieutenant governor Defies Constitution," Opinion, *The Buffalo News*, 7/15/09, http://www.buffalonews.com/149/story/733825.html. The decision by New York's highest court to uphold the constitutionality of the appointment of Richard Ravitch as Lieutenant Governor was reported, for example, in Dionne Searcey, N.Y. Court Upholds Lieutenant Governor Appointment, *The Wall Street Journal*, 9/22/09, http://online.wsj.com/article/SB125362688632130689.html.

Joseph Spector and Cara Matthews, "Democrats regain control of state senate," *Pressconnects.com*, 7/10/09, http://pressconnects.com/article/20090710/NEWS01/907100 333/1112, in a sidebar headed "Timeline," offered a day-by-day list of the events in the Senate crisis, including a description of the period in which the even split allowed both sides to claim majority control.

"Editorial, Liars and bullies: State Senate Democrats become ever more disgraceful," *New York Daily News*, 7/10/09, http://nydailynews.com/opinions/2009/07/16/ 2009-07-16_liars_and_bullies_state_senate_democrats_become_ever_more_ disgraceful.html; Editorial, Chamber of horrors, *New York Daily News*, 6/23/09, http:// nydailynews.com/opinions/2009/06/23/2009-06-23_chamber_of_horrors_gov. . . ; Editorial, Albany's Madhouse, *The New York Times*, 6/10/09, http://www.ny-times.com/2009/06/10/opinion/10wed1.html?_r=1&ref+opinion&pagewanted. . . ; Editorial, As bad as government gets, *Albany Times-Union*, 6/12/09, http://www.time-sunion.com/AspStories/storyprint.asp?StoryID=809540; Danny Hakim, "Albany Impasse Ends as Defector Rejoins Caucus," *The New York Times*, 7/10/09, http://www.ny times.com/2009/07/10/nyregion/10albany.html?_v=1& pagewanted=print . . . all ferociously criticized both Senate parties and listed the variety of ways in which their behavior damaged the interests of the public.

The Spector and Matthews "Timeline," noted above, also detailed the elements of agreement that allowed the Democrats to reunite to reestablish control.

Chapter 11 offers a more detailed discussion of the end of the Spitzer governorship.

Interviews with both Warren Anderson and Stanley Fink may be found in Gerald Benjamin and Robert Nakamura (eds.). *The Modern New York State Legislature: Redressing the Balance* (Albany: Rockefeller Institute of Government, 1991) quotations are from pp 73–74, 119.

Tom Robbins, Senate Coup Plotters' Hidden Agenda, *The Village Voice*, 7/1/09, http://www.villagevoice.com/content/print/Version/1235318, first offered the unusual perspective on the Senate crisis explored here. For an example of criticism of the budget process under the Senate Democrat's pre-coup leadership, see, e.g., Rick Karlin, Secrecy still shrouds budget talks, Albany *Times-Union*, 3/19/09, http://timesunion.com/Asp Stories/storyprint.asp?StoryID= 781388. Chapter VII described in more detail the 2009 reforms of the Rockefeller drug laws. The Robbins article noted above New York State 2009–10 Enacted Budget: Financial Plan, 4/28/09, David Paterson, Laura L. Anglin, Director of the Budget Page 97, http://publications.budget.state.ny.us/budgetFP/ 2009–10EnactedBudget-FINAL.pdf, reports the increase in the basic welfare grant in New York's 2009–10 budget. For a discussion of the new public authorities reform law, see Nicholas Confessore, Paterson Signs Bill to Rein in State's Free-Spending Public Authorities, *The New York Times*, 12/12/09, http://www.nytimes.com/2009/12/12/ny region/12authorities.html. and Editorial, "Do It for Olga: State Senate Must Pass Farm Labor Bill to Honor Trailblazer Mendez," *New York Daily News*, 7/31/09, http:// www.nydailynews.com/opinions/2009/07/31/2009-07-31_do_it_for_olga_state _senate_must_pass_farm_labor_bill_to_honor_trailblazer_mende.html, listed legislation likely to come to fruition with the Democrats controlling the Senate. However, a *New York Daily News* editorial later excoriated the State Senate Democratic leadership for backing off its pledge to pass the farmworkers bill out of fear of losing one of its upstate Democratic Senators, representing a marginal rural district, to a Republican opponent: Editorial, Plowed under by Sampson: State Senate boss' lie buries hope of farm worker bill, 1/ 25/ 10,   http://nydailynews.com/ opinions/ 2010/ 01/ 25/ 2010-01-25_plowed_under_ by_sampson .html. Editorial, New York's Phantom Government, *The New York Times*, 7/ 23/ 09, A30, c.1, applauded legislation to impose transparency and accountability on public authorities, passed when the Democrats regained control of the Senate.

Senator Espada's comment on rules reform indirectly empowering the public appeared on CBS 6 Morning Update, 7/ 9/ 09, www.cbs6albany.com/ video/?bcpid. See, e.g., Editorial, Senate embraces democracy, *The Buffalo News*, 7/ 20/ 09, http://www .buffalonews.com/ opinion/ editorials/ story/ 738664.html; Elizabeth Benjamin, The Daily Politics: Early Morning Reform on Tap in the Senate, *Daily News Blogs*, 7/ 16/ 09, http:// www.nydailynews.com/ blogs/ dailypolitics/ 2009/ 07/ early-morning-reform-on-tap-in.html described those rules reforms. Governor Paterson's criticism of the behavior of the Senate was quoted in Alan Chartock, Opinion: "The Capitol's red light district," *Daily Freeman*, 7/ 19/ 09, http:// dailyfreeman.com/ articles/ 2009/ 07/ 09/ opinion/ doc4a5b5feea561c850888505.prt. The blunt characterization of Espada and Monserrate was quoted in Danny Hakim, In the New York Senate, Order is Restored, but Decorum Isn't, *The New York Times*, 7/ 18/ 09, http:// www.nytimes.com/ 2009/ 07/ 18/ ny region/ 18notebook.html?_r=1&ref=nyregion&pag. . .

As to the history of the "sausage" comment attributed to Bismarck, Fred R. Shapiro, in *The Yale Book of Quotations*, Yale University Press, New Haven, Connecticut 2006, 86, quotes the *McKean Miner* of Smethport, Pennsylvania, of April 22, 1869, as follows: "Saxe says in his new lecture: 'Laws, like sausages, cease to inspire respect in proportion as we know how they are made.'" Shapiro thinks "Saxe" may have been the lawyer-poet John Godfrey Saxe, whose grandson, according to Wikipedia, http:// en.wikipedia.org/ wiki/ John_Godfrey_Saxe, became a New York State Senator! The first attribution of a similar comment to Bismarck, "To retain respect for laws and sausages, one must not watch them in the making," according to Shapiro, was not until 1958, sixty years after Bismarck's death, in the 104th volume of *Southern Reporter, 2d Series*, page 18.

Chapter I. New York State and Public Safety: Tales from the Sausage Factory

The map of Brooklyn Assembly districts comes from the 1981 edition of *They Represent You*, published by the League· of Women Voters of the City of New York. Norman Adler and Blanche Blank's *Political Clubs in New York City*, New York: Praeger Publishers, 1975, provides good background for our discussion of regular and reform Democratic clubs. Kenneth Silver, New York's Nightmare Legislature, *City* Journal, Spring 1995, v. 5, #2, http:// www.city-journal.org/html/ 5_2_new_yorks.html, visited 11/9/04, offer an example of the perennial criticism of the overwhelming majorities by which most New York State legislators win reelection. The various election results in the 45th Assembly District to which we make reference can be verified by means of the records of election results maintained by the New York City Board of Elections. The Board provides more recent results, currently back to 1999, on its web site, at http:// vote.nyc.ny.us/ results.html, visited 2/ 24/ 08; their headquarters at 32 Broadway, New York, N.Y. 10004 will guide researchers to older results from their paper records.

Some articles describing the Parking Violations Bureau controversy include Tom McMorrow, "Victims of Parking Bureau may soon get some relief," *New York Daily*

News, 7/24/85, K2; Tom McMorrow, *New York Daily News,* City "Parking Bureau gives its side of collection story," 8/5/85, K2; Dan Janison, "State lawmaker says Koch rejected early PVB warnings," *The Staten Island Advance,* 3/13/86, 1; Ray Kerrison, "'Payback' bill just the ticket for PVB," *The New York Post,* 6/21/86, 8. Feldman's law making the PVB pay motorists who could prove they were harassed unduly was enacted as Chapter 338 of the Laws of 1987.

Sam Roberts, in *The Brother,* New York: Random House, 2001, sets forth the basis for serious doubt that Ethel Rosenberg was guilty, at page 487, and explains the unprecedented nature of the Rosenbergs' execution, at page 414. Mr. Roberts' *New York Times* article, "57 Years Later, Figure in Rosenberg Case Says He Spied for Soviets," 9/12/2008, A1, c.3, reports and reinforces the consensus that Ethel was not guilty. Ronald Radosh and Joyce Milton, in *The Rosenberg File,* New Haven: Yale University Press, 1997, report the improprieties by Judge Irving Kaufman that deprived the Rosenbergs of a fair trial, from pages 277 through 282.

On the rarity of consistent and coherent ideological commitments among United States citizens, see G. Terry Madonna and Michael Young, "American Temperament," Franklin & Marshall Center for Political & Public Affairs, 6/28/06, http://www .fandm.edu/12075.xml, visited 2–28–08. David Mayhew's seminal study, *Congress: The Electoral Connection,* New Haven: Yale University Press, 1974, explains legislative behavior in terms of self-interest. For an example of scholarship supporting an alternative argument, that strong commitments to public service and to the public interest substantially motivate legislators, see Grant Reeher, *First Person Political,* New York: NYU Press, 2006.

For a scholarly discussion of our reference to "professional" legislators, see Keith Hammond and Gary Moncrief, "Legislative Politics in the States," in Virginia Gray and Russell L. Hanson, eds., *Politics in the American States: A Comparative Analysis,* 8th ed., Washington: CQ Press, 2004, 158 and 171ff.

Our comments about the 1960s legislator, George Michaels, as well as the discussion of intuitionist and utilitarian value systems, drew on an article Feldman wrote for Volume 15 of *Policy Studies Journal,* 441–460, in March 1987, called "Ethical Analysis in Public Policymaking." The description of a typically American set of regime values and universal values for use as measures of utility took some additional material from that article and some from Chapter One of his book, *Logic of American Government* (hereafter "LOAG"), New York: William Morrow and Co., 1990. Our understanding of "values" in this context owes much to John Rohr, especially Rohr's books *Ethics for Bureaucrats,* New York: Marcel Dekker Inc., 1978, and *To Run a Constitution,* Kansas: University Press of Kansas, 1986. Charles Lindblom's article, "The Science of 'Muddling Through,'" 19 *Public Administration Review* 79 (1959), reprinted in A. Etzioni, ed., *Readings in Modern Organizations,* Englewood Cliffs, New Jersey: Prentice Hall, 1969, 154, famously explained how legislators seem to alter their values as well as their policy goals in efforts to reach workable compromises.

Ruth Benedict described the potlatch ceremony of the Kwakiutl Indians in her anthropology classic, *Patterns of Culture,* Boston: Houghton Mifflin Co., 1959, 2d edition. The federal courts' refusal to intervene in the Terri Schiavo case was reported by Abby Goodnough, "Supreme Court Refuses to Hear the Schiavo Case," *The New York Times,* 3/25/05, A1, c6.

Chapter II. What Counts When Legislators Decide

Hannah Pitkin's *The Concept of Representation,* Berkeley: University of California Press, 1967, provides a classic discussion of the complexities. Feldman chose values, legal principles, inside politics, and outside politics as the four headings under which to categorize elements of the legislative process based on his own experience as a New York legislator for eighteen years. The non-reporting of troop movements has long served as an example of when freedom of the press should bow to security concerns, but a few years ago Feldman learned that this happens to be the example that at least one prominent newsroom uses itself. At the annual conference of the New York Fair Trial Free Press Conference, at the New York University School of Law on April 6, 2005, Michael Oreskes, the deputy managing editor of *The New York Times*, noted that an "old saying" in that newsroom is "one of the things we don't publish is troop movements."

The discussion of the clash of values behind the abortion and death penalty debates again draws heavily on Feldman's 1987 article for *Policy Studies Journal* cited earlier. The story about Al Smith in that section comes from Robert Caro's *The Power Broker*, New York: Alfred A. Knopf, 1974, 124. The description of the *Boreali* case appears at greater length in *LOAG*, as does the discussion of the legislative effort to protect free speech and petition rights in privately-owned shopping malls, including the reference to *Marsh v. Alabama*.

Feldman's "counter-offer" to Mario Cuomo's proposal to create a commission to investigate the Legislature, and his response, was covered by Adam Nagourney in *The New York Daily News*, "Gov blasts proposal for SIC probe," 4/7/87, p. 7, and "It's Hurly-Burly-on-Hudson," 4/9/87, p. 21. Further and somewhat more detailed discussion of the incidence of criminal and unethical behavior of Albany officials appears below in Chapter III. The Public Employee Ethics Reform Act was enacted as Chapter 14, Laws of 2007. The NYS Legislative Ethics Commission Home Page, http://www.legethics.state.ny.us/home.aspx, includes an explanation of how its members are appointed. Governor Paterson described his ethics reform bill in his Press release, Executive Chamber, Governor Patterson Announces Sweeping Ethics Reform Legislation, 5/26/09, http://www.state.ny.us/governor/press/press_0526091.html, and explained his veto of the Legislature's bill in Jimmy Vielkind, "Ethics Bill Faces Veto Pen," Albany *Times Union* 1/21/10, http://www.timesunion.com/AspStories/story.asp?story ID=891370 and Jeremy W. Peters, Patterson Vetoes Ethics Bill Saying It Isn't Real Reform, *The New York Times*, 2/2/10, http://www.nytimes.com/2010/02/03/nyregion/03ethics.html. Jay Jochnowitz commented on the unsuccessful attempt to override the Governor's veto in N.Y. still needs ethics reform, Albany *timesunion.com*, 2/10/10, http://blog.timesunion.com/opinion/n-y-still-needs-ethics-reform/2383/. Examples of news coverage of the behavior of Governor Paterson that gave rise to ethical and legal questions and investigations include Danny Hakim and Jeremy W. Peters, Under Fire, Paterson Quits Governor's Race, *The New York Times*, 2/27/10, A1, c6; Jeremy W. Peters and Danny Hakim, Paterson Says He Has No Plans to Quit, and Will Clear His Name, *The New York Times*, 3/6/10, A19, c1; and Reuters, NY Gov Says May Seek Extra Power to Cut Spending, *The New York Times*, 3/9/10, http://www.nytimes.com/reuters/2010/03/09/politics/politics-us-newyorkstate-debt.html. Articles describing the new depths apparently plumbed by New York State government in March 2010 include Jeremy W. Peters, Some Black Democrats Suggest Race is Factor in Pressure on the Governor, *The New York Times*, 3/1/10, http://www.nytimes.com/2010/03/02/ny region/02race.html; and see Michael Powell and Nicholas Confessore, Dysfunction Edges Out Work In a Deeply Distracted Albany, *The New York Times*, 3/6/10, A1, c.4. Discussions of recent scandals involving governors of other states include Alan Ehrenhalt, Are Baby-Boom Governors More Prone to Scandal? *Governing*, 10/29, http://www.governing.com/column/are-baby-boom-governors-more-prone-scandal; and Peter Applebome, In Governors, the Averages Aren't Good, *The New York Times*, 4/3/10, http://www.nytimes.com/2010/03/04/nyregion/04towns.html.The *Jewish Press* covered the law establishing permanent state funding for the transportation of handicapped students to religious schools, "Major Gain for Disabled Yeshiva Students As NY Gov Signs Busing Bill Into Law," 8/7/92, p. 25.

The story of the decision by District Council 37 of the American Federation of State, County, and Municipal Employees to endorse majority Senate Republicans for pragmatic political reasons, and how this helped entrench divided partisan control of the Legislature, is told in an interview with Adler published in Gerald Benjamin and Robert Nakamura, *The Modern New York State Legislature: Redressing the Balance*, Albany: The Rockefeller Institute of Government, 1991, 463-485. New York Court of Claims Judge James Lack, at that time chair of the State Senate Labor Committee, described his central role and confirmed the pragmatic considerations on both sides, in an in-person conversation with Feldman, 2/15/08.

Feldman's effort to reform the local finance law was reflected in Assembly Bill Number 76 of the 1981-1982 session. The story behind the basis for Feldman's doubts about of the New York State Education Department can be found in his 1981 book, *Reforming Government*, New York: William Morrow & Co., in the chapters covering the Summer Food Program scandal of 1976.

Chapter III. How Things Work

Bill Passanante's role in the "baby carriage" victory over Robert Moses was noted in Christopher Lemak's doctoral dissertation, *Urbanism as Reform*, Florida International University, 2004, chapter 4, 156-7, www.fiu/%7Eklemek/Lemekdissertation.html, visited 7/30/06. Robert Caro also discusses the incident in *The Power Broker*, 984-1004, but does not mention Passanante.

Seymour Lachman and Robert Polner, in *Three Men in a Room: The Inside Story of Power and Betrayal in an American Statehouse*, New York: New Press, 2006, argue an extreme version of the thesis that the Governor, the Assembly Speaker, and the Senate Majority Leader make all significant decisions in New York State government without allowing individual legislators any significant opportunity to influence those decisions. The present volume recounts instances when individual legislators have overcome the opposition of a member of the "troika" either by persuasion or by political force, and thus while acknowledging that individual legislators could and should exercise more power, presents a far more nuanced thesis.

A report illustrating an instance of Speaker Silver's willingness to bow to the will of the majority conference he leads, perhaps in response to the attempted coup in 2000 by former Assembly Majority Leader Michael Bragman, was reported in *The New York Observer* web site "The Politicker," noting Silver's support for the inclusion of civil remedies in legislation limiting the use of the statute of limitations in rape cases. http://216.70.73.119/mt/mt-tb.cgi/entry/convincing_Shelly, visited 8/15/06.

For the discussion of Albany officials whose ethics were exposed to public question in recent years, some of the many possible news sources include Helen Kennedy's "1 in 5 Albany legislators break the law—study," *New York Daily News*, 3/16/08, at http://www.nydailynews.com/news/2008/03/16/2008-03-16_1_in_5_albany_legislators _break_the_law_-1.html, accessed 10/13/08, including the names and infractions of many of the officials on our list; other officals on the list were mentioned in Azi Paybarah, "Reactions to Spitzer: Karben Feels Bad, Stone Doesn't," *New York Observer*, 3/10/08, http://www.observer.com/2008/reactions-spitzer-karben-stone, accessed 10/13/08; Irene Jay Liu, "Hoyt reprimanded for "inappropriate personal relationship," *Capitol Confidential*, 9/26/08, http://blogs.timesunion.com/capitol/archives/8832, accessed 10/13/08; and Errol Cockfield Jr., "Hevesi to Resign," *Newsday*, 12/22/06,

http://www.newsday.com/news/local/newyork/ny-stheve1222,0,7997791.story?coll=ny
-top-headlines, accessed 10/13/08. The seminal work on political culture in the states is
by Daniel Elazar, *American Federalism: A View From the States*, 2nd ed., Thomas Y.
Crowell, N.Y. 1972. Our discussion of Lincoln and FDR in this context relies on, respectively, Doris Kearns, *Team of Rivals*, Simon and Schuster, N.Y. 2005, and Conrad
Black, *Roosevelt: Champion of Freedom*, Public Affairs, N.Y. 2003.

Compare Feldman's description of his living accommodations in Albany in the
1980s and 1990s with the remarks of the late Senate Majority Leader Warren Anderson
describing an earlier period, in Anderson's interview in Benjamin and Nakamura, cited
earlier, page 67: "All the social functions in the fifties and sixties were in the same ho-
tels. There was an awful lot of mixing. You could more easily keep up with what was
going on; if something happened in the Assembly that day you knew it right away.
Now, the minute the day's session is over, people take off for events all over town. They
live in motels on the outskirts of town. Some live in apartments. They're all over the
place so there is a lack of communication."

Stanley Fink's comments about his getting more leverage, not less, from the relative
scarcity of attractive assignments in the Assembly came from his interview in Benjamin
and Nakamura, 120.

Note that references to "Hispanic" population figures do not refer to a racial classification; people of Hispanic origin are counted in several racial categories. For a good description of the demographic differences between the population of Democratic and Republican Senate Districts in New York State See Andrew Beveridge "The Senate's
Demographic Shift" *Gotham Gazette*, November 24, 2008, http//www.gothamgazette.com
/article/fea/20081124/202/2767.

For a discussion of the vast variety within the ethnic and racial population figures
noted, see New York City, Department of City Planning, *The Newest New Yorkers,
2000: Immigrant New York in the New Millenium*. Party enrollment figures in New York
City and statewide, as of November 2007, come from the New York State Board of
Elections, at http://www.elections.state.ny.us/NYSBOE/enrollment/county/county_nov
08.pdf, accessed 11/8/08. We acquired 2006 figures party enrollment figures that year,
when the Board of Elections had a slightly different web site address, at http://www
.elections.state.ny.us/enrollment/county/county_nov06.pdf.

An astute pre-publication reviewer of our manuscript for the publisher pointed out
the significance of the Supreme Court's greater liberality in allowing population variation among state legislative districts, as compared with congressional districts, and supplied the contrasting average population numbers for upstate and New York City State
Senate districts. The tally of the partisan affiliation of elected officials comes from a variety of sources, including the *New York State Directory*, Empire State Report Inc., Albany, New York, 2004–5 edition; and the *Green Book: Official Directory of the City of
New York*, New York City Department of Administrative Services, New York, New
York, 2004–5 edition. Figures marking the decline in the population of Buffalo come
from Bruce Jackson, Buffalo in Black and White, *CounterPunch*, 8/10/02, at http://
www.counterpunch.org/jackson0810.html, accessed 3/31/05. Edward Schneier and
John Brian Murtaugh, in *New York Politics*, Armonk, New York: M.E. Sharpe, 2001,
74, explain how New York State's demographics renders New York Republicans as
well as Democrats somewhat more liberal than most of the United States; and also provide a chart setting forth the periods of control of the respective houses of the Legislature by the two major parties between 1933 and 1998, 95.

The quotation from Elihu Root comes from Ruth S. Silva, "Legislation Representation—With Special Reference to New York," *Law & Contemporary Problems*, Durham,
North Carolina: Duke University School of Law, Summer 1962, 408, at 410; and the

comparison of Senate and Assembly representation to population quotes Silva directly, at 408. Schneier and Murtaugh, at page 85, also discuss legislative apportionment in the context of the 1894 Convention, as does Joseph Zimmerman, in his *Government and Politics of New York State*, New York: New York University Press, 1981, at 118. See also Peter Galie, *Ordered Liberty: A Constitutional History of New York*, New York: Fordham University Press, 1996, 166–8; and Gerald Benjamin and Charles Brecher, editors, *The Two New Yorks: State and City in a Changing Federal System*, New York: Russell Sage Foundation, 1988, 129, for further discussion of the impact of the 1894 constitutional convention on legislative apportionment in New York State.

Chapter 45 of the New York State Laws of 1978 established the Legislative Task Force that subsequently drew district boundary lines. New York's highest court upheld bizarre boundary lines for legislative districts in *Schneider v. Rockefeller*, 31 N.Y. 2d 420 (1972). Victories by Republican State Senate candidates in districts with wide Democratic enrollment margins are reported in Blair Horner and Michael Hartwell, *Unfair Advantage: New York State's Redistricting Process*, New York Public Interest Research Group, April 2006, 6, www://nypirg.org/goodgov/redistrictnReport4.20.06.pdf, visited 2/24/08. The Commission included in the 1967 constitution is discussed in Henrik N. Dullea, *Charter Revision in the Empire State* (Albany: Rockefeller Institute Press, 1997) pp. 204–208. The Gennaris bill calling for the establishment of an independent reapportionment commission was A.6287 of the 2005–2006 legislative session. Stephen Lefevre's article, "Independent Legislative Redistricting is Needed," *Ventura County Star*, 9/28/08, at http://www.venturacountystar.com/news/2008/sep/28/independent-legislative-redistricting-is-needed, accessed 10/26/08, noted that Hawaii, Arizona, and Idaho are among the twelve states that "have adopted independent redistricting commissions."

Chapter IV. Playing by the Rules, and Changing Them

For a discussion of the controversies arising out of the subject matter title, single object, or public purpose requirements, see Peter Galie, *Ordered Liberty*, cited above, or Gerald Benjamin and Henrik N. Dullea, eds., *Constitutional Change in New York*, Albany: Rockefeller Institute Press, 1997. Jeremy Creelan and Laura Moulton's report, *The New York State Legislative Process: An Evaluation and Blueprint for Reform*, New York: Brennan Center for Justice at NYU Law School, 2004, provides a wealth of information, including the current list of "professional" state legislatures taken from Sarah McCally Morehouse and Malcolm E. Jewell's *State Politics, Parties, and Policy*, 2d ed. 2003. We drew upon Alan Rosenthal *et al.*, *Republic on Trial*, Washington, D.C.: CQ Press, 2003 for other statistical comparisons of state legislatures as well as for insights into the nature of modern-day legislatures. Jack Davies' *Legislative Law and Process*, 2d edition, St. Paul, Minnesota: West Publishing Co., 1986, an older book, nevertheless offers useful comparisons of various state legislatures and an interesting discussion of the role in committees played by inertia in keeping bills from the floor.

The quotations in the text concerning the legislation to "privatize" Empire Blue Cross came from James McKinley, "Before Bills Move in Albany, 3 Leaders Cut Deals in Secret," *The New York Times*, 10/21/02, http://query.nytimes.com/gst/fullpage.html ?res=9B0CE1DA1F3DF932A15753C1A9649C8B63&sec=health&spon+&page wanted=print, visited 2/24/08. John Sheffer's 1985 proposals for reform of the Assembly rules can be found in New York State Legislature, Assembly Republican Study Group, *Project 1990: the challenge of effective legislative management in the state of New York: a report of the Republican Study Group of the New York State Assembly*. On file at University of Buffalo Law Library, KFN 5722 N49 1985.

For criticisms of the New York Legislature, we drew first of all on the Brennan Center report by Creelan and Moulton cited above, but also on an excellent series in *The New York Times*: Richard Perez-Pena, "Legislating the New York Way In a Chronic Case of Gridlock," 10/20/02, 1, c1 and 38, c1; James C. McKinley Jr., "Before Bills Move in Albany, 3 Leaders Cut Deals in Secret," 10/21/02, A1, c1 and B7, c1; Richard Perez-Pena, "Lax New York Rules Make Big Money Talk," 10/22/02, A1, c1 and B2, c1; and on a strong editorial in *Newsday*, "To Make State Government Work, Albany Must Embrace Reform," 11/11/02, which we quoted in the text. James C. McKinley, Jr., "Bruno Rejects Silver's Call for Conference Committees," *The New York Times*, 6/26/03, B10, c3, reports the Legislature's continued rejection of that mechanism.

Eric Redman's classic *The Dance of Legislation*, the story of the enactment of the National Health Service Corps legislation in 1970, was originally published in 1973 but, we were delighted to discover, reissued by University of Washington Press in Seattle and London in 2001. Our quotations from Redman's imaginary Senator's speeches against a floor amendment appear in his book on pages 59 and 61.

Eric Lane, former counsel to the New York State Senate, presented an impressive array of criticisms of the Legislature at the Bar Association of the City of New York on March 26, 2003. The "message of necessity," was originally intended to waive the rule that bills must be available at their desks for three days for perusal by legislators *only* in circumstances of grave necessity. Among other interesting items, Lane reported that eighty percent of the legislation enacted in one two-year session was introduced on one day and passed that same day or the next day, with messages of necessity. This case is discussed in by Peter Gailie in "The New York Constitution and the Federal System" in Benjamin (ed.) *Oxford Handbook of New York State Government and Politics* (New York: Oxford University Press, forthcoming, 2011) typescript, p. 43.

Michael Cooper's articles in *The New York Times*, "In Radical Shift for Assembly, To Vote, They Must Show Up," 1/7/05, B1, c1, and "State Senate Leaves Open Negotiations on Legislative Rules," 1/11/05, B6, c1; Patrick Healy, "For Republicans, Albany Reforms Go Just So Far," *The New York Times*, 4/20/05, B6, c4; an email of 1/7/05 from Assembly Member Scott Stringer to Feldman and others, Subject: Progress on Albany Reform; a *New York Times* editorial of 1/10/05, "Going by the Rules," A18, c1; a *New York Times* regional editorial of 2/6/05, "The Ruling Party," LI 7, c.1; and a *Newsday* editorial, "State Senate's Baby Steps," 2/1/05, A34, c1, all provided useful discussions of the rule changes finally adopted by the Assembly and Senate in January 2005, upon which we drew.

Articles reporting New York's on-time 2005 budget include Al Baker, "Albany Passes Budget on Time, A Feat Unequalled Since 1984," *The New York Times*, 4/1/05, A1, c5; Fredric U. Dicker, "Miracle in Albany: Budget is on time," *New York Post*, 4/1/05, 4, c2; and Errol A. Cockfield, Jr., "State budget on time!,: *Newsday*, 4/1/05, A14.

Among the many articles, editorials, and columns indicating that disgust with the New York State Legislature reached unprecedented heights, or depths, in 2004, including an explosion of such commentary all over the State after the release of the Brennan Center report, were Michael Cooper, "Albany Legislature Set to Adjourn Without Doing Much of Anything," *The New York* Times, 6/21/04, A1; John Caher, "Albany is Awash in Blame for Fruitless Legislative Session," *New York Law Journal*, 6/24/04, 1, c3; Michael Schenkler, "I'm Mad As Hell And I'm Not Going to Take It Anymore," *Queens Tribune Online*, 7/22/04, www.queenstribune.com/not4pub/ImMadAsHell AndImNotGoingT. . . , accessed 7/23/04; Editorial, "New York's Shame," *The Buffalo News*, 8/1/04; Editorial, "The worst legislature in America," *New York Daily News*, 7/25/04; Editorial, "The trouble with Albany," *Newsday*, 1/22/04; Editorial, "Worst in the Nation," *New York Post*, 1/26/04; Editorial, "New York's Fake Legislature," *The New York Times*, 7/25/04; Editorial, "Albany emperors," Binghamton *Press & Sun-Bulletin*, 7/25/04; Editorial, "More proof," Rochester *Democrat and Chronicle*, 7/22/04; Jay Gallagher, "Perspective: State in a league of its own for dysfunctional Legislature," *Poughkeepsie Journal*, 7/25/04; Editorial, "A Legislature in Denial," Albany *Times Union*, 7/25/04; Michael Cooper, "Calls Increase for Overhaul In Albany," *The New York* Times, 9/28/04, B1, c6; Jonathan "Hicks, "New Political Tactics for State Races: Everybody's a Reformer," *The New York Times*, 10/22/04, B1, c2; and Elizabeth Benjamin, "Reform or face wrath, state warned," Albany *Times Union*, 10/10/04.

The anonymous reader for the publisher who provided numerous helpful suggestions commended our attention to the discussion of conference committees in the Library of Congress, at Thomas Home, "From a Bill to a Law, How Our Laws Are Made," XV. Final Action, at http://thomas.loc.gov/home/lawsmade.bysec/final.action .html, accessed 11/9/08. A press release issued by jointly by both Houses of the New York State Legislature on 12/7/04, "Bruno and Silver Announce Agreement on Partial Rockefeller Drug Law Reform," included Senator Michael Nozzolio's statement crediting the criminal justice conference committee of the two Houses for work on Rockefeller drug reform. Malcolm Smith's pledges of procedural reform in the Senate were reported in Danny Hakim, "Senate Minority Leader Vows to Share Power if Democrats Take Reins," *The New York Times*, 11/2/08, 39, c.1.

The comment by Assembly Member Charles Lavine, the erstwhile reformer, quoted in the text, appears in Edward Isaac Dovere, "The Young Turks: How the Reformers Are Changing Albany—And How Albany is Changing the Reformers," *City Hall*, March 2007, http://cityhallnews.com/covere_031207.html.

The quotation from *H.M.S. Pinafore* can be found in Bennett A. Cerf and Donald S. Klopper, eds., *The Complete Plays of Gilbert and Sullivan*, New York: The Modern Library, 1936, 111. The George Washington Plunkitt comment quoted can be found in William L. Riordan, *Plunkitt of Tammany Hall*, 1963, Chapter 4, recorded by The Project Gutenberg, 2001, http://www.marxists.org/reference/archive/Plunkitt-george/tammany -hall/index.htm#s04, visited 2/24/08.

Chapter V. The Organized Crime Control Act

The crime statistics noted at the beginning of the chapter come from Patrick A. Langan and Matthew R. Durose, "The Remarkable Drop in Crime in New York City," 10/21/04, paper delivered at the International Conference on Crime, Rome, Italy, 12/ 3–5/03, sponsored by the Italian National Institute of Statistics (ISTAT). http://samoaiistat.it/Eventi/sicurezza/relazioni/Langan_rel.pdf.

Assembly Bill Number 12A of the 1987–88 Session is the earliest version of Feldman's use immunity bill currently available; he had introduced a very similar if not identical predecessor, A.5317, in the 1983–84 Session; and an earlier version in the 1981–82 session, for which a bill number is no longer available. Some of the discussion covering the controversy surrounding this bill includes Catherine Shattuck, "Assembly Gets Grand Jury Proposals," *The Legislative Gazette* Albany, N.Y.], 3/5/84, 3; Editorial, "To reform the courts, let's forget Millertime," *The New York Post*, 2/25/84, 32; Editorial, "Not Too Much Immunity for Grand Jury Witnesses," *Newsday*, 4/18/84; and Bob Keeler, "Standoff Jeopardizes Plans to Tighten Immunity Law," *Newsday*, 5/8/84, The State (page). Some of the discussion of use immunity and of the Organized Crime Control Act appeared in Feldman's article, "Criminal Justice—Liberal Principals, Conservative Policies," in *The New York Law Journal*, 11/2/84, 1. The New York District Attorneys Association report, The Case for a New Immunity Law in New York,

March 1988, provides a strong defense of use immunity, as well as excellent source material on the bill, including references to the Delissa Carter case and the other cases
cited, as well as to the later police union opposition that emerged a year after the 1983
defeat in the Codes Committee. Copies of the memoranda in opposition to A.12-A from
the Police Conference of New York and from the New York Civil Liberties Union are
on file with the authors. Leonard W. Levy's *Against the Law: The Nixon Court and
Criminal Justice*, Harper & Row, Publishers, New York, 1874, provides strong arguments against use immunity, in favor of transactional immunity.

Sam Roberts, "Now, City Party Bosses Do Little Moving and Shaking, *The New
York Times,* 5/23/10. http://www.nytimes.com/2010/05/24/nyregion/24bosses.html attributes to John P. O'Brien, the new mayor of New York City in 1932, the "they haven't
told me yet" response to the police commissioner appointment question, and implies
that the "they" were Tammany Hall political bosses. For the first published version of
the story of the threat from the corrupt union in the asphalt case, see Feldman's 1981
book, *Reforming Government*, New York: William Morrow & Co. For background on
federal RICO, see John L. McClellan, "The Organized Crime Act (S.30) or Its Critics:
Which Threatens Civil Liberties?" 46 *Notre Dame Lawyer* 55 (Fall 1970); and G. Robert Blakey and Ronald Goldstock, "'On the Waterfront'": RICO and Labor Racketeering," 17 *Amer. Crim. L. Rev.* 341 (1980). For background on New York's OCCA, see
Steven Kessler, "And a Little Child Shall Lead Them: New York's Organized Crime
Control Act of 1986," 64 *St. John's L. Rev.* 797 (1990); and Martin Marcus, Chapter 36:
"Enterprise Corruption—– Article 460," in Richard Greenberg et al., *New York Crimi-
nal Law*, 2002 edition, West Group, Eagan, Minnesota. For discussion of the Parking
Violations Bureau controversy, see references cited above where that matter is men-
tioned in Chapter 1. Some of the discussion of the negotiating process came from Chapter Seven of LOAG, which also includes references to much useful source material on
RICO and OCCA. In the discussion of shared values between the prosecutors and the
Assembly Democratic leadership, survey data support for the proposition that government professionals strongly value fairness can be found in John Rohr, *Ethics for Bureaucrats*, Basel and New York: Marcel Dekker, 1978, 67. OCCA itself, of course, was
enacted as Chapter 516 of the Laws of New York of 1986.

Chapter VI. Getting Into the Prisons and Drugs Business

For a discussion of the immediate aftermath of the 1986 campaign for Speaker of the
Assembly, see Elizabeth Kolbert, "Deposed Panel Chief Assails Speaker of Assembly,"
The New York Times, 1/9/87. The text of this book sometimes uses the correct, official
title of the Assembly Committee on Correction, but sometimes calls it the "Corrections" Committee, which is technically incorrect, but widely used.

Although early in the chapter Feldman refers to debating Mel Miller on the 1981
prison construction bond issue at Kingsborough Community College, he says he has the
odd recollection that Miller did not show up, and that Feldman actually supplied both
sides of the debate, even shifting to the chair that had been assigned to Miller when
Feldman presented what he thought Miller would argue. The decades past have clouded
Feldman's memory of the event, so he is no longer sure what happened.

For an interesting view of criminal justice policy and practice regarding illegal drugs
in the United States, see Joseph T. Hallinan, *Going Up the River*, Random House, New
York 2001. Hallinan refers to Feldman's relatively early research, "20 Years of Prison
Expansion: A Failing National Strategy," 53 *Public Administration Review* 561, 1993,
and we have drawn on that research in this chapter as well, especially where in our discussion of addict population and inmate population statistics state by state, and prison

location within New York State. In the latter discussion, we listed the eight most populous counties in New York. We did not explain there, however, that while the five counties of New York City each constitute the respective boroughs of that City, the other three counties include more territory than the cities associated with them. The State prison population in New York in 2009 came from the home page of the New York State Department of Correction, http://www.docs.state.ny.us/. As an example of the emergence of voting rights for convicted felons, see John Fund, "My Fellow Americans," *Wall Street Journal*, 3/7/05 http://www.opinionjournal.com/diary.?id=110006382.

An anonymous reviewer for the publisher reminded us to check the New York State Department of Correction website for recent figures identifying State prison inmates as African-American, Hispanic, and White. http://www.docs.state.ny.us/Research/Reports /2008/Hub_Report_2008.pdf., page 7.

We also relied on Judith Greene and Vincent Schiraldi, "Cutting Correctly: New Prison Policies for Times of Fiscal Crisis," Washington, D.C.: The Justice Policy Institute, 2002. The 1997 version of Feldman's legislation to reform the Second Felony Offender Law, Assembly Bill Number 55 of the 1997–98 Session, is available, and is similar to the earlier versions dating back to 1991 that we cite. We also cited a letter from Matthew Crosson, chief administrator of the courts for the New York State Office of Court Administration, to the chair of the Senate Finance Committee and the Assembly Ways and Means Committee, April 10, 1991, analyzing proposals to reform Second Felony Offender.

Alfred Blumstein's research underlies the best analysis of the impact of increased penalties for illegal drug transactions on urban ghetto youth violence in the late 1980s and early 1990s, especially his articles "Youth Violence, Guns, and the Illicit-Drug Industry," 86 *J. Crim. L. & Criminology* 19, 1995; and "The Context of Recent Changes in Crime Rates," Panel Paper, National Institute of Justice and Executive Office for Weed and Seed, Washington, D.C., Jan. 5–7, 1998. Michael Smith and his colleagues at the Vera Institute wrote an extremely useful report on their research on the impact of law enforcement on the illegal drug trade in New York City, "The Neighborhood Effects of Street-Level Drug Enforcement," revision #1, New York, 1992. Lieutenant Governor Richard Ravitch's Five Year fiscal Plan for the state, released on March 10, 2010, may be found at http://www.state.ny.us/governor/press/pdf/FIVE%20YEAR %20FISCAL%20PLAN.pdf.

Chapter VII. Reforming the Rockefeller Drug Laws

One anonymous reviewer for the publisher noted that Daniel Frisbie of Schoharie County was the one exception to the rule that in the twentieth and twenty-first centuries all Democratic speakers of the Assembly came from New York City.

For those not familiar with the relevant history, the "Nixon-in-China" reference apropos of Pataki's potential for liberalizing the drug laws may need some explanation. Richard Nixon, throughout most of his political career, fiercely opposed communism. His vicious, ill-founded attacks on political opponents like Jerry Voorhees, whom he defeated for his congressional seat, and Helen Gahagan Douglas, whom he defeated for his Senate seat, were based on allegations that they were "soft" on communism. When Nixon began to normalize relations between the United States and China, this background immunized him (for the most part) against right-wing critics who might otherwise have attacked him for his embrace of a communist regime.

Feldman's constitutional attack on the post-1981 method used to finance prison construction was reported in Sarah Metzgar, "Democrats may leave prison plan to the voters," *Albany Times Union*, 4/26/96, B2, and in an editorial, "Wasteful Criminal Justice," *The New York Times*, 5/14/96, A22. The figures cited for the total off-budget borrowing by New York State entities as of 2005, of which prison borrowing was one variety, come from the Office of the State Comptroller, at http://www.osc.state.ny.us/debt/index.htm, visited 8/15/06. Litigation to block UDC borrowing for prison construction failed. See New York State Coalition for Criminal Justice, Inc., et al. v. Thomas A. Coughlin, III, as Commissioner of the New York State Department of Correctional Services, 103 A.D.2d 40; 479 N.Y.S.2d 850; 1984 July 26, 1984.

Newspaper coverage of the moves of Governor Pataki and Speaker Silver toward a compromise on Rockefeller drug law reform in June 2002 when the momentum for agreement seemed at its peak, and then failed, includes John Caher, "Drug Reform Takes Step Forward," *New York Law Journal*, 6/5/02; Assembly Press Release, attachment, Assembly's Rockefeller Drug Law Reform Compromise Bill [A. 8888A] Addresses Major Issues Raised by Governor's Framework, 6/5/02; Executive Chamber Press Release, George E. Pataki, Governor, Governor Proposes New Rockefeller Drug Law Reform Bill, 6/7/02; and James C. McKinley Jr.'s articles in *The New York Times*, "Democrats Try to Break A Deadlock on Drug Laws," 6/6/02, B6, c6; "Senate Passes Pataki's Drug Laws Bill [S.7588], Forcing Talks With Assembly," 6/13/02, B4, c1; "In Effort to Change Drug Law, Some See Too Little Change," 6/18/02, B1, c2; "Swapping Blame as Drug Law Rift Widens in Albany," 6/20/02, B5, c1.

Coverage of the 2003 negotiations includes John Caher, "State Bar Pushes Pact Seeking Rockefeller Drug Law Reform," *New York Law Journal*, 6/4/03, 1–2; "A Sense of Urgency Grows for Lawmakers in Albany" (no by-line), *The New York Times*, 6/19/03, B5, c1; James C. McKinley, Jr., "Time Running Out, Albany is Stymied on Major Measures," *The New York Times*, 6/20/03, A1, c6, B6, c1; Al Baker, "Albany Leaders Say They Fell Just Short on Drug-Law Deal," *The New York Times*, 6/20/03, B6, c5; James C. McKinley, Jr. with Lynette Holloway, "Rap Impresario Meets With Albany Leaders and Learns a Hard Lesson About Politics," *The New York Times*, 6/25/03, B5, c1.

The article cited claiming that legalized abortion contributed to reductions in crime is John J. Donohue and Steven D. Levitt, "The Impact of Legalized Abortion on Crime," 116 *Quarterly Journal of Economics* 379, 2001. Vivian Berger discussed that article in "Abortion and Crime," *The National Law Journal*, 6/26/02.

The *New York Post* editorial calling for repeal of the Rockefeller drug laws was headlined "Getting Rid of Rockefeller," and appeared on 9/13/04. Articles discussing the impact of David Soares defeat of Paul Clyne for Albany District Attorney, and Manhattan District Attorney Robert Morgenthau's call for reform of the drug laws, as spurs to the Legislature in late 2004 include Elizabeth Benjamin, "Accord Reached on Rockefeller Drug Law Reform," *The New York Times*, 12/7/04; and John Caher, "Election Fears Seen Behind Drug Law Shift," *New York Law Journal*, 12/9/04, 1, c8.

Articles reporting the 2004 agreement on the drug law reform, as well as criticisms of that agreement, include Leslie Eaton and Al Baker, "Changes Made to Drug Laws Don't Satisfy Advocates," *The New York Times*, 12/9/04, B1, c1; Robert Gangi, "Doing Time: Drug laws are still too harsh," Opinion Page, *Newsday*, 12/9/04, A51, c1; and the Elizabeth Benjamin article cited in the preceding paragraph. The inmate population figure for January 1, 2008 came from Hub System: Profile of Inmate Population Under Custody on January 1, 2008, State of New York, Department of Corrections, 3, www.docs.state.ny.us/Research/Reports/2008/Hub_report_2008.pdf, accessed 10/5/08.

Governor David Paterson's announcement that he had signed into law the legislation repealing the Rockefeller Drug Laws appeared in his Press release, State of New

York Executive Chamber, "Governor Paterson Signs Rockefeller Drug Reforms Into Law," 4/24/09, http://www.ny.gov/governor/press/press_0424091.html. Specifics of the bill signing, such as the actual signing date and Chapter number, can be found at David Badertscher, New York Law Librarian, New York Legislation: Update to Legislation Regarding Rockefeller Drug Law Reform, *Criminal Law Library Blog*, posted 4/21/09, http://www.criminallawlibraryblog.com/2009/04/new_york_legislation_update_to_1.html. That information, as well as the text of Chapter 56, Laws of 2009, can be found through Westlaw, at http://web2.westlaw.com/Find/default.wl?bhcp=1&cite=2009+NY+Laws+56&rs=LAWS2.0&strRecreate=no&sv=Split&vr=1.0, or presumably at any other legal research service. The *New York Times* article comment on the law's impact on first-time offenders was Jeremy W. Peters, "Albany Reaches Deal to Repeal 70s Drug Laws," *The New York Times*, 3/26/09, p. 1, c. 6. The estimate of the maximum number of inmates potentially released as a result of the new law, as well as the designation of second offenders as "hard-core criminals," came from an editorial, "First, Free the Felons?", *New York Post*, 3/27/09, http://www.nypost.com/php/pfriendly/print/php?url=http://www.nypost.com/seven/03272009), and the likely more accurate characterization of such offenders appeared more generally, e.g., Editorial, "End the Rockefeller Drug Laws," *The New York Times*, 3/10/09, A26, c.1.

Kenneth Lovett, "Clause in new Rockefeller laws could allow legal — and illegal — immigrants to escape deportation," *New York Daily News*, 4/1/09, http://www.nydailynews.com/news/2009/04/01/2009-04-01_clause_in_new_rockefeller_laws_could_all-1.html reported the criticisms of the new law by the president of the District Attorneys Association and the New York City Police Commissioner, while the D.A. Association president's pre-enactment warnings can be found at Daniel M. Donovan Jr., "Imprisoned Drug Felons at a Twenty-Year Low," web site, New York District Attorneys Association, 2/2/09, http://www.nysdaa.org/detail.cfm?page=224.

The inmate bragging how he would take advantage of the new law was quoted in Editorial, "Unleashing the Beast: Proof that relaxed Rockefeller laws really are Drug Dealer Protection Act," *New York Daily News*, 6/9/09, http://www.nydailynews.com/opinions/2009/06/09/2009-06-09_unleashing_the_beast_proof_that_relaxed_rockefeller_laws_really_are_drug_dealer_.html.

The criticisms of the law from Robert Gangi and Randy Credico were reported, respectively, in Adam Serwer, "Reversing Rockefeller," *Prospect.Org*, 4/1/09, http://www.prospect.org/cs/articles?article=reversing_rockefeller, and in Jennifer Gonnerman, "Addicted: The myth of the Rockefeller-drug-laws repeal," *NYMag.com*, 4/29/09, http://nymag.com/news/intelligencer/55693/.

The 2009 Pew Center report quoted is Pew Center on the States, *One in 31: The Long Reach of American Corrections* (Washington, DC: The Pew Charitable Trusts, March 2009), page 21 http://www.asca.net/documents/Pew1in31Report_002.pdf.

The news sources from upstate rural counties quoted criticizing the Rockefeller drug laws themselves were Editorial, "New focus on local prisons," *PressRepublican.com*, 5/5/09, http://www.pressrepublican.com/0201_editorials/local_story_124232613.html, and Daily Messenger: "State prisons can't be solely job centers," *MPNnow.com*, 4/30/09, http://www.mpnnow.com/opinions/x1194147907/State-prisons-cant-be-solely-job-centers.

Chapter VIII. Beating the Leadership, Winning in the Courts: Sex Offenders and Megan's Law

Since news outlets closely covered the Megan's Law controversy, much of the material in the chapter can easily be documented. See, for example, support for Megan's

Law in response to the murder of Megan Kanka, Paul Browne, "Gov vows to name 'beasts,'" *New York Daily News*, 8/5/94 (also noting Silver's promise to "introduce his own community notification bill," because mine "wouldn't accomplish anything because its confidentiality provisions restricted availability to police"); Editorial, "Protect Kids, Not Sex Offenders," *New York Daily News*, 8/11/94, 40, c1; Kimberly J. McLarin, Fast [NJ] Assembly Passes 7 Bills on Sex Abuse, *The New York Times*, 8/30/94, B1, c1; Feldman's letter in *The New York Times* questioning why the Assembly had failed to pass the bill in the 1994 session, 8/29/94, A14, c1; a news column exploring that question as well, "A Shift Toward a Stronger Bill For a Sex-Offender Registry," *The New York Times*, 9/4/94, 36 (Sunday Metro section); discussion of legal challenges to the New Jersey statute, Robert Hanley, "Sex-Offender Disclosure Law Hitting Snags in New Jersey," *The New York Times*, 1/9/95, A1, c5; AP, Federal Judge Tosses Part of Megan's Law, *New York Daily News*, 3/1/95, 12, c1; discussion of vigilante attacks on identified sex offenders, Jon Nordheimer, "Vigilante' Attack in New Jersey Linked to Sex-Offenders Law," *The New York Times*, 1/11/95, A1, c5; Editorial, "Megan's Law Needs Fixing," *The New York Times*, 1/13/95; the Feldman-Skelos press conference in Manhattan with the parents of Megan Kanka, Karen Friefeld, "Pols to Abusers: Call Home," *New York Newsday*, 3/6/95, A19, c1; AP, "New York Bill Calls for a 'Megan's Law,'" *The New York Times*, 3/6/95, B2; their press conference in Albany with the parents of Sara Anne Wood, AP, "Sex crime victims' families press for notification law," *Schenectady Daily Gazette*, 3/8/95; article reporting Mindy Bockstein's prediction that Silver would support our bill, Lorelei Palmer, "Early approval expected on sex crimes bill," *Legislative Gazette* [Albany], 3/13/95, 2 & 15; description of interruption of Silver's press conference by parents of slain children, James Dao, "Relatives of Slain Children Join Albany Lawmakers to Push for Bills Aimed at Violent Crime," *The New York Times*, 6/15/95; Nekesa Mumbi Moody, AP, "Silver put on defensive on sex-crime legislation," *The Troy Record*, 6/15/95, A3, c1; Nicholas Goldberg, "Speaker Silver Gets Compassionate Plea," *Newsday*, 6/15/96; Editorial, "So there will be no others," *New York Daily News*, 6/18/95, 34, c1; and its result, Jeff McLaurin, "Silver Says Assembly will pass Megan's Law," *Legislative Gazette*, 6/19/95, p1, c3; Kevin Sack, "Bill to Track Sex Offenders Nears Passage," *The New York Times*, 6/27/95, B1, c6; praising enactment of New York's Megan's Law, Editorial, "Megan's NY Law," *Newsday*, 7/27/95; discussion of Silver's order to boycott Pataki's Megan's Law press conference, Fredric U. Dicker, "Silver: Gov's inviting trouble," *The New York Post*, 1/22/96; reaction to Judge Chin's decision holding the notification aspects of New York's Megan's Law unconstitutional, Editorial, "Rogues Gallery of Junk Judges," *New York Daily News*, 3/31/96, 40, c1; Editorial, "Junk Justice: Now It's Megan's Law," *The New York Post*, 3/26/96, 22, c1.

For a summary of research on diffusion of policy innovation see Michael A. Minstrom and Karen Mossberger "Tthe Politics of Ideas and the Diffusion of Policy Innovations," (Unpublished paper delivered at the annual meeting of the American Political Science Association, Boston Ma, August 28–31, 2008). http://www.allacademic.com//meta/p_mla_apa_research_citation/2/7/9/4/1/pages279414/p279414-24.php., last visited on November 28, 2008.

Assembly Bill Number 1059-B/Senate Bill Number 11-B became Chapter 192 of the Laws of 1995. Other 1995 Assembly bills intended to address sex offender registration and notification, presented in the Assembly Steering Committee meeting described, included #770 (Matusow); #5035 (Morelle), and #6077 (Schimminger).

The Assembly and Senate debates on the bill played a role in the constitutional challenge to New York's Megan's Law, the District Court decision, and the Circuit Court reversal. The Assembly debate can be found on pages 286 through 418 of the transcript of the June 28, 1995 session; the Senate debate, pages 6564 through 6670 of the Stenographic Record of the May 24, 1995 session.

Discussion of the legal issues involved is based on Feldman's article, "The "'Scarlet Letter Laws'" of the 1990s: A Response to Critics," 60 *Albany Law Review* 1081 (1997), sources cited therein, on the Second Circuit Court of Appeals decision reversing the District Court and upholding the constitutionality of the notification provisions of New York's Megan's Law, *Doe v. Pataki*, 120 F.3d 1263 (2d Cir. 1997), which was issued subsequently; and on two United States Supreme Court decisions on March 5, 2003, respectively upholding Alaska's and Connecticut's Megan's Laws, *Smith v. Doe*, 538 U.S. 84, and *Dep't of Pub. Safety v. Doe*, 538 U.S. 1.

Chapter IX. Guns — The Struggle in the Legislature and Courts

The quotation from Thomas Jefferson can be found in his Papers, 334, cited, among other places, at http://www.buckeyefirearms.org/article3464.html, visited 2/26/08. The quotation from Hubert Humphrey comes from "Know Your Legislators," *Guns Magazine*, February 1960, 6. We drew on two of Feldman's articles, "Not Quite High Noon for Gunmakers, But It's Coming," 67 *Brooklyn Law Review* 293 (2001), and "Legislating or Litigating Public Policy Change: Gunmaker Tort Liability," 12 *Va. J. of Social Policy and the Law* 140 (2004), and sources cited therein, for discussion of the legal issues, the statistical information provided by the Federal Bureau of Alcohol, Tobacco and& Firearms (ATF), the American cultural history, and the competence of the respective institutions dealing with the issues. The most recent comparison of gun-related and automobile-related fatalities in the United States came from the listing for firearm deaths in Table 18 of the National Vital Statistics Report, Volume 56, #10, by the National Center for Health Statistics, April 24, 2008, at www.cdc.gov/nchs/data/nvsr/nvsr56/nvsr56_10.pdf, accessed 10/5/08, reporting 30,694 such fatalities in 2005, and the Fatalities Analysis Reporting System Encyclopedia of the National Highway Traffic Safety Administration, at www.-fars.nhtsa.dot.gov/Main/index.aspx, accessed 10/5/08, reporting 43,510 such fatalities in 2005.

Robert J. Spitzer, *The Politics of Gun Control*, 3d ed., CQ Press, Washington, D.C. 2004, provides a discussion of the political pressures on ATF for and against providing crime gun tracing data, as well as much other useful information. As in Chapter VI, we relied on Alfred Blumstein's research and analysis of increases in urban ghetto youth violence in the late 1980s and early 1990s, especially his articles Youth Violence, Guns, and the Illicit-Drug Industry, 86 *J. Crim. L. & Criminology* 19, 1995; and The Context of Recent Changes in Crime Rates, Panel Paper, National Institute of Justice and Executive Office for Weed and Seed, Washington, D.C., Jan. 5–7, 1998. Two invaluable sources of data on the gun industry, as well as the costs of gun violence, are Tom Diaz, *Making a Killing*, The New Press, W.W. Norton & Co., N.Y. 1999, and Trudy Karlson and Stephen W. Hargarten, *Reducing Firearms Injury and Death*, Rutgers University Press, New Brunswick, N.J. 1997. Chapter Five, Costs, by Ted R. Miller and Mark A. Cohen, in R.R. Ivatury and C. Gene Cayton, *Textbook of Penetrating Trauma*, Wilkins and Wilkins, Baltimore, 1996, also provides useful information on the costs of gun violence. Peter Squires, *Gun Culture or Gun Control? Firearms, Violence and Society*, Routledge, New York and London, 2000, at page 5, compared the British response to the Dunblane massacre to the relatively feeble American response to gun violence.

The report referred to from Elizabeth Holtzman's office with the initial proposal for the gun manufacturers' tort liability bill came from David Eichenthal, Taking the Profit Out of Firearms Violence, Office of the Comptroller of the City of New York, June

1991. The initial 1991 bill was Assembly Bill 3572 of the 1991–92 Session; the more restricted 1992 version was Assembly Bill 9408. News and editorial coverage of the legislation, and later legislation in the New York City Council, appeared in "Gun Control, Privatized," *The New York Times*, editorial, 2/1/92; Jacques Steinberg, "Dinkins Promises Money for Safety in Violent Schools," *The New York Times*, 3/2/92, p.1, c1; Jim Dwyer, "Don't Be Fooled: *Guns* Kill People," *New York Newsday*, 3/2/92; "Where Kids Get Their Guns," *The New York Times*, editorial, 3/7/92; "Hitting Gun Profits," *New York Daily News*, editorial, 3/2/92, 14C; "Bill Would Penalize Gun Makers for Deaths," *The New York Times*, 3/30/95.

The NRA lobbyist improperly cited James A. Henderson and Aaron D. Twerski, "Closing the American Products Liability Frontier: The Rejection of Liability Without Defect," 66 *NYU Law Review* 1263 (1991), as Henderson and Twerski pointed out in their letter to Feldman of 5/15/92.

A record of the Assembly votes to ban assault weapons can be found in Legislative Bill Drafting Commission, *State of New York Legislative Digest*, Albany, New York for each 1993, 1995, 1996, and 1997, respectively tracking Assembly bills 7118, 6821, 6821 (same bill, following year) and 1268. The legislation was enacted as Chapter 189 of the Laws of 2000.

News coverage of the Long Island Railroad, California, and Brooklyn gun victim lawsuits appeared respectively in John T. McQuiston, "Victims Sue Arms Makers in Shooting on L.I.R.R.," *The New York Times*, 10/27/94, B8, c6; AP, "Lawyers for Shooting Victims Seek to Sue Gun Manufacturer," *The New York Times*, 2/19/95, 37, c1; and Barry Meier, "Victims Can Sue Gun Makers Over Sales, Judge Rules," *The New York Times*, 5/3/96. The federal district court rendered its opinion in *McCarthy v. Sturm, Ruger & Co.*, 916 F. Supp. 366 (S.D.N.Y. 1966). The appellate affirmance cited was *McCarthy v. Olin Corp. 119* F. 3d 148 (2d Cir. 1997). The Michigan decision the trial court distinguished was *Moning c. Alfono*, 254 N.W. 2d 759(1977) and the New York state court decision upon which the federal courts most clearly relied was *Forni v Ferguson*, 232 A.D. 2d 176, 648 N.Y.S. 2d 73 (1st Dept. 1996)n.

The 1993 legislation, Assembly Bill 6395-B/Senate Bill 5510-B, to remove firearms from the hands of domestic abusers likely to use them, was enacted as Chapter 498 of the Laws of 1993. Statistics and other background on domestic violence used in the discussion of that legislation can be found in Chapter Law Memoranda, 1993, Memorandum of Assemblyman Daniel L. Feldman, Orders of Protection: Violation, 374–375; AP, "Domestic Violence Bill Approved," *The Sunday Gazette* [Schenectady], 7/4/93; and AP, "Women protected by new state law," *Times Union* [Albany], 11/2/93, B2. The editorial commending the law but seeking an end to the loophole for police officers was "Law adds protection from violent spouses," *Gannett Suburban Newspapers*, 11/5/93, 14A, c1.

People v. Sturm Ruger is reported in *New York Law Journal*, 8/17/01, 17 (Sup. Ct. N.Y. Co., York, J.) Lexis reports the Appellate Division's decision affirming the trial court's decision for the gun manufacturer defendants at 2003 N.Y. App. Div. LEXIS 7304 (1st Dept., June 24, 2003), with the dissent beginning on page 30. Spitzer's previous efforts to reach a national settlement with the gun manufacturers were reported in, for example, Barbara Vobejda and David Ottaway, "Gunmakers Discuss Possible Deal With New York," *Washington Post*, 7/22/99, A10; Barry Meier, "In Seeking Firearms Deal, Spitzer May Set Standard," *The New York Times*, 7/22/99, B5, c5; Paul Barrett, "New York's Spitzer Seeks to Resolve Municipal Suits Against Gun Industry," *The Wall Street Journal*, 8/17/99, Paul M. Barrett and Vanessa O'Connell, "White House and Gun Industry May Discover Some Talking Points to Reach Deal on Lawsuit," *The Wall Street Journal*, 12/13/99, A36, c1; James Dao, "Under Legal Siege, Gun Maker Agrees to Accept Curbs," *The New York Times*, 3/18/2000, A1, c6; and (suggesting Andrew Cuomo's efforts to steal the limelight) Paul M. Barrett, Joe Matthews, Vanessa O'Connell, "Arms Deal—Behind the Gun Pact: mixing legal hardball with personal bonds," *The Wall Street Journal*, 3/22/2000, reporter-news.com/guns/texnews/news/dealo322.html, 9/5/02.

The discussion of a potential design defect claim draws on Hillel Deutsch's unpublished study, "Gun Safety: Myth or Reality," Program Development Unit, Office of the New York State Attorney General, New York, summer 1999; *Voss v. Black & Decker Mfg. Co.*, 59 N.Y.2d 102, 463 N.Y.S. 398 (1983); Karlson and Hargarten, *op. cit.*; Barry Meier, "Gun Makers' Approach to Basic Safety Feature Varies Widely," *The New York Times*, 3/19/99, A12; Krista Robinson et al., "Personalized Guns," Johns Hopkins Center for Gun Policy and Research, Baltimore, Md., Sept. 1996; Kristen Rand, Memorandum, "'Tort Reform'" is Bad News for Gun Control," Violence Policy Center, Washington, D.C. 9/8/98.

Two law review articles make especially valuable contributions to the discussion of proportional causation, Aaron D. Twerski and Anthony Sebok, "Liability Without Cause? Further Ruminations on Cause-in-Fact as Applied to Handgun Liability," 32 *Conn. L. Rev.* 1379 (2000); and John C.P. Goldberg and Benjamin Zipursky, "Concern for Cause: A Comment on the Twerski-Sebok Plan for Administering Negligent Marketing Claims Against Gun Manufacturers," 32 *Conn. L. Rev.* 1411 (2000).

The discussion of law and values draws on Lon L. Fuller's work in Collective Bargaining and the Arbitrator, 1963 *Wis. L. Rev.* 3, 32–33 and *The Morality of Law*, rev. ed., Yale University Press, New Haven, Conn. 1969. Some discussion of the budget-making function comes from LOAG, 56–57. Ross Sandler and David Schoenbrod's *Democracy by Decree*, Yale University Press, New Haven, Conn. 2003, provides valuable and more recent criticism of judicial overreach beyond the judiciary's area of institutional competence. An excellent discussion of the inherent difficulties in achieve budget equity appears in Deborah Stone, *Policy Paradox*, W.W. Norton & Co., New York 1997, especially at pages 39–60. The cases cited in that discussion are *Lochner v. New York*, 198 U.S. 45 (1905), *Roe v. Wade*, 410 U.S. 113 (1973), and *Brown v. Board of Education*, 347 U.S. 483 (1954).

Timothy Lytton, "Lawsuits Against the Gun Industry: A Comparative Institutional Analysis," 32 *Connecticut Law Review* 1247 (2000); John Ferejohn, "The Law of Politics: Judicializing Politics, Politicizing Law," 65 *Law and Contemporary Problems* 41 (Summer 2002); and Howard Gilman, "How Political Parties Can Use the Courts to Advance Their Agendas: Federal Courts in the United States, 1875–1891," 96 *Amer. Pol. Sci. Rev.* 511 (Sept. 2002) provide additional source material for the discussion of the appropriateness of going beyond the legislative arena to address gun manufacturers' liability in the judicial forum. Mancur Olson first described the "free rider" problem distorting the results of legislative combat in his classic *The Logic of Collective Action*, Harvard University Press, Cambridge, Massachusetts 1965. A more recent discussion of the same problem appears in Note, "Examining Senate Procedure Through Narrative," 116 *Harvard Law Review* 1499, 1502–3 (March 2003).

Fox Butterfield, "Gun Industry is Gaining Immunity From Suits," *The New York Times*, 9/1/02, p. 27, c1, and Sheryl Gay Stolberg, "Senate Leaders Scuttle Gun Bill Over Changes," *The New York Times*, 3/4/04, A1, described the back and forth efforts to cut or add court jurisdiction over lawsuits against gun manufacturers. Other articles on later developments in the law and politics of handgun litigation include James Gordon Meek, "Gun Supporters Return Legal Fire," APBnews.com, kyfirearms.org/news/return fire.htm, 9/30/02; Jim Oliphant, "How the Gun Debate Died," *Legal Times*, law.com, 10/22/02; Jill Barton, AP, *The New York Times*, 11/15/02, A26, c1; Fox Butterfield, "Despite Violations, Gun Shop in Sniper Case Continued to Operate, Records

Show," *The New York Times*, 11/19/02, A19, c1; William Glaberson, "Gun Strategists Are Watching Brooklyn Case," *The New York Times*, 10/5/02, B1, c1.; "Gun Distributor Held 5% Liable in Killing," *The New York Times*, 11/15/02, A26, c1; William Glaberson, "Trying Again to Make Gun Makers Liable for Shooting," *The New York Times*, 3/23/03, A35, c1; Vanessa O'Connell and Paul M. Barrett, "NAACP Lawsuit Puts Gun Makers in the Cross Hairs," *The Wall Street Journal*, 3/10/03, B1, c2.

The creation of Mayors Against Illegal Guns by New York City Mayor Michael Bloomberg in response to the enactment of the federal Protection of Lawful Commerce in Arms Act is described in http://mayorsagainstillegalguns.org/html/about/principles.shtml; see also Courtney Gross, Taking Aim at Guns, http://www.gothamgazette.com/article.20070710/200/2225. The ultimate defeat of New York City's lawsuit against gun dealers was reported in David Stout, U.S. Justices Decline New York' Suit Against Gun Makers, *The New York Times*, 3/10/09, A23, c3.

NAACP v. Acusport Corp., 2003 U.S. Dist. LEXIS 12421 (E.D.N.Y.) records the plaintiffs' defeat in the NAACP gun case in federal court in Brooklyn, along with *dicta* setting forth criteria for plaintiff victory in hypothetical or future lawsuits brought by victims of gun violence or their representatives. Robert Ricker, the former industry insider who testified in that case, first came to prominence with his deposition in a California case, *Firearm Case*, Judicial Council Coordination Proceedings No. 4095, DiFiglia, J. (Super. Ct. San Diego Co., Cal.), Declaration of Robert A. Ricker in Support of Plaintiffs' Opposition to Defendants' Motion for Summary Judgment, March 7, 2003, discussed in Fox Butterfield, "Gun Industry Ex-Official Describes Bond of Silence," *The New York Times*, 2/4/03, A14, c1.

Plaintiffs's success in the Bull's Eye Shooter case was reported in Sue Reisinger, "High Noon," law.com, 10/29/04, and in a press release from the Brady Center to Prevent Gun Violence, "Gun Dealer, Manufacturer Pay $2.5 Million to Sniper Victims to Settle Lawsuit," 9/9/04. The expiration of the Assault Weapons Ban was reported in Fox Butterfield, "As Expiration Looms, Gun Ban's Effect is Debated," *The New York Times*, 9/10/04, A14.

The enactment of Council Member Yassky's Intro 354, the New York City tort liability law, was reported in Tom Topousis, Mike opens fire on gun makers, *New York Post*, 1/19/05, 25, c1. Winnie Hu, "Accord Reached on Bill to Make it Easier to Sue Gun Makers," *The New York Times* 1/5/05, B2, c3 discussed the bill and reported the comments by Patrick Brophy and Laurence Keane. Jacqueline Kuhls, representing New Yorkers Against Gun Violence, discussed the enhanced provisions and the prospect for enactment of the 2005 version of Senator Craig's national immunization bill as an invited guest at the meeting of the New York District Attorneys Association Legislative Committee in the conference room of the Brooklyn District Attorney's Office March 29, 2005. Ian Urbina, in "City Urges U.S. Senate to Reject Bill on Gun Suits," *The New York Times*, 2/25/05, B6, c8, discussed the Senate's then-likely vote on the bill and its projected impact on the new 2005 New York City law.

Justice White's dissent suggesting a constitutional objection to medical malpractice caps appeared in *Fein v. Permanente Medical Group*, 474 U.S. 892, 894-5 (1985). Since then, courts in a half dozen states have struck down their malpractice caps on constitutional grounds, most recently in Illinois and Georgia, respectively in February and March 2010. See Robbie Brown, Ruling Strikes Down Georgia's Cap on Malpractice Awards, *The New York Times*, 3/23/10, A19, c1; *Lebron v. Gottlieb Mem. Hosp.*, 2010 Ill. LEXIS 26, 2010 WL 375190 (Ill. Feb. 4, 2010); *Smith v. Baptiste*, 2010 Ga. LEXIS 215 (Mar. 15, 2010).

Chapter X. Politics and Lawmaking

The estimate of the average number of bill introductions covers the two-year period of a legislative session. In the 2007–2008 session, for example, Jay Gallagher and Brian Sharp of the Gannett News Service reported that New York State legislators had introduced a total of 18,239 bills, of which 1634 were passed by both houses, and 537 were signed into law by the Governor as of the date of the article, "New York Legislature Leads Nation in Bill Introductions," *Rochester Democrat & Chronicle*, 9/24/08, http://www.democratandchronicle.com/article/20080924/NEWS01/809240363, accessed 10/6/08.

The second edition of Murray Edelman's book, *The Symbolic Uses of Politics*, was published by University of Illinois Press, Chicago, in 1985. The original edition was published in 1964.

Comments here on the Rockefeller drug laws should not be interpreted to suggest that further reforms would not be useful. Many mandatory sentences remain excessive. See Martin Espinosa, "Name by Name, a Push to Change Drug Laws," *The New York Times*, 10/5/08, 46, c.1.

Thoughts on the methamphetamine epidemic were prompted by Mark Schone's article, "The Epidemic on Aisle 6," in *LegalAffairs,* a Yale Law School publication, New Haven, Conn., Nov./Dec. 2004, 30. Mark Woodward, a spokesperson for the Oklahoma Bureau of Narcotics and Dangerous Drugs Control, supplied Feldman with much additional information on the subject when he was researching it for then-Attorney General Spitzer in early March 2004. Information on the federal statute restricting access to pseudoephedrine appeared in General Information Regarding the Combat Methamphetamine Epidemic Act of 2005, Drug Enforcement Administration, May 2006, at www.deadiversion.usdoj/meth/cma2005_general_info.pdf, visited 7/9/07.

The discussion of recent statistics showing lower rates of recidivism among sex offenders than previously thought possible was based on a study by the Patrick A. Langan, Ph.D., Erica Schmitt, and Matthew R. Durose, Bureau of Justice Statistics, U.S. Department of Justice, Recidivism of Sex Offenders Released from Prison in 1994, November 2003, NCJ 198281, Washington, D.C.

On the effect on gun control on the 2000 and 2004 presidential elections, and on future prospects for gun control, useful sources included Nicholas Kristof, "Lock and Load," Op-Ed, *The New York Times*, 11/13/04; Ruy Teixera, "Cultural Alien," AlterNet, 11/11/04, www.alternet.org/module/printversion/20464, accessed 11/16/04; Christine Hall, CNSNEWS.com, "As Elections Near, Democrats Rethink Opposition to Gun Rights," www.newsmax.com/archives/articles/2002/5/25/l, accessed 11/16/04.

A discussion of the federal Hillory J. Farias and Samantha Reid Date Rape Drug Prohibition Act of 2000 can be found in Asjylyn Loder, "Date Rape Drugs Still Available, Despite Crackdown," *Women's eNews*, 1/16/04, at http://womensenews.org/article/cfm/dyn/aid/1677/context/archive, accessed 4/21/05.

The statistics on improved conditions for mentally ill outpatients in New York since the enactment of Kendra's Law come from E. Fuller Torrey, "Remembering Kendra: Keeping all New Yorkers safe," New York *Post* Opinion, 4/18/05, 25, c1. Other sources for the discussion of Kendra's Law included John McManamy, McMan's Depression and Bipolar Web, Kendra's Law, www.mcmanweb.com/article-66.htm, updated through 10/10/04, accessed 11/24/04; Laura Newman, WebMD Medical News, "Can Tragedy Spur Revamping of the Mental Health Care System?", 1/19/00, http://my.webmd.com/content/Article/21/1728_54190.htm, accessed 11/24/04; Press release, Governor Pataki Announces Major New Mental Health Package, November 1999, www.cqc.state.ny.us/newsletter/77gov.htm, accessed 11/24/04; David Kellogg, $126 Million More?, New York City Voices, November/December 1999, www.newyorkcityvoices.org/nov99a.html, accessed 11/24/04; Governor of the State of New

York, 2001–02 Executive Budget, Office of Mental Health, pages 163–171; Mental Health Association in New York State, Policy Paper: The Unfinished Promise of Willowbrook, October 18, 2002, www.mhanys.org/pubpol/pp_willowbrook.htm, accessed 11/24/04. For additional background on deinstitutionalization in New York in the 1970s, see Robert H. Connery and Gerald Benjamin, *Rockefeller of New York*, Ithaca, New York: Cornell University Press, 1979, 167–175. The estimate of inmates with serious mental illnesses in state prison came from an editorial, "Better Care for Mentally Ill Inmates," *The New York Times*, 12/19/04, Long Island/Opinion, LI 15, c1.

On the relatively minor impact of the assault weapons ban, see Deborah Sontag, "Many Say End of Firearms Ban Changed Little," *The New York Times*, 4/24/05, 1, c3.

H. Mark Roelofs' *The Poverty of American Politics*, 2d edition, Temple University Press, Philadelphia 1998, provides a very good explanation and description of legislators' relationships with colleagues in government (pages 146–50) and with others (144–5). Alan Rosenthal et al., *Republic on Trial*, CQ Press, Washington, D.C. 2003 eloquently defends the legislative institutions of the United States against the almost constant attack to which they have been subjected in recent times. Bernard Crick's profound and more broadly applicable *In Defense of Politics*, 2d edition, Penguin Books Ltd., Harmondsworth, Middlesex, England 1982 (a fourth edition was published by the University of Chicago Press in 1992) well justifies its title. His warning about liberals' excessive attachment to honesty and sincerity appears on page 126 of the 1982 edition; the quotation from "Boss" Richard Croker appears on page 125 (where Crick, in turn, cites M. T. Werner, *Tammany Hall* (New York 1928), p. 449). For a brief history of the Brighton Baths, see Francis Morrone, "Abroad in New York: Brighton Beach is Blooming," *The New York Sun*, 8/2/04, at http://www.muss.com/news/080204.phtml, accessed 4/21/05.

In the discussion of inside politics, Feldman acknowledges that Codes Committee chair Joe Lentol might deserve credit for protecting the Democratic majority in the Assembly by keeping the gun manufacturers' tort liability bill off the floor. Professor John Hibbing of the University of Nebraska at Lincoln pointed this out when he served as the discussant for papers presented on August 30 at Panel 22–18, "Congressional Responsiveness," at the 2003 Annual Meeting of the American Political Science Association, including Feldman's paper, "Legislating or Litigating Public Policy Change: Gunmaker Tort Liability," a precursor of the law review article of the same name cited earlier, in the source notes for Chapter Nine.

Chapter XI. The New York State Legislature, On Balance

Jay Jochnowitz, in "Hevesi's Ride Ends, Capitol Confidential," *Albany Times Union*, 12/22/06, http://blogs.timesunion.com/capitol?p=3092, visited 7/18/07, reports on the end of Alan Hevesi's political career.

The New York State Constitution references are to Article V, Section 1. New York's Public Officers Law, Section 41, provides the statutory authority for the Legislature's method of filling vacancies in the offices of Attorney General and Comptroller.

Background on Sheldon Silver was obtained from Geoffrey Grey. "The obstructionist," *New York Magazine*, June 1, 2008 http://nymag.com/news/politics/47409/; James C. McKinley. "Silvers is an Albany Strongman, and It's Not Because He's Flashy" *New York Times*, February 11, 2003 http://query.nytimes.com/gst/fullpage.html?res=9500E7D81E3BF932A25751C0A9659C8B63&sec=&spon=&pagewanted=print; and Joyce Purnick., "Silver Wields Power by Keeping Albany Guessing," *New York Times* June 20, 2007. http://www.nytimes.com/2007/06/20/nyregion/20silver.html?_r=1.

Sources on the developments leading up to the Legislature's selection of Tom Di-Napoli as New York's Comptroller include, New York State Legislature, Legislature Sets January 23 Interview Date for Comptroller Candidates, *Press Release* of January 17, 2007, http://assembly.state.ny.us/Press, visited 3/2/08; Wayne Barrett, "Too Smart by Half: How Spitzer Rigged the Build-Up to the War With the Assembly," *The Village Voice*, 2/16/07, http://www.villagevoice.com/news/0708,barrett,75838,2.html, visited 7/18/07; and Nicholas Confessore, The Pushback, *The New York Times*, 1/26/07, http://empirezone.blogs.nytimes.com/2007/01/26/thepushback/#more, visited 7/18/07; Office of the Governor, Spitzer Urges Lawmakers to Honor Comptroller Selection Agreement, *Press Release*, 2/6/07, http://www.ny.gov/governor/press/0206071.html, visited 3/2/08. Details of the Legislature's vote to select DiNapoli came from Elizabeth Benjamin, By the Numbers, Capitol Confidential, *Albany Times Union*, 2/10/07, http://blogs.timesunion.com/capitol/?p23688, visited 7/18/07. In her column under the same heading two days earlier, Ms. Benjamin had noted that although the Assembly Democratic Conference had 108 members until shortly before the DiNapoli controversy, the untimely passing of Assembly Member John Lavelle reduced that census by one, and Assembly Member Pete Grannis, whose forthcoming appointment as Commissioner of the New York State Department of Environmental Protection, was absent. http://blogs.timesunion.com/capitol/archives/3688, visited 11/9/08.

Discussion of Spitzer's effort to replace a Republican state senator with a Democrat appear above in Chapter 3. Bruno's conviction is detailed in Glenn Blain and Ken Lovett. "Former Senator Majority Leader Joseph Bruno Convicted on 2 of 8 Felony Federal Corruption Counts" *New York Daily News*, December 7, 2009 http://www.nydailynews.com/news/ny_crime/2009/12/07/2009-12-07_former_senate_majority_leader.html.

Governor Spitzer's criticism of the Legislature's choice for Comptroller was reported at http://www.northcountrygazette.org/articles/2007/020707NamesComptroller.html, visited 7/19/07. The editorials criticizing the choice appeared respectively in the New York *Post*, 2/8/07 at 36 and 2/20/07 at 26; the Syracuse *Post Standard*, 2/13/07 at A11; the *Buffalo News*, 2/10/07 at A6; and *The New York Times*, 2/8/07 at A20. *Newsday*'s editorial, complimentary to DiNapoli although not to the Legislature's process, came out on 2/8/07.

State Senator Joseph Griffo and Assembly Member Kevin Cahill introduced a constitutional amendment providing for a special election to fill any vacancy in the offices of Comptroller or Attorney General, S.2724/A.5703 of the 2007–2008 session.

Spitzer's attacks on the Legislature after the vote were reported in Michael Cooper, "Lawmakers Feel Heat Over Comptroller Choice, And Not Just From Spitzer," *The New York Times*, 2/14/07, B5.

Poll results for the New York State Legislature were reported in Quinnipiac University Poll, Spitzer Approval Bounces Back in New York, Quinnipiac University Poll Finds; State Voters Prefer Congestion Pricing to Fare Hike, *Press Release*, 6/19/07, http://www.google.com/search?sourceid=navclient&ie=UTF-8&rlz=1T4IBMA_en_US225&q=Quinnipiac+poll+June+19%2c+2007, visited 3/2/08. Similar findings appeared in 2005 and 2006 in the New York Times/ CBS poll, http://graphics8.nytimes.com/packages/pdf/nyregion/20060927_nys_poll.pdf, visited 3/2/08. Polling results for Congress come from http://www.pollingreport.com/institute.htm, visited 8/27/07. The comments quoted about the generally low opinion of legislatures held by the public come from Karl Kurtz, The Public Standing of Legislatures, http://ncsl.typepad.com/the_thicket/2006/05/the_fiscal_con.html, May 15, 2006, visited 7/3/07. For polling results for other states, see http://pollingreport.com/CongJob1.htm, visited 8/27/07.

Keith Hamm and Gary Moncrief, Legislative Politics in the States, in Virginia Grey and Russell L. Hanson, eds., *Politics in the American States*, cited above in source notes to Chapter I, supply at page 160 the comment about legislators who "run against the institution." The assessment of New Yorkers' low level of confidence in their Legislature comes from Christine Kelleher and Jennifer Wolak, "Citizen Confidence in State Governmental Institutions," unpublished paper delivered to State Politics and Party Conference, East Lansing, Michigan, May 13–14, 2005, on file with present co-author Gerald Benjamin.

For discussion of late budgets in New York, see Gerald Benjamin, "Reform in New York: the Budget, the Legislature, and the Governmental Process," 67 *Albany Law Review* 1021–1069, 2004; for New York's late compliance with federal voting technology requirements, see Howard Stanislevic, New York: Last in HAVA Compliance or First in Election Integrity?, Verified Voting Foundation, http://www.votetrustusa.org/index.php?option=com_content&task=view&id=1436&itemid=113.

The comments rejecting the attribution of dysfunctionality to the Legislature come, respectively, from Joe Mahoney and Elizabeth Benjamin, "Try li'l luv, gov: experts tell how he can make amends," *New York Daily News*, 12/30/07, 28; and Nicholas Confessore, "Perception of Being Slighted Stoked Revolt by Lawmakers," *The New York Times*, 2/9/07, B7.

Daniel Elazar discusses local political cultures in *American Federalism: A View from the States*, New York: Thomas Y. Crowell, 1972.

Baker v. Carr, the seminal one-person one-vote decision, is reported at 369 U.S. 186, 82 S. Ct. 691 (1962). The New York State constitutional requirement of residence for New York State legislators appears in Article III, Section 7 of the State Constitution. Material on building local support in congressional districts can be found in Richard Fenno, *Homestyle: House Members in their Districts*, Boston: Little Brown & Co., 1978.

Robert Miraldi, Ulster Seeks Real Estate Tax, *Kingston Freeman*, 8/2/07, 1, reported that Ulster County's attempt to win new taxing authority. Michelle York, "Unwanted Results of Ballot Confusion: A Dry Town," *The New York Times*, 6/19/07, http://www.nytimes.com/2007/06/19/nyregion/19beer.html?_r=1&pageswanted=print&oref=slogin, reported a town's attempt to obtain state authorization to evade an unintentional local ban on beer sales. Article IX, Section 2b2 of the New York State Constitution allows the State Legislature to provide such relief to localities.

Statistics on African American, Latino, and women members of the New York State Legislature comes respectively from http://www.ncslor/programs/legismgt/about/afrAmer.htm; http://www.ncslor/programs/legismgt/about/Latino.htm; and http://www.ncslor/programs/w/n/WomenInOffice2006.htm.

Appendix

Some Notable Changes in Employment

Balboni, Michael: was appointed Deputy Secretary for Public Safety by Governor Spitzer in January 2007, and resigned in February 2009.

Barbaro, Frank: left the Assembly in 1996 to serve as a New York State Supreme Court judge in Brooklyn until 2002. In 2004, at age 78, he won 41 percent of the vote against then-incumbent Member of Congress Vito Fosella in a district primarily based in Staten Island, although Fosella lived in Staten Island and Barbaro in Brooklyn.

Bockstein, Mindy: was confirmed by the New York State Senate as Chair of the Consumer Protection Board on February 27, 2007, after having been nominated by Governor Spitzer for the post.

Crosson, Matthew: became president of the Long Island Association, a business group, after he left the Office of Court Administration in 1993.

Cuomo, Andrew: was elected Attorney General of the State of New York in 2006.

Feerick, John: was appointed Chair of the Public Integrity Commission by Governor Spitzer in April 2007, and resigned in February 2009. He remains on the faculty of Fordham Law School.

Grannis, Alexander "Pete": was confirmed by the New York State Senate as Commissioner of the Department of Environmental Conservation on March 31, 2007, after having been nominated by Governor Spitzer.

Johnson, Sterling: became a judge of the federal district court for the Eastern District of New York in 1991.

Lippman, Jonathan: was appointed presiding justice of the First Department of the Appellate Division of the New York State Supreme Court in 2007, and Chief Judge of the State of New York in 2009.

Lopez, Vito: remains chair of the Assembly Housing Committee, but also became chair of the Kings County Democratic Committee ("Democratic county leader") in 2005.

Marcus, Marty: became a judge of the Court of Claims in 1999.

Meeks, Gregory: was elected to Congress from Queens in 1998.

Nadler, Jerrold: was elected to Congress from Manhattan in 1992 and as of 2008 chairs the House Judiciary Subcommittee on the Constitution, Civil Rights and Civil Liberties.

Pope, Peter: was appointed Policy Director by Spitzer, who announced the appointment in December 2006 shortly before taking office as Governor. Within a month of assuming the governorship in March 2008, David Paterson accepted Peter Pope's resignation.

Serrano, Jose: was elected to Congress from the Bronx in 1990.

Stringer, Scott: was elected Borough President of Manhattan in 2005.

Tallon, James: became president of the United Hospital Fund in 2002 and was elected by the Legislature to a five-year term as a member of the New York State Board of Regents. He was reelected to the Regents post in 2007.

Tonko, Paul: was appointed C.E.O. and President of the New York State Energy Research and Development Authority by Governor Spitzer on June 18, 2007, but resigned and was elected to Congress in 2008.

Vitaliano, Eric: became a judge of the federal district court for the Eastern District of New York in 2006.

Wesley, Richard: was nominated by President Bush as Judge of the Second Circuit Court of Appeals for the United States and was confirmed by the Senate in 2003.

Yates, James: was appointed as judge of the Court of Claims in 1992 and became a New York State Supreme Court judge in 1998. In 2008, he was asked to become Counsel to Governor David Paterson but decided to remain on the bench instead.

Index of Names

Subject Index

Index of Cases